D1557069

THE DARKENED LIGHT OF FAITH

The Darkened Light of Faith

RACE, DEMOCRACY, AND FREEDOM IN AFRICAN AMERICAN POLITICAL THOUGHT

Melvin L. Rogers

PRINCETON UNIVERSITY PRESS

PRINCETON & OXFORD

"Strange Fruit." Words and music by Lewis Allan, copyright 1939 (renewed) by Music Sales Corporation. All rights outside the United States controlled by Edward B. Marks Music Company. International copyright secured. All rights reserved. Used by permission. Reprinted by permission of Hall Leonard LLC.

Published by Princeton University Press
41 William Street, Princeton, New Jersey 08540
99 Banbury Road, Oxford OX2 6JX

press.princeton.edu

Library of Congress Cataloging-in-Publication Data

Names: Rogers, Melvin L., author.
Title: The darkened light of faith : race, democracy, and freedom in African American
    political thought / Melvin L. Rogers.
Description: Princeton : Princeton University Press, 2023. | Includes bibliographical
    references and index.
Identifiers: LCCN 2022040775 (print) | LCCN 2022040776 (ebook) |
    ISBN 9780691219134 (hardback) | ISBN 9780691220758 (ebook)
Subjects: LCSH: African Americans—Politics and government—Philosophy. | Democracy—
    Moral and ethical aspects—United States. | Political science—United States—Philosophy. |
    African Americans—Intellectual life. | African Americans—Civil rights—Philosophy. |
    African American leadership—Philosophy.
Classification: LCC E185.96 .R58 2023 (print) | LCC E185.96 (ebook) |
    DDC 320.089/96073—dc23/eng/20221109
LC record available at https://lccn.loc.gov/2022040775
LC ebook record available at https://lccn.loc.gov/2022040776

British Library Cataloging-in-Publication Data is available

Editorial: Rob Tempio and Chloe Coy
Production Editorial: Sara Lerner
Jacket Design: Katie Osborne
Production: Erin Suydam
Publicity: Alyssa Sanford and Carmen Jimenez

Jacket Credit: Nikola / Adobe Stock

This book has been composed in Miller

Printed on acid-free paper. ∞

Printed in Canada

10 9 8 7 6 5 4 3 2 1

To Roosevelt and Yvonne Rogers

CONTENTS

[vii]

ACKNOWLEDGMENTS

THIS BOOK WAS completed over many—perhaps too many—years. I have secured new jobs, moved across the country and back again, and along the way acquired a great many debts. Among those include administrative staff in the various departments where I have spent time as well as the various librarians at the University of Virginia, Swarthmore College, Emory University, UCLA, and now Brown University. I will not be able to say thank you to all by name. I hope that the substance of the book is thanks enough.

Parts of the book develop ideas I have explored elsewhere. Portions of chapters 1 and 2 incorporate elements from "David Walker and the Political Power of the Appeal," *Political Theory* 43, no. 2 (2015): 208–33 and "David Walker: Citizenship, Judgment, Freedom, and Solidarity," in *African American Political Thought: A Collected History*, ed. Melvin L. Rogers and Jack Turner (Chicago: University of Chicago Press, 2021). Chapter 3 includes modified selections from "Race, Domination, and Republicanism," in *Difference without Domination: Pursuing Justice in Diverse Democracies*, ed. Danielle Allen and Rohini Samanathan (Chicago: University of Chicago Press, 2020). Chapters 4 and 5 contain modified and expanded sections from "Race and the Democratic Aesthetic: Jefferson, Whitman, and Holiday on the Hopeful and the Horrific," in *Radical Future Pasts: Untimely Political Theory*, ed. Romand Coles, Mark Reinhardt, and George Shulman (Lexington: University Press of Kentucky, 2014), 249–82. Chapters 6 and 7 contain modified and expanded sections from "The People, Rhetoric, and Affect: On the Political Force of Du Bois's *The Souls of Black Folk*," *American Political Science Review* 106, no. 1 (2012): 188–203.

Portions of this project have been shared with audiences at the following institutions and organizations: Cornell University; University of California, Riverside; Arizona State University; American Philosophies Forum; Britain and Ireland Association for Political Thought, University of Oxford; University of Massachusetts-Amherst; St. John's College; University of Richmond; Linfield College; University of Chicago; University of San Diego; Mississippi State University; University of Cambridge; Institute of Historical Research; Princeton University; Miami University; University of Texas-Austin; University of Victoria; Emory University; Yale University; University of Memphis; Amherst College; University of Oregon; Columbia University; Georgetown University; University of Wisconsin-Madison;

Hamilton College; University of California, Irvine; Stanford University; Washington University; University of California, Berkeley; Society for the Study of Africana Philosophy; Morehouse College; University of Alabama; University of Washington; University of Maryland, College Park; Rutgers University; History of Philosophy without Gaps podcast; What's Left of Philosophy podcast; University of Vermont; King's College London; University of Pennsylvania; Edmond and Lily Safra Center for Ethics.

I started thinking about this project while on leave as a visiting faculty member in the Department of Political Science at Swarthmore College in 2010–11. I also made significant progress as a Distinguished Visiting Scholar at the John W. Kluge Center at the Library of Congress in the summer of 2019. I finally completed the project while on the faculty at Brown University. I thank all three institutions for their support and stimulating intellectual environments. During my time at Kluge, I was assisted by the careful research of Shannon Dawe.

Rob Tempio at Princeton University Press is a gift. We started a conversation about this book very early on, and over the years Rob nurtured our relationship, periodically checking in to see how I was progressing. And even amid delays, he continued to believe in the project. I thank him for his commitment. Hank Southgate was an invaluable copyeditor before I sent the manuscript to Princeton to begin production and Jenn Backer thereafter. Special thanks to the team at Princeton University Press: Chloe Coy, Sara Lerner, Katie Osborne, and Erin Suydam.

So many people provided assistance along the way, but a few key individuals offered critical advice. They include Danielle Allen, Lawrie Balfour, Elvira Basevich, Adrian Blau, Corey Brettschneider, Nick Bromell, Nicholas Buccola, Alan Coffee, Tommy Curry, Jason Frank, Robert Gooding-Williams, Alex Gourevitch, Bonnie Honig, Juliet Hooker, Humeira Iqtidar, Chike Jeffers, Colin Koopman, Sharon Krause, Meena Krishnamurthy, Ainsley LaSure, Jared Loggins, John Lysaker, Minkah Makalani, Patchen Markell, Utz McKnight, Anthony Sean Neal, Larry Perry, Diana Popescu, Neil Roberts, Corey Robin, Michelle Rose, Ian Shapiro, George Shulman, Siraj Sindhu, Quentin Skinner, Rogers Smith, Jason Stanley, Jeffrey Stout, John Stuhr, Brandon Terry, Ian Ward, Cornel West, Sarah Wilford, Deva Woodley, and Alex Zamalin.

Davide Panagia provided advice and excellent feedback. He was a fantastic colleague while I was at UCLA, and he has become a wonderful friend.

Eddie Glaude, that masterful teacher, first introduced me to the intellectual and philosophical contributions of black people many years ago in college. He takes my calls and replies to my text messages, and after each, I always find my spirit renewed, my mind alive and ready to write again. He continues to model for me a way of reading widely and thinking deeply, and I hope the book honors the lessons I have learned.

Jack Turner, my dear friend Chip. He has listened to my worries, endured my doubts, challenged my arguments, and encouraged my vision. As this project reached its end and I worried whether it would be completed, he steadied and encouraged me until the final page. His last set of comments on the conclusion was just brilliant. I am grateful for his friendship.

In his work and spirit, Chris Lebron knows this project intimately. I have appreciated our many conversations and his listening as I read a paragraph or a few pages over the phone. And as I read, periodically he would say, "Okay, let's come back to that sentence," or "I have a thought about that paragraph." We all should have friends to whom we can read our sentences. He helped bring philosophical precision and beauty to many of the sentences in this book.

My partner, Frederick Godley Rogers, has sustained me throughout the many years of writing this book. When I needed time away to get a chunk of writing done, he supported me without complaint. When I could not go somewhere or do something because the book needed attention, he understood without resentment. For his love and his friendship, I am forever grateful. Our son, Isaiah August Godley-Rogers, seemed to understand the significance of this book and patiently waited for me to take breaks. He has added a joy to my life that I did not know was possible and has anchored me to this world just as I seemed to be slipping away from it. He has renewed my life and purpose. Let all my best sentences now be written on your heart, and in acceptance, revision, or rejection, you will forge who you are meant to be.

This book was just getting underway when my father passed away, and it was coming to a close as my mother departed this world. This book is dedicated to them. My life is good because they were great. I miss them every day.

THE DARKENED LIGHT OF FAITH

An Introduction

The Timeliness of Democratic Faith

In *Darkwater* of 1920, W.E.B. Du Bois offers incisive commentary on the meaning of democracy. Against those who would restrict the franchise, he remarks: "Such arguments show so curious a misapprehension of the foundation of the argument for democracy that the argument must be continually restated and emphasized."[1] Although the context of this statement is about voting, Du Bois emphasizes the principle of equality as the foundation of democracy throughout his work, treating the equal standing of persons in and outside the voting booths as part and parcel of a democratic ethos—a way of life. Du Bois's statement and the views that underwrite it are arresting given the historical setting. He wrote these words at a time when the insecurity of black life was always on display—a period in which, despite the Civil War amendments, Jim and Jane Crow were the law of the land and lynching a daily reminder of one's vulnerability to premature death. Defending democracy against the persistence of racial violence, exclusion, and domination raises an important question that haunts the struggle for racial equality and, indeed, the legitimacy of the American polity. What is it about democracy that justifies our faith, especially African Americans' faith, in it? This is the question to which this book attempts a response.

This question will seem untimely. Given how frequently the police kill African Americans, the ongoing structural inequality they experience, and housing and food insecurity suffered by so many from city to city and state to state, it is difficult to suggest commitment is ever justified. It may seem more appropriate to interpret the United States as working according to plan, connecting the horror of the earliest periods of African American life to the present moment in one story about the nation's presumed

[1]

foundational commitment to racism. Writing, for example, in response to
the 2012 killing of African American Florida teen Trayvon Martin, journalist Ta-Nehisi Coates describes Martin's killing as the natural consequence of the functioning of American society:

> When you have a society that takes at its founding the hatred and deg-
> radation of a people, when the society inscribes that degradation in its
> most hallowed document, and continues to inscribe hatred in its laws
> and policies, it is fantastic to believe that its citizens will derive no ill
> messaging. It is painful to say this: Trayvon Martin is not a miscarriage
> of justice, but American justice itself. This is not our system malfunc-
> tioning. It is our system working as intended.[2]

There is little to deny in Coates's analysis. To his claims, we can add
other voices trying to get us to see that racism functions as a precondition
for American progress. As Calvin Warren tells us: "It is the humiliated,
incarcerated, mutilated, and terrorized black body that serves as the ves-
tibule for the Democracy that is to come."[3] Warren stands in a tradition
of thinking known as Afro-pessimism, including scholars such as Jared
Sexton and Frank Wilderson. All view the persistence of racial inequality
and the vulnerability of black life as the *inescapable* "after-life" of slavery.[4]
These thinkers raise the haunting suggestion that modernity—that period
running roughly from the Glorious Revolution to the American and French
Revolutions—specifies an ontology that "requires an alterity, a referent outside itself"[5] for its conceptualization of identity, freedom, and progress. The
thirst for mastery Max Horkheimer and Theodor Adorno famously identified as part of the European Enlightenment has played itself out through
the logic of racial domination in the Afro-pessimists' view. This ontological
framework in which African Americans work, live, and struggle leads, as
Juliet Hooker and Barnor Hesse tell us, to a central problem: "One of the
fundamental paradoxes of black politics is the invariable futility of directing activism toward a racially governing regime historically founded on the
constitutive exclusion and violation of blackness."[6]

The cold, cruel reality of American life often undercuts moments of
hope.[7] It is no wonder we find it hard to stabilize our faith in creating a
racially just society. Here, in brief, is a version of how the historical narrative goes. In the wake of black Americans' participation in the American
Revolution, the nation witnessed a slow denial of their standing and contribution to the polity. With the ongoing development of slavery in the South,
Northern states in the nineteenth century slowly rescinded rights previously
extended to African American men. Although the Civil War amendments

sought to acknowledge black people's equal status, the nation-state denied the worth of African Americans through the ascendancy of debt peonage, economic exploitation, lynching, and Jim and Jane Crow. The civil rights movement killed Jim and Jane Crow. Still, the policing of black people reemerged through the rise of the carceral state, the welfare state, and the underfunded public education system that has been exacerbated by residential segregation. Whatever one might think of his success, the fact remains that the election of the first black president was followed by another figure who dedicated himself to removing any trace of its previous occupant. That figure's success was, without exaggeration, cultivated through the tropes of white supremacy, nativism, and the commitment to police black and brown populations. Claims of white supremacy's death—of the post-racialism supposedly evidenced by Barack Obama's presidency—have proven false.[8]

This is not merely *a* feature of the American story—this is *the* American Story, Afro-pessimists contend. For them, the historical record is not simply a collection of events that hang together one way rather than another given the interpretative framework one brings to it. Instead, the historical record reveals the deeper logic of America's self-understanding—indeed the self-understanding of the West—that is reflected in the facts regarding the status of black people and the standing of whites. Or to put it differently, one can infer from the facts the commitments held by the American community. This allows someone like Coates to call those struggling for racial justice "dreamers" in a pejorative sense and encourages Warren to do the same with those, especially black people, who deploy the language of hope. The Afro-pessimists' story functions as a making-it-explicit story.

This way of seeing things is powerful. Its power derives from the frequency with which the United States cycles through the emergence, decline, and reemergence of white supremacy. The appeal to transform the nation into a society that is racially just, I imagine, can all be so exhausting. I am sympathetic to this view; I see its allure. At a basic level, we might even think that for the sake of collective self-care, accepting the story as accurate may alleviate the disappointment that is likely to come for those who believe in the possibility of racial justice.

Even as I see the power of this position, I also see how it nonetheless relies upon, to appropriate Hayden White's thinking, a metahistorical framework. Herein lies the problem. By metahistorical, White means the kind of expectations or predictions built into "the content of the [narrative] form."[9] The appeal to history that we often see in Afro-pessimism obscures a background determinism—the past's relationship to the present resolves itself in the form of a fixed future. This is what is on display in Wilderson when he says, "Blackness is coterminous with Slaveness," or appropriating Hortense Spillers, he tells us that "Black . . . is not an arc at all, but a flat line . . . 'historical stillness.'"[10] Facts about the past of racial injustice function as the immovable markers of American society. The result arrests the "distinctive story-potential" of development.[11] Where black lives are concerned, the story of the United States' moral and political growth necessarily becomes a *closed tragedy*.[12] The citizenry is closed off from tragedy's insights and we deny its educative function. In the case of black life in America, we cannot see that the scope and constraints of human flourishing follow from living under emergent white supremacist conditions. Institutions, norms, practices, and sensibilities seemingly follow some inevitable logic and are not the result of choices, unintended consequences, and unconscious decisions. Human agency dissolves altogether, and we fail to acknowledge that our institutions are what they are and our culture is what it is because we have made them so.

But if we step back a moment from determinism—if we allow ourselves to see our societies as something we have a hand in shaping—I think we can ask some critical questions. Is American democracy constitutionally at odds with our goals? Or might it be conducive to building a society in which we all can live equally and at peace with one another? Are there normative resources on which one can rely to advance affirmative claims regarding racial equality? Or must the resources of modern American democracy remain forever premised on racism?

These are not merely historical questions, the answers to which are wholly settled by empirical facts. Rather, what is at stake is the form of narration that already contains closures, openings, possibilities, and even settled futures. What do I mean by this? Consider two ways of telling the story of racial struggle. In our historical narration, we might emphasize the reconstitution of white supremacy amid persistent attempts to achieve racial equality. This is the story of Afro-pessimism. But we could just as easily, and often do, emphasize how multiple waves of racial inclusion disrupted white supremacy. In the end, the story goes, the true American Creed will win the day.[13] The first story has a dark, tragic conclusion that seems inescapable. The second is a romantic story of inevitable progress. Those who embrace the first of these as our "true" racial reality find themselves trying to prove to those of us who have benefited from racial struggle why our success is illusory or, at best, temporary. Those who locate America's identity in its resistance to white supremacy have another problem. They cannot see the evidence of institutional racism,[14] or they readily describe it as anomalous, foreign to the political and economic structures of society and culture.

If the first posture seems unsatisfying because it denies human agency and gives the past too much power over the present and future, the second risks ignoring how institutional logics and state-sanctioned violence emerge from a culture that disregards black people. Both sides fail to distinguish between the somewhat different tasks of *studying* the past and *narrating* the past in a useful way for moving society in a promising direction. In Frederick Douglass's felicitous formulation of the matter: "We have to do with the past only as we can make it useful to the present and to the future."[15]

These words come from Douglass's famous 1852 address, "What to the Slave Is the Fourth of July." This address, I suggest, has an important philosophical insight regarding the normative infrastructure of democracy; it contains, in abbreviated form, much of a response to the question with which we began. In that address, Douglass does not dismiss the past. He stands in a line of thinkers who see in America's past a vital principle that is both visionary and realistic. His intuition is that he can deploy the principle of making and remaking that underwrites the American polity—what political theorists call the people's constituent power—to reimagine who constitutes the civic "we" of society. The idea of the people forms part of the tradition of American life; it is often used to combat the white supremacist tendencies of the American polity. We see it in the abolitionist movement, the long civil rights movement, and the Black Lives Matter movement most recently. Douglass retrieves this principle from the past; he counsels his fellows to place it in the service of the present and future. This implies that acting and reimagining the future is worthwhile and meaningful, but progress is not inevitable.

Douglass was not alone in his thinking. He belongs to a complicated tradition of African American political theorizing that includes nineteenth-century abolitionists David Walker, Maria Stewart, Hosea Easton, and Martin Delany and twentieth-century figures such as Anna Julia Cooper, Ida B. Wells, W.E.B. Du Bois, Alain Locke, Billie Holiday, and James Baldwin. Often, they see their efforts as forming part of the very complex tradition of American moral and political language. They are fully aware of the entanglement of democracy and white supremacy, freedom and slavery, even as they seek to pull from and transform those portions of America's traditions that might support a racially just society. America's meaning—its past, present, and future—is, for them, something over which to struggle. They see "struggle" as an emergent property of the contested notion of the people central to democracy. This at once acknowledges both their place within and contested relationship to American political and moral thought more broadly.[16]

In one sense, entanglement tells us something—namely, that for these thinkers, they recognize a connection between the United States' style of democracy and white supremacy. But in another sense, it does not tell us anything at all. In just what sense are they connected? On the reading of the thinkers I advance, most of them see American democracy and white supremacy as what Rogers Smith calls a "contingent symbiosis." Although discussing the discourse of rights in America, I think we can expand Smith's reflections. The thinkers I discuss largely interpret "America's historical partnership" of democracy and white supremacy "as a profoundly constitutive but still contingent political alliance that has never been inevitable or unalterable." As Smith explains, thinkers who subscribe to the contingent symbiosis thesis "stress how efforts to deny rights [and standing] on racial grounds have always been contested."[17]

As African Americans grappled with the permutations of white supremacy, theirs was not a quest to recover a vision of the exalted America from which we have strayed. After all, the origins of the United States were not merely evidenced in the idea of a free republic but also and more importantly in the exercise of arbitrary power over indigenous populations and black people. The Janus-faced character of the American polity means that the interventions of African Americans are less of a recovery than a reconstruction. Gathering the symbols of their present and America's past, they deploy them and speak through them, but always to authorize something that never truly existed. In this, the general tenor of their outlook rarely treats white supremacy as anomalous to America, but nor do they see the connection between it and democracy as inescapable.

The question of what America *is* or *can be* may defy articulation, but we cannot get on with figuring out where we should go and who we ought to be without narrating the past to which we belong. Worrying, however, about offering the *True* or *Final* description of that past (whether in the form of a closed tragedy or a romance) may miss the point: we ask questions of the past (Who are we, really?) less to understand our identity once and for all and more to aid us in making decisions about who we should become. The meaning of the past is forever being revised in light of an unsettled future. This is the aspirational character of the American imagination; it forms the foundation on which African Americans have often relied to make sense of their appeals to the nation. In this, they have placed their faith.

In the remainder of this introduction, I lay out a more specific set of questions that structure the book and the problem space they suggest, consider the relationship between history and political vision against which the thinkers in this book emerge, specify the key animating concepts that ground the answers to the book's central questions, and outline the path forward.

The Central Questions

The Darkened Light of Faith offers a philosophical-historical reconstruction of the shared normative vision of the thinkers listed above: David Walker, Maria Stewart, Hosea Easton, Martin Delany, Anna Julia Cooper, Ida B. Wells, W.E.B. Du Bois, Alain Locke, Billie Holiday, and James Baldwin. It aims to distill these thinkers' philosophical and rhetorical arguments as they sought to transform America into a racially just society.

I opened this introduction with a question about what justifies faith in the American polity. I suggested that the answer is tied to an aspirational view of the people. This offers a more focused set of questions that animate the book:

- How should we understand the political-philosophical thinking of African Americans (i.e., the thinkers above) who so often found themselves dominated by the American society they so diligently sought to transform?
- What must their vision of democracy presuppose about the people to whom they appealed and the society in which they stood?

In focusing on these two questions, this book intends for its readers to understand the broadly ethical account of political life these thinkers defend. An ethical account offers an orientation for guiding interactions among persons outside of state or federally recognized institutions. An ethical account is broadly social, and not merely a description of programmatic points to inform our political-institutional environment (e.g., political parties, branches of government, and legal institutions). The idea, however, is that the latter political-institutional account is embedded in and draws support from the social vision.

In this book, an ethical account of democracy refers to those features of action, self-understanding, and the value attached to others that are themselves guided by the norms of *freedom* and *equal regard*. Freedom here refers to the ability to pursue one's plans of life without fear or threat of being subjected to the use of arbitrary power—that is, without being dominated.[18] Equal regard is a term of specific importance. To regard someone or community is to show concern for them. To modify regard with the word "equal" means that the concern you extend is not comparatively diminished in relation to others. Invidious racial distinctions, for example, violate the norm of equal regard because they presuppose status hierarchies (sometimes grounded in a story about biology or culture).[19] Equal regard can thus have different modalities, displaying itself in electoral politics, the distributive logic of economic systems, and the social organizations of society. This should not obscure what we are paying attention to—a way of regarding persons not diminished by social hierarchies that attach higher and lower values as if people were set upon a scale of measurement. Equal regard can inform institutions, but the thinkers we consider throughout this book emphasize its role in shaping social life—the character and culture of its inhabitants. To think of democracy in ethical terms is to understand freedom and equal regard as forming key features of a cultural horizon to which we can become habituated.

Given this framework, questions such as "who are we" and "who should we be" figure centrally as these thinkers confront and seek to upend the workings and habits of white supremacy. White supremacy thus functions not as anomalous to American culture but as part of its historical workings, thus necessitating a deep reconstitution of society.[20] The book insists on this view against overly legalistic and institutionalist accounts of democratic theory in circulation. It also advances this view against pessimistic accounts that see in American democracy a fundamental commitment to white supremacy that renders appeals for racial justice naïve. Finally, the book treats the questions of "who are we" and "who should we be" as necessitating a form of responsiveness that guards against romantic or triumphalist narratives of progress.

Notably, the book is selective and does not treat the many complex "ideologies" that define this tradition of thinking—what Michael Dawson calls "Black Visions."[21] It is a selective interpretation of African American political thought from the perspective of a quest to transform the American polity—my central preoccupation. The omission, for instance, of Marcus Garvey or the later work of W.E.B. Du Bois is not a negative commentary on their significant contributions. Similarly, my emphasis on Frederick Douglass or Ida B. Wells or the early to middle Du Bois in their aim to improve the polity does not mean they are more deserving of attention than others. Rather, it speaks to my inquiry into how a group of intellectuals, activists, and, in some cases, artists found a way to commit themselves to make the United States a racially just society. In focusing on this thread of the tradition, one comes to discover the normative vision of democracy that sustained them and that they helped shape and articulate.

Two concepts present themselves—democracy and tradition—and deserve additional comment. The first is explicit throughout the book. The second is implicit in how I proceed. Democracy[22] does not, as just mentioned, exclusively refer to the institutions and procedures specified in the U.S. Constitution. As I read them, these thinkers see democracy as a way of relating to one's fellows that acknowledges their freedom and equal ethical and political standing and shows care and concern in that acknowledgment. "Relating to" is embodied fundamentally in action and comportment. This explains why the archive of African American political and literary reflections is often characterized by a persistent request, often demand, that their white counterparts be more than they are in their treatment of black people, or to see themselves as having betrayed equality, freedom, or justice. Democracy is an embodied and acted upon way of life that black people are often trying to realize mainly because the existing way of life involves violence, exclusion, and domination. The idea of democracy functions as both a presumption of these thinkers' practical and philosophical orientation and a way of relating that they seek to elicit from their fellows. This account is commensurate with the representative institutions of a constitutional order, but democracy's meaning exceeds the workings of those institutions as it seeks a home in the habits and sensibilities of the community.

By tradition—the idea implied in how I proceed—I mean an ongoing practice of inquiry that emanates from a set of historical concerns and problems and their role in shaping the community's ethos. Understanding tradition in this way draws on the very different thinking of post-colonial scholar David Scott and the Aristotelianism of Alasdair MacIntyre. Traditions, as MacIntyre argues, are often defined "retrospectively," but they are nonetheless expressive of a set of themes immanent to communal life and structure the purposes of individuals within the community, even as they disagree on how one ought to understand those themes and on what are the best approaches to addressing them.[23] This is what Scott calls the "problem-space" of language and action—"an ensemble of questions and answers around which a horizon of identifiable stakes . . . hang."[24] Traditions have a dynamic character; their unfolding involves "an argumentative retelling" that assumes the possibility of conflict, harmony, abandonment, and growth.[25] Members of what we think of as intellectual traditions can be understood as responding to, elaborating, criticizing, or wholly rejecting claims put forward by parties to the conversation.

Here now is the problem space. The figures in this book belong to a wider "Afro-modern tradition of political thought" that first emerged in response to eighteenth-century slavery and colonialism.[26] But they specifically and critically engage with the practices and habits of domination that emerge from white supremacy's hierarchy of value in the United States and believe they can use and redeploy the normative resources of democracy to imagine society anew. These two features bind them together across time that justifies speaking of something like African American political thought, while also marking them off from other problems that define the tradition of political philosophy.

Of course, it is significant that the collection of thinkers I take up in this book direct their reflections to the status of black people in the United States and do not concede ground on the ethical and political meaning of democracy. The first narrows the focus area, which means the book does not follow the current drift of important scholarship on black internationalism and transnational influences on African American political thought.[27] The second centers the book's goal to recover a thread of thinking within African American political thought that sees the practice of contestation as central to the legitimacy of the American democratic project.

Legitimacy is not a way of talking about adherence to a de facto polity but a way of marking the principle of revision and invention that can connect what the nation *is* to what it *may be*, and do so within the very boundary of the background norms with which the citizenry is familiar. In basic electoral terms, for example, this means losing need not be a permanent condition. In broad ethical-political terms, it means the culture of a democratic society is ideally open to development as a condition of its legitimacy. The criterion of legitimacy is the norm of openness, with freedom and equal regard guiding the purposes to which openness should be put.

The principle of openness provides political actors entitlement to improve the polity. This is not to suggest that existing institutional configurations and laws are insignificant. Rather, it claims that citizens will typically act in the name of a future-not-yet and treat responsiveness to that imagined future as the grounds for the legitimacy of democracy. This is because our institutions are not perfectly organized, our laws are never consistently followed, and the virtue of justice is always in short supply. This avoids any suggestion that these thinkers subscribe to democracy's inherent goodness.[28] Instead, I focus on what African American thinkers believe to be possible, given how they understand democracy (i.e., its commitments) and our capacities.

In using the language of a future-not-yet, the book follows a naturalistic line of thinking latent in these thinkers' writings. Their naturalism mingles with a perfectionist impulse regarding self and society's capacity to improve. By naturalism, I mean the basic claim that society's norms emerge from our interactions with each other and the wider world to which we belong. Our norms do not sit outside our everyday practices of critical evaluation—they exist in the space of reasons.[29] An ethical quality, as denoted in the utterance "that was a mean thing to do," is susceptible to being a true or false statement on par with the claim "that dog is brown." Notice, both intend to reference something in the world, although we treat human beings as natural parts of that world.

I use the language of perfectionism to track a way of thinking about the *existing* features of democratic life (e.g., norms, beliefs, and social practices) and the cognitive-affective dimensions of human beings that make possible imagined futures.[30] Importantly, I do not define perfectionism by referencing some static vision of the good or human excellence, even as perfectionism sits within a regulatory framework. Seeing self and society as subject to improvement takes off right at the point where the norms of freedom and equal regard function as regulative goods. These norms discipline the character and content of society's responsiveness and development, while opening intense debate about how to understand the meaning of those norms and who can lay claim to them. African American political thought often intervenes with creative reconfigurations and resignifications of the existing features of democratic life. But what they are often doing is directing their readers and listeners to an incompleteness to life as found in the treatment of black people. The aversion to or shame of this incompleteness, they hope, will push individuals beyond themselves (as a form of education) toward new patterns of living and ways of seeing one's fellows. Their perfectionist contributions are at once internal to American culture, even as they transcend the empirical realities black and white people live.

History and Vision

The studies in this book are not exhaustive of the authors and texts under consideration. Some of the thinkers I consider have written only one main text (e.g., Walker) and others have written numerous works (e.g., Du Bois and Baldwin). In cases where I take up a thinker who falls into the second camp, I am not especially interested, as a biographer might be, in holding the entirety of a thinker's corpus in view and exploring the relationship between context and ideas throughout a life. As political theorists often do, I am not attempting to articulate the philosophical holism of these thinkers. I do not claim to represent the ultimate integrity of their views throughout their careers. The book invites the reader to think about the themes here in the context of a single figure in just the way suggested by the biographer or the political theorist, but that is not my task.

Moreover, since I am interested in their thinking when they believed democracy susceptible to being improved and realized, I do not pursue those moments when despair set in. Here, "despair set in" refers narrowly to those moments when the quest to transform the United States was abandoned, never to be pursued again. Those moments are important and worthy of study. Reflecting on them, however, is not the task here. This book is after what, in their estimation, is necessary to transform the United States into a polity that affirms the self-worth and normative standing of black people and that grounds self-worth and standing in a firm basis of proper care and concern. Since the inception of this project, my thinking has been to proceed candidly regarding my approach and prepare the reader for precisely what they will receive from beginning to end. Suppose it turns out, at the very start, that my mode of proceeding stands in violation of the methodological commitments of the reader and the book is therefore unlikely to get a fair hearing. In that case, it stands to reason that this book is not for you and you should promptly put it to the side. But I hope you will instead stay and journey with me.

Notwithstanding, my historical sensibilities guide the method of engagement with these thinkers and I attend to the context. The working assumption is that what these thinkers are *saying* is coextensive with understanding what they are *doing* vis-à-vis their context. I treat their texts as ethical and political interventions seeking to transform their communities and as containing insights for us today.[31] Here, history becomes a means to envision a different community.

How we should stand to the past and allow it to inform our orientation toward the future has always been a lively debate within African American political thought. An example of the importance of this is in order. In his 1885 Storer College address, "The Need for New Ideas and New Aims," African American minister and nationalist Alexander Crummell worries about black people's constant "recollection" of slavery and domination, for "as slavery was a degrading thing, the constant recalling of it to the mind serves, by the law of association, to degradation."[32] Crummell attempts to free black Americans from what he calls the "commanding" thought of slavery and domination so that they may imagine new ideas and new aims regarding their freedom. After all, Storer College was created in the wake of the Civil War to educate and usher black men into a bright future of freedom. "You will notice here," Crummell argues, "that there is a broad distinction between memory and recollection. Memory . . . is the necessary and unavoidable entrance, storage and recurrence of facts and ideas to the understanding and the consciousness."[33] But he seems to think that meditating on the past will only constrain the imagination of black Americans and serve to diminish them in their own eyes.

Douglass, who was in attendance, greeted Crummell's remarks with "his emphatic and most earnest protest."[34] But why protest? The reason is that Douglass wants both black and white Americans to keep in view (that is, recollect) the harms of slavery in order to discipline present and future action but also to ensure that one acknowledges the problems to which he and others were called to respond. Recollection is the process of bringing back to mind that which lives in our memory. Douglass, of course, was also after what scarred that past. Recollecting the past recognizes what Wells, Du Bois, Baldwin, and Morrison go on to observe: the past lives in us (Du Bois, explicitly, refers to this as the "present-past"), subtly shaping our habitual and perceptual capacities.[35] For them, the past functions as funded experience, making a claim on Americans and against which a properly imagined future comes into view.

This, too, is Douglass's position. Speaking only two years earlier on the twentieth anniversary of the Emancipation Proclamation, with the Civil War still fresh in his mind, Douglass tells his audience: "Man is said to be an animal looking before and after. To him alone is given the prophetic vision, enabling him to discern the outline of his future through the mists of the past."[36] He binds the future and past together, as he says elsewhere, if only to hold back the "many disguises" deployed by the "South" to explain away slavery as the reason for the Civil War and with it "influences, which will remain with us . . . for generations to come."[37]

Douglass makes an important observation. The influence of the past is not merely something that we need to reckon with in order to imagine the future. The future itself (even in its imagined form) will likely bear the trace of the tragic past—the betrayals, the violent acts, and the deaths. The issue is how shall we stand in relation to this fact. Will we disavow, allowing the past to wreak havoc on our lives? Or will we try to be responsive and accountable to it, thus placing the past in a productive relationship with the future?[38] Throughout the book, I will insist that this second position runs through most, if not all, of the thinkers we consider and finally leads to the idea of responsiveness to the past as a feature of democratic life given our racial history. We will see this most powerfully on display in the critical essays of James Baldwin.

The Animating Concepts

I have provided a set of questions that motivate the book, but *The Darkened Light of Faith* also revolves around several concepts that serve as guides for addressing the questions above—"the people," "rhetoric," "affect," "aesthetics," "character," and "faith"—concepts that find powerful defenders in the thinkers that animate the book. The book argues that the workings of these concepts capture the deeper meaning of much of what African Americans are after. These concepts help disclose their understanding of the interiority of democracy and the resources that can enrich and extend its reach. I do not structure the book according to these concepts. Instead, they unfold throughout the book. Sometimes they emerge for analysis, and, at other times, they serve as presuppositions of the argument. They nonetheless work as substantive frameworks that shape these thinkers' understanding of the problem-space. These concepts are not unique to African Americans, but they redeploy them because they see in them the means for articulating social forms and ways of living not yet realized.

The book centralizes the meaning of "the people" as the animating ethical and political category of democracy. Although there is a historical lineage regarding the importance of the people, the term has received renewed interest in recent decades.[39] I join others in emphasizing the constitutive futurity of the people in American discourse. Critically, I add to that discussion by showing how African Americans put the concept of the people to work. The people function as both a descriptive term (referring to those with rights and privileges per the Constitution) and an aspirational term (a category in which new visions of self and society might be reimagined). The latter view captures the discontinuity between an evolving idea of the people and the relative stability of political society (i.e., governmental institutions, laws, and the policing apparatus) that claims to speak and act in the people's name and on their behalf.

The aspirational view gains the power that it does because it involves claims about the malleability of our cognitive and emotional faculties— that is, it presupposes the people's susceptibility to being transformed, expanded, and improved. This is a feature of American political and moral discourse generally, running from Thomas Jefferson through the transcendentalists to the pragmatists. As with them, the aspirational view of the people forms a central thread in African American political thought. Democracy derives its legitimacy from this aspirational description, and thus the principle of openness forms a constitutive feature of democracy's self-understanding. This normative perspective imagines the American polity capable of receiving new visions of how it ought to be organized and how it ought to understand itself.

Rhetoric, as a mode of persuasion, is how these thinkers seek to induce their fellows to embrace new visions of the nation and their place therein. Throughout the book, rhetoric refers to a practice of speaking and writing that seeks to persuade one's audience. Simple enough. But one of the critical insights of scholarship on rhetoric is that it is neither an idiosyncratic feature of democracy nor a strategic framework of manipulation.[40] For our purposes, rhetoric functions in a twofold sense. First, rhetoric is a means to honor the judgment of one's interlocutors as well as denote the absence of sovereign control over those with whom we engage and on whom we depend for nurturing a safe and nourishing community. This is also true, as I read the tradition, of its religious prophetic form and its secular variety.[41] To say "I am persuaded" is not to make a claim about what the rhetorician has achieved, and so my account here disciplines the presumptive and coercive role the charismatic leader is thought to serve in African American political thought. On the account of rhetoric I use, the person who is persuaded is making a claim about their abilities—they have turned things over in their mind, they have used their judgment, and they have decided to live their lives in the light of that judgment. Rhetoric's internal logic thus invites contestatory engagement. It honors the reflective and affective agency of those to whom the rhetorician appeals.

In the second sense, rhetoric functions as a means to enter the discursive field of America's ethical and political life. We see this quite consistently when African American thinkers appeal, for example, to the Declaration of Independence or the American Founders or they figuratively place themselves into the story of Exodus (not uniquely American).[42] At just these moments, they pay deference to the legitimating languages of society. For without some horizon of legitimation, they can scarcely be thought persuasive in their appeal. In fact, it is unlikely they would be intelligible at all. But importantly, this is always the first step to transforming the reach of society's discursive and practical symbols. They thus understand rhetoric as a form of power.

We clearly see this idea of rhetoric as power if we focus on the cultural and characterological significance of white supremacy and racial domination. Here, rhetoric's ethical dimension is most clearly visible. African

American thinkers direct their rhetorical appeals to the affective dimension of persons, and personhood, for many of them, presumes a cognitive-affective bind. I run these two together (cognitive and affective) so that the reader understands that for the thinkers I discuss in this book, emotions do not merely lead to physical disturbances of the body (e.g., recoiling in horror or lowering one's head in shame) but significantly are also evaluative (e.g., I lower my head in shame because I stand in violation of my commitments or the commitments I should hold).[43]

As I maintain throughout, from Walker to Baldwin, these thinkers believe that human sensibilities perform a central role in our comportment toward the world and others. Whether it is in Walker's graphic invocations of the suffering slave, Du Bois's textured narrative of black life, or Wells and the NAACP's deployment of the lynched black person to reveal the horrors of America's character, they all see themselves as trying to reeducate the sensibilities of their white counterparts. Their deployment of fear, sympathy, love, shame, and horror is part and parcel of the normative infrastructure of human life. These emotions help us in our process of marking out just what kinds of life are worthy of inhabiting and what forms of life we should abandon.

For them, democratic politics is not merely an arrangement of institutions and procedural functions but a means for rearranging and transforming our sensibilities. Rearrangement and transformation are focused on having our perceptual capacities (i.e., the senses that enable us to perceive and respond to the world) attuned to the claim black Americans make and the pain they endure, thus locating them within rather than outside our cognitive-affective field. For example, Billie Holiday's late 1930s orchestrated performances of the haunting song about lynching, "Strange Fruit," in New York's Café Society provoke her audiences into displaying the appropriate emotions to lynching through a mimetic display of the horrific. The meaning of the song contains a somatic-affective road map that Holiday's gestures make explicit for consideration. Her words and performances reach out toward the audience, asking them to think and feel the norm being conveyed—that we should look at these events in horror. Or to put it differently, she performs the very thing she hopes to arouse in her listeners. This is not an evasion of politics but engaging politics at the deepest level of self and society. This is what Baldwin has in mind when he says in *The Fire Next Time*: "that we, with love, shall force our brothers to see themselves as they really are, to cease fleeing from reality and begin to change it."[44] As with Holiday and Baldwin, the goal of this tradition is to cultivate new sensitivities toward black people (sometimes by seeing things as we should and other times by seeing who we are in our treatment of black people) and to do so such that they emanate from white Americans' self-understanding.

In saying that *democratic politics is not merely an arrangement of institutions and procedural functions,* I do not mean to deny the necessity of regulation. I accept as settled Martin Luther King Jr.'s point that "judicial decrees may not change the heart, but they can restrain the heartless." There are many practices—slavery, racial segregation, unfair treatment based on race or gender differences—that are demonstrably wrong and thus require prohibitions and sanctions. For just this reason, the franchise has functioned and continues to do so as a tool of self-defense for African Americans. There is a place, then, for what King calls the "force of law" in realizing justice. But we must not be misled into believing that restraining the heartless is sufficient for rightly orienting us to the values the law defends. "We must admit," King continues, "that the ultimate solution to the race problem lies in the willingness of men to obey the unenforceable."[45] Here, the subjects of engagement are not the unfeeling actors—the heartless that King speaks about—but the ones whose hearts have not yet been touched. These are the people to whom King speaks when he says, "our goal is to create a beloved community and this will require a qualitative change in our souls as well as a quantitative change in our lives."[46] This qualitative change in our souls—this perfectionist ethic—informs many of the thinkers we will take up.

In proceeding this way, my reading of these thinkers overlaps with political theory's turn toward ethos, but my most proximate fellow-travelers emphasize the "habits" of racial disregard (e.g., Eddie Glaude, Danielle Allen, and Christopher Lebron) and the "culture" of racial ideology (e.g., Cornel West, Iris Marion Young, and Imani Perry).[47] Ethos refers to the "characteristic spirit . . . of a people or community."[48] African American political thought aims to uncover one kind of ethos that sustains what Allen calls the habits of "dominance and acquiescence."[49] These habits often structure the relationships and orientations among black and white citizens and narrow the cognitive-affective field of regard. But given that African Americans stand within the very community whose particular way of life they seek to transform, it is appropriate to frame their resistance as pressing against a *specific form* of American life.[50] Seen in this light, African American thinkers seek to engender feelings of horror (in some cases) and shame (in other instances) regarding the people we are when the habits of acquiescence and dominance are at play. They aim to cultivate an alternative ethos that affirms black Americans' social standing and proper regard for them. It is not only then that these thinkers direct their reflections to the affective basis of self and society, but they see both as artistic productions in a fundamental sense—that is, as configurations that intend to "engender a certain sensibility toward" the reality they describe.[51]

By focusing on the importance of character as a site where affect and aesthetics combine, I resist accounts that confine political and ethical development to the domain of legality. One prominent contemporary thread in thinking about constituent power restricts its meaning to constitutional or, more broadly, juridical processes.[52] For the thinkers considered in this book, it leaves little room for addressing the political and ethical culture of society to which they direct their attention.

I have frequently invoked the language of character. In following King (although we see this in earlier African American thinkers), I have also used character's semantic cognate—soul—to convey those ethical characteristics that define who we are. The soul functions as the bearer of the attributes we typically associate with character. I have used these terms to make clear what these thinkers are trying to transform.

The use of character or soul often makes many anxious because they worry it will only serve to indict those who are often the victims rather than those responsible for the harms. The nineteenth- and early twentieth-century version of this among African Americans was decidedly mixed. Uplift ideology or respectability politics by African American thinkers—an ethical-political orientation that centers the practices and culture of black people as essential to their freedom—was consistently structured by criticisms of white supremacy.[53] From Walker to Douglass to Cooper to Du Bois, the emphasis was on black agency and on black people's role in their own advancement, while also engaging in criticisms of the psychological, social, and institutional workings of white supremacy that constrained black flourishing. As African American thinkers struggled to articulate a robust vision of self and society necessary to sustain freedom and equality, they contended with dominant cultural norms that linked freedom to sovereignty on the one side and to crass individualism on the other.

Admittedly, against the backdrop of a culture that devalued black life and also affirmed ideas of sovereignty and individualism, the politics of respectability often produced its own irony. As Kevin Gaines puts it: "Elite Blacks replicated, even as they contested, the uniquely American racial fictions upon which the liberal conceptions of social reality and 'equality' were founded."[54] The historical downstream result of this is the following: the context of domination falls from view, leaving only the will and character of the victims in place. Failing to free oneself from domination, or so the argument goes, is a problem with you, not with the society to which you belong. Historically, the result of this, argues Adolph Reed, led to a vision of racial custodianship—a set of political and cultural actors that broker for black freedom while reinscribing worries of black people's preparedness, especially poor black people, for freedom.[55]

While I am sympathetic to these worries, especially given how easily character-talk lends itself to conservative approaches to addressing the inequities in black life, I ultimately think leaning too heavily on this framework distorts the thinkers under consideration in this book. For on their account, they intend to get us to see that our political and economic institutions are not structurally immune from our faults. This claim, and primarily because of where power resides, is consistently directed at the failure of character and the short supply of virtue of white Americans. All of the thinkers considered in this book have something to say about black people regarding their role in securing their own freedom, but those claims are always housed within a critical analysis of the United States' culture of devaluing black people that shapes institutions and, significantly, the outlook of white Americans. The implication, I hope, is clear: it is a mistake to think we can realize and institutionalize a healthy and inclusive democratic society without a set of habits and orientations that support the equal standing of citizens.

The emphasis in this book on character or soul is fundamentally about centering a question: *Who do we take ourselves to be in the lives we live and the practices in which we participate?* The "we" here is a general kind; the question is for members of the United States. The question deliberately does not focus on discrete actions of persons and, instead, emphasizes the patterns of living that shape and give expression to the lives we do live in relation to our black counterparts. As I interpret the thinkers in this book, it seems that what they have in mind above all else is the character of our lives, whose very workings often frustrate the flourishing of black lives.

Throughout, I invoke the use of character or soul, to use John Dewey's language, to refer to "an acquired predisposition to ways or modes of response"[56] in how we think, feel, and act. To say "acquired predisposition" is to say there are general patterns to our attitudes and actions that are themselves shaped by background beliefs. This is what gives our way of acting in the world a kind of predictive quality.[57] I shall assert that this notion of character or soul is applicable to communities—indeed, whole nations—as when we speak of fighting for or improving the "soul of the nation." It is just simply possible for us to talk about the character of the American polity—its predicative tendencies toward black people and, even, its countervailing tendencies. It is even possible to speak, as the language of countervailing tendencies suggests, of the national character warring against itself.

This view of character sits in the background of a great many African American thinkers. This is why Baldwin says that the "business of the writer is to examine attitudes, to go beneath the surface, to tap the source."[58] Here, Baldwin discusses the writer's goal as a social critic and as a model for democratic citizenship. We must go beneath the surface because it shapes how we see, hear, and think: "The things that people really do and really mean and really say and really feel are almost impossible for them to describe, but these are the very things which are most important about them. These things control them and that is where reality is."[59] But we ought to be careful. White supremacy does not merely obstruct democracy because it shapes the institutional and economic structures through which we move (although it does) but, significantly, as Baldwin suggests, because it molds the orientation of white Americans who come to see themselves as more worthy than others, and certainly as more emblematic of the "True" or "Real" America.[60] White supremacy thus functions as a feature of the American character, and it is what makes that character an object of horror, of shame, of profound disappointment, and, dare I say, as something from which we must revolt.

Amid the workings of Jim and Jane Crow and the horror of lynching, Ida B. Wells points us to the logic of white supremacy in the form of the "unwritten law" that defines much of what African Americans intend to upset. Lynching, she explains in her 1900 article "Lynch Law in America," represents "the cool, calculating deliberation of intelligent people who openly avow that there is an 'unwritten' law that justifies them in putting human beings to death without complaint under oath."[61] The passage is gripping; she intends to capture the unstated habits of American life. It denotes the ever-present force of white supremacy (that which is unwritten) that shapes white Americans' outlook and polices the boundaries between them and blacks (thus functioning as law). White supremacy forms a collection, as Baldwin tells us, of "habits of thought [that] reinforce and sustain habits of power." For that reason, "it is not even remotely possible for the excluded to become included, for this inclusion means, precisely, the end of the *status quo*."[62] At a basic level, by status quo Baldwin means the habits of believing white Americans are worthy of care and concern while non-whites, especially black folks, are not. In his last book, King points to this same force when he explains that "white America is not even psychologically organized to close the gap" between themselves and black Americans to realize equality.[63] Wells's, Baldwin's, and King's remarks could have come from Walker or Easton or Du Bois. Precisely because the unwritten law informs white people's identity, African American intellectuals often direct their reflections to the characterological and psychological foundations of American life.

These thinkers are not naïve; they know that success is not assured. The reason is simple but often ignored: African Americans depend on the judgment and actions of those over whom they exercise no control. For this very reason, they rely on faith to sustain themselves during their struggles. However, the grand illusion of American popular thinking is in believing that it grants to its participants sovereign control over their lives. This belief is heightened by the specific ways white supremacy immunizes some segments from the racial harms experienced by other segments of society. In their struggles to contest white supremacy and transform society— in their dependence on those over whom they do not control—African Americans often model a form of non-sovereign existence that mirrors the interdependence and uncertainty of democratic life.[64] In other words, the specific and heightened state of vulnerability black people experience bespeaks a general form of vulnerability that all democratic citizens must confront in their reliance on their fellows.

There is, of course, an important caveat to this point. As it relates to black Americans specifically, the aim is to disentangle their vulnerability from their blackness. But they nonetheless ask us to remain attuned to the general vulnerability that comes with being reliant on one's fellows in a democratic society. In grappling with experiences of disregard, they reveal for themselves and their white counterparts that the logic of white supremacy turns on a fundamental rejection of the dangers (and the benefits) that come with democracy—with working in concert and community with others in contexts of uncertainty.

This uncertainty heightens the necessity of faith. Admittedly, "faith" is a term that does not seem like the kind of thing one would want to invoke where political life is concerned. On one level, faith readily brings to mind dependence on a non-human entity such as God. On another level, faith seems to involve us in holding beliefs that appear irrational for people to hold. This may unwittingly tether us to an irredeemably unjust polity. For example, Martin Delany worried that black people take their religious faith "too far," preventing them from acknowledging that their white counterparts are beyond repair.[65] Or, one might think that the need for faith is pointless precisely because of the existing legal and institutional safeguards that sidestep a game of chance that faith would seemingly involve us in.[66]

Faith, in the first instance, need not work in that way. People have faith in God's redeeming power, a naturalistic faith in humans' collective capacities to be better than what they are, and faith in the power of a political vision to capture the imagination of others and direct their actions. Throughout this book, I shall often emphasize the cooperative relationship between the last two objects of faith as forming part of one coherent whole.

Regarding the second worry—faith as holding beliefs that appear irrational—I also do not think this is necessarily true. I generally agree with Robert Merrihew Adams that "faith is, or involves, believing something that a rational person might be seriously tempted to doubt."[67] As we will see with Douglass, but especially Cooper, faith in a vision of life will always be in danger of giving the society to which one belongs and the capacities of one's fellow citizens too much credit. Since our political and ethical standing is always in need of social support, it is not clear how we avoid uncertainty by emphasizing institutional configurations or constitutional norms.

As I interpret the thinkers throughout this book, faith is a stance toward a vision of life that one projects into a world at variance with that vision and for which one is willing to struggle in the service of and often against the odds. Faith, as theologian Paul Tillich famously tells us, is a matter of "ultimate concern."[68] And "our ultimate concern is that which determines our being or non-being."[69] There is, then, a stubborn attachment to a vision of life precisely because were one to lose faith in it or come to think it could never be, one would lose something of constitutive significance. Precisely because faith takes uncertainty as a central feature of its existential and epistemic logic, faith-holders are capable of struggling in the face of democracy's likely compromises with injustice and disregard without giving in to pessimism or withdrawal.

Faith is less a species of a particular religion, although religious commitments may be involved, and more a function of the imagination seeking to realize the good related to one's very standing. Two observations about this point are worthy of note. First, given the connection between faith and ethical and political standing, it should be unsurprising that faith forms a central thread in African American political thought and action. As James Cone tells us, for an "abused and scandalized people—the losers and the down and out," the formal structure of faith provides black people with the strength to struggle against the odds.[70] This need not depend on the thick eschatological framework informing Tillich's and Cone's reflections, if we see the general framework of faith as a feature of perfectionist longings in both sacred and secular forms. For African Americans, worrying about their political and ethical standing is a matter of ultimate concern.

Second, in struggling against the odds, the ethical and political imagination is a central feature of perfectionist longings. The imagination figures prominently in African American political thought, carrying a role similar to that Percy Shelley assigned to the imagination in poetry—namely, that "a man, to be greatly good, must imagine intensely and comprehensively; he must put himself in the place of another and his own. The great instrument of moral good is the imagination."[71] For this reason, Douglass, to take just one example, tells us that the most interesting side of human beings, even as complex as we are, is our "dreamy, clairvoyant, poetic . . . side . . . the side which is better pleased with . . . things as they seem, than things as they are."[72] For Douglass and others, this is not a retreat from reality but a confrontation with it and an attempt to fight against the deadening forces of "things as they are." The imagination, as I use it throughout, is the ability to see the *not yet*. Faith becomes the imagination's expression, and the courage to act functions as faith's executive virtue.[73] When bound to the imagination, faith looks on the present from the perspective of the future. The vision of the future becomes part of the reason for resisting present actions that frustrate flourishing. This does not, however, involve denying the present (and, as a result, the past) since the ethical and political imagination always carries the ghostly after-effect of the reality that gave it life.[74] Resistance involves working through the present and past such that one is no longer under their control. The disciplined quality of faith comes from taking bits and pieces of the existing culture of American life (things as they seem, in Douglass's language) and reweaving them into a narrative about freedom's realization and equal regard. It is a way of helping others imagine more comprehensively than they do and from positions they do not occupy.

Both here and throughout, I invoke culture as a way to understand (once more) the register on which these thinkers work. Culture is the web of beliefs, norms, and values that shape from below and above the social-psychological horizon in which we forge our characters and understand our place and the place of others in society.[75] As Imani Perry puts it: "we have common ways of thinking that are reflective of a racial ideology and that sustains a belief in or an assumption of White superiority."[76] These common ways of thinking provide the context in which ideas of who is worthy of regard and disregard form. Therefore, culture is not about the "best which has been thought and said";[77] rather, culture embodies ways of living and the patterns of that life whose meaning is captured in the complex whole of society's social understanding.

Importantly, in a diverse society, culture is always internally differentiated as it reflects the inner tensions and pressures of a community. I thus treat these thinkers as interested in focusing our attention on ways of living that disregard black life. They seek to offer alternative patterns of proper regard to reshape the culture of American life. In this sense, from Walker to Baldwin, and in political pamphlets, treatises, and music, the idea of democracy—how to understand it and its location—spans the field of culture itself. This explains why they often concern themselves with the normative underbelly of political life, speaking both to and beyond society's institutional and juridical practices. They concern themselves with trying to figure out just how it is that white Americans come to think of themselves in the way that they do and just how white Americans could come to choose to be something other than the false ideas they hold, the cruel actions they often commit, and the dehumanizing practices in which they participate.

The Path Forward

Here now is the unfolding of the path of this book. Because of the book's internal complexity, I have found it necessary to preface each part with introductory remarks to remind the reader of where we have been and what we still have left to traverse. Part 1 outlines the central concerns of the first three chapters. It begins with a question: How did African Americans in the nineteenth century come to imagine themselves as political agents amid their exclusion and domination? In answering this question, I track the power of rhetoric, how it centralizes the capacity for judging as the essence of the citizenly standing of persons, the ability for transformation and improvement as a result, and the form of domination against which black Americans struggled.

Chapter 1 centralizes the importance of nineteenth-century abolitionist David Walker. There I offer a reading of his widely circulated 1829 pamphlet. Walker's famous and infamous *Appeal to the Colored Citizens of the World, But in Particular, and Very Expressly, to Those of the United States of America* expresses a puzzle at the very outset. What are we to make of his use of "citizens" in the title given the denial of political rights and equal standing to African Americans? The chapter argues that the pamphlet relies on, because it emerges within, the cultural and linguistic norms associated with the term "appeal" in the eighteenth and nineteenth centuries. This allows Walker to call forth the political standing of black people. Walker's use of the term "citizen" dispenses with the recognitive legal relationship we usually associate with constitutionalism. In contrast, it is the practice of judging that grounds one's citizenly standing. This, I argue, is the pamphlet's political power; it exemplifies the call-and-response logic of rhetoric as a feature of what Walker calls a republican society.

Chapter 2 extends the previous analysis by explaining the relationship between responsiveness (as embodied in Walker's goal to stimulate his readers' judgment) and political action. If the first chapter illuminates how rhetorical engagement affirms the political standing of addressees in a republican polity, chapter 2 asks what entailments follow from political standing in the face of domination. Walker tells us that he seeks to awaken his fellows. We must ask: To what is he trying to awaken them? His answer, I argue, is what I call the demand of freedom. To stand within the normative horizon of taking oneself to be free involves, quite simply, but powerfully, the demand to resist domination.

Walker's text is about freedom and how one can awaken blacks and whites—men and, importantly, women—to its demand. This is the place of his perfectionism but also that of several other prominent nineteenth-century thinkers such as Maria Stewart, Hosea Easton, and Frederick Douglass. All of them help fill out my discussion of the period. All are concerned with how domination distorts the aspiring feature of the self—what they call the soul—and how we are to guard against distortion. This involves thinking through black Americans' relationship to themselves amid domination but also, and critically, the comportment of white Americans. It is this second issue where the cognitive-affective features of self and societal improvement come into view as Walker appeals to fear, shame, and integrity. In this, we see the ethical character of the tradition with which we will be concerned.

Chapter 3 brings Walker's and others' reliance on republicanism, with its idea of freedom as non-domination, under critical scrutiny. The point of doing so is to explain how character and culture—the sites of perfectionist intervention—function in the criticism of white supremacy. This chapter pursues two arguments. First, the chapter contends that we should read nineteenth-century African American thinkers as resituating republicanism's idea of civic virtue in the context of chattel slavery and racism. The result transforms civic virtue into a defense of racial solidarity. This was supported by the various political activities of the nineteenth century that we see in periodicals by African Americans, literary societies, and the Negro Convention movement beginning in the 1830s. But it also found philosophical articulation and defense in various thinkers running from the 1830s to the 1850s.

The chapter enriches the meaning of non-domination (beyond its normal descriptions in the contemporary literature) by placing it in the context of white supremacy. In doing so, we see how these thinkers illuminate an essential difference between political slavery and chattel slavery that is often missing from defenses of republicanism. Political slavery involves denying a standing previously had (think, for example, of the British American colonists). In contrast, chattel slavery refers to beliefs that one was never *naturally* fit for standing at all.

These two different forms of slavery generate different responses. Historically, most variants of republicanism tie mastery to identifiable persons or institutions. This largely shapes the legalistic or institutionalist responses of redress. In contrast, African American thinkers see domination as emanating from the community—its culture—given the hostile and demeaning ideas about black people in circulation. Easton will refer to this as "public sentiment" in the 1830s, Douglass in the 1840s will refer to blacks as being the "slaves of the community," and Frances Ellen Watkins Harper will say in the 1850s that blacks are enslaved to a "vitiated public opinion."[78] In all instances, what they have in mind is the culture of disregard and they see it as the site on which transformation must occur.

By the end of part 1, we will be left with an important set of questions that frame the four chapters of part 2. We can state the questions as such: Can the account of our cognitive-affective capacity for transformation suggested by the previous chapters find support in the normative foundation of American life? Is there a way of understanding the norms of legitimacy and justification central to American political life as supporting the plasticity of the self as suggested by the appeals of many of these thinkers? How to effect a transformation in the citizenry's cognitive-affective capacities to bring the life of African Americans into proper view? These questions are of utmost importance because by the end of chapter 3, a disagreement opens between Delany's forceful rejection of the idea that the American polity is susceptible to transformation in the 1850s and Douglass's (and others') faith in the opposite claim.

Chapter 4 begins to answer these questions by turning to the idea of the people central to American political discourse—the people in its descriptive and aspirational modes. The chapter also addresses a concern that emerges with this account of the people—the way the aspirational account leaves black people open to abuse—by revisiting the debate between Delany and Douglass in the 1850s over emigration. I treat accounts of the people as a means for thinking about ethical and political transformation. But I do so by recovering and using Thomas Jefferson as a proxy for a

general way of thinking in which the idea of the people is tied to openness—an idea internal to early American revolutionary discourse. Instability sits at the core of the idea of the people central to popular sovereignty.
As we will see, this undermines determinant descriptions of the people,
both the version found in Jefferson's unsavory moments and the version
found in Delany's writings of the 1850s.

The chapter also takes up a critical issue, one that remains with us today.
In orienting African Americans to a future that may never arrive, they may
unwittingly become reconciled to their condition as they long for a future-
not-yet. Returning to Delany and Douglass, but now with the insights
of Anna Julia Cooper's seminal text of 1892, *A Voice from the South*, the
chapter maintains that this problem denotes the uncertainty that defines
political life and necessitates faith. On this account of the people, faith
becomes an intrinsic feature of democratic life.

Chapter 5 revolves around a series of questions that think through the
process by which the people are called to a higher vision of themselves
in late nineteenth- and early twentieth-century America. How should we
read Ida B. Wells's rich and detailed journalistic narrations of lynching?
How should we understand the deployment of lynching photographs by
the NAACP? How should we interpret Billie Holiday's powerful and culturally significant protest song "Strange Fruit" and explicit performances
of it throughout her career?

The chapter explores the horror of lynching events (as described or
photographed) as part of a politics of reeducation. Just as lynching events
and photographs tied white participants together in a community organized around norms and practices that involved policing and brutalizing
black Americans, antilynching activists see the same photographs as a visible testimony to the moral depravity of white Americans that might galvanize the black community and shame the polity into a new, higher mode
of living. The chapter maintains that Wells, the NAACP, and Holiday presuppose the people as an unsettled category and understand the image (in
fact or imagined) as part of calling a people into existence.

The first part of the chapter begins with a stylized account of the relationship between aesthetics and democracy as distilled from Walt Whitman's *Democratic Vistas*. In that work we see the centrality of aesthetics
and the power of the image in political society, and Whitman's attempt to
make the viewer perceptually sensitive to the equal standing of persons.
With the idea of the aspirational people on the one side and the account
of democratic aesthetics on the other, we discover our angle of vision for
understanding Wells, the NAACP, and Holiday. Recasting lynching as a

story about the horrific features of American life functions to generate not attraction but horror and revulsion. This occurs in both Wells's detailed depictions of lynching and the NAACP's antilynching campaign and the use of lynching photographs. Wells, the NAACP, and Holiday aim to make the reader, listener, and viewer perceptually sensitive to black pain, thus creating a new ethical economy that endows African Americans with a standing otherwise flagrantly denied by lynching.

Chapter 6 continues the themes of the previous chapter with a discussion of the relationship between aesthetics and rhetoric in W.E.B. Du Bois's political philosophy. This is the first of two interpretative engagements with Du Bois. I ask the reader to follow me from Du Bois's seminal 1926 essay "Criteria of Negro Art" and the debates about the role of art in responding to racial inequality during the Harlem Renaissance to his 1903 work, *The Souls of Black Folk*. I maintain that what he says in his 1926 essay is a formalization of an approach already at work in 1903. In this chapter, rhetoric functions less as a stylized description as used in part 1. It now involves technical elements that align Du Bois with the classical accounts of eloquence. It seems important to stress this difference if only to foreground Du Bois's education in rhetoric and deployment of its techniques in his writing.

The chapter aims to show that he aestheticizes politics as an instrument of cultural transformation—what I refer to as Du Bois's defense of positive propaganda. Aestheticizing politics functions as a way of training the senses to be perceptive to the whole environment in which one is located, thus cutting against the one-sided and stereotypical views of black people in circulation. By focusing on the idea of training the senses, I will also suggest that the supposed divide between Du Bois and other key figures of the Harlem Renaissance, principally among them Alain Locke, is not as wide as often thought. For both, the aesthetic character of politics becomes the means for combating white supremacy—that is, a means for helping one's counterparts imagine a vision of themselves not yet. I insist that Du Bois sees aesthetics and rhetoric as tools of political power.

Chapter 7 turns directly to *The Souls of Black Folk* and offers an interpretation of three of its chapters—"Of Our Spiritual Strivings," "Of the Meaning of Progress," and "Of Alexander Crummell"—as a model for reading the entire work. On my reading, attending to the first of these chapters brings into sharper relief the book's central problem—namely, the problem of frustrated and unrealized souls. For Du Bois, the soul functions as the seat of aspiration, and reading the soul in this way enables a discussion of the emotional and ethical dimensions of the self that aspire for objects in this world, the realization of which exceeds the abilities of the self. This at once points inward to character and self-description necessary to realizing the soul's aims and outwardly to the importance of a community of support to create the conditions to aspire with the possibility of success. The first of these is fundamentally about black people's relationship to themselves amid white supremacy. The second is about white Americans' role and complicity in domination.

To the first, Du Bois offers his reader models through which black Americans might relate to themselves in healthier ways than provided by the broader culture of disregard. Here, one thinks of Josie Dowell in "Of the Meaning of Progress" but especially Crummell in the chapter "Of Alexander Crummell." To the second, Du Bois invites his white reader to journey through the tragedy of black lives. This journeying is a way of seeing the whole of the environment, the result of which is to bind blacks and whites together as part of a shared quest for self-development, while awakening white Americans to their role in frustrating that pursuit in the lives of black people. Together, Du Bois seeks to stimulate sympathy and shame as part of a praxis of transformation.

The conclusion raises a final, critical issue given the United States' history of racial disregard and thirst for absolution. How can the American polity remain committed to the progressive character of aspirational politics in matters of racial justice without simultaneously seeing development as redeeming the moral and political sin of white supremacy and black domination? I treat this as a problem that runs through the public philosophical narrative of the United States' moral and political development—America's specific quest for what Dewey called certainty. In this case, certainty of racial progress and certainty of racial redemption that informs the polity's self-description—that defines the American Creed. This common quest—progress-as-entailing-redemption—ironically undermines the capacity of Americans to remain responsive to the ongoing problem of racial disregard while absolving them of responsibility for its continual role in shaping the structures of social and political life.

Something must be said in response and it is the goal of the conclusion to do so. There I offer a careful reading of James Baldwin's reflections on American democracy. The chapter uses his writings to stage a confrontation between the mythos of American redemption that shapes the postwar landscape and the persistence of racial disregard. The first is captured in the quest to secure equality that we see in Gunnar Myrdal's modern racial liberalism that involves minimizing the centrality of white supremacy to America's self-understanding, while the second is expressed in the demand that the nation reckon with its racial past as the basis for addressing the persistence of disregard. I ask: What does it mean to remain committed to the aspirational view of the American polity amid the history of black pain? What does it mean to live with the horror of one's past without succumbing to an ill-formed perfectionism of postwar liberalism?

Baldwin's answer is that we must abandon our quest to measure progress based on its success in achieving redemption from the sins of white supremacy and racial domination. The reason is that the deed of white supremacy and racial domination, for him, is irrevocable and the polity bears the imprimatur of its horror. This theme functions in Baldwin as a means for articulating what I call critical responsiveness—that is, a form of agency that resists being merely the reproduction of the past, that aims to take control over the development of one's character, but that acknowledges that the motivation for development often follows from constitutive failures. Critical responsiveness keeps alive our capacity to properly listen, see, and feel—all of the senses the previous thinkers have emphasized in their attempts to transform the polity. Baldwin thus offers us an epistemic and ethical orientation, forcing us to be on constant alert for the dangers posed to freedom and equal regard. He offers us an appropriate posture toward the American polity as a condition of democratic citizenship.

In those final moments, we will encounter an important observation. Our positive responses to dismantling white supremacy only make sense because we remember (recollect) the nation's constant attraction to racial disregard. This leads to an unsettling, but generative, conclusion: black Americans must always look on their white counterparts with suspicion and white Americans must always look on their antiracist activities and those of the country with doubt. With this we do not overcome the ever-present danger of racial disregard, but we may just confound its workings.

PART I

Situating Oneself in the Political World

———◆———

IMAGINE THAT YOU ARE RIPPED violently from those you love, denied the ability to form bonds of affection, and that you live daily at the whim of a world that regards you with contempt and whose members can extinguish your life with impunity. Imagine further others who look like you being born into a condition of indignity, made to live in a community in which they are politically alienated from the institutions of governance and denied opportunities for self-direction, and confronted with daily reminders that they secure neither care nor concern from those whose society they are excluded from. Can you see it? Can you imagine what life would have been like for others like you?

This was the modern condition of being black in the Western world—a state of experiential precarity that shaped not only the dreams imagined but also the bodily comportment that would bring those dreams to fruition. For the enslaved, one sees institutionalized freedom that one cannot enjoy. For the nominally free, one knows all too well that theirs is an ephemeral condition, and to that extent, it is not freedom at all.

And yet, as if by some magical act of mind and heart of what is rightly deserved and what social and political life should be, one refuses to allow precarity to define human existence. In that moment of refusal—in that instance of a momentous proclamation of one's existence—black people situated themselves in the Western political world without having a law or constitution affirm their status, thus creating the condition for transformation. This marks a fundamental rejection of social death—the sense in which one is merely an instrument of the master's will—indicating that the image just described was not total in its realization.[1]

The power of reflective self-assertion cannot be understated, for although its ethical and political significance has classical roots (think, for instance, of the Socratic injunction: an unexamined life is not worth living),[2] it achieves its true meaning through the project of Enlightenment, the intellectual zenith of modernity. It connects the individual and the social order by virtue of the capacity of ordinary human beings to render judgments about the lives they lead and the world they inhabit. "In the power of human reason," to positively appropriate one historian, lies the ability to "change society and liberate the individual from the restraints of custom or arbitrary authority."[3] And while the social and political order may well draw its institutional and juridical content from the capacity to judge, the faculty of reason itself does not depend on institutional recognition. Self-determination, freedom, autonomy—the watchwords of the modern period—gain their power because one can reflect on what is good and right, and in what virtuous conduct consists. Unshackled from the necessity of blind deference, one's judgment covers not only what is but what may be, emanating from the self like a spell seeking to subtly but affirmatively remake society. The power of human reason, as the American philosopher John Dewey observed, is thus inextricably bound to the imagination—the ability to envision the *as yet* from the fragments within the community one inhabits. "The aims and ideas that move us," Dewey explained in *A Common Faith*, "are generated through imagination. But they are not made out of imaginary stuff. They are made out of the hard stuff of the world of physical and social experience."[4]

But if one is to be honest, the famous and much-discussed wars of liberation in the modern period—the American and French Revolutions—are narrowly construed expressions of modernity. For while they most certainly involved struggles for freedom—to have one's capacity to judge institutionally affirmed—the question of whether white people could judge was never in doubt. What was in doubt was whether the lowborn could judge carefully and calmly, without being overtaken by their passions. But never was it a prominent question of whether white people could judge at all. Although the monarchical societies of Britain and France may well have ruled over subjects, they could not do as they pleased without violating the status of their subjects—their recognized *human* subjects. Such constraints followed from the complicated logic of religion, the complex systems of authority, and the normative expectations that regulated proper conduct toward one's subjects.

In contrast, black people in the West radicalized modernity and, to that extent, invested it with a meaning hitherto unimagined. By this I mean the deployment of the discourse of modernity involved a revision. To understand this, one must keep in view the system of racialized domination against which black people struggled. White supremacy, in its emerging form, involved an "animalization" of black persons that denied their basic capacity to judge.[5] The first American edition of the *Encyclopedia Britannica* of 1798 clearly captures this animating view:

> Negro, *Homo pelli nigra*, a name given to a variety of the human species, who are entirely black, and are found in the torrid zone, especially in that part of Africa which lies within the tropics. In the complexion of negroes we meet with various shades; but they likewise differ far from other men in all the features of their face. Round cheeks, high cheek-bones, a forehead somewhat elevated, a short, broad, flat nose, thick lips, small ears, ugliness and irregularity of shape, characterize their external appearance. The negro women have the loins greatly depressed, and very large buttocks, which give the back the shape of a saddle. Vices the most notorious seem to be the portion of this unhappy race; idleness, treachery, revenge cruelty, impudence, stealing, lying, profanity, debauchery, nastiness and intemperance, are said to have extinguished the principles of natural law, and to have silenced the reproofs of conscience. They are strangers to every sentiment of compassion, and are an awful example of the corruption of man when left to himself.[6]

What is of note here is not that black people were thought to be animals (although some held that view) but rather that their reflective and moral characteristics—honoring the principles of natural law and hearing the call of conscience—placed them closer to unreflective animals than thoughtful humans. For this reason, they seemed, or so the argument went, to be without the characteristics that would make them worthy of respect.

Here, two tracks emerge that permit the affirmation of freedom for some and the denial of it to others. The denial to black people of the capacity to judge involved a categorical distinction—a class of persons (i.e., black people) whose natural or normal position was confined to servility and obedience, and a class of persons (i.e., white people) whose rightful place was defined by superiority and dominance. This categorical distinction shaped from above and below the etiquettes of citizenship and social engagement, filtering throughout the social-psychological horizon of modern life and conditioning the philosophical and practical landscape of the West. Examined from this point of view, the assertion by black people of their ethical and political standing was not merely against a king who violated codes of conduct vis-à-vis fellow human beings (as in the American and French Revolutions) but against a way of seeing and feeling that confounded what otherwise was meant to be distinct: man and beast.

It is for this reason that the Haitian Revolution marks the third critical revolution of the modern period. This much was observed in 1857 by African American abolitionist and bishop James Theodore Holly, who noted the distinction between the American and Haitian Revolutions:

> The Haytian Revolution is also the grandest political event of this or any other age. In weighty causes, and wondrous and momentous features, it surpasses the American revolution, in an incomparable degree. The revolution of this country was only the revolt of a people already comparatively free, independent, and highly enlightened. . . . But the Haytian revolution was a revolt of an uneducated and menial class of slaves, against their tyrannical oppressors. . . .
>
> The American revolters had their colonial government in their own hands, as well as their individual liberty at the commencement of the revolution. The black insurgents of Hayti had yet to grasp both their personal liberty and the control of their colonial government, by the might of their own right hands, when their heroic struggle began.[7]

Implicit in Holly's reflections on the Haitian Revolution is the distinction between political slavery and chattel slavery. Acknowledgment of the first sharpened the meaning of freedom and equality by bringing into view those who had political standing that was now denied or in doubt. But the second revealed the inadequacy of the practical workings of the ideals of freedom and equality by alerting us to those who were never thought fit to have political standing at all. In this, the significance of the Haitian Revolution comes into view. As Vincent Brown remarks, "Over the course of nearly fifteen years of deadly turmoil in the French Atlantic culminating in genocidal warfare, a hardened country of former slaves emerged as the first nation in the Americas to conclusively abolish slavery and white supremacy."[8]

The Haitian Revolution, which partly inspired African Americans and their self-description, helped bring into focus a critical inquiry about U.S. black-white relationships. For the question was not whether one belonged to a society that engaged in self-determination but whether one belonged to a community in which self-determination evidenced itself in honoring the equal *human* standing of those not previously seen in that light. This is the backdrop of Afro-modern political thought. As Robert Gooding-Williams observes, it aims to upend white supremacy and the practices of domination it creates, and Afro-modern political thought does so both in the service of black folks and, often, even if not consistently, in the service of white people as well.[9]

To invoke white supremacy and its tendency to animalize and dominate black people is to mark the distinction between forms of enslavement at work in the modern imaginary and to refocus our attention on one of the significant purposes of politics—namely, to secure freedom and the equal standing of persons.[10] The contemporary revival of republicanism rightly points to being under arbitrary power as the defining trait of the master-slave relationship. Freedom is realized when one avoids not merely interference but also the ever-present threat of illegitimate interference—a danger that leaves one in a condition of psychological and bodily uncertainty.[11] And yet, the idea of domination in the context of colonialism and chattel slavery denoted a naturalization of the subordinate condition of nonwhites. This logic of enslavement did not principally orient modern and contemporary philosophical defenses of republicanism. For whereas the American revolutionaries largely claimed that their condition as slaves involved a violation of the political standing they previously enjoyed within the structure of British monarchical society, black people's status as slaves was understood to follow from their natural condition. From the start, the organization of American society bore the trace of an older, vertical structure for organizing society but now channeled through "ascriptive hierarchy."[12] This is the point Holly makes in the quoted passage above. Domination functioned through chattel slavery, even as it extended well beyond it into the inner workings of modern society. Repairing the first—American colonists experiencing domination—involved a restoration of standing now denied, while correcting the latter required a radical transformation of the cultural logic of racial domination to realize freedom. For black people, this involved belonging to a culture in which the presumption of their very capacity for freedom was no longer doubted and therefore a culture in which dominating black people could no longer coexist with those who enjoyed freedom. It required that they belong to a society in which they enjoyed equal regard—a form of care and concern not comparatively diminished in relation to others because of one's racial designation.

The ethical and political language of black Americans followed that of their white counterparts to be sure. Still, the normative vision offered by black people sought to reshape the ethos of American society. The language of modernity functioned as a discursive field. Common terms (i.e., democracy, equality, freedom, justice, domination, virtue, character, etc.) worked as rhetorical devices within that field. The terms of modernity at once marked the familiar, even as political and intellectual actors prevented from enjoying the benefits of modernity were transforming the reach of those terms.

The deployment of modernity's language by African Americans was a practical endeavor in the service of ethical and political improvement, or what I shall otherwise refer to as *perfectionism*. In calling it perfectionism, I merely take my direction from novelist and social critic Ralph Ellison:

> Actuated by passionate feats of revolutionary will which released that dynamic power for moralizing both man and nature, instinct and society, which is a property of linguistic forms of symbolic actions, these principles—democracy, equality, individual freedom and universal justice—now move us as articles of faith. Holding them sacred, we act (or fail to act) in their names. And in the freewheeling fashion of words that are summoned up to name the ideal, they prod us ceaselessly toward the refinement and perfection of those formulations of policy and configurations of social forms of which they are the signs and symbols. As we strive to conduct social action in accordance with the ideals they evoke, they in turn insist upon being made flesh.[13]

Perfectionism does not denote some fixed place to which one is destined to arrive; it is not, in this regard, a teleological description. Nor is it a claim about the imposition of state power in the service of a coherent vision of the good. Instead, perfectionism is the ongoing development of self and society, whose possible unfolding has empirical and historical anchors in the capacities of human beings and the social life to which they belong. Historically, this fueled (some) African Americans' faith that America could be a better polity.

The ability to critically assess political society, to require evidence of its moral legitimacy, and to help society imagine differently sits at the core of what shapes a just polity. The German critical theorist Axel Honneth is right: "individual self-determination, i.e. the power to arrive at one's own judgments, is not just some contingent human quality, but the essence of our practical-normative activity."[14] We see the force of this point when we focus on a class of persons who experienced categorical alienation and devaluation. In other words, we put to the test the idea of the capaciousness of judgment as well as its ability to produce materially embodied forms of freedom, equality, and justice by focusing on those who have otherwise stood beyond the pale of consideration. To put it in the form of a question: Are white Americans capable, vis-à-vis their black counterparts, of being something other than what they seem to be in the lives they lead and the institutions they produce? Asking this question involves centering Afro-modern thinking and elevating it to a level of philosophical consideration that has not been consistently recognized.[15] In thinking about this question, we come to see the framework on which African Americans relied to affirm their ethical and political standing in the nineteenth century amid white supremacy (part 1). This will also position us to understand the normative presuppositions that sustained their faith in the possibility of transformation throughout the twentieth century (part 2).

We begin with how it was that amid domination and exclusion African Americans were thought capable of situating themselves in the political world. Upon closer inspection, I argue, one sees that this is tied to the cognitive-affective capacity to judge. No thinker in the American context better captures this than David Walker in his intensely radical and incendiary *Appeal to the Colored Citizens of the World*. In this 1829 text, situated at the end of earlier deferential appeals by African Americans and standing at the beginning of forceful criticisms that became the hallmark of the struggle for freedom, Walker seeks to elicit from African Americans a way of seeing themselves and tries to properly calibrate the actions of white Americans to the demand of what he calls republican liberty. Walker and others in the nineteenth century (e.g., Maria Stewart, Hosea Easton, Martin Delany, and Frederick Douglass) direct their energies to the characterological level of American life—its ethos—seeking to reshape the foundation that can support broad-based flourishing. Character thus functions not as a passive dimension of the self but as one that can be reflectively guided and emotionally enlightened—that is, perfected. Understanding their approach requires a more explicit elucidation of the nature of racialized domination than we will get if we focus exclusively on the traditionally recognized modern political philosophers for whom domination often involved a denial of a political standing one was otherwise presumed to have.

Within this discussion, we will only indirectly address whether this cognitive-affective capacity can find support within the normative structure of American society or whether it should lead to a form of racial solidarity among African Americans to create a separate sovereign nation-state. Part 1 will leave us with a question about how we can decide between those who seek to transform the American polity (Walker, Stewart, Easton, and Douglass) and those who see white supremacy as so constitutive of the nation that transformation is deemed unlikely (Delany). Only in part 2 will we confront whether it can be normatively assumed that

African Americans belong to a society for whom the condition of ethical and political possibilities is central to the legitimacy of the polity. This will involve explicating more carefully an implicit claim of part 1—namely, the idea that democratic legitimacy in the American context is tied to an aspirational view of the people—and tying it to the ongoing affective and aesthetic appeals that African Americans advanced in the twentieth century. But I am getting ahead of myself. We must first begin with David Walker.

CHAPTER ONE

My Judgment Makes
Me Political

DAVID WALKER'S TRANSFORMATIVE APPEAL

Yet I have planted thee a noble vine, wholly a right seed: how then art thou turned into the degenerate plant of a strange vine unto me?

—JEREMIAH 2:21

WHEN FREDERICK DOUGLASS, now in the twilight of his life, reflected on the abolitionist movement, he acknowledged David Walker as one of its earliest defenders. There were others before him, but there was little doubt regarding the significance Douglass attached to Walker's 1829 *Appeal to the Colored Citizens of the World*. Walker's "appeal against slavery," Douglass said to his Washington, D.C., audience in 1883, "startled the land like a trump of coming judgment."[1]

Douglass was not alone in holding this estimation of Walker. We can find similar claims in Henry Highland Garnet, Maria Stewart, and, of course, W.E.B. Du Bois.[2] And yet, like so many others who do not enjoy the prominence accorded Douglass or Du Bois in American philosophical letters, Walker's place in African American political thought has slowly slipped from view, maintained, dare I say, by only a handful of scholars.[3] Even then, the political philosophical significance of this single text has escaped even the most sophisticated among us.[4] In turning back to this pamphlet, we recover a capacious way of thinking about political standing amid domination that marks a radical moment in African American political thought—a moment in which the basic capacity to judge, rather than mere recognition from a constitution, serves as the hallmark of citizenship.

———————

Walker's pamphlet confronts the reader with an immediate puzzle. Consider the title in its entirety: *Appeal, in Four Articles; Together with a Preamble, to the Colored Citizens of the World, but in Particular, and Very Expressly, to Those of the United States of America.*[5] How should we understand the phrase "citizens" in this title? By the late 1820s, we see a diminution or removal of the rights otherwise extended to black men in Northern states. This calls into question the accuracy of the attribution of "citizens" to "colored" individuals.[6] As suggested by Samuel Johnson's 1755 *Dictionary of the English Language*, the term "citizen" refers to "a freeman of a city; not a foreigner; not a slave" (although we can find a similar definition in antiquity).[7] To be a citizen is to enjoy a legal status of duties, rights, and privileges constitutive of belonging to a city and taken by that city as having that status. This stands in contrast to persons who are legally outside the community (e.g., foreigners) or legally at the will of another (e.g., slaves). As suggested by Johnson's definition, citizenship depends on what we might call a recognitive legal relationship.[8] The task for Walker is to show that one need not rely on legal recognition to underwrite one's status as a citizen. Put differently, how can one situate oneself in the political world in the absence of the recognized structures necessary to affirm one's standing as a citizen? Walker's answer to this question is connected to the other significant term in the title—the word "appeal." "Appeal" presupposes the capacity to judge.[9]

In focusing on the practice of appeal and its connection to our capacity for judgment, I mean to argue that Walker's text engages the dominant ideas regarding the presumed cognitive deficiencies of African Americans used as obstacles to their citizenship by calling them to perform their political standing. To use "citizen" to address "colored" folks at a time when those two terms were seen as incompatible calls out a form of political activity that is not itself dependent on the juridical framework that excluded blacks. His use of these words—"citizen" and "appeal"— exemplifies the ways blacks constituted themselves as political actors at the very moment their ability to do so was called into question or denied. The use of those terms brings into sharp relief a presupposition of republican politics—namely, that ordinary individuals are capable of judging their social world—to which he means to awaken his audience.

In this chapter, I explore the presupposition of republican politics implicit in Walker's deployment of the term "appeal." My claim is that *appealing to* is a bidirectional rhetorical practice that affirms the political standing of the claimant and the one to whom the appeal is directed.[10] The word "appeal" is not idiosyncratic; it captures a way of thinking about one's political standing that is not itself dependent on constitutional endorsement. In fact, this is the same logic that the American revolutionary generation employed to contest monarchical domination and that African Americans, particularly Walker, used to contest white supremacy (although the forms of domination, as I argue in chapter 3, were markedly differently). "When people use particular words," writes legal scholar Mary Bilder, "they choose among different cultural scripts—they select and create meaning" *of* possibility in which they embed themselves and the recipients of those words.[11]

Walker's approach is of broader significance given that most contemporary reflections tend to define "citizenship" as a form of "legal status."[12] This need not be at odds with the obvious point that historically excluded groups such as African Americans have argued for the necessity of formal inclusion for much of the United States' history. But connecting citizenship exclusively to legal status will blind us to the fact that through activities of contestation African Americans have sought to model a vision of citizenship alongside their plea for inclusion. Although it may well be the case that, as Rogers Smith suggests, "through most of U.S. history, lawmakers pervasively and unapologetically structured U.S. citizenship in terms of illiberal and undemocratic racial, ethnic, and gender hierarchies," we should not interpret this as exhausting the meaning of citizenship in American moral and political practice.[13] Using "colored citizens," as Walker did, directs our attention to a kind of activity—namely, the judging that precedes and contests practices of exclusion that were (and remain) part of the fraught discussion about what it is to be a citizen. Who among us would deny that the practice of judging helps create conditions for realizing the civil, political, and social rights famously identified by T. H. Marshall?[14] And just as the Declaration of Independence relies on this capacity, so too does Walker's *Appeal*. Appealing to one's fellows, as Walker does, is a rhetorical move to be sure, but it is one that reflects the political possibility latent within us all—a way of capturing citizenship as an activity.[15]

Few scholars attend to what I am here calling the rhetorical quality of Walker's appeal and the inherent political power of the practice of appealing—its desire to call into existence a political status that is denied.

More often, the *Appeal* is read as espousing a militant form of black nationalism with an emphasis on violent resistance.[16] This, of course, is a questionable reading, since it is not at all clear given Walker's rejection of leaving the United States what kind of black nationalist he could possibly be. Still others read it as continuous with the American jeremiadic tradition, even as this tradition is seen as being tied to an elitist vision of leadership.[17] This second approach is troubling precisely because it is susceptible to the criticisms of custodial black politics voiced by a diverse range of scholars.[18] But if the practice of the appeal entails a commitment to engage the judgment of the audience, as I contend, then situating the pamphlet in this *specific* rendering of the jeremiadic tradition and the custodial politics that it entails will be a nonstarter.

I focus on the practice of appealing that frames the pamphlet to reject these claims but also to elucidate the "principle of demotic rationality"— the commitment that the masses' reasoning abilities are up to the task of rendering social and political judgments.[19] On my reading of Walker's *Appeal*, demotic rationality sits at the heart of his thinking—a principle that honors the reflective agency of his audience regardless of station in life or racial designation. There is an important connection among the constellation of concepts thus far referenced—"appeal," "citizen," and "demotic rationality"—that must be kept in view to orient the reader to Walker's pamphlet. *The practice of "appealing to" does not merely affirm the political standing of claimant and recipient (as embodied in Walker's use of the word "citizens"), but it presumes the equal capacity of actors to judge (the principle of demotic rationality).* The horizontal standing of persons becomes the basis for vertical relationships of authority.[20]

Walker's approach presumes the capacity of ordinary people to be self-reflective and self-governing that was the hallmark of many, although not all, during the revolutionary period. Importantly, however, he extends that thinking to black people in ways that were otherwise resisted or denied. This is a significant move, for the radicalism of Walker's work lies not with his call to destroy the still emerging American polity but to change it such that African Americans are rightly acknowledged as its members. The largely nationalistic reading of Walker's text denies his attempt to achieve broad-based ethical and political transformation.[21]

In arguing that Walker's position entails the principle of demotic rationality, I mean to say two things, the second of which explicitly recasts the meaning of the prophetic stance and aligns it with the practice of the appeal. First, for him, African Americans did not need a prophet to whom they should *blindly* defer. Rather they were in need of a community willing to confront practices of domination, capable of being responsive to their grievances, and susceptible to transcending America's narrow ethical and political horizon. In other words, the American jeremiad appropriates the prophetic form (although not necessarily substance) of the Hebrew tradition to awaken America to its failure to live up to its commitments like Jeremiah sought to rouse his fellows for falling away from the righteous path of God.[22]

Second, I join George Shulman and Eddie Glaude in arguing that, in appealing to his readers, prophecy functions as a position or "office" to be authorized by those to whom the prophet speaks.[23] The prophetic intervention is one that seeks to awaken a spirit of what Walker calls "inquiry and investigation," and it awaits a response that might unify in public life the visions of the prophet and the audience.[24] The metaphor of slumber that appears throughout the *Appeal* and its connection to moral and affective failings or the language of inquiry and investigation and its relationship to the weaknesses of judgment more broadly ought to be read as a plea to use one's senses that have otherwise become dull. Walker, therefore, speaks as Jeremiah once did—"Hear now this, O foolish people, and without understanding; which have eyes, and see not; which have ears, and hear not"—the response to which sublates the need for the prophet in the first instance.[25] To tease out the inherent political power of Walker's pamphlet, I take up the cultural and linguistic practices associated with the term "appeal." In so doing, this chapter explores what people typically meant in the nineteenth century and earlier when they used the word "appeal." I maintain that these meanings are in the background for Walker, finding institutional support in the emerging Northern black institutions such as the first African American newspaper, *Freedom's Journal*. This will allow us to see in the first three sections how the term is associated with a larger rhetorical tradition, how it is capable of calling into existence a political status otherwise denied to African Americans, and how that status affirms the equality between claimant and recipient.

With this settled, I argue in "Aligning Prophecy and the Practice of Appealing" that the practice of the appeal clarifies the democratic character of Walker's prophetic stance. Just as "appealing to" illuminates and honors the judgment of the audience, so too does the prophetic stance depend on an endorsement from those to whom the prophet speaks, disrupting any commitment to what Wilson Jeremiah Moses calls the "messianic leader."[26] This reading of prophetic speech acts as depending on and affirming demotic rationality helps us resist the subtle alignment between prophecy as hierarchical rule and custodial black politics.

Walker's goal, however, is far more ambitious than merely calling into existence a political stance. There is, we might say, a conclusion that he wants to persuade his audience to adopt. As I argue in the next chapter, to be awake or to be free (Walker collapses these two ideas) is to resist domination. The absence of domination requires not only that one oppose it but that one belongs to a culture in which the conditions for domination no longer obtain. Walker's ambition is similar to the ambition of his white counterparts who resisted monarchical domination. The significant difference is his deployment of this mostly republican view of liberty to reimagine the polity along racially inclusive lines. In fact, by the time we reach chapter 3, we will see that Walker and others also mean to highlight the specific nature of racialized domination. But before we get there, we need to be rightly oriented to the *Appeal*, and this requires elucidating the theoretical apparatus that was otherwise part and parcel of nineteenth-century America.

To Appeal: Rhetorical Posture and Demotic Rationality

Walker was born legally free in 1796 to an enslaved father and free mother in Wilmington, North Carolina. During his early years, Walker traveled throughout the South where he witnessed firsthand the horrors of black life. By 1825, he moved to Boston with the aim of addressing racial domination. He was a respected member of the Boston community not merely because of his business as a secondhand clothing dealer but also because of his leadership role in the Massachusetts General Colored Association (MGCA), an organization that sought to unite black Americans and combat domination, because of his membership in the African Masonic Lodge, and because of his work as an agent for the newly established black newspaper, *Freedom's Journal*. Published in Boston, his famous 1829 pamphlet traveled along the eastern seaboard through a loose interracial network, encouraging some and sparking the indignation of others. The pamphlet traveled well into Georgia and as far west as Louisiana. Because of the earlier foiled insurrectionist plot by Denmark Vesey in 1821 and the nature of Walker's text that called for rebellion if the nation did not reform, Georgia and North Carolina (among other states) banned incendiary documents. Violation of those laws came with harsh penalties.[27] Of course, Walker anticipated this response, writing in the preamble of the *Appeal*, "I am fully aware, in making this appeal to my much afflicted and suffering brethren, that I shall not only be assailed by those whose greatest earthly desires are, to keep us in abject ignorance . . . and who are of the firm conviction that Heaven has designed us and our children to be slaves."[28]

Because of the actions and emotions it sparked on both sides of the slavery debate, the text remains a compelling work in the tradition of American pamphleteering aimed at addressing the physical and mental slavery of black Americans. Walker knew the importance of the oppressed assuming a public voice.[29] This did not, of course, preclude cooperation with whites. In his 1828 address to the MGCA, he encouraged blacks to "cooperate with them [white Americans] as far as we are able by uniting and cultivating a spirit of friendship and of love among us."[30] Still, assuming a public voice, he argued, served as the vehicle through which blacks might perform their freedom and thereby lay claim to it more firmly. In this context, the *Appeal* is a rhetorical performance—seeking to call out and honor the demotic capacity of black people.

This connection between rhetoric and demotic rationality has achieved renewed interest among philosophers of democracy,[31] and with good reason: the art of persuasion abounds in our contemporary democratic society no less than in America's past. The battle for America's soul—whether it would extend freedom and equality and tighten the nation's grip on justice or flaunt its articulated principles—was and continues to be waged through the following question: Who among us is more persuasive? We can understand rhetoric in simple terms. Rhetoric is a practice of speaking and writing that seeks to persuade one's audience; it relies on the audience to judge the content of what is being offered. As Ronald Beiner observes, rhetoric reveals the faculty of judging "by which we situate ourselves in the political world. . . . [It] open[s] up a space of deliberation. In respect of this faculty, the dignity of the common citizen suffers no derogation."[32]

Rhetoric does important work. To say that rhetoric situates us in the political world is another way of capturing the idea that authority is answerable to our judgment independent of and prior to legal recognition. That rhetoric foregrounds demotic rationality as central to the practice of legitimizing authority points to a philosophical and institutional alignment at the heart of the modern notion of politics—namely, that politics should offer its members a means to direct the forces that guide their lives. When Thomas Jefferson, for example, remarked in 1824, "in a republican nation, whose citizens are to be led by persuasion and not by force, the art of reasoning becomes of first importance," we should understand him as acknowledging this alignment rather than asserting that the practice of judging emerges only after one is legally endowed with standing.[33] In just this way, historians and literary scholars of the antebellum period rightly highlight rhetoric's role as a political art form through which the public voice of African Americans emerged. Through their public voice, they reimagined themselves as a political community, affirmed their equal standing, and offered trenchant criticism of American society.[34] This begins to illuminate how Walker's title can refer to "colored *citizens*." For him, it is from the perspective of judging that our citizenly status emerges. And what invites the judgment of the reader—what elicits their citizenly status—is Walker's appeal to them.

Rhetoric is at work in another equally important sense that reflects the complexity of being answerable. Appealing to someone is crucially about giving and asking for reasons for what we do or the beliefs we hold. The idea is that we are subjects of normative evaluation, not merely the ones who are appealing but also the ones who receive. It is precisely this idea that stimulates Walker's engagement with his African American audience: "Are we Men!!—I ask, O my brethren! Are we MEN?"[35] Or his claim, directed to both blacks and whites, that the "miseries and wretchedness" of African Americans take place "in this *Republican Land of Liberty*!!!!"[36]

These formulations, especially the use of exclamation marks and declarative sentences, stage a call-and-response relationship that is both deliberative and combative. "What are we really," his African American reader and listener are asked to consider, given how we comport ourselves in the face of domination? Is this truly a *"Republican Land of Liberty?"* both blacks and whites are urged to question, given the practices of domination at work. Italics, capitalizations, and exclamation marks register the emotional gravity of the issue. They prompt the recipient to linger and probe—to probe their actions and inactions and the surrounding social and political context. As Walker says, he offers his reflections and questions for you to "digest."[37]

Readers and listeners are pushed to grapple with these considerations because the impassioned and accusatory tone of the text is directed to issues that matter to the recipient. The pamphlet relies on the audience's deliberative capacities; its queries are meant to induce thoughtful consideration. And the text uses compositional practices that stage argumentative exchanges with readers and listeners. Taken together, they form one mode of rhetorical engagement. This is part of the practice of giving and asking for reasons: provide an account, Walker is asking, of *why* we should think we "are men" or *why* we should believe we live in a *"Republican Land of Liberty."* To say one must provide an account is to treat the recipient as one from whom reasons can issue—one capable of judging.

Precisely because citizenship and judgment are connected through the principle of demotic rationality, Walker intends his pamphlet not merely to be read *by* educated blacks but also to be read *to* uneducated and often illiterate black people. In contrast to arguments by Elizabeth McHenry and Timothy Patrick McCarthy, both of whom tightly connect freedom and literacy in their interpretation of the pamphlet, Walker discourages his audience from tying the civic significance of the *Appeal* to a literate public.[38] Hence he says at the very outset, "It is expected that all colored men, women and children, of every nation, language and tongue under heaven, will try to procure a copy of this Appeal and read it, or get some-one to read it to them."[39] He offers a way of understanding his *Appeal*: it is a tool to vivify one's political standing. As a journalist confirms in the *Boston Daily Evening Transcript* of 1830 regarding the impact of the *Appeal* and the transformed self-conception that developed in its wake, "It is evident they have read this pamphlet, nay, we know that the larger portion of them have read it, or heard it read, and that they glory in its principles, as if it were a star in the east, *guiding them to freedom and emancipation.*"[40] Note that reading the pamphlet and having it read to them seem to function on black people in the same way, enlivening their judgment regarding the possibility of their freedom. Focusing on the linguistic and cultural norms associated with the practice of appealing will help us understand the status it calls into existence and its demotic character. As we shall see, there is an alignment between the practice of appealing and what I shall want to call Walker's prophetic stance.

Norms of an Appeal

The term "appeal" is commonly used in the eighteenth and nineteenth centuries as part of the petitionary genre and carried a distinct meaning. Some of the more famous texts of this genre, although not exhaustive, include Samuel Adams's "An Appeal to the World or a Vindication of the Town of Boston" (1769), Isaac Backus's "An Appeal to the Public for Religious Liberty" (1773), Moses Mather's "America's Appeal to the Impartial World" (1775), James Lowell's "An Appeal to the People on the Causes and Consequences of a War with Great Britain" (1811), Robert Purvis's "Appeal to Forty Thousand Citizens, Threatened with Disfranchisement, to the People of Pennsylvania" (1837), and Angelina Grimke's "Appeal to Christian Women of the South" (1838). It should not be surprising that the last two authors—Robert Purvis, an African American abolitionist, and

Angelina Grimke, a women's rights advocate and abolitionist—are members of historically excluded groups. In citing these texts, I mean to direct attention to the shared aim of enlisting the judgment of their audience, understood in various ways as a locally defined community or larger collectivity such as "people" or "impartial world."

Central to the petitionary genre of the day, these documents presuppose an authority whose judgment is capable of deciding the matter at issue. As Susan Zaeske explains, "At its core a petition is a request for redress of grievances sent from a subordinate (whether an individual or a group) to a superior (whether a ruler or a representative)."[41] This way of understanding a petition is folded into the appeal itself. In John Cowell's 1637 legal dictionary, *The Interpreter*, for example, we find the following definition: "appeal is used in our common law . . . as it is taken in the civil law: which is a removing of a cause from an inferior judge to a superior."[42] In Nathan Bailey's 1721 text, *An Universal Etymological English Dictionary*, we find a similar definition: "a removing of a cause from an inferior judge or court, to another."[43] More than a century after Cowell's description, Johnson defines appeal as "a provocation from an inferior to a superior judge, whereby the jurisdiction of the inferior judge is . . . suspended, in respect of the cause."[44]

While there are legalistic and hierarchical dimensions to these definitions that do not cohere with the democratic character of Walker's *Appeal*, we should begin by observing the shared sense that some issue is to be reheard or retried. When Walker says in what might be considered the second preamble of the 1830 edition of the *Appeal*, "all I ask is for a candid and careful perusal of this third and last edition," he too means to have a retrying of the issue.[45] When he recounts the tragic facts of black subordination (Article I), restates what he perceives as Jefferson's demeaning descriptions of blacks and their complicity in their subordination (Articles I and II), details the role of preachers in sustaining slavery (Article III), and levels criticism against the presumed legitimacy of various colonization plans to remove blacks from American soil (Article IV), he should be read as re-presenting facts that might be heard anew.

No place was this more clearly on display than in *Freedom's Journal*—the first African American periodical with which Walker was closely associated and that emerged only two years before the original publication of the *Appeal*. As Samuel Cornish and John Russwurm explained to their patrons in the first issue of the paper in 1827,

> In presenting our first number to our Patrons, we feel all the diffidence
> of persons entering upon a new and untried line of business. But a

moment's reflection upon the noble objects, which we have in view by
the public of this Journal . . . encourage us to come boldly before an
enlightened publick. For we believe, that a paper devoted to the dis-
semination of useful knowledge among our brethren, and to their
moral and religious improvement, must meet with the cordial appro-
bation of every friend of humanity.

The peculiarities of the Journal, renders it important that we
should advertise to the world our motives by which we are actuated,
and the objects which we contemplate.

We wish to plead our own cause. Too long have others spoken for
us. Too long has the publick been deceived by misrepresentations, in
things which concern us dearly.[46]

As this passage suggests, *Freedom's Journal*, in its very construction,
responds to practices of racial degradation and systematic racial exclusion. After all, markers of African descent denoted a blight: the creation of
a virtual social identity indicating "legal, moral, and intellectual incapaci-
ties" that stigmatized its bearers.[47] Replicating Cornish and Russwurm's
approach, Walker prods black folks: "We, and the world wish to see the
charges of Mr. Jefferson refuted by the blacks *themselves, according to
their chance; for we must remember that what the whites have written
respecting this subject, is other men's labors, and did not emanate from
the blacks.*"[48] The practice of an appeal—in both its implicit use by Cornish and Russwurm and its explicit invocation by Walker—was a "second
chance to cry injustice" and, importantly, to have it properly redressed.[49]
This practice served, crucially, as a method for forging a collective identity
against misrepresentations in circulation.[50]

To retry the issue brings to mind the term's jurisprudential associations. But we conclude hastily if we confine our thinking in this way and,
in turn, obscure what Walker is doing. Both *Freedom's Journal* and the
Appeal move within the public rather than the legal sphere. As Bilder
argues, the term "appeal" is inseparable from colloquial—that is, publicly
familiar—usage that transcends legal recognition, informs a discursive
community, and frames their understanding.[51] This endows the conduct
and experiences of individuals with significance and intelligibility irreducible to a legalistic framework. The legal definitions above rely on but do
not adequately capture this background culture.

We can see the more capacious usage of the appeal among the American revolutionary generation and the way it extends beyond the legal
domain. Consider, for example, when Congregational minister Moses

Mather "appeals to the impartial world" or when African American abolitionist James Forten "appeal[s] to the heart."[52] Their appeals are obviously directed to perceived authorities. This is especially so in Forten's case. His *Letters from a Man of Colour, on a Late Bill before the Senate of Pennsylvania* (1813) speaks directly to a proposed state law in Pennsylvania that, if passed, would abridge the rights of African Americans. Forten addresses himself most immediately to the Pennsylvania General Assembly. But the reach of authority, as suggested by Mather's term "impartial world" or Forten's language of "heart," is not properly captured through a narrow jurisprudential lens; rather, both seek to mobilize a wider public. The most famous of these appeals is the Declaration of Independence: "We, therefore, the Representatives of the united States of America, in General Congress, Assembled, appealing to the Supreme Judge of the world for the rectitude of our intentions." Similar to *Freedom's Journal* and Walker's *Appeal*, Mather, Jefferson, and Forten intend to capture the attention of a broader audience than could be enshrined in a legal framework.

From the perspective of the American and African American pamphleteer tradition, the term "appeal" carries an expansive vision of political power. The term is also emblematic of an underlying political reorientation. We shall have an occasion in the next section to reflect on the changed political orientation from which the appeal emerged. What should be noted at this juncture is that both the American colonists and the antebellum African American activists are united by the experience of having their political standing denied. But ironically, to petition or to appeal involves performing a status that is otherwise not legally endorsed or recognized.[53] To petition is to see oneself as an agent, a person for whom something is at stake and in need of attention. The action and attitude of the addresser (i.e., appealer) do not merely function in the subjective "I-mode," in which *mere* performance by an individual brings that role into existence; rather, the cultural and linguistic norms denote the background presence of a "we-mode" (i.e., thinking and acting in light of a shared understanding).[54] The reason why "*mere* performance" is inadequate to capture the meaning of petitioning is that it obscures the normative backdrop that renders the practice intelligible. It also ignores the broader social preconditions for the assertion of agency that are at work when one petitions. Petitioning proceeds from a social practice suffused with shared norms and expectations about what one is doing when one petitions.[55] In this case, the shared understanding is that to petition or to appeal means seeking redress from an authority regarding one's grievances. To petition tacitly reflects a normative attitude *about* oneself but also *about* one's social and political world—that is, as being capable of responding appropriately to the claims being advanced.

This carries political implications for those who found themselves alienated from power to give direction to their lives (e.g., the American colonists) and was of crucial importance for historically excluded peoples (e.g., African Americans). By virtue of appealing to "colored citizens," Walker combined a designation that marked exclusion (colored) with one that denoted inclusion (citizens), both criticizing the America polity for its horrific treatment of blacks while endowing those same individuals with a political status otherwise denied. To interpret Walker's *Appeal* as moving within the public sphere is also to take note of its countervailing goals. Similar to *Freedom's Journal*, Walker sought to generate "a parallel discursive arena" in which to "formulate oppositional interpretations" of the identity, interests, and needs of black people.[56] This oppositional interpretation begins with the very affirmation of voice and judgment.

Whereas laws of citizenship, as embodied in the federal Naturalization Act of 1790 or Militia Act of 1792, for example, sought to tether the meaning of political standing to "free white persons" or "free able-bodied white male citizen[s],"[57] Walker returned his audience to the presupposition upon which American civic activity was based: the capacity and activity of judging. Through his *Appeal*, one can hear that famous Kantian injunction: "Have the courage to use your own understanding!"[58] The critical difference, of course, is that as a radical proclamation Walker directs it to his African American counterparts.

His appeal to the capacity and activity of judging might well strike us as odd given the degree to which we currently define citizenship through the federal government and statutory law. But in the early nineteenth century, as William Novak and Stephen Kantrowitz argue, the meaning of who counted as a citizen and for what purposes was unsettled and contentious.[59] Walker's pamphlet comes prior to the constellation of court cases that sought to settle citizenship and confine it to free white persons.[60] His emphasis on the activity of persons—indicative of his pamphleteering activity and support of and participation in black organizations—rather than legal recognition was not without good reason. But the focus on activity explains how formal denials of citizenship to blacks were questioned. The term "colored citizen," then, took advantage of a capacity that even Walker's white fellows assumed to make sense of their actions against the British Crown. And with that assumption came the entailments of judgment—that is, the power to assess one's actions, the actions of others, and the rules by which one would live one's life. Unsurprisingly, this view informed the salutation of Walker's preamble—"My dearly beloved Brethren and *Fellow Citizens*"—framing the pamphlet as a submission to the judgment of the audience.[61] It is no wonder that upon reading the pamphlet or hearing it read, as suggested by the *Boston Daily Evening Transcript*, African Americans felt liberated and empowered.

The status Walker's text means to elicit from blacks—that they are judgment-making beings and therefore citizens—is strikingly reinforced by the responses the text generated from whites. Since Walker offers the text for the "inspection" of the reader, it is no wonder that his accusations and queries generated an equally strident set of disavowals and responses. As one commentator, simply named Leo, remarks in his letter of 1831 to William Lloyd Garrison, editor of *The Liberator*, I am "opposed to [the production of the *Appeal*] not because he is a man of color, but because I do not believe that he wrote it."[62] The letter disputes not the claims advanced but their authorship by an African American. Later that year, Garrison published a review of the *Appeal*. In the review by an author identified merely as "V," we find the following remark regarding his transformed self-understanding:

> I have often heard, and constantly believed, that *Walker's Appeal* was the incoherent rhapsody of a blood-thirsty, but vulgar and very ignorant fanatic, and have therefore felt no little astonishment that it should have created so much alarm in the slaveholding states. . . . It has been represented to me as being . . . worthy of contempt. I have now read the book and my opinions are changed. . . . It is vain to call him incendiary, ruffian, or exciter of sedition. Let those who hold him such, imagine the circumstances of the two classes of our people reversed, and those who now rise up and call him cursed will build him a monument, and cry hosanna to the patriot, the herald of freedom.[63]

Still others sought to fortify slaveholding states by passing legislation that would ban the circulation of the text.

These responses are not without irony. As Walker says, "they [whites] beat us inhumanely, sometimes almost to death, for attempting to inform ourselves . . . and at the same time tell us, that we are beings void of intellect!!!! How admirably their practices agree with their professions in this case."[64] As Frederick Douglass would do only two decades later in his famous "What to the Slave Is the Fourth of July?" Walker baits his white reader. The general inconsistency that Walker identifies is a theme he emphasizes throughout his pamphlet. Either African Americans are devoid of rational powers that make them judgment-making beings (in which case the pamphlet requires no response at all) or they have the very capacity that is otherwise denied (in which case their claims regarding their status must be addressed). Herein lies the rub: taking the pamphlet to be a site of evaluation regarding the reasons and arguments offered (as white Americans did), holding, in other words, the text responsible for the claims advanced, is to treat the author as not merely something (e.g., property) but a judgment-making being and, to that extent, one who enjoys equal standing—who is like *us*.[65]

An Appeal as a Horizontal Relationship

Yet describing his pamphlet as an appeal seems a strange sort of thing to do, especially given that he means to challenge the domination of African Americans. Let us recall the definition of an appeal from Samuel Johnson: "a provocation from an inferior to a superior judge, whereby the jurisdiction of the inferior judge is . . . suspended, in respect of the cause."[66] Why use a term that is historically located in a tradition of hierarchy as suggested by this and other legal definitions? Why work out of a genre that, as historian Edmund Morgan rightly explains, involves "supplication" and reinforces "subjection"? Morgan's analysis sees the petitionary genre as emerging most clearly "from the days when authority rested in the hands of God's lieutenants" such as popes and kings.[67] Correspondingly, the legal definitions associated with the "appeal" carry this hierarchical imprint.

Yet we move too quickly if we conclude in this way and miss the underlying political reorientation to which the larger petitionary genre as well as the practice of the appeal belong. By the eighteenth century, the petitionary genre emerges out of a political culture that views the source of power as no longer emanating from the figure of the king but as arising from those who are the subjects of power. The king, as it were, can no longer command blind deference. Rather, authorization is tied to reflective assent commensurate with the "morality of self-governance" in which we each may claim to give direction to our lives.[68] This does not prevent others from suggesting (as we will see Walker do in the next chapter) that the genuineness of direction may be called into question if the appropriate conditions do not obtain. Nonetheless, to the extent authorization depends on reflective assent, authorization recasts the meaning of the appeal.

Of course, this logic fuels the American Revolution (that is, reflective assent must underwrite legitimate power), as well as the petitionary genre to which Walker's pamphlet belongs. To appeal does not refer to a social practice of supplication—a subordinate position of being *merely* ruled. Instead, the practice of an appeal presupposes a relationship among equals—Aristotle's ruling and being ruled in turn. To appeal denotes not only the rhetorical posture of speaking to but also a posture that authorizes the power of another, seeking a judgment regarding the issue at hand.

The hierarchical imprint remains, but its logic is transformed in light of this other, more democratic orientation. The horizontal standing among persons (i.e., addresser and addressee) frames how vertical relations of authority emerge. Walker's salutation speaks to "fellow citizens" because he means to signal that individuals enjoy equal status, and he must, therefore, as John Schaar and George Shulman note, "elicit [their] assent."[69] This is the hallmark of demotic rationality—that each of us can reflectively engage the important decisions of our political world. We can state this in a more formulaic manner:

A. The appeal affirms the political standing of claimant and recipient.
B. Citizenship is a designation of that political standing.
C. The principle of demotic rationality equalizes the standing between claimant and recipient.
D. This equal standing becomes the basis for vertical relations of authority.

Walker authorizes his audience, and he, in turn, must await their judgment regarding the claims advanced. The reason, to cite Shulman, is that "the capacity of persons, ideas, or institutions to elicit assent is always at risk, always in need of recommitment."[70] The logic of "being ruled" most certainly reflects a posture of submitting oneself to a higher authority, but it is a higher authority that alternates between the collective judgment of black people and the wisdom of those who claim to lead. This point is evident in the original preamble, when Walker describes his role vis-à-vis his fellow citizens as one who seeks to "awaken a spirit of inquiry and investigation respecting our miseries and wretchedness . . . !"[71] In this, he takes it upon himself to assume a position of authority, but one always in need of recommitment. The ability and power to arouse his audience point to the significance of their role in bringing about lasting social and political transformation.

Walker does not intend for his audience to submit their judgment to his authority. Nor does he mean to alienate his judgment to them. Instead, he asks readers to put their capacity to judge to work. Recalling the passage from the second preamble of the third edition where he requests a "candid and careful perusal" of the text, Walker importantly adds that in closely considering his pamphlet, the "world may see" the harms done to "Colored People."[72] That they "may see" denotes his quest to persuade as much as it reflects the possibility of refusal by his audience. Because demotic rationality affirms the equal capacity of the people to judge, one cannot be relieved from the uncertainty that results from dependence. This sensitivity to uncertainty is one that Du Bois makes known decades later in *The Souls of Black Folk* (1903) to indicate the lack of authorial control: the danger and possibility of democratic engagement. "Herein lie buried," he explains, "many things which if read with patience *may* show the strange meaning of being black here in the dawning of the Twentieth Century." Like Walker, Du Bois recognizes that the quest to persuade denotes his role as a participant in this process. He thus encourages the reader to study his words "with" him.[73] What Beiner rightly said of the rhetorician's audience might well be said of Walker's and Du Bois's: "the dignity of the common citizen suffers no derogation."

Aligning Prophecy and the Practice of Appealing

Thus far I have explained the cultural and linguistic norms associated with the term "appeal" and the way Walker relies on it to call into existence the political status of black Americans. That political status depends on the practice of judging. Citizenship turns out to be a designation of that status—a status that is intelligible even when shorn of legal recognition. I have further maintained that appealing to the judgment of the audience reflects a horizontal relationship of equality—demotic rationality—that legitimizes vertical relationships of authority.

The account thus far troubles those arguments regarding the hierarchical quality of the African American prophetic tradition that seemingly runs roughshod over democratic commitments. As Wilson Moses writes in his reflections on this tradition,

> An authoritarian collectivist ideal was evolved, a belief that all black people could and should act unanimously under·the leadership of one powerful man or group of men, who would guide the race by virtue of superior knowledge or divine authority towards the goal of civilization. . . . *Racial obligation was an important theme in the writing of black nationalist pamphleteers, Robert Young and David Walker, who urged subordination to the worthy messianic leader who they assumed was to come.*[74]

Although Walker is not the primary target of this description (after all, Moses is defining an entire tradition), he is nonetheless considered to be part of it. For Moses, the meaning of black nationalism is consolidated through the political vision of a leader who occupies a position of authority because of intellectual expertise or divine endorsement.

As I read Moses, the religious inflection of the *Appeal*, for example, assumes the force that it does for Walker precisely because God has anointed it. I say "religious inflection" because throughout the *Appeal*, Walker often describes himself as speaking the word of God. The prophetic stance, on Moses's view, is largely defined by what the prophet does to his followers rather than what the prophet does in concert with those he seeks to guide. The logic of authorization seemingly shifts from the people to something that stands outside of them, ultimately making the relationship between the prophet and black people, in Adolph Reed's felicitous phrase, "custodial."[75]

My reference to Reed captures a trend in the scholarship on African American political thought and already at work in Moses's reading of Walker. Reed views this custodial vision of politics as consolidating in the wake of the Civil War, and Robert Gooding-Williams, for example, sees in Du Bois its greatest spokesperson.[76] The logic of custodial politics is that blacks are in the care of a leader mainly because they are unable to direct their own political lives. We hear a similar concern as it bears on the prophetic tradition in Rom Coles's criticism of Martin Luther King Jr., who, he remarks, "barely grasped" the "receptive relational practices" of democratic politics. By "receptive relational practices," Coles means attunement to and reception of those ordinary, everyday black people who will be subject to political decisions when made.[77] Such figures swing free of accountability, establishing vertical relations that do not proceed from the horizontal standing among equals. It is precisely this logic at work in Moses when he latches on to the following passage from the *Appeal* to validate his reading of the messianic and elitist tendencies in Walker: "The Lord our God . . . will give you a Hannibal, and when the Lord shall have raised him up, and given him to you for your possession, O my suffering brethren! Remember the divisions and consequent sufferings of Carthage and of Hayti."[78] If correctly attributed to Walker, it undermines the practice of the appeal thus far laid out. Since scholars see Walker as belonging to this tradition, it would be remiss to ignore this attribution. We would also miss an opportunity to explore Walker's democratization of the prophetic. We need to attend to the prophetic in the American tradition and how Walker's text exemplifies it before confronting Moses's worry.

The prophetic tradition is best embodied in the American jeremiad. As David Howard-Pitney explains, it is "rhetoric of indignation, expressing deep dissatisfaction and urgently challenging the nation to reform."[79]

There are three elements at work. First, the jeremiad presupposes a promise, for example, that all men shall be respected as equals, that the nation has failed to keep. This is the source of indignation. Second, failure to keep the promise results in warnings of moral deterioration and divine retribution. Third, and importantly, warnings denote possibilities yet to be realized rather than the foreclosure of transformation altogether. At the very moment criticism seems to signify a point of no return, awareness of deterioration opens up the possibility that the community may yet pull itself back from the precipice. The prophetic intervention occupies the imagination of the audience, projecting from a world now in ruins a future yet to be realized. Prophecy always functions, then, in the aspirational mode. This *form* is most clearly at work in the Hebrew prophet Jeremiah. To be sure, Jeremiah laments the Israelites' rejection of the Covenant God made with Abraham. But God encourages him to hope for the emergence of a new land: "See, I have this day set thee over the nations and over the kingdoms, to root out, and to pull down, and to destroy, and to throw down, to build, and to plant."[80] This form—promise, failure to keep the promise, and redemption—suffuses American moral and political discourse.

When we overlay this form on Walker's pamphlet, we see the following. First, the background promise for Walker is the Declaration of Independence, allowing him to say, "Compare your own language above, extracted from your Declaration of Independence, with your cruelties and murders inflicted by your cruel and unmerciful fathers and yourselves on our fathers and on us—men who have never given your fathers or you the least provocation!!!!!!"[81] Second, Walker criticizes the nation for inviting God's vengeance and black rebellion, but more significantly a vengeance and violence that bespeak the moral decay of the country as exemplified in slavery. Although the American jeremiad means to suggest a divine offense, the emphasis is not placed exclusively on contemplating one's relationship to God but rather directs us inward to reflect on our relationship to ourselves. It is that relationship that reflects our adherence to or rejection of God's law. Walker not only says to his white counterparts, "do you understand your own language" as found in the Declaration, but strongly counsels black people to "look into [their] freedom and happiness, and see of what kind they are composed."[82] In both instances, he means for whites and blacks to consider their relation to themselves in the light of their failure to honor the logic of the Declaration or respond adequately to the fragility of their presumed freedom. This internal failure—a failure of character—marks a tragic departure from God's law. For Walker, only in properly honoring who we are in our treatment of others and ourselves do we fulfill God's expectation of human existence.[83] Third, and relatedly, criticism opens up an interpretative space regarding what may yet heal the wounds of the nation. If white Americans, for instance, properly understand the Declaration, they will find resources contained therein that may be tapped for addressing the suffering of blacks. If black Americans, specifically those in the North, carefully examine their freedom, they may yet come to see how uncertain their grasp on it is. I will consider the fullness of these three points in the next chapter where they relate to what Walker takes to be the entailments or demands freedom places on us. Suffice it to say, there is a clear correspondence between Walker's thinking and the American jeremiad.

What does this mean for understanding his preamble and Moses's criticism? First, it makes sense that Moses would read the prophetic as containing a hierarchical imprint. After all, the Hebrew prophets are chosen or called not by the people but by God. They stand above the people, demanding that they submit to their vision. But by working in the genre of the appeal, Walker specifically locates himself among equals, making his status as well as the full meaning of his vision dependent on those to whom he speaks. The meaning of the appeal and the prophetic achieve alignment. Both presuppose the principle of demotic rationality. As Walker says, "It is not to be understood here, that I mean for us to wait until God shall take us by the hair of our heads and drag us out of abject wretchedness and slavery."[84] The significance of the passage is the contrast between "God" and "us." For him, African Americans must decide their fate, just as white Americans must decide if they will transform.

I turn to this passage above by Walker to trouble imputed connections between the prophetic tradition and custodial black politics. African Americans were struggling for freedom. It would be an odd occurrence indeed if, given this background, African American leaders made their case for freedom by counseling blind subordination. It is true that Walker envisions a vital role for the black educated elite. He says explicitly in Article II of the *Appeal*, "Our Wretchedness in Consequence of Ignorance," "Men of colour, who are also of sense, for you particularly is my APPEAL designed. Our more ignorant brethren are not able to penetrate its value."[85] In this context, he literally means they are unable to penetrate its value because they are unable to read its words. Walker did not make the mistake, however, of believing that those who were illiterate were also without the ability to judge, as indicated by his insistence to have the pamphlet read by and to black people. The pamphlet is for the educated, but not exclusively so. Thus Walker says, "I call upon you therefore to cast your eyes upon the wretchedness of your brethren, and to do your utmost to enlighten them."[86] I do not want to overstate the point. Walker is deeply concerned that less educated blacks will ignore his claims. Still, he does not conceive the process of enlightening black people as precluding their capacity to judge what they are receiving.

Walker's text uses the prophetic form to enlighten his audience but tilts in a democratic direction. His orientation toward his audience necessarily rejects custodial black politics and does so as a precondition for the expression of freedom by black people in the first instance. Walker's prophetic stance means to educate black individuals so that they may act and judge appropriately. The full meaning of the future depends on the choices the people make for themselves, even if the prophet is a participant in helping them see those choices. If the prophet occupies the imagination of the audience, what, if not the actions of the audience (the full audience), can bring that vision to fruition? To be sure, Moses is correct to say African Americans, as Walker understands the matter, depend on a prophet for their salvation, but he is wrong in how he conceives of the political authorization of prophecy. It is located within the self, rather than from without. The prophet's role, no less than the educated elites', is to enable them to see and hear the vision more clearly. Contained within the role of being a participant is its limiting function that results from respecting the audience's reflective capacity, disabusing us of the idea that the motor for political change can be identified with a singular figure. As he says, his goal is to "penetrate, search out, and lay . . . open for your inspection" the "sources from which our miseries are derived." Consistent with the power of independent inspection, he writes, "If you cannot or will not profit by them, I shall have done *my* duty to you, my country, and my God."[87]

What should we say, then, of Walker's direct reference to the Carthaginian commander and statesman Hannibal? Hannibal lived during a time when the Roman Empire exerted enormous influence and threatened societies such as Carthage. Walker cites the example of Hannibal to capture something about leadership. But what does he mean to capture? He first takes up the case of Hannibal in Article II of the *Appeal* where he discusses the conduct of African Americans as a result of their ignorance. We can make two observations. First, he appears to have in mind Hannibal's defeat during the Second Punic War partly owing to internal conflicts in Carthage that halted support. I say "appears" because it is not clear what Walker was reading to support this claim, although the closest account to Walker's description can be found in Titus Livy's *The History of Rome*.[88] Regardless of his sources, what is certain is that Walker believes that "had Carthage been well united and had given him [Hannibal] support, he would have carried that cruel and barbarous city [Rome] by storm."[89] Second, it is the absence of unity among the Carthaginians that Walker wants to use as a lesson for African Americans, leading to the claim cited above and by Moses: "The Lord our God . . . will give you a Hannibal, and when the Lord shall have raised him up, and given him to you for your possession, O my suffering brethren! Remember the divisions and consequent sufferings of Carthage and of Hayti." This leads to an important conclusion. When Walker invokes Hannibal, it is in the context of seeing him as an offer or gift from God to the people. He means to say to African Americans that it is up to them, as was the case with Carthage, to willingly take "possession" of the leadership being offered. Carthage failed, he argues; we must not.[90]

When he speaks of God sending a leader, it is in the context of imploring his fellows to lay claim to the figure. Presumably, this extends to the prophetic intervention Walker himself represents—a response that intends to redound to the benefit of the community. He aims to provide reasons, then, for why one would submit to a leader. After all, Hannibal is described in Article II as engaging a "cruel and barbarous" Rome. Similarly, any leader sent to black people must be assessed based on the goal of engaging what Walker refers to in Article I as the "barbarous cruelties" of the nation.[91] It is the context that creates the conditions for leadership to emerge rather than something inherent to or essential about a leader. (And it will be to this context, rather than something essential about blacks, that Walker will turn to defend the necessity of racial solidarity [see chapter 3].) Importantly, Article I lays out the depth of the cruelty of American slavery in comparison to the historical domination of other peoples. His aim, as he says, is to

> demonstrate to the satisfaction of the most incredulous, that we, (colored people of these United States of America) are the *most wretched, degraded* and abject set of beings that *ever lived* since the world began, and that the white Americans having reduced us to the wretched state of *slavery*, treat us in that condition *more cruel* (they being an enlightened and Christian people,) than any heathen nation did any people whom it had reduced to our condition.[92]

When we take Articles I and II together, Walker recounts the intensity of black domination and the story of Hannibal to enlighten his audience regarding what is in their best interest. His use of the term "incredulous" both here and elsewhere indicates his opinion that the facts will be so forceful that they will penetrate a mind that was otherwise unwilling to believe. The meaning of submission looks radically different on this view. If the people are to submit, as Moses understands Walker, it must be a free submission that is ostensibly consistent with the spirit of inquiry and investigation that he seeks to stimulate in the first instance.

The strongest point of comparison one might make here to capture the force of Walker's point is with John Stuart Mill's and Du Bois's reflections penned decades later, when they independently reflect on the role of the leader. As Mill says in his classic work, *On Liberty*, "I am not countenancing . . . 'hero-worship' which applauds the strong man of genius for forcibly seizing on the government. . . . *All he can claim is freedom to point out the way*. The power of compelling others into it is not only inconsistent with the freedom and development of all, but corrupting to the strong man himself."[93] But Mill is not alone: Du Bois also argues that because "the sufferer knows his suffering," the "choice of rulers must fall on electors."[94] Du Bois does not mean this in a narrow political sense; rather he intends to affirm the experiential content of the sufferer that serves to contextualize and is used as a measure for assessing would-be leaders. In Mill's case, it is the role of the leader to help us realize something about who we are and our condition, whereas Du Bois adds that it is because of our condition that we must be left to decide whether the leader's vision will be beneficial. Akin to both these positions, Walker counsels deference, but it is reflective deference consistent with an understanding of the best interest of individuals and the community to which they belong. The best interest of both the community and the individuals that comprise it is to free itself from the barbarous cruelties that result in the domination of the mind and the body of black people.

———————

What does it mean to be awake? As we will see in the next chapter, Walker answers that it is to be free. Freedom requires that we see ourselves as thinking, intending, feeling, and norm-obeying individuals. For him, being free involves a kind of comportment in the face of forces that aspire to distort one's life through domination. Freedom is a precondition for living a life that we would properly recognize as human—a life consistent with the demand of our nature as God created us—without which one can only be viewed as a slave. The internal logic of freedom involves certain entailments about our conduct, indeed, our self-description. If this is correct, Walker is not exclusively interested in the use of our judging

capacity (although necessary); he also means to indicate a proper alignment between the responsiveness of judging and action. This, Walker
believes, is essential if blacks are to address their treatment, but it also
depends on their white counterparts being able to hear the aggrieved not
as a foundation of their freedom but as a consequence of it. How he man-
ages both is the issue to which we now turn.

CHAPTER TWO

Living an Antislavery Life

WALKER ON THE DEMANDINGNESS
OF FREEDOM

*The common utility that is drawn from a free way of life is . . . being able
to enjoy one's things freely, without any suspicion, not fearing for the
honor of wives and that of children, not to be afraid for oneself.*

—NICCOLÒ MACHIAVELLI, *DISCOURSES ON LIVY*

FEW DENY David Walker's reliance on God as the foundation of his defense
of the freedom of blacks in America. It is difficult to bracket the place of
God in his thinking and have a recognizable picture of a free society.[1] The
religious content of the *Appeal* is internally connected to our nature as
human beings such that without the stipulation of God, liberty makes little
sense. Walker relies on the proposition that we are created in the image of
God as a reason for why our nature is constituted the way it is.[2]

We might think that the mere assertion of God's role in creating us
as free creatures is enough to sustain Walker's argument that blacks be
treated equally. Regardless of how blacks comport themselves in the face
of domination, we might say that whites are obliged to abstain from practices of enslavement. Or to put the matter differently, the meaning and
protection of freedom need not depend on our affirmation of it. If this
were the case, there would be little reason for Walker to argue that it is
ignorance that distorts the self-understanding of black people or to insist
on the necessity of black people acting in a way commensurate with the
demand of freedom. And yet Walker does make these arguments. The reason for doing so is essential; he means to underscore the importance of
cooperation between God and humans and ultimately among themselves.

[63]

Although the "spirit and feeling"[3] of freedom that constitute humans cannot be erased, he is aware that their role in making us the creatures we are does not mean we will always recognize the demand of our nature. Our nature is not self-executing. The spirit and feeling of freedom do not mean we will always comport ourselves in the light of it. This gap introduces interpretative space that the *Appeal* means to fill; we must, as it were, assume a standpoint from which the meaning of human nature, and in turn the force of freedom, comes into view. This is why Walker insists on the need to remove ignorance, and it explains his goal to awaken among his audience a "spirit of inquiry and investigation."[4]

In emphasizing his quest to enlighten his reader, I do not mean to downplay the religious dimension of the *Appeal*; I mean to put it in its proper place. For him, black Americans must resist the idea that just because God is foundational, they are relieved of their responsibility to address their unjust conditions.[5] As argued in the previous chapter, prophetic intervention does not mean to replace the judgment of the audience; instead, it appeals to and depends on that judgment. The question of whether black people are free human beings does not exclusively depend on the religious claim about human nature (which is still important) but on a normative view about oneself as a human being that Walker seeks to persuade his reader to adopt. This explains his aversion to acting slavishly—a criticism directed to those blacks within and outside the formal institution of slavery. For him, African Americans must perform their freedom to lay claim to it. This is what he means to awaken black Americans to—the demandingness of freedom.

This suggests that Walker has a rich notion of what constitutes freedom. His persistent attack on servility and ignorance throughout the *Appeal* means to illuminate a form of enslavement that distorts the humanity of the enslaved person, not exclusively because individuals are treated as "*merchandise*"[6] but also because of the narrowing effect it has on one's self-understanding. To free oneself from this notion of slavery is to move toward human flourishing; it is to resist domination. By "domination," I mean black Americans live at the arbitrary mercy or whim of their white counterparts, what Walker refers to, as do classical and contemporary thinkers, as the absence of republican liberty.[7] Importantly, domination radiates outward into the elusive social and cultural horizon of the community, subtly shaping and disciplining one's comportment even in cases where there is no apparent master. The principal worry, in this context, relates to the effects of domination on African Americans' self-understanding; it obscures the necessity of racial solidarity.

(A full defense of racial solidarity will have to await discussion in the next chapter.)

It is common to demand "proper" comportment from black Americans while losing sight of how white supremacy shapes, distorts, and destroys their lives. Both then and now, we have a propensity to pathologize black Americans. Walker is neither politically nor sociologically naïve. He knows that the full realization of freedom does not solely depend on the actions of blacks, even if it is a condition for their freedom to acquire meaning in the world. Of course, he often has harsh things to say to his black audience regarding their servility and their willingness to set their goals based on the proscriptions of white Americans rather than on the reach of their imaginations. Yet, he levels some of his harshest criticisms against white Americans, both threatening a violent revolution and excoriating their moral hypocrisy for denying to blacks what the nation so vigorously fought to secure only a few decades earlier. For this reason, although the *Appeal* is largely aimed at black folks, Walker also seeks to reclaim whites by enlightening them regarding what they otherwise recognize in themselves—namely, the demandingness of freedom. The *Appeal*, to use Danielle Allen's language, is directed to the established "etiquettes of citizenship" on display—the one of servility and the other of dominance—with the aim of reorienting the habits of the audience.[8]

To make good on these claims, the argument here extends the analysis of the previous chapter by elucidating the connection between responsiveness (as embodied in Walker's goal to stimulate the judgment of his readers) and action (as embodied in his claim that blacks and whites must comport themselves as freedom demands). The reader can think about the connection this way: if the last chapter sought to explain how rhetorical engagement affirms the political standing of addresser and addressee, this chapter draws out the implication that follows from that political standing. The first section of this chapter takes up Walker's invocation of God for understanding the relationship between nature and development. That we are created in God's image highlights an affordance of our nature, but that claim only matters if we properly see and comport ourselves.

The previous argument will set the stage for Walker's perfectionist intervention in the section "Demandingness of Freedom." His argument about transformation allows for a careful elucidation of two examples that sit at the heart of Article II of the *Appeal*—the complicit slave woman and the enslaved free man. When placed against the backdrop of Thomas Jefferson's demeaning claims about black Americans, the examples centralize the importance of blacks acting as free individuals should. Walker does not rely primarily on his religious argument about how we are created to motivate action; instead, he means to persuade black Americans to inhabit a kind of identity that is commensurate with that nature as a step toward human flourishing.

In keeping with broader abolitionist appeals, the examples are negative illustrations or warning signs that attempt to capture the imagination of the audience—to get them to see and *thereby* feel appropriately regarding the lives on display. This power of seeing is not something Walker puts into his audience, or at least this is not how he talks about it. Rather, he intends to *turn* the audience toward the horror of black life. This is part of what I referred to in the last chapter as the rhetorical practices of the text. The struggle is not over our capacity for seeing but over the proper direction of our gaze. Walker thus uses narratives to illuminate what happens in the absence of adopting a particular normative attitude—black Americans will become accessories to their domination. They will, to use Machiavelli's thinking from the epigraph, be unable to freely enjoy their property; they will fear for the lives of friends and family, and they will suffocate under the weight of existential terror.[9] The examples intend to serve an educational role that fills out the moral point of view of his audience.

Finally, the section "Understanding One's Language" completes the movement or turn toward freedom's demand—a movement dependent on the comportment of white Americans. Whereas the first two sections of the chapter stage a cooperative relationship between God and African Americans, and then again among themselves, the third takes up the comportment of whites toward blacks. His argument seeks not only to induce fear but to get them to seriously consider the shamefulness of their actions and the lack of ethical integrity those actions represent. Just as Walker seeks to capture his African American audience regarding the meaning of their condition, he equally attempts the same with white Americans regarding their practices of tyranny.

Nature and Development

The *Appeal* is not exclusively about freedom for blacks and the moral depravity of whites. Walker's pamphlet is also an articulation of a religious anthropology of human nature—his vision of personhood, we might say. *This account highlights an affordance of our nature provided we adopt a standpoint from which to see the meaning of that nature.* This sentence contains two claims. The first is a description of human nature that *affords* us a capacity for freedom. "Affordance" is a not a term that readily comes to mind when we think of human nature. But consider it this way: a door-knob, for example, affords us with an opportunity for twisting. The rela-tionship is between an object and us. We can similarly interpret human nature if we also treat our nature as an object of reflection. We do this all the time when we think about what we take ourselves to be doing as the people we are and in the lives we lead. It should not be mysterious for us to think, then, that given the capacities we have as humans, our nature affords us with an opportunity for acting freely. Just as twisting is a function of a doorknob, so too, we might say, freedom is a function of our nature.

The second claim is an argument about occupying a perspective for understanding the meaning of that nature and in turn the capacity it affords us. Consider the doorknob once more. Twisting does not inhere in the knob itself; after all, if you remove it from the door, it may well be used as a weapon. The idea that the doorknob affords us with an opportunity for twisting makes sense only because we hold that possibility in view. We understand the relationship that connects the knob, the door, and our-selves. Similarly, human nature is a site of possibilities, among which is the opportunity for freedom, provided we see our nature in its proper light. Here, we come to understand a specific kind of relationship that obtains between ourselves, the descriptions of ourselves, and the world. Take these two points together, and they capture the connection between our nature (as free creatures) and our epistemic development (that rightly holds that nature in view).

Consider, for a moment, a passage that appears in Article IV of the *Appeal*, although Walker echoes the meaning in earlier articles:

> Man is a peculiar creature—he is the image of his God, though he may be subjected to the most wretched condition upon earth, yet the spirit and feeling which constitute the creature, man, can never be entirely erased from his breast, because the God who made him after his own image, planted it in his heart; he cannot get rid of it.[10]

The pain and suffering we endure as part of this world may be exact-ing, but it can never reach the substance of our nature. This too, Walker argues, applies to the reach of slavery and domination. But what consti-tutes the nature of man? (I shall return to Walker's gendered language in the next section.) His answer is freedom: "if we lay aside abject servility, and be determined *to act* like men, and not brutes—the murderers among the whites would be afraid to show their cruel heads."[11] Walker contrasts abject servility—a characteristic suitable of a slave—with being a man. The latter is not merely meant as a descriptive term (i.e., what one finds in nature) but more importantly as a normative one (i.e., how we should understand humans).

This normative picture of "man" explains why Walker is concerned about an important element of modern slavery—the goal to animalize black people. He takes up this point specifically in Article I, "Our Wretchedness in Consequence of Slavery," and repeats the point in Article II, "Our Wretchedness in Consequence of Ignorance." Whereas classical slavery, he contends, merely confined itself to the subordination of different peoples (Egyptians subordinating the Israelites, for instance), it did not include the "insupportable insult upon the children of Israel, by telling them they were not of the human family."[12] Modern slavery, he maintains, differs on just this point. "Can the whites deny this charge? Have they not, after having reduced us to the deplorable condition of slaves under their feet, held us up as descending originally from the tribes of Monkeys or Orang-Outangs?"[13]

Of course, slavery is an evil, but he is primarily concerned with the additional claim that animalizes black Americans. Why is this so important? The answer has to do with the dehumanizing quality of slavery in its racialized form. Slavery is an institution of exploitation as well as debasement (not only an "insupportable insult" but what he calls a "gross insult").[14] But the nature of debasement, Walker argues, disavows the ethical standing of persons by confounding their status with that of animals. As David Brion Davis notes, this carries a distinct meaning; it denotes "eradication not of human *identity* but of those elements of humanity that evoke respect and empathy and convey a sense of dignity."[15] This is precisely the concerning aspect of slavery to which Walker directs our attention—what his friend Hosea Easton would call only a few years later "mind act[ing] on matter."[16] We will have a chance to return to Easton in the next chapter, but this bit of philosophical idealism refers to the power of our mind and its categories to give shape to the perceptual world, including our relationship to ourselves. Walker and Easton, then, concern themselves with the dehumanization of black people also, in part, because of how black people might come to see themselves.

When one's status as a slave is accepted—whether reflectively or unreflectively—it has catastrophic ethical consequences; it narrows one's normative field of vision and deforms—what we might call following Walker—the *soul*. Walker was not alone in his thinking. In a series of lectures delivered between 1832 and 1833, Maria Stewart, a prominent member of the Boston community who was influenced by Walker, centralizes the soul. In her African Masonic Hall address, she asks her audience: "Have the sons of Africa no *souls*? Feel they no ambitious desires?"[17] These two sentences run on the same track, as it were, so that the soul functions as the seat of desire. Easton, in his 1837 *A Treatise on the Intellectual Character, and Civil and Political Condition of the Colored People of the United States*, speaks about the soul-destroying power of slavery that subjects the "soul to a morbid state of insensibility."[18] Here, slavery seemingly leads to a lack of concern or indifference toward oneself. In his autobiography of 1845, Frederick Douglass powerfully captures the worry of these earlier thinkers as he describes one of his encounters with Edward Covey, a man known for disciplining "problem" slaves: "Mr. Covey succeeded in breaking me. I was broken in body, soul and spirit. My natural elasticity was crushed, my intellect languished, the disposition to read departed . . . behold a man transformed into a brute!"[19]

Douglass's use of the words "soul" and "spirit" is important because they relate directly to the thinking of Walker, Stewart, and Easton. Although the word "soul" has a complicated philosophical and theological history, it seems that what all of these thinkers have in mind is the idea that human beings are souls fueled by an energy of life or spirit. When Walker refers to the "spirit and feeling" of freedom, when Stewart refers to the "spirit of men," or when Easton tells us that the soul can be reduced to insensibility, they are, in essence, referring to soul as the longing and aspiring feature of the self. Or to put it more plainly, to talk about the soul is to refer, in essence, to the life force that drives the person. Douglass's description, then, strikes me as a perfect example of what these earlier thinkers have in mind about being overtaken by or accepting the normative status of the slave. He is referring to the daily cruelties of slavery and also the internalization of degradation that is the source of those cruelties and that arrests the soul's longings. We will come back to the idea of the soul much later in the book, as this becomes the centerpiece of W.E.B. Du Bois's thinking, but for now we can say that Walker's focus (and Stewart's, Easton's, and Douglass's as well) is on how African Americans understand themselves given the description they come to accept and how acceptance of that description opens or closes possibilities—that is, releasing or constraining their "natural elasticity," to use Douglass's formulation.[20]

There seems to be a problem with this account. On the one hand, humans have an "unconquerable disposition" or free nature.[21] On the other, this account seems to be flimsy, since we might very well come to accept some other description of our nature. We are not instinctually drawn to take up one view rather than another. The issue at hand bears on the force of our nature. For our nature to be unconquerable, it seems to lack the power that term implies.

If this worry is correct, then it appears Walker is asking us to rely on the very thing (i.e., our nature) that now appears to be without power. I think the reason he takes this path is to help us understand the importance of education and performance in bringing the force of our nature to fruition. Nature is only one part of what he means to illuminate. This points to a task—work to be done. As we will see, the work to be done highlights the importance of action that Walker calls for in the *Appeal*.

But before we get there, we need to deal with the weakness of our nature. Consider Walker's language from an earlier section of Article II: "Ignorance, my brethren, is a mist, low down into the very dark and *almost* impenetrable abyss in which, our fathers for many centuries have been plunged."[22] Or let us return to the sentence quoted above, paying attention to its structure: "Man is a peculiar creature—he is the image of his God, though he may be subjected to the most wretched condition upon earth, *yet* the spirit and feeling which constitute the creature, man, can never be *entirely* erased." The conjunction "yet" is meant to capture something taking place at the same time, as when one says, "the path was dark, yet I slowly found my way." Similarly, Walker does not mean to diminish the difficulty at work. His point is that despite that difficulty, there are limits to how far distortion and ignorance can go.

Consider the example of Douglass once more. For all of his talk about his soul and spirit being broken, he nonetheless tells us, "From my earliest recollection, I date the entertainment of a deep conviction that slavery would not always be able to hold me within its foul embrace; and in the darkest hours of my career in slavery, this living word of faith and spirit of hope departed not from me, but remained like ministering angels to cheer me through the gloom."[23] What Douglass has in mind when he discusses Covey and what Walker means to convey by the spirit and feeling of freedom is the following: the unconquerable disposition of freedom remains, but our understanding of our nature can be deformed because of slavery or hidden from view because of ignorance. The path back to our nature may be dark (as it was for Douglass), but we may yet find our way. The *Appeal* is therefore a text seeking to inform the political and ethical activities of his readers and listeners.

I have been discussing the role of nature in Walker's thinking, but I want to be careful about how we finally understand its status. Thinking about the status of nature will help clarify how Walker is proceeding. He presupposes an alternative position from which he articulates his critique of the social and political order. That alternative view is grounded in a religious-anthropological account of human nature, as we have thus far examined. But he does not derive the requirements of being free from the description "man," independent of how we think and act concerning that description. "Man" is not a value-neutral term for him that one finds in nature. The point is that the concept "man" is partly shaped by a normative description as being created as a free creature by God and cannot be understood once that description is removed.[24] Remove the description, and one may well have servile creatures, but not humans. The point comes into sharp relief if one recalls that Walker's pamphlet is a text that appeals to the judgment of the reader. He is exhorting African Americans to assume a specific normative point of view that he claims is their nature—a view that is meant to contrast with the description of them that is currently in circulation.

I do not doubt that Walker believed God created humans as free creatures. However, the truth of his belief is beside the point. Philosophically salient here is that his audience *believes* it to be so. In Article I, for instance, he emphatically intones, "Are we MEN!!!—I ask you, O my brethren! Are we MEN?"[25] This is not a rhetorical question, since he seemingly answers in Article IV: "But O, my God!—in sorrow I must say it, that my color, all over the world, have a mean, servile spirit."[26] How is this possible? How can Walker concede that African Americans have a "servile spirit" in the very same paragraph where he asserts that a "feeling and spirit" of freedom constitute them? Walker uses "spirit" in this context to denote a vital principle or animating force, and yet his reflections denote contradictory principles—one of freedom and the other of servility. Here we confront the ambivalence of our nature once more. Is he confused?

I propose that we resolve the confusion if we see that the mere fact that God constituted us as free is of little consequence by itself. Similar to later figures such as Anna Julia Cooper and William James, action, for Walker, becomes denotative of beliefs held. "*Live* your creed," Cooper puts it in 1892 as she explains how one enacts beliefs in the world.[27] James puts the point more dramatically in 1897: "Our only way, for example, of doubting, or refusing to believe, that a certain thing *is*, is continuing to act as if it were *not*."[28] For Walker, the only way of doubting, or refusing to believe, that we as African Americans are men is to continue to act as if we were not. Thus Walker says, recalling the line cited earlier, "be determined *to act* like men." Since the subject "man" cannot be separated from the normative status of "being free," accepting that one is a man, for him, performatively entails its own truth. This is why he is so concerned about the description we accept of ourselves. For the description shall be true just to the extent African Americans performatively affirm it.[29]

Walker's emphasis on performativity constitutes his response to Jefferson's demeaning views of blacks rather than a direct argumentative refutation. Written in 1780 and 1781, and published in 1787 in London, Jefferson's *Notes on the State of Virginia* is described as "the most important scientific and political book written by an American before 1785."[30] Jefferson's claims in Query XIV of his *Notes* engage in what was taken for the time as a scientific analysis regarding the physical, intellectual, and moral endowments of African Americans.[31] Even if Jefferson did not place blacks outside the human family, he nonetheless views them as distinct within it, contributing to the perceived bestial nature of blacks.[32] For him, the inner workings of blacks are taken to be determinative of their outer comportment. It is then possible to speak, as others did, about specific black individuals—their character and mental endowments—by virtue of the broader racial classification to which they belong. The classification becomes shorthand for making ethical judgments about particular black persons. Jefferson thus concludes his reflections with an important claim that Walker cites: "This *unfortunate* difference of color, and *perhaps* of *faculty*, is a powerful obstacle to the emancipation of these people."[33] Because someone of Jefferson's status backs the claim, Walker rightly perceives it (regardless of what Jefferson says or intended elsewhere) as causing harm to the status of freedom. He remarks, "Mr. Jefferson . . . has in truth injured us more, and has been as great a barrier to our emancipation as anything that has ever been advanced against us."[34]

Walker does not respond to Jefferson's arguments by offering a contrasting "scientific" analysis, although he often plays fast and loose with similar language. That said, he more often appears uninterested in waging the battle on the grounds of physiology specifically or natural history more generally. Proceeding differently, he quips: "I'm glad Mr. Jefferson has advanced his positions for your sake; for you will either have to contradict or confirm him by your *own actions*."[35] Walker reverses the mode of inquiry, treating activity as indicative of their nature.[36]

The emphasis on performance or activity is not meant to downplay Walker's religious commitments. The latter does work in two important respects. First, it allows him to argue that "God made man to serve Him *alone*, and that man should have no other Lord or Lords but Himself— that God Almighty is the *sole proprietor* or *master* of the WHOLE human family, and will not on any consideration admit of a colleague."[37] The claim, not unlike John Locke's in the *Second Treatise of Government*, is that because we each belong to God, we are each protected from being the property of another.[38] Those who abandon their freedom or deny freedom to others invite God's wrath. The claim was of some significance, prompting abolitionist Henry Highland Garnet to remark in 1843, "the forlorn condition in which [blacks] are placed, does not destroy [their] moral obligation to God."[39] The line comes from an address Garnet delivered at the National Negro Convention and was the same address he would append to an edition of Walker's *Appeal*, for which he also wrote a biographical sketch. Second, and again similar to Locke and echoed by Garnet, Walker is clear that although we owe the source of our freedom to God, the custodianship of that freedom rests with us. Hence, although God is foundational, the stipulation of God underdetermines how we perform, leaving the normative capacity of self-reflection and its relationship to action up to us to work out.

We must take care in understanding how moral obligation vis-à-vis God functions. Duty is not a freestanding idea; it does not exist apart from our orientation to the larger framework that grounds any specific duty. If one reflectively accepts that we are created in God's image, thereby having a special obligation, the conditions we find ourselves in (horrible though they may be) do not absolve us of that obligation. Whether this position has force depends on us occupying a normative standpoint from which its obligatory quality (or demandingness) makes sense.

This way of stating the matter, I admit, may seem too philosophical. What does it mean to occupy a standpoint from which an obligation makes sense? Here we need to consider the experiential dimension of obligation. Consider an example to illustrate the point. Think of the shame we feel when we fail to fulfill an obligation we have freely undertaken, such as failing to attend a friend's birthday party, despite having said we would be there when asked. Shame only makes sense because we conceive our situation in terms stipulated by a particular ethical point of view that we have failed to affirm. The ethical point of view is not merely making good on our promises but doing right by the demand of friendship.[40] The idea of friendship marks out an especially significant area of human concern that one embraces and that has urgency and a demanding quality to it. This does not mean friendship inheres in nature apart from us but that friendship takes on the urgency it does because we are part of the natural world.

This last point prepares the way for Walker's question. What does it mean to do right by our nature as free creatures? Whatever the answer is to that question, which we will take up in a moment, his point is that what follows from the standpoint of our nature is currently not in view because of slavery and ignorance. As he has been saying, the habits of dominance and servility obscure the affordance of human nature to which African Americans must be awakened. It is to this issue we must now turn.

The Demandingness of Freedom: On the Complicit Slave Woman and the Enslaved Free Man

For Walker, our nature is of little significance apart from a normative attitude that is commensurate with it—an attitude expressed in performance. Hence he says, "It is not to be understood here, that I mean for us to wait until God shall take us by the hair of our heads and drag us out of abject wretchedness and slavery."[41] There are, we might say, Divine sanctions against slavery. But whatever those sanctions are, Walker is clear that human agency is the best vehicle for decisively responding to domination. God's work is done, and we must now do the rest. To adopt a normative attitude denotes Walker's goal to get African Americans to exercise their capacity for freedom, and in that moment they will have become the picture of their nature he describes. The first step in doing so is to see what happens in the *absence* of assuming such a standpoint. The thrust of his approach turns on two of the examples central to Article II: the complicit slave woman and the enslaved free man.

Apart from portraying black life in bondage, Walker relies on *stories* not merely to illuminate the capacity to judge but to enrich or educate the judgment of his audience. This is especially so given the centrality that storytelling and the practice of *seeing* assumes in the thinkers we will take up later. For Walker, the use of examples is not merely descriptive; rather, it appeals to readers and listeners, asking them to judge the situations. Judgment, in this context, has a cognitive-affective character that moves the audience. I will first say a word about this process of enriching judgment that will prepare the way for his examples.

ENRICHING JUDGMENT

My use of the word "standpoint" relates to Walker's folk moral psychology. The use of "folk" denotes his commonsensical approach; his moral psychology does not depend on questionable assumptions—at least to his nineteenth-century audience—about forming moral judgments. This informs his approach to freedom. Although one can advance an affirmative argument for freedom, one can also, as Walker does, defend freedom from the perspective of negation. Here Walker paints pictures of lives and experiences in which docility and domination are the norms. Do these lives, we should read Walker as asking, not appear morally impoverished? He intends to metaphorically place the audience in "conversation" with perspectives that may not readily be considered. Storytelling is a tool for focusing the audience's perception—to get them to see and feel in a certain way in the light of those stories. The aim, as the rhetorician intends, is to move the audience. Consider Walker's words:

> Any man who is curious to see the full force of ignorance developed among the colored people of the United States of America, has only to go into the southern and western states of this confederacy, where, if he is not a tyrant, but has the feelings of a human being, who can feel for a fellow creature, he may see enough to make his very heart bleed![42]

This passage conveys the complex interaction between Walker's commitment to republicanism and sentimentalism: first, by centralizing the master-slave image in his analysis to illuminate the meaning of freedom; second, by placing affect in a productive relationship to one's self-understanding as a human being responsive to the claims of one's fellows. This second point, I argue, has an affinity with the Scottish sentimentalist tradition, especially given the tight connection that tradition draws between moral judgment and the emotive dimension of the self. For like that tradition, Walker means to use the imagination as both a vehicle and productive agent of phenomenological knowledge. I will take each in turn.

In the passage, Walker has in mind the conventional idea of the master-slave relationship central to republicanism's idea of freedom. Just as he defines a human being in contrast to a slave, he also contrasts being a human to a tyrant. To be a human being is to occupy a position between these two extremes—the slave who lives at the mercy of another and the tyrant who lives only to dominate. This in-between position is the standpoint of what Walker calls republican liberty, understood as the absence of arbitrary power. He means to relocate his audience to that position by showing them what happens when freedom goes unrealized.

Second, the lines occur in the sixth paragraph of Article II of the *Appeal* and form part of what we might call the introduction to that article. Here, Walker is trying to orient his reader and listener, to whom he repeatedly refers in that paragraph as "my observer" or "observer."[43] In its Latin formulation, to observe is "to watch over, [to] note, [to] heed."[44] No wonder the word "observer" is regularly used as part of newspaper titles, indicating that one should pay careful attention to what one is about to witness.

For all of its importance, the *Appeal* was not novel in its emphasis on vision and sight. In fact, it was central to the Western classical rhetorical tradition, and scholars identify the "ubiquity of vision as the master sense of the modern era."[45] It figures quite importantly as Walker and others aim to help their audiences "see" the horror of black life under conditions of enslavement.

The idea of observing, watching, and seeing figured prominently in antislavery writing and its iconography, and activists often described in graphic details scenes of slavery's horror. Writing under the pen name Zillah, Sarah Mapps Douglass, a prominent Philadelphia black abolitionist, describes the hardship of black mothers under the system of slavery. Black mothers were especially, although not exclusively, torn between protecting their lives or the lives of their children. In her 1832 short essay, "A Mother's Love," published in William Lloyd Garrison's *Liberator*, Mapps Douglass provides in vivid detail slavery's cruelty on a mother. After painting the picture of horror and pain, she appeals: "American mothers! Can you doubt that the slave feels as tenderly for her offspring as you do for yours? Do your hearts feel no throb of pity for her woes?"[46] A year later in 1833, women's rights activist and abolitionist Lydia Maria Child famously remarked in *An Appeal in Favor of That Class of Americans Called Africans* that one must "follow the poor slave through his wretched wanderings, in order to give some idea of his physical suffering, his mental and moral degradation."[47] Her graphic recounting, like that of Mapps Douglass, sought to remove the divide between the reader and the subjects of her appeal. In 1834, argues Radiclani Clytus, the American Anti-Slavery Society launched a pamphlet campaign to put before the eyes of observers the horrors of slavery. Their slogan—"KEEP IT BEFORE THE PEOPLE"—turned on the belief that "engravings . . . bring home to the bosom of the reader a full conception of the wrongs and sufferings of his fellow-men."[48] In his 1837 work, Easton asked his readers to "think of a poor [black] woman, a prospective mother . . . see her weeping eyes fixed alternately upon the object of her affections and him who accounts her a brute . . . the latter wields the accursed lash, until the back of a husband indeed the whole frame, has become . . . mangled flesh."[49] And in his 1861 speech "Pictures and Progress," Douglass describes the "moral and social influence of pictures" as of greater importance than "the making of . . . laws" in shaping the nation.[50] Like the spectators of Greek tragedy, the Greek and Roman rhetoricians, and eighteenth-century moral sense theorists, Walker, Mapps Douglass, Childs, Easton, Douglass, and the American Anti-Slavery Society intended for the audience to play witness to the lives on display and heed the lessons contained therein. In this, they envisioned ethics, to positively appropriate Karen Halttunen's language, "as a matter of sentiment, sentiment as a matter of sympathy, and sympathy as a matter of spectatorship."[51]

This emphasis on vision combined several different elements at once: sentimentality, the idea of the horrific, and action. The first two functioned to educate adult citizens as well as children to the horrors of domination. As Glenn Hendler makes clear of the eighteenth and nineteenth centuries, in the "culture of sensibility, feelings were not primarily the sorts of unique, individualized interior emotions they are in our more psychologized culture. Rather, sentiments required the cultivation of a moral and proper repertoire of feelings, a sensibility."[52] The cultivation of one's sensibility was a public practice. This is precisely what Theodore Dwight Weld has in mind when, in 1842, he explains that the sympathetic imagination develops in children by showing "them suffering objects."[53] Earlier in 1836, children learned of the "wicked Mrs. Lalaurie of New Orleans, who chained slaves in her garret—and refused to free them when her house caught fire."[54] The narrative detail of the images was part of a general goal to educate the citizenry regarding the demand of sympathy. However, this was not meant to be a passive education but, as with Walker's general approach, meant to translate into action.

When Walker remarks, then, that one's standpoint is enriched if they "go into the southern and western states"—a formulation he will repeat—he does not simply mean to provide direction; he is also telling us something about his approach. His vision of traveling seeks to expand the imagination of the audience and thereby inform their judgments. The position of the observer is not inert; as he says in the preamble, "I shall endeavor to penetrate, search out, and lay [our miseries] open for your *inspection*."[55] This way of speaking fits with what it means to observe. To properly inspect requires that one "lay aside prejudice long enough to view candidly and impartially."[56] He has in mind not only white Americans who benefit from dominating black Americans but also those black Americans who are either "in league with tyrants" or who "are said to be free" because they are not subjected to the horrors of slavery in the South.[57] These last two positions roughly correspond to the two examples central to Article II.

Walker's language of "candid" and "impartial" seeks to remove prejudice that would close the observer off from what is on display. He therefore wants black Americans, especially those in the Northeast, to be clear about the conditions of blacks in the South and West as well as the evaluative structure of the society in which those conditions emerge. Blacks in the

Northeast may well avoid the first but cannot avoid the second because, as Walker makes clear, the racial classification system informs the evaluative structures of American life. To be impartial is to be fully alive to the world in which one is located. He knows we cannot abandon the position we occupy, but he hopes the force of our position can be lessened "long enough" so that we may imagine the position of our fellows and, as a result, come to understand our position.

There is a conceptual affinity between Walker's thinking and sentimentalism; it frames his stories about the complicit slave woman and enslaved free man. I use "conceptual affinity" here to avoid claims about philological filiation. I do not mean to argue that Walker was directly influenced by the moral sense tradition (despite its primacy during this period) by reading this or that passage in the work of this or that author. But every age has its circulating languages that are used and reused, forming a conceptual field in which others move. Conceptual affinity implies similar characteristics that mark out relationships and connections. In this sense, the importance of occupying the standpoint of others to inform the moral perspective is as central to Walker's thinking as it was to the tradition of moral sentimentalism. What he expects of the observer is reminiscent, for example, of Adam Smith's remark that "the spectator must, first of all, endeavour as much as he can to put himself in the situation of the other" if the deliverances of the situation are to be rightly received.[58] Through "the imagination," says Smith, "we place ourselves in his situation . . . and become in some measure the same persons with him, and thence form some idea of his sensations, and even feel something which, though weaker in degree, is not altogether unlike them."[59] Relatedly, the significance of affect to moral judgment figures prominently in Walker as it did in the Scottish moral sense tradition and earlier American thinkers.[60] Here one is reminded of an affinity with David Hume's earlier comment when thinking of Walker's deployment of feeling. As Hume remarks, "where the objects [of reason] themselves do not affect us, their connexion can never give them any influence" in our conduct.[61]

This affinity frames the contrast he draws between having the feelings of a human being and having the feelings of a tyrant. His point is that being inattentive and insensitive to the pain of others defines the character of the tyrant—that is, the tyrant tracks only his own concerns, interests, and feelings. From the perspective of the tyrant's actions and judgments, the world seems to lack anyone who might make a claim worthy of a response. The world may well include others, but it most certainly is not shared or held in common. In contrast, Walker seems to be saying that being human entails having what we might call "a shared physiology of feeling" that we recognize, and that unless we are somehow emotionally broken or inveterately prejudiced, we readily feel for our fellows. This first portion is noteworthy. Walker's language of "feelings of a human being" in the quoted passage above seems interested in marking (albeit without specifying) a universally pervasive catalog of feelings that we, as humans, are capable of deploying and acknowledging.[62] This second portion is also significant, but it works in tandem with confronting specific situations. Feeling, as a sensory experience, depends on the revealed texture of life. Indeed, in the nineteenth century, abolitionists often targeted slavery by targeting its cruelty. They sought to destabilize the institution through the growing revulsion to pain and suffering otherwise central to punishment.[63] For Walker specifically, attentiveness to the lives of others enables the audience to "see the full force of ignorance" and have their "heart bleed." Attentiveness teaches what observation means: take heed of these examples, Walker says to his African American audience, lest you suffer the same fate. To have the feelings of a human being, then, seems to presume a shared community that can be brought into view for our fellows.

We can further sharpen this affinity with sentimentalism. Walker refers to the importance of feeling for a fellow creature. His point is that if the audience feels appropriately for their fellows, this will cause them emotional pain ("he may see enough to make his very heart bleed"). Feeling, as Walker is using the term, involves sensations or physiological disturbances (captured, metaphorically, in the bleeding heart). This is brought on by a set of experiences that he believes an honest and impartial audience would readily disapprove of. This is why it seems appropriate to call this folk moral psychology; there is something strikingly ordinary about what Walker has in mind. After remarking that "he may see enough to make his very heart bleed," he briefly specifies what experiences would generate such pain:

> He may see there, a son take his mother, who bore almost the pains of death to give him birth, and by the command of a tyrant, strip her as naked as she came into the world, and apply the cow-hide to her, until she falls a victim to death in the road! He may see a husband take his dear wife, not unfrequently in a pregnant state, and perhaps far advanced, and beat her for an unmerciful wretch, and until his infant falls a lifeless lump at her feet! . . . My observer may see fathers beating their sons, mothers their daughters, and children their parents, all to pacify the passions of unrelenting tyrants.[64]

That one would readily disapprove of what he describes is not Walker's individual wishes dressed up as public concerns. The reason is that our affective judgments are rarely the reflection of mere private considerations but are socially constituted. This is why he speaks of having the "feelings of a human being."

He presents these examples because he believes they tap into a proper alignment between experience and our affective judgments of them that is part of the social order. Consider the thrust of the passage: Walker is not merely saying some random person stripped some random woman on command by some random individual and proceeded to beat her. While this may very well be abhorrent, he wants to direct our attention to son, mother, and the commandments of the tyrant, for it is by virtue of those relationships that the emotions we feel take on the texture that they do. Only a decade later, and similar to Walker, abolitionist Weld says to his audience in *American Slavery as It Is: Testimony of a Thousand Witnesses*:

> Reader, you are empannelled [*sic*] as a juror to try a plain cause and bring in an honest verdict. . . . Look at it. TWENTY-SEVEN HUN-DRED THOUSAND PERSONS in this country, men, women, and children, are in SLAVERY. Is slavery, as a condition for human beings, good, bad, or indifferent? We submit the question without argument. You have common sense, and conscience, and a human heart;— pronounce upon it. *You have a wife, or a husband, a child, a father, a mother, a brother or a sister—make the case your own, make it theirs, and bring in your verdict.*[65]

The entailments of these roles as Walker and Weld understand them are distorted or more significantly go unrealized owing principally to the scene in which they are located—a scene of enslavement and domination. Citing these relationships is meant to focus attention on the examples so that the audience adequately perceives the texture of cruelty and, perhaps, their complicity. To recall Mapps Douglass once more, after describing the horror black mothers experience, after laying out how their ability to care for their children is denied, she concludes: "Calumniators of my despised race, read this and blush."[66] The relationships described by Walker, Weld, and Mapps Douglass function as causes for why one should be horrified by the violation of what those relationships demand. This should cause shame, what Mapps Douglass here refers to with her use of "blush." But the point is that these relationships have explanatory and normative power. Walker, Weld, and Mapps Douglass thus invoke these examples because they contain within them standards that constitute social life, reflect shared concerns, and capture social mores. To the extent that they do, neither they nor the emotions that emerge from the distortion of those relationships emanate from the "phantasm of the senses," as Hume rightly observed.[67]

Walker's emphasis on physiological disturbances—his use of the word "pain"—does not exhaust his meaning. As suggested in the previous paragraph, feeling is also about something—a judgment about the world and the lives on display. Since he has more in mind than sensations, one wishes Walker would have specified the relevant emotions: does he mean anger, indignation, sadness, sympathy, or something else? Or, does he mean the word "feeling" to serve as the general term for what are otherwise specific emotions? This, perhaps, is to demand too much of a pamphlet and to be too little aware of how the idiom typically functions. To say "My heart bleeds for you" is to express sadness and sympathy at once. Although Walker does not specify these emotions, it seems clear he has in mind a structured sensitivity to the world that involves an appraisal. And we can say for sure that a bleeding heart is not a good thing for the person whose heart it is and the individuals to whom sympathy and sadness are directed.

In deploying stories as he does, Walker's analysis of affective judgment moves in two different directions. To appropriate the language of one scholar, Walker's reflections contain both mind-to-world and world-to-mind relationships.[68] The first of these is seeking to get into right relationship with the world, understood as appropriately perceiving the cruelty on display. Hence if one has the feelings of a human being and not a tyrant, one's heart cannot help but bleed because that is the appropriate response given the situation. But to feel appropriately is simultaneously to wish that those cruel experiences were no longer part of the social and political order to which one belongs. Affective judgment is about not merely adjusting one's mind to the world but also expressing a longing that the world adjust itself to the aspirations of one's mind.

COMPLICIT SLAVE WOMAN

Walker transitions from his introductory remarks to "show the force of degraded ignorance and deceit among" black Americans. He refers to an article of 1829 from the *Columbian Centinel*—a prominent Boston newspaper—that recounts the details of sixty slaves, some of whom managed to get free in Kentucky, while being transported from Maryland to Mississippi. Those responsible for the slaves included Gordon and his two

companions, Allen and Petit. Although Walker transcribes the entire article, it is worth looking at a small selection:

> The men were hand-cuffed and chained together, in the usual man-
> ner for driving those poor wretches, while the women and children
> were suffered to proceed without incumbrance [*sic*]. It appears that,
> by means of a file the negroes, unobserved, had succeeded in separat-
> ing the iron which bound their hands, in such a way as to be able to
> throw them off at any moment. . . . At this moment, every negro was
> found to be perfectly at liberty; and one of them seizing a club, gave
> Petit a violent blow on the head and laid him dead at his feet; and
> Allen, who came to his assistance, met a similar fate. . . . Gordon was
> then attacked, seized and held by one of the negroes, while another
> fired twice at him with a pistol, the ball of which each time grazed his
> head, but not providing effectual, he was beaten with clubs and left for
> dead. . . . Gordon . . . not being materially injured, was enabled, by the
> assistance of one of the women, to mount his horse and flee.[69]

After quoting the article Walker writes, "I want you to notice particularly
in the above article, the *ignorant* and *deceitful actions* of this colored
woman. I beg you view it candidly. . . . [W]hat do you think of this?"[70] His
query is sincere, but he provides some guidance in assessing the situation.

Although Walker goes on to discuss the actions of the black men also
mentioned in the newspaper article, it is the black woman to whom he
first directs the observer's attention. His point is that black women also fall
prey to ignorance, which implicates them in their own domination and the
domination of those similarly situated. When Walker refers to the woman
as ignorant, he means she is unaware of what the situation demands. We
might liken the situation, to borrow a modern example, to a blind spot: an
area just outside a driver's visual field.[71] Analogously, the woman displays
the normative attitude of a slave, leading to a moral blind spot. As Walker
says, despite the freedom that the context creates, the "servile woman"
nonetheless assists Gordon *as if* she were not "perfectly at liberty" to do
otherwise. But the observer is also meant to bear witness to something
else, having to do with the relationship of the other slaves to the woman:
there was no good reason for the men to believe that one who was equally
enslaved would act in a way to aid the enslaver. This is why the *actions* are
considered deceitful; they deceive those who rightly expect her actions,
given the context, to be otherwise.

What is the observer to make of all this? The woman is caught in a
double bind. She is bound by an expectation she does not see and therefore

bound by a betrayal she does not acknowledge. She is unwittingly complicit in the domination of herself and others. Nonetheless, it may strike us as deeply unsettling and unfair that Walker blames her, labeling her actions "deceitful." Difficult as it may be to note, he is very much concerned to distinguish between making a normative judgment about the woman's actions and making a normative judgment about her capacity for freedom. Her actions are inconsistent with what it means to be a free human being, and this is because she lives under the weight of slavery. Her moral blind spot does not prevent us from seeing either the harm she does or the tragedy of her double bind.

Despite the woman's position, Walker refuses to pity her; as he tells his audience, "The actions of this black woman are really insupportable."[72] Here again, the target is her actions. The rationale is not as callous as it may first appear, and it connects to the epistemic egalitarianism of the last chapter. As he says, one who "will stand still and let another murder him, is worse than an infidel, and, if he has common sense, ought not to be pitied."[73] We often extend pity to those whose condition, although unfortunate, we believe can never be like our own. Pity is a way of looking down on the condition of others, often smuggling in condescension toward the suffering person and affirming feelings of deserved advantage in oneself. When applied to this context, it takes on a specific meaning. To pity the woman is to pity the absence of common sense; it ironically reaffirms the subordinate position of black people.[74] This is precisely what Walker rejects. Such a position may reinforce the view of blacks often used to challenge their equal standing.

The term "common sense" and the related formulations that appear throughout the *Appeal*, such as "sense," "sound sense," and "good sense," are not unusual in the nineteenth century.[75] They are common in the American revolutionary generation, as well as among African American abolitionists with different political programs such as Daniel Coker, Robert Purvis, and William Whipper.[76] "Common sense" means for Walker, as it did for many, an ordinary way of seeing things, about which there is no need for debate and to which we all have access. The epistemological significance of the term extends to political life precisely because of its social leveling implication—the belief that regardless of our station in life, we are all endowed with a basic and equal capacity for understanding and assessing the world around us. This logic, as argued in the last chapter, is the hallmark of the practice of the appeal.

There is something odd at work when common sense is mentioned, as we see in Walker's text. As Sophia Rosenfeld more generally says of the term, no one invokes "common sense who is not convinced that it is under assault or fast disappearing."[77] Walker is no different. He mentions this capacity precisely to deny the claim that black Americans are without it. Paradoxically, he discourages pity in order to affirm the equal access by the black woman and those like her to common sense. His argument is undoubtedly directed to his listening and reading public, and its upshot should not be understated. Despite the view of African Americans in circulation, he contends, common sense belongs to black women and men alike and therefore is not the sole property of whites.

We should linger a bit longer on this point. Walker is outlining something important for his reader about the connection between equality and liberty, tying together his reflections here with those discussed in the last chapter. By invoking common sense, he reminds the audience of the norm implicit in the practice of appealing, namely, our equal capacity to judge. Recall that it is the capacity to judge that is the foundation of our status as citizens and explains the title of his pamphlet. He now connects this argument to his claim about freedom. The defense of common sense as a property of black people runs alongside his claim that although the feeling and spirit of freedom may well be silenced, it can never disappear from our nature. To say the woman's actions are ignorant and deceitful is not to say she is without a basic and equal capacity to recognize the offense against freedom that domination represents. And more importantly, Walker suggests, neither is his audience.

The point is less about the woman described in the story and more about the readers and listeners of the *Appeal*. After all, she is a stand-in for Walker's audience, an embodied identity through which the effects and affects of servility and domination are discernable. Her example thus serves to disrupt the logic of these forms of comportment. For him, so long as black people—men and women alike—think of themselves as unresponsive to the injury of racial domination because they lack common sense, the more they must see whatever limitations they have (even when brought on by the institutions of slavery and practices of domination) as limitations for which they cannot be held partially responsible and from which they cannot be freed. For Walker, this concedes too much ground; it invites the claim that blacks are incapable of acting as free humans should and therefore are rightly treated as unequal. This rejects what our nature affords us as human beings—a capacity for freedom and therefore a capacity to recognize when that freedom has gone unrealized.

We have now arrived at a four-part lesson for the observers.

(1) The observers should see the self-deception and betrayal on display in the example.

(2) The observers should judge the position of the woman tragic given the habits of dominance and servility responsible for her condition.

(3) The observers should nonetheless judge her and those like her as unpitiable precisely because of the capacity for transformation— that is, the basic and equal capacity to reflectively align one's actions with the demand freedom makes.

What, finally, does this mean for the position of the observers?

(4) Although this appropriate alignment may well be too late for the black woman, it need not be too late for those who have now witnessed what servility and domination have created.

There is still the lingering issue of gender to which I said I would return. One might wonder why Walker focuses on the black woman given that he seems to tie liberty to manliness. Against the backdrop of discussing the story, he writes, "Oh! Colored people of these United States, I ask you, in the name of that God who made us, have we, in consequence of oppression, nearly lost the spirit of man . . . ?"[78] Consistently he encourages his audience to act like men, with the presupposition being that to act as men do is to assert one's freedom. This seems to undermine the argument laid out thus far; it may invite not only a hierarchy based on gender differences but a new form of domination.

Despite the gendered language throughout the *Appeal* that connects manliness to liberty, it is a mistake to think about this in oppressive terms. But we need to begin with an honest reading of the period and ultimately expand Walker's thinking. Among nineteenth-century black Americans, "equality" did not mean sameness. Black men and women intellectuals regularly spoke about the importance of black women to the future of the race and regularly affirmed what Maria Stewart called in 1833 the "natural force and energy" that belong to a "man."[79] Distinct notions of womanliness and manliness were part and parcel of the culture.

Stewart, for example, readily asserts these distinctions. But she also rejects the notion that women must be "willing to spend their lives and bury their talents in performing mean, servile labor."[80] She is not objecting to the labor that women do, even if often confined to the household (something Stewart affirms). Rather, her criticism is directed to the fact that the labor of women is subjected to the arbitrary rule of men. Women live, Stewart argues, at the will of their male counterparts, and thus their own actions must always carry the silent permission of those on whose will they depend. They are, in essence, unfree. This is, of course, what

Cooper means when she turns the point around in her famous 1892 text, *A Voice from the South*: "Only the BLACK WOMAN can say 'when and where I enter, in the quiet, undisputed dignity of my womanhood, without violence and without suing or special patronage, then and there the whole *Negro race enters with me.*'"[81] While Cooper, like Stewart, endorses a version of gender essentialism, she thinks this has no bearing on the integrity of their freedom. Although Walker does not use the commonly used distinction, it is fair to say that he was not immune to its social and cultural force.

Notwithstanding, and consistent with the example above, he nonetheless encourages black women to resist those who would dominate them. The slide from Walker to Stewart and Cooper is not meant to provide Walker with a feminist defense but to focus our attention. Even if all subscribe to something like a division of labor between men and women, Walker, Stewart, and Cooper affirm the equal right of men and women to be free from domination. This, of course, carries with it the earlier claim: the equal capacity of men and women to judge and assess the world in which they live as the basis for their freedom. Yoking together "man" and "liberty" should not be read as Walker saying that liberty is only the right of males. We therefore should not read Walker's call for outward, physical engagement to resist domination as implicitly coded as male from which women are denied participation. A more accurate reading is that the term "men" is meant to denote all people. The final proof of this, of course, comes from the fact that the text is directed to men, women, and children.[82]

ENSLAVED FREE MAN

After leaving the example of the complicit slave woman, Walker turns his attention to the enslaved free man. The analysis seeks to reveal how racial domination radiates outward, influencing the standards black Americans set for themselves, thus extending the analysis of the complicit slave woman. But Walker also asserts the necessity of racial solidarity as a result of racialized domination. This second point doubles back to his example of the complicit slave woman, since she is seemingly unaware of the need to stand in solidarity with those equally enslaved. At this stage, racial solidarity will only function as a mere assertion. In the next chapter, I will sharpen the defense of racial solidarity and extend the argument as part of a larger reconfiguration of republicanism to which Walker and other African American intellectuals contributed.

Walker's treatment of racial domination points to the constraints on those blacks who are putatively free. He means to illuminate the way racial domination infiltrates the very self-understanding of black Americans. Consider the following example of what I call the "enslaved free man":

> I met a colored man in the street a short time since, with a string of boots on his shoulders; we fell into conversation, and in course of which, I said to him, what a miserable set of people we are! He asked, why?— Said I, we are so subjected under the whites, that we cannot obtain the comforts of life, but by cleaning their boots and shoes, old clothes, waiting on them, shaving them &c. Said he, (with the boots on his shoulders) "I am completely happy!!! I never want to live any better or happier than when I can get a plenty of boots and shoes to clean!!!!" Oh! How can those who are actuated by avarice only, but think, that our Creator made us to be an inheritance to them forever, when they see that our greatest glory is centered in such mean and low objects?[83]

There are two arguments here, the last of which will lead to a third. The first is captured by the last sentence. Precisely because the man is only concerned with monetary gain, Walker argues, he is unaware of the evaluative structure in which his status as a bootblack is located. This directs us to the second argument relating to the force of racial domination, the way it constrains and conditions one's self-description. The second point underscores how racial domination limits even where there is no obvious person acting in the role of a master. This should bring to mind the example of the complicit slave woman, who, in a condition of perfect liberty, nonetheless runs to the aid of her enslaver. This leads to the third point, not referenced in the passage, regarding Walker's assertion of racial solidarity.

Similar to Stewart who follows only a few years later, Walker does not have an aversion to labor that helps provide for one's family and basic subsistence. "Understand me, brethren," Walker insists, "I do not mean to speak against the occupations by which we acquire enough and sometimes scarcely that, to render ourselves and families comfortable through life."[84] As Stewart says at a New England Anti-Slavery Society meeting: "I do not consider it derogatory, my friends, for persons to live out to service. There are many whose inclination leads them to aspire no higher; and I would highly commend the performance of almost anything for an honest livelihood."[85] But what they both object to is setting one's sights no higher than cleaning and shining the shoes of white people. "My objections are," Walker explains, to us "looking forward with thankful hearts to higher attainments than *wielding the razor* and *cleaning boots and shoes*."[86] Stewart puts the point differently, worrying less about what black people aspire to achieve and more about what would happen if they did otherwise: "As servants, we are respected; but let us presume to aspire any higher, our employer regards us no longer."[87]

The focuses in some of these lines point in different directions. Nevertheless, Walker's and Stewart's outlooks are part and parcel of the complicated politics of racial uplift or respectability politics common among Northeastern black intellectuals. But this politics was not always exclusively, or even primarily, about white people and what white people thought of black people. More often, it was about what Erica Ball rightly refers to as the "intrinsic value of respectability"—what do black people think of themselves.[88] As a result, Walker and Stewart think there is more to life than shining shoes and shaving faces.

Two observations should be noted. First, Walker's (as well as Stewart's) uplift ideology must be appropriately contextualized. The concern is with a class of persons (e.g., blacks) who are structurally confined to occupy specific positions in order to serve another class of persons (e.g., whites). When he argues that black Americans are not an inheritance to whites, he does so in order to upset the link between America's economy and white supremacy. The most intense form of this connection, Walker says, is having us "work without remunerations for our services." "May I not [be] asked," he queries, "to fatten the wretch and his family?"[89] On the one side, then, Walker's criticism of the bootblack might well appear complicit with the dominant descriptions of blacks because of the ease with which it marks this man as comfortable with his position. And yet, on the other side, it subverts such descriptions by calling into question the genuineness of the man's freedom. Uplift ideology or respectability politics was a way to highlight the transformative power of freedom: "its ability to remake an individual into a new being elevated to a higher state" that was not itself determined by the standards of white Americans.[90]

That the bootblack is actuated by avarice only serves to obscure the limit that has been placed on his aspirations and in turn the structural inequality in which he participates that is fundamentally shaped by white supremacy. The black man confuses the fact that he cleans shoes because he has no choice with the idea that he cleans shoes because he has freely chosen that profession. Or to turn the matter around, the black man cleans because he does not have the freedom—that is to say, the power—to do otherwise. The bootblack's aspirations are unwittingly tethered to the constrained expectations that are generally set for blacks in America—namely, that they are meant to serve precisely because their lives are worth less than those of their white counterparts. Walker's point is that black Americans are perceived as only useful for work of this kind and that acceptance of this view (blacks "*glorying* and being *happy* in such low employments") merely reaffirms their unequal and unfree standing.[91] The evaluative structure that deems blacks as inferior and that is responsible for Southern and Western enslavement thus radiates outward, influencing one's own self-description.

Second, one might think that Walker's conception of freedom places an inordinate demand on black Americans, undercutting their ability to isolate those moments of liberty, however slight, under conditions of domination. In this context, one cannot help but think of Douglass's final passage of his 1845 autobiography, where he describes feeling a "degree of freedom" while addressing white people at an antislavery convention in New Bedford, Massachusetts. It is worth citing the passage at length:

> But, while attending an anti-slavery convention at Nantucket, on the 11th of August, 1841, I felt strongly moved to speak, and was at the same time much urged to do so by Mr. William C. Coffin, a gentleman who had heard me speak in the colored people's meeting at New Bedford. It was a severe cross, and I took it up reluctantly. The truth was, I felt myself a slave, and the idea of speaking to white people weighed me down. I spoke but a few moments, when I felt a degree of freedom, and said what I desired with considerable ease.[92]

Walker's analysis seems not to admit of such gradations—a "degree of freedom," as Douglass says—that might explain the reaction of the bootblack to his situation. But this is to miss the crucial distinction at work in comparing Douglass and the bootblack. Douglass stood before a white audience and spoke his mind, and at that very moment he felt empowered. He and the words he spoke existed without the permission, even if silent, of those he now addressed. He did not feel himself a slave at that moment because the idea that he lived at the mercy of his white audience no longer figured in his mind and therefore did not constrain his power in speaking his mind. This is why he spoke with "considerable ease." But unlike the bootblack, Douglass is well aware that the resilience of his freedom—its stability in the world—is all too often dependent on the permission of those who think African Americans unworthy of freedom. He often refers to this in different ways as being "the slaves of the community" (1848) or "the slave of society" (1855).[93] This is precisely why he says, following the quoted portion above, "From that time until now, I have been engaged in pleading the cause of my brethren."[94] What is striking about the boot-black is that he believes his situation exhausts what freedom means and what it makes possible. By virtue of this belief, he ironically participates in his domination. This much Walker says to his audience: "You may there-fore, go to work and do what you can to rescue, or join in with tyrants to oppress them [black Americans] and yourselves."[95]

This last point moves us to his affirmation of solidarity. What, then, is demanded of the bootblack and those like him? What should the observer make of all of this? Walker's response to those who are putatively free is precisely what he thinks one should rightly expect from the complicit slave woman—that is, to ally with those similarly situated. Speaking of the boot-black, Walker says to his audience, "I advanced it therefore to you, not as a *problematical*, but as an unshaken and forever immovable *fact*, that your full glory and happiness, as well as all other colored people under Heaven, shall never be fully consummated, but with the entire emancipation of your enslaved brethren all over the world."[96] This is a clarion call for soli-darity as a fundamental element in securing black liberation.

Understanding One's Language:
Fear, Shame, and Integrity

We have come a long way—from discussing the relationship between God and African Americans to the necessity of acting as freedom demands. There are some final questions to be asked. Given the intensity of domination that Walker describes, why should we read the *Appeal* as a pamphlet that also seeks to transform white Americans? Answering this question requires us to address the complex themes of fear, shame, and integrity and how Walker intends for them to function in his appeal.[97]

To get a handle on this, we need to briefly restate points made in the last chapter. You will recall that the *Appeal* functions as an American jer-emiad. The American jeremiad works on three levels. First, it presupposes a promise. Second, it highlights the failure to keep the promise, and this is expressed in the form of warnings regarding retribution. Third, the warn-ings are meant to focus attention—they are a catalytic agent—preparing the ground for transformation. Transformation is treated as a historical possibility, not a metaphysical certainty.

Against this backdrop, we should begin by comparing the *Appeal* to another revolutionary document, which Walker references: the Declara-tion of Independence. The latter is clear that the colonists sought a divorce from Great Britain—its king and British subjects. We see a transition from members belonging to colonies, having allegiance to a superior power, to becoming "Free and Independent States." The document indicates that the character of the king provides no good reason to believe he will act in a way commensurate with the character of a free people. Similarly, Walker regularly speaks about the tyrannical actions of whites and even refers to them as the "natural enemies" of blacks.[98] This ostensible correspondence between Walker's *Appeal* and the Declaration seems to imply the inability of whites to be transformed.

Comparatively speaking, despite the similarities between his pamphlet and the Declaration, the *Appeal* is a different text. Even as Walker pushes for solidarity, he does not mean for blacks to take up a separate and equal station among the "white" powers of the earth. In this regard, he does not sound the alarm of separation in the way Martin Delany or Mary Ann Shadd will do in the 1850s but rather recommits to the idea that the polity also belongs to African Americans. We see this in Walker's rejection of the American Colonization Society (ACS) and its plans to relocate blacks— plans that he rightly interprets as an attempt to remove the influence free black people may have on the slave population.[99] The *final call* of the pamphlet does not mirror the Declaration in its conclusion. Despite the fact that the *Appeal* concludes with embracing the revolutionary tone of the Declaration, Walker's insurrectionist argument should be understood within an if-then propositional framework—that is, *if* white Americans do not transform, *then* black Americans will rebel. He has not abandoned faith, even as he struggles to embrace it, that white Americans may yet be transformed.

There is, after all, a differential appeal at the heart of the pamphlet. Walker's target is not only the docility of blacks but also the tyrannical actions of whites. His early appeal to the "observer" marks this distinction: "He may see some of my brethren in league with tyrants."[100] There is a clear division between the "he" that stands apart from members of "my" or Walker's brethren. The aim is not only for blacks to see the practice of slavery and white supremacy but also for whites to ethically consider the tyranny with which they may bear witness or commit.

Walker's first purpose is to say to white Americans that tyranny only serves to prepare black Americans for a violent revolution. Here we come face-to-face with the practice of warning so central to jeremiadic appeals: "They have newspapers and monthly periodicals," he writes in Article III, and the reader "scarcely ever finds a paragraph respecting slavery . . . and which will be the final overthrow of its government, *unless* something is very speedily done; for their cup *is nearly full*."[101] Citing the Declaration in Article IV, he reminds white Americans of their justification for revolution: "Hear your language further! 'But when a long train of abuses and usurpation, pursuing invariably the same object, evinces a design to reduce them under absolute despotism, it is their right, it is their duty, to throw off such government, and to provide new guards for their future security.'"[102] Walker wants his white audience to understand that insofar as freedom is as central to human existence as they claim, the logical conclusion, given racial domination, can only be a violent exchange between themselves and blacks.

What is striking about Walker's use of the Declaration is what he leaves out. That the Declaration outlines the justification for revolution, understood as a "long train of abuses and usurpation," is not yet to declare a break with Great Britain. This comes in the lines that follow the portion above, which Walker does not cite: "Such has been the patient sufferance of these Colonies; and such is now the necessity which constrains them to alter their former Systems of Government." The Declaration is clear; the colonists mean to announce what they have already done.[103]

In contrast, Walker speaks differently. After citing the justification for revolution, he writes, "Some of you, no doubt, believe that we *will never* throw off your murderous government and 'provide new guards for our future security.'"[104] He says again in a footnote: "The Lord has not taught the Americans that we will not *some day or other* throw off their chains and hand-cuffs."[105] Using the possibility of revolution to induce fear is meant to focus attention on the present and one's actions therein that may yet prevent an imaginable future from coming to fruition.

Fear seems to stand in a productive relationship to our reasoning capacities. Walker is not the first to understand fear in this way. "Fear was given to us," says Locke, "as a monitor to quicken our industry." The most significant defender of the role of fear in informing our judgment is obviously Thomas Hobbes; it leads, he says, to "Articles of Peace, upon which men may be drawn to agreement."[106] This theme also figures prominently among African American thinkers and activists who followed Walker. It is at work in Frederick Douglass, Harriet Tubman, W.E.B. Du Bois, Malcolm X, and even Martin Luther King Jr. What African American theorists share with Walker is the idea that fear can clear the ground of factors that entice white Americans to stand idly by in the face of racial domination or to engage in the practice themselves. It does this by treating self-preservation as a necessary, even if insufficient, condition for enjoying the goods life provides. The urgency with which he argues for the eventual coming of violence—an urgency that cuts through all four articles of the

Appeal—is meant to heighten the place of fear in the minds of his readers and open them to what may address it.

The function of fear is not merely self-referential; it directs one's attention to the condition and subjectivity of black Americans in part by tapping into white Americans' sense of self-worth. There is danger here. For it may well be the case that black Americans are reduced to wild animals to be put down, returning the reader back to the tendency of white supremacy to animalize those over whom it exacts its greatest harm. It is most certainly the case that fear prompted legislative bodies in the South to ban documents they considered incendiary.[107] And Jefferson's own sense that blacks and whites were located in a Hobbesian state of war most certainly fueled his desire to free blacks and place them beyond the reach of the United States.[108] But these interpretations are too narrow a construal of how Walker understands fear. For him, it may yet serve as a ground-clearing device. As one white reader, previously skeptical of the truth of the *Appeal*, observed, "Let those who hold him such [i.e., "incendiary, ruffian, or exciter of sedition"], imagine the circumstances of the two classes of our people reversed, and those who now rise up and call him cursed will build him a monument, and cry hosanna to the patriot, the herald of freedom."[109] Another possible outcome—but only a possibility—is that the complex subjectivity of black Americans and their desire for freedom come into sharp relief. Fear focuses one's attention on the primacy of freedom that now goes unrealized because of tyranny. On this reading, the likelihood of violent rebellion comes not from wild beasts unaware of their place but from political agents demanding to be treated accordingly.

In directing the attention of the reader to the present moment, we can explain the second way Walker deploys his criticism of tyranny. In this, he follows the revolutionary tone of the Declaration, but it is of a kind that points to the constituent powers of the people to reimagine themselves. This takes us to the promise that has gone unrealized, but importantly it is the basis for reconstituting the American polity. What Jack Turner says of James Baldwin can equally be said of Walker: he "does not offer specific institutional or policy proposals. He seeks, rather, to reconcile citizens to their power to reconstitute society anew."[110] Reconstituting society depends on the extent to which the audience feels the pull of their ethical failure and the demand that honoring freedom makes on them.

Feeling the pull and demand of one's ethical failures and commitments is precisely the rhetorical register on which Walker argues. In the *Appeal*, ethical disapprobation is about the character of the audience, one that is intimately connected to affect. Here Walker seeks to shame the reader into action. If fear works to discipline one's reflective attention, shame represents an affective judgment regarding the ethical gap between one's settled beliefs and practices. "Affective judgment" sounds odd to our contemporary ears only if we think our emotions are noncognitive. Walker does not think in these terms. As he says in a passage from Article II, cited earlier, "if he is not a tyrant, but has the feelings of a human being, who can feel for a fellow creature, he may see enough to make his very heart bleed!"[111] The metaphorical use of the bleeding heart, as previously noted, turns out to denote an affective value judgment regarding what one is witnessing. The reasons why one ought to be fearful send white Americans back to their ethical failure. The standard against which that failure comes into view is the Declaration, and this anchors the very deployment of shame.

But the deployment of the Declaration, which we will see again with Douglass, involves an important revision that dethrones its primary author: Thomas Jefferson. Throughout the *Appeal*, we have seen Walker attack, again and again, Jefferson's thinking, his words, and his practices. When Walker invokes the Declaration as the ethical foundation of the polity, but refuses to encourage black emigration, he revises the function of the document to include African Americans as its heirs on American soil. Insofar as the legacy of Jefferson is followed, the polity will be tarnished, in violation of its deep commitments. And this must be the source of profound shame.

Shame is an uncertain but nonetheless important emotion. It involves falling below standards to which one otherwise takes oneself to be committed. This internal logic points to its uncertainty. Walker must take as settled the unrealized values of those to whom he appeals. And yet it is the actions of white Americans that suggest that they are not committed to those values at all.

Walker locates himself squarely within this uncertain arena. Hence he asks in Article IV, "Do you understand your own language? Hear your language, proclaimed to the world, July 4th, 1776—'We hold these truths to be self-evident—that ALL men are created Equal!! That they are endowed by their Creator with certain unalienable rights; that among these are life, liberty, and the pursuit of happiness.'"[112] He then invites his white audience to compare the language of the Declaration to the factual treatment of black Americans: "Compare your own language above, extracted from your Declaration of Independence, with your cruelties and murders inflicted by your cruel and unmerciful fathers and yourselves on our fathers and on us."[113] This comparative moment, as much as it highlights the uncertainty of shame, for Walker, also marks the importance of the emotion. For the comparison is seeking to generate ethical dissonance given the words of the Declaration. This is the moment of possibilities not yet realized—a world in which deeds and actions may rightly correspond.

We should take note of his approach. This is the rhetorical posture of what Michael Walzer calls "connected criticism"—an approach in which the critic sees his or her views as emerging out of the traditions, values, and histories of their society.[114] But importantly, they reweave the internal web of those traditions, values, and histories that at once connects with the recipients but provides them with a way of seeing their society in a novel way. Douglass will do this in his famous Fourth of July address. And this is what Martin Luther King Jr. classically achieves in his "I Have a Dream" speech, as he reweaves a story of the American Founders in which African Americans now appear to be heirs to the rights of the Declaration of Independence. None of them are naïve regarding the "singular truth" of moral persuasion and its relationship to politics: "that an injustice you aim to correct had better be seen not from the point of view of the victim, but from the perspective of the agent who commits the injustice." One comes face-to-face, as David Bromwich remarks, with "some contrast between what I am and what I ought to be" that "startles me and leads to self-discontent, which then issues in remedy or redress."[115]

The force of ethical dissonance cannot be disentangled from its companion character trait, integrity. Integrity is not merely about an internal ethical uprightness but about the way that internal wholeness displays itself in conduct. Treating black people as you do, Walker says to his audience, makes you untrue to yourself, and for that you ought to be ashamed. The proper treatment, to borrow from one scholar, that you extend or do not extend to black Americans says something about them to be sure, but it does so "only after it has said something" about you. For in withholding freedom and equality from them, you at once fail to confirm the place of these commitments in your own life.[116] To take seriously one's own language as expressed in the Declaration must reject the differential application of its values as they are currently practiced.

An immediate and difficult question emerges. How can shame function in a context of intense racial domination? Given the structure of shame, the use of it as a technique may seem poorly suited for the practices of slavery and domination at work. Surely, we might say, Walker is underestimating the deep-seated nature of white supremacy that does not merely blunt the force of equality and liberty but transforms them altogether. For if the logic of white supremacy devalues black life, the differential application of equality and liberty makes perfect sense. The invocation of shame and integrity is pointless because there is no gap between ideals and practices. As we know, many white Americans did not see the domination of blacks as inconsistent with their commitment to equality and liberty. What Walker is after—a theme that will echo across the struggle for racial equality and haunt the chapters of this book—may seem impossible.

Walker might respond to this by relying on the very agency in both whites and blacks he means to guide and inform. In fact, he expresses it in the preamble to the *Appeal*:

> The sources from which our miseries are derived, and on which I shall comment, I shall not combine in one, but shall put them under distinct heads and expose them in their turn; in doing which, keeping truth on my side, and not departing from the strictest rules of morality, I shall endeavour to penetrate, search out, and lay them open for your inspection. If you cannot or will not profit by them, I shall have done *my* duty to you, my country, and my God.[117]

Walker's use of the word "inspection" makes clear that he believes blacks and whites may yet learn something about their condition. The very structure of the *Appeal* attempts to establish the conditions for its proper reception. But this mundane point also presupposes that despite the habits of servility and dominance that police the relationships between whites and blacks, those habits need not run so deep as to make one immune to appeals for transformation.

Walker's belief in transformation contains within itself a cognitive-affective claim about the malleability of persons. But we still need some way to connect that claim to the normative structure of republican politics that can underwrite the broad-based commitment of African Americans to the polity given white supremacy and racial domination. If we are unable to do so, the idea that persons are malleable, susceptible to hearing the claims of others and transforming in the light of those claims, will be unable to find support within the political culture to which they belong. Emigration, as Martin Delany and others call for, may well be the best way for blacks to display their sense of self-worth. If Walker's thinking is to make sense, at a minimum, African Americans must belong to a political and ethical community for whom the condition of possibility functions as a foundational part of what makes society legitimate. The condition of possibility creates the space for positive transformation of self and society, even as it perpetually contains danger. Seeking the former and trying to manage the uncertainty of the latter is, quite simply, a matter of faith.

Before turning to this issue in part 2, I want to trouble the discussion of republicanism in the next chapter. As it stands now, Walker's deployment of freedom has largely functioned as a ready-made concept within republicanism for criticizing the comportment of both blacks and whites. This obscures how the very deployment of freedom by African American intellectuals and activists involved them in properly calibrating the usefulness of republicanism to the conditions of racial domination. For them, responding to racial domination involved more than constitutional rearrangements and political procedures (although important) but significantly turned on addressing the lower position of worth that black Americans occupied. This second issue was not merely an institutional problem but a cultural issue that shaped habits and sensibilities and structured the precarity of black life.

CHAPTER THREE

Being a Slave of the Community

RACE, DOMINATION, AND REPUBLICANISM

Having been instructed from youth to look upon a black man in no other
light than a slave, and having associated with that idea the low calling of
a slave, they cannot look upon him in any other light.

—HOSEA EASTON, *A TREATISE ON THE INTELLECTUAL*
CHARACTER, AND CIVIL AND POLITICAL CONDITION
OF THE COLORED PEOPLE OF THE UNITED STATES

ONE STARTLING FACT about racial disregard is how deep it runs in our
ethical and political life. For this reason, black Americans appeal to the
character of the nation or they invoke the culture of the polity to indicate to their audiences the depth of the problem. To be sure, questions of
who we are as a nation and who we should be mingle with more narrowly
focused questions of what policies we should endorse and what laws ought
to be on the books. Focus too long on the latter, though, and you are likely
to miss the importance of the former.

Political societies are, after all, ethical ventures. Contained within them
are traditions and ways of being, sometimes at odds, which not only reflect
the standing of persons but also guide how to treat others with whom we
share society. This way of seeing the matter is not new; we can trace it back
to the ethical and political philosophies of Aristotle, Jean-Jacques Rousseau, and G.W.F. Hegel and the Scottish moral sense tradition of David
Hume and Adam Smith. In the American context, we see it at work in
Thomas Jefferson in the eighteenth century and the pragmatists such as

William James, John Dewey, Anna Julia Cooper, George Herbert Mead, Jane Addams, and Alain Locke in the nineteenth and twentieth centuries. For all these thinkers, the meaning of society is developed and expressed through the cultural norms that shape the social practices in which members of the polity participate—the social-psychological horizon of human life, we might say. The most visible version of this is when classes of persons in political society are not, for example, permitted to vote or hold office as part of the taken-for-granted workings of society. Subtler and more insidious versions of this are at play when one refuses, as an affirmation of role expectations, to have intimate and mundane interactions with those classes of persons on the streets, in classrooms, in stores, and in churches. We also see this when one's aspirations are circumscribed at the moment of inception, reflecting one's subordinate standing in society.

This reminds us of David Walker's worry about the "enslaved free man" as discussed in the last chapter. Walker's reflections on domination, his discussion of republican liberty, his affirmation of racial solidarity, and his invocation of and appeal to character were all part of his attempt to get his fellows to address the social-psychological norms of black servility and white supremacy. Walker was not alone. He belongs to a tradition of thinking that draws on and reconfigures republicanism.

Whereas the previous reflections have taken republican thinking for granted, this chapter brings it under critical scrutiny, to tease out precisely why character and the cognitive-affective dimension of those who inhabit the American polity figure so prominently. I do not merely claim that Walker and others used republicanism on par with their white revolutionary counterparts; I insist that they reconfigured its meaning in the service of political transformation. This recasting by African Americans is not without its internal disagreements over how deep the problem runs. While some envision white Americans as susceptible to transformation, others are doubtful about the likelihood of a racially inclusive society. Nonetheless, each holds in view the ethical life of the polity and does so from within a republican framework. In part 2, we will better understand the normative basis on which African Americans stood (and continue to stand) to adjudicate between these two positions.

———◆———

Early African American political thinking draws on two different strands of republicanism. The first emerges from the emphasis placed on the civic character of the citizenry. For African American thinkers, this emphasis directs attention to the character mostly of white citizens and a failure of the republican tradition to foster an appropriate manner of behavior— what I shall call "comportment"—toward their black counterparts. Black thinkers in the early nineteenth century see exclusion as rooted in white citizens' motivations and attitudes, which in turn shaped the character of the citizens and the laws of the polity. These thinkers ask questions about who we are and who we ought to be. This is because they see the community as an ethical enterprise of invention and development rather than the expression of so-called prepolitical values we discover. African Americans direct their intellectual energies to the ethos of the American polity, treating laws and institutions as necessary but nonetheless derivations from the characterological propensities of the nation. They did not, in other words, expect institutions to run on their own; instead, they connect the goal of realizing a just society to citizens' comportment. This thread of republicanism has its roots in ideas of civic virtue, political participation, and character as central to a self-determining polity.[1]

The second strand African Americans deploy emphasizes freedom as nondomination. The use of this strand emerges in African Americans' desire to escape the internal tyranny of the United States. On the republican definition of freedom, one is free if one does not live at the arbitrary mercy of another. Republicanism in this guise, as Quentin Skinner and Philip Pettit argue, thinks of arbitrary power exercised over another as the worst form of enslavement.[2] This iteration of republicanism has its roots in classical Rome. It is rearticulated by Machiavelli during the Renaissance and is defended by thinkers in the modern period, such as James Harrington, Montesquieu, John Adams, and Thomas Jefferson. For this strand, the security of freedom depends on (a) a republic imposing constitutional constraints that guard against arbitrary power and (b) providing institutional spaces that allow citizens disputative power to ensure the proper functioning of a constitutional order. As one commentator explains, for the Romans "full *libertas* [or liberty] is coterminous with *civitas* [or citizenship]."[3] The two strands connect in the following way: the characterological orientation of the first helps to realize and stabilize the institutional meaning of freedom found in the second. That is, civic virtue is the necessary foundation for free institutions.

It is a mistake to say that republicanism exhausts the tradition of African American political thinking.[4] That is not my claim. Republicanism nonetheless serves as an essential resource on which some of the earlier thinkers relied to contest the reach of white supremacy. But we move too quickly if we see a seamless transition from republicanism to its deployment by African Americans. What matters is not which political-philosophical model exhausts our understanding of the tradition but how the tradition redirects or extends the categories central to any specific model deployed. Furthermore, the language of character, virtue, and solidarity has more often than not been associated with the republican tradition rather than the liberal one. We can acknowledge that without falling prey to the dubious claim that focusing on the first means the second did not exist.

African American thinkers add to the meaning of both strands of republicanism. Sometimes the addition consists of using republicanism's concepts (e.g., civic virtue) in a situation or context not otherwise addressed in the tradition. In other instances, it involves complicating its central concepts, such as freedom and nondomination, by situating them within a different experiential context. This second approach involves not merely redeploying republicanism but supplementing its toolbox so that it can work properly in a context of racial domination.

This chapter expands our conversation partners while simultaneously deepening the considerations taken up thus far. If the last chapter focused on the demand republican liberty places on us, this chapter helps us understand that the demand takes on the form that it does because of the specific racialized quality of domination. This necessitates critically assessing the idea of republicanism. Early nineteenth-century African American thinkers should be read as resituating republicanism's concepts or complicating those concepts through necessity. I do not doubt that these thinkers were deploying republicanism, but I am not here claiming that they were concerned with the meta-issue of how to enable republicanism to work for them. I take it as settled that they believed it useful and the urgency of the moment forced them to bypass intellectual debate. My claim is that despite their self-understanding, they were not deploying a tradition conceptually ready for their situation; rather, their very use of the tradition involved conceptual reconfiguration.[5] This allows us to revise the history of political republicanism, particularly in its American context.

This enables me to advance an important point that remains hidden from view if our primary thinkers are Machiavelli, Harrington, or Jefferson. Despite the neorepublican revival in political theory and history and the significance of the United States as a primary historical site for understanding the meaning of republicanism, African Americans have been oddly out of view. What slips into the neorepublican revival is an implicit acceptance of criteria of validation of whose thoughts and expressions count as philosophical in the first instance and therefore worthy of historical attention and explication.

If, however, we treat theoretical reflections, regardless of their form of expression, as modes of political participation, we need not allow prior criteria of validation to constrain what thoughts count as worthy of attention or whose voices count as worthy of consideration. We avoid the troublesome claim by contemporary thinkers that by the nineteenth century republicanism was in retreat or already eclipsed. We need not find ourselves saying, as Pettit does, that "not only did the conception of freedom as non-interference displace the republican idea in the new liberal tradition. It apparently succeeded . . . without anyone's noticing."[6] Nor should we be persuaded by Skinner's claim that "with the rise of classical utilitarianism in the eighteenth century," the idea of republicanism "eventually slipped almost wholly out of sight."[7] For a contemporary intellectual revival that means to free people from domination, effectively acknowledging their equal standing, neorepublican defenders oddly find themselves reaffirming the unequal intellectual worth of black thinkers in the nineteenth century, and many others addressing themes of slavery, colonialism, and patriarchy. For surely when we attend to the ongoing problem of slavery in the United States and the ascendancy of Jim Crow in the wake of the Civil War, we shall find the language of republicanism very much alive. This suggests that we need only unshackle ourselves from the chains of authorial status, a move that can only lead to the expansion of our narratives of the past and an avoidance of the blind spot at work in the present neorepublican revival.[8]

From the 1830s to the 1850s, thinkers such as Walker, Maria Stewart, Hosea Easton, Martin Delany, and Frederick Douglass—all black and all abolitionists—reconfigure civic virtue under conditions of racial domination as the justification for solidarity among blacks, since they are likely to be harmed by the ill effects of racism. This discussion sharpens and better elucidates Walker's earlier affirmation of racial solidarity, while expanding its defenders.

As these thinkers use it, republican liberty involves an important insight. Whereas variants of republicanism typically describe the necessity of civic virtue to the republic, these thinkers direct their black audiences to the necessity of solidarity with the race given the racialized nature of domination. For them, domination absorbs the identity of individuals into a broader racial classification that is itself associated with specific negative attributes. This classification system becomes the basis for treating blacks unequally. Importantly, justifications for inequality and domination extend beyond the formal shackles of slavery into the cultural sphere of American life. This permits the following question: *What entailments follow from civic virtue under conditions of racial domination?* The answer turns out to be an endorsement of racial solidarity.

Yet, even these thinkers disagree about the political implications of their positions, offering weak and strong versions of racial solidarity.[9] Whereas some see racial solidarity as a temporary position on the road to reimagining an inclusive society and in turn transforming the polity, it is Delany who understands racial solidarity as a permanent state, leading to an endorsement of emigration in the 1850s. Here we see a redirecting of republicanism's resources that reveals its political potential for redressing the status of African Americans. Critically, the redirection involves these thinkers in developing conflicting claims, first, about the possibility of transforming white Americans, and second, and consequently, about the fate of African Americans in the United States.

These thinkers also complicate republicanism's commitment to freedom from domination by assessing it in the context of racial exclusion. The specter of slavery looms large for them, but the meaning of slavery—being subject to a master who exercises power arbitrarily—extends beyond the formal practices of enslavement. In their analyses, slavery's reach is dispersed through the cultural sphere of American life, circumscribing African Americans even in instances where there is no obvious master. In the last chapter, we observed the psychological effects on black Americans that condition their comportment and arrest their souls. Here we consider the way they shape the social epistemic context in which black Americans live out their lives. Frederick Douglass succinctly captures the point in his 1848 speech to the National Negro Convention in Cleveland to which he was appointed president: "In Northern States, we are not slaves to individuals, not personal slaves, yet in many respects we are the slaves of the community."[10] African Americans highlight their domination by attending to the imbrication of race and white supremacy. To enjoy liberty requires not merely freedom from the caprice of particular agents or laws that limit arbitrary power but a transformation of the system of cultural value in which blacks occupy a lower position of worth. Theirs was a desire for a form of citizenship found not only in the law but also in the heart.[11] This could not be achieved by tracking institutional domination but only by also attending to its racialized form that corrupted the soul of the nation.

When republicanism encounters racialized domination, the question turns out to be the following: *How might we add to the conceptual toolbox such that freedom as nondomination can do its distinctive work for*

African Americans? In the republican theories I introduce, freedom is still understood as *nondomination*, but against the backdrop of race, it requires that African Americans acquire freedom through means that are not exclusively about formal positive laws. Here we confront the limits of republicanism as traditionally understood. Pettit, for instance, identifies the project of republicanism with seeking to satisfy the "range of constitutional Constraints associated broadly with the mixed constitution." He links subordination, as the Romans did, to the presence of a *dominus* or master.[12] This definition of republicanism and these formal requirements obscure the question addressed in African American political thought. That is, Pettit and the tradition of republicanism fail to deploy a more expansive notion of slavery—one that focuses not on those whose political standing is formally in doubt or denied but on those who are not seen as fit for freedom in the first place. Walker's challenge, for example, to the cultural animalization of black folks discussed in the last chapter was part of a broader critique of categorical inequality. Satisfying one's constitutional standing is a necessary but insufficient indicator of regard. But even in instances where Pettit highlights the importance of norms of proper regard—what he calls civility—he seems to overlook that insofar as one's status as a slave is taken to be natural or normal, it will be difficult for one to be seen as a fit object of proper regard. A cultural habit of viewing blacks as natural slaves or subordinates to be controlled follows from the logic of white supremacy—a logic in which republican principles can simultaneously be "honored" and limited in their application to whites. Focusing on this issue explains the concern of black Americans to transform the cultural logic of American life. Theirs is a wish to avoid being the slave of the community, as Douglass says.[13]

Civic Virtue as Racial Solidarity: Intimations of Republicanism

It is difficult, if not impossible, to read early African American thinkers and not be struck by the rich literary portraits of American society and the horror of black life therein. The point of such descriptions is to dramatize the differential application of care and concern in American society. In marking the difference, however, between blacks and whites, African American thinkers point to the characterological distortion of the citizenry and simultaneously seek to transform it.

As argued in the last chapter, this is nowhere more clearly on display than in Walker's incendiary 1829 *Appeal to the Colored Citizens of the World.* The *Appeal* confronts the reader with the shocking details of being black in the United States and, in doing so, calls into question the very humanity of white Americans. The invocation of sentiment, captured metaphorically in the bleeding heart as previously discussed, should not be separated from the theme of character. Walker participates in the broader intellectual culture of sentimental appeals central to early American moral and political thought.[14] In this, he too believes sentimental exchanges reveal "the underlying commonality of human potential across artificial status divides" such as race.[15] He thus aligns the capacity for fellow feeling with the image of being a human, and then uses this as a normative compass to orient readers to the daily treatment of black people. The aim is to cultivate proper comportment toward the harm of black bodies that can in turn produce a just society in which all can share.

Walker directs his reflections to the normative foundation of American life. His pamphlet prefigures Hosea Easton's remark in his 1837 *A Treatise on the Intellectual Character, and Civil and Political Condition of the Colored People of the United States* that "a government like this is at any time liable to be revolutionized by the people, at any and every time there is a change of public sentiment. This, perhaps, is as it should be."[16] Like Walker, Easton also joined the Massachusetts General Colored Association, an organization dedicated to combating slavery and racism. Easton was politicized in the 1820s by the discrimination and exclusion his family experienced.[17] Walker and Easton knew that institutional organizations were not the only way to combat exclusion and, in any case, should function as discursive arenas in which black folks sharpened their ethical and political skills. Easton is not as significant as Walker, but his invocation of public sentiment (as well as his thinking on prejudice) expresses an underlying orientation that captures much of African American political thinking, from its slave narratives to its political pamphlets. All provide vivid displays of the condition of life to move the people to embrace a new view of themselves. I return to this in the next chapter, but the idea of the people functions in an aspirational sense—that is, it denotes a people not yet in existence. Both Walker and Easton presuppose this account in their interventions.

The emphasis on character and public sentiment was not new, even if it took on a different articulation in Walker and Easton. Some of its most important expressions appeared among classical republican thinkers such as Aristotle and Cicero and were reaffirmed in American thinkers such as Jefferson and Adams. We are likely to miss the difference if we conclude here. Thinkers such as Jefferson, in particular, appealed to character and public sentiment to affirm and stabilize the white male portion of the polity, which they imagined as constituting the whole of society. In contrast, nineteenth-century African American intellectuals emphasized character and public sentiment to highlight the fracture at the core of the American demos.

The emphasis on character and public sentiment combines with republicanism's commitment to the common good. For Aristotle, Cicero, Jefferson, and Adams, the stability of the polity depends on proper attentiveness. They each interpret civic virtue as a form of attentiveness that leads to the social integration of the community. Citizens must, as Cicero writes in *On Duties*, "fix their gaze so firmly on what is beneficial to citizens" and "care for the whole body of the republic rather than protect one part and neglect the rest."[18] As Adams explains to political writer Mercy Otis Warren in 1776, civic virtue, or what he calls public virtue,

> is the only Foundation of Republics. There must be a positive Passion for the public good, the public Interest, Honor, Power, and Glory, established in the Minds of the People, or there can be no Republican Government, nor any real Liberty. And this public Passion must be Superior to all private Passions. Men must be ready . . . and be happy to sacrifice their private Pleasures, Passions, and Interests, nay, their private Friendships and dearest Connections, when they stand in Competition with the Rights of Society.[19]

Civic virtue infuses and underwrites political participation and grounds solidarity among citizens. There can be no equal institutional compensation, despite James Madison's promises, for the deficiencies of civic virtue.[20] A constitutional order thus depends on the attitudinal orientation of the citizenry of which civic virtue is its crowning achievement.

What is one to do in the face of the differential application of care and concern? After all, racism constrains the idea of *common* in the term "common good." How might one enact political agency when the polity protects one part of society, as Cicero worried, and the other is neglected? These questions animate thinkers like Walker and Easton, allowing them to redirect the gaze of republicanism to the condition of internal slavery and the absence of mutual recognition.

Walker and Easton challenge their fellows to confront the comingling of an exclusionary vision of the common good with freedom that does not guard against domination but entrenches it. The distinction between blacks and whites—the habit of servility by the one and the practice of domination by the other—marks the source of America's moral corruption and with it the circumspection of republicanism's theoretical possibilities. Freeing the idea of republicanism cannot be realized through the thinkers typically associated with the tradition. Instead, it requires us to attend to those who remain hidden from view or ignored. It is no wonder, then, that Easton, for example, reflects on the "condition and character of the colored people" in the United States and uses the status of black people as the measure of a healthy republic.[21]

Easton worries, and far more intensely than Walker, about the possibility of redeeming the nation. As he says, "But when the subjects of a republican government become morally and politically corrupt, there is but little chance remaining for republicanism." The reason for this, he goes on to say, is that "good laws, and a good form of government, are of but very little use to a wicked people."[22] Elsewhere, and in what appears to be a settled conclusion, he writes: "There can be no appeals made in the name of the laws of the country, of philanthropy, or humanity, or religion, that is capable of drawing forth any thing but the retort,—*you are a negro!*"[23] In speaking this way, Easton rejects the logic of the Federalists and Immanuel Kant, both of whom see the constitutional framework as compensation for the deficiencies of character. This is not because Easton is politically naïve; rather, he maintains that laws are not self-executing and depend on proper motivation for their faithful execution. Hence his use of the word "wicked" to describe motivational distortion. The term "wicked" may seem archaic, but in this context, it is an ethical predicate, denoting an impoverished character. To become the opposite of a wicked people requires the American nation to address the standing of African Americans. And yet, despite his worry, Easton's pamphlet is meant to get the nation to address this issue: "Let the country, then, no longer act the part of the thief. . . . Let them rather act the part of the good Samaritan."[24]

In light of black subordination and slavery, civic virtue no longer requires attentiveness to a social whole that excludes. Rather, civic virtue *among* the excluded becomes the foundation for responding to the polity as a whole. Civic virtue, now directed to the condition of African Americans, generates a form of solidarity grounded in one's identity. There can be no presumptive retreat to the common good since its internal meaning at the level of American ethical life is partial, that partiality determines social integration, and institutional and juridical practices turn out to express domination. This need not imply (although Delany will suggest otherwise) an unbridgeable divide between blacks and whites. However, the existing culture of domination does motivate a defense of racial solidarity.

In the nineteenth century, arguments for solidarity among African Americans emerge in two separate spheres—what we might call the *performative* and *explanatory* spheres of early black politics. The first results from the memory of the Haitian Revolution as the performance of solidarity among slaves and the creation of self-directed organizations—churches, newspapers, literary societies, and benevolent organizations.[25] The Haitian Revolution is especially significant; it exhibits the same logic of the modern self-understanding as the American and French Revolutions. This is the idea that political deference can no longer be forced or demanded; rather, political authorization must be tied to reflective assent and answerability in which agents may claim to give direction to their lives. But there is an undeniable difference. The capacity for self-governance among the Haitian people served as a powerful rejoinder to the historical, philosophical, and scientific animalization of black people that otherwise functioned to deny them freedom. For African Americans in the nineteenth century, Haiti is at once "distinct yet inseparable from the flawed world that its singular example had the power to change."[26]

The second, explanatory sphere is captured by the intellectual intervention among the black intelligentsia—an attempt to *explain* rather than *perform* solidarity. It is this second dimension to which these thinkers most clearly belong (even as they were often members of the organizations stipulated by the first point). For them, racial solidarity is less of a departure from republicanism and more of an entailment of civic virtue under conditions of racial domination. I say "less of a departure" because I reject the idea that political-philosophical ideas can be claimed or owned, even as I subscribe to the obvious point that they can be reconfigured and, perhaps, improved. Nonetheless, racial solidarity comes in weak and strong versions, and the description of the two has less to do with the meaning ascribed by each thinker to "blackness" as essential and fixed; instead, the weak and strong versions of solidarity follow from what each thinker believes is possible of white Americans.[27] This is because chattel slavery (rather than political slavery) is not easily rectified by the extension of the franchise since the status of an enslaved person was thought to be consistent with the natural order of things. Chattel slavery—in its racialized variety—thus poses a distinct ethical problem whose resolution depends on either a characterological transformation of those who were once masters or the acquisition of a separate geographical territory to realize sovereignty by those previously enslaved.

CIVIC VIRTUE AS NASCENT RACIAL SOLIDARITY

In the last chapter, I argued that Walker supported the necessity of racial solidarity. I merely asserted the claim and did not adequately provide his defense of it. I now offer that explanation, with reference to a broader constellation of thinkers. How precisely did nineteenth-century African Americans understand racial solidarity?

To answer this question, we need to clarify what we mean regarding the functioning of racial classification. Briefly, racial classification takes the form of assigning meaning to what Paul Taylor refers to as "human bodies and bloodlines" that permits one to "draw inferences about more distant, often non-physical matters" such as intelligence, imagination, and moral agency.[28] The meaning of one's racial classification in the eighteenth and nineteenth centuries functions as a global category: it allows one to make judgments about particular individuals that fall under specific racial categories. As Jefferson, for example, argues in *Notes on the State of Virginia* (1787), especially Query XIV, regardless of the biological source of one's blackness, its meaning is important for understanding the capacities of black Americans.[29] Although Jefferson advances it as a "suspicion," no one doubted the force of his claim that "whether originally a distinct race, or made distinct by time and circumstances, [the blacks] are inferior to the whites in the endowments of body and mind."[30]

The second point involves treating the broader category as the primary target of analysis. This involves accepting the covering-law universalism of the category—that is, its reference to groups rather than individuals—not the content of the universalism. The idea is that since race refers to groups rather than individuals, the broader attributions that apply to the race effectively ignore one's subjective identity. Thus, blacks literally become interchangeable, no matter where they live in the country. This is because it is the covering-law universalism of the category of race that defines their proper status as unfree. Recall the way Walker refused (as we saw in the last chapter) to distinguish between the complicit slave woman and enslaved free man as a way to focus attention on the logic of American life for black people.

The point I want to emphasize is less about the shared position of enslaved and nominally free blacks and more about the logic of solidarity that emerges from this account. To quote a passage previously used: "I advanced it therefore to you, not as a *problematical*, but as an unshaken and forever immovable *fact*, that your full glory and happiness, as well as all other colored people under Heaven, shall never be fully consummated, but with the entire emancipation of your enslaved brethren all over the world."[31] Maria Stewart shares this outlook, imploring her audience to remain "united [with] hearts and souls" as they make "mighty efforts to raise [their] sons and daughters from the horrible state of servitude and degradation."[32] Behind these claims is a rich notion of race. Precisely because one's subjectivity as a black person is not in view due to the workings of one's racial designation, it is a mistake to assume that mere self-assertion is sufficient to secure freedom. To think otherwise is to deny the depth of the problem.

What, then, is required to generate and sustain a flourishing black community? Part of the answer, these thinkers argue, is a coordinated effort with other blacks to resist racial domination and transform the system responsible for it, since African Americans individually are likely to suffer when racial designations are at work. For Stewart's part, her greatest critiques, even more intensely than Walker's, are directed at a failure of African Americans to stand with each other in solidarity in addressing their condition of oppression: "The general cry among the people is, 'Our own color are our greatest opposers.'"[33] For Easton's part, his endorsement is implied by both his reflections in the *Treatise* and his involvement in antislavery and moral uplift organizations during the 1830s. For all, solidarity is a functional outgrowth of racial categorization, aiming to create a stable context in which one's "full glory and happiness" can find support. But we should proceed with care. As Eddie Glaude argues, this view of racial solidarity uses the covering-law universalism of racial classification, but it rejects the idea of essentialism.[34]

There was, of course, disagreement about whether one could successfully deploy race-talk and avoid essentialism. This was one of the themes that emerged during the life of the National Negro Conventions, hosted in various cities, starting with Philadelphia in 1830. In fact, the Fifth Annual Convention for the Improvement of the Free People of Color, "after an animated and interesting discussion . . . unanimously adopted the motion" to remove the words "colored" and "Black," mainly because they viewed such terms as inimical to the cause for freedom.[35] The motion, proposed by William Whipper, an abolitionist and member of the convention, and seconded by fellow Philadelphian Robert Purvis, sought to eliminate race-talk. However, they did so out of a desire to focus attention on the universal dignity of black and white people and the life they shared. As Whipper explains at the 1835 Convention meeting, if we place our "institutions on the high and indisputable ground of natural laws and human rights actuated by the law of universal love to our fellow men," then we must abolish "those hateful and unnecessary distinctions by which the human family has hitherto been recognized."[36] The invocation of race, Whipper believes, only serves to reinforce prejudice against blacks in part because there is no way to make use of race language without it carrying the baggage of hate that brought the language into existence.[37] Whipper's racial eliminativism follows from a desire to align one's language with the notion of the common good that theoretically, at least, aspires to include the polity as a whole and that is otherwise central to republicanism.

This marks a difference between himself and Walker, Easton, and Stewart (although to a lesser degree). For them, just as race is the organizing principle of domination, it becomes the organizing principle that colors civic virtue. If civic virtue is fundamentally about the habits necessary to sustain and realize a political community, these thinkers now give it a particular bent. For them, civic virtue does not point toward habits necessary to sustain the American polity as a whole, especially given that society is internally divided. Instead, they racialize civic virtue; it now expresses itself as solidarity in order to fortify African Americans and contest the logic of racism and white supremacy. Ethical and political transformation must first attend to the source of the corruption. Simply put, African Americans must be able to name the problem, and that requires the language of race. If this is right, it is not race understood as a substantive natural kind but race understood as an experiential outgrowth of domination. If the discourse of race is the basis for one's domination, it must now serve as the foundation for the coordinated efforts by black Americans.

This is nonetheless a weak form of racial solidarity, pointing in different directions. Stewart, for example, often deploys racial solidarity to fortify African Americans; it is a means for them to reflect on how they appear in their own eyes. To be sure, it does function as a stepping stone toward transformation of the polity—that is, white Americans are, as Carla Peterson puts it, "textually present as internal addressees" in Stewart's writings—but her emphasis is on its internal benefit among African Americans.[38] Walker and Easton, especially, endorse racial solidarity as the initial move toward a more racially inclusive society. They more explicitly hold out the possibility of ethical and political transformation. Walker and Easton seek to awaken their white counterparts—to get them to see that in dominating black folks, they betray the meaning of their republicanism. Thus Easton:

> I have taken this course to illustrate the state of a people with a good government and laws, and with a disposition to explain away all their meaning. My conclusions are, that such republicans are capable, like the angel about which I have spoken, to carry out their republicanism into the most fatal despotism. A republican form of government, therefore, can be a blessing to no people, further than they make honest virtue the rule of life.[39]

Similar to Walker's reflections in the last chapter, Easton intends to generate reflective dissonance that may provoke a reorientation toward black Americans. But all three are not committed to the notion that the practice of domination by whites fully exhausts the ethos of the nation. Precisely because they do not subscribe to the latter idea, racial solidarity only expresses itself for them as a nascent form of group unity that aspires toward a society in which all enjoy freedom and equality. How they can hold this view and steel themselves in the face of disappointment is tied to the aspirational view of the people on which republicanism relies and the idea of faith to which it is bound, which I take up elsewhere. Suffice it to say, this idea of the people presupposes both a political and ethical elasticity to the polity that helps fuel the perfectionist or developmental vision at work in Walker and Easton—a position that marks a substantive break from the radical outlook of Martin Delany.

Racialized Domination and America's Ethical Life

On the evening of December 13, 1850, the faculty of Harvard's Medical School met at the house of then dean Oliver Wendell Holmes Sr. to discuss various petitions regarding the admission of three African Americans and one woman to the school. Although Holmes had already granted admission to the students and the men would be allowed to attend for a semester (the woman had already withdrawn), it was ultimately deemed "inexpedient, after the present course, to admit colored students to attendance on medical lectures."[40] Holmes explains his position in a letter of 1850: the faculty is convinced "that the intermixing of the white and black races in their lecture rooms, is distasteful to a large portion of the class and injurious to the interest of the school."[41] Holmes was expressing and affirming views articulated in an earlier resolution passed by a majority of the students:

> Whereas blacks have been admitted to the lectures of the medical department of Harvard University
> Therefore
> *Resolved* That we deem the admission of blacks to the medical Lectures highly detrimental to the interests, and welfare of the Institution of which we are members, calculated alike to lower its reputation in this and other parts of the country, to lessen the value of a diploma from it, and to diminish the number of its students.

Resolved That we cannot consent to be identified as fellow students with blacks; whose company we would not keep in the streets, and whose Society as associates we would not tolerate in our houses.[42]

Martin Robison Delany, one of the four admitted students, left Harvard Medical School in March 1851. He was not permitted to return.

Delany, defender of black nationalism and subsequently certified physician, follows the logic of solidarity to its natural conclusion given the seemingly fixed quality of racial domination. I am less interested in the logic of black nationalism (a well-trodden theme) and more concerned to discuss the ethical presupposition regarding white Americans specifically, and the American polity more generally, that pushed Delany to embrace that political ideology. His signature political-philosophical text, *The Condition, Elevation, Emigration, and Destiny of the Colored People of the United States*, published in April 1852, represents a powerful indictment of American life.[43]

Delany was born in 1812 in Virginia, the youngest of five children.[44] Although his father was a slave, the legal norms of the state meant that Delany's status followed that of his free mother. After being threatened for teaching her children how to read, Patti Delany moved her family to Chambersburg, Pennsylvania, in 1822. She was subsequently joined in 1823 by her husband, who had purchased his freedom. Unlike in Virginia, Delany attended school and, according to one biographer, deepened his mind with the great literary and philosophical texts of the West. In 1831, Delany headed west to Pittsburgh, where he became an active member in antislavery circles, joining the African Education Society, the Moral Reform Society, and the Pittsburgh Anti-Slavery Society. His 1852 text, however, represents a significant shift away from his earlier attempts to transform the polity from within to locating salvation beyond American shores.[45]

Delany's book is separated from Walker's *Appeal* by more than two decades and Easton's *Treatise* by a little less. The transformation of the racial context by the 1850s was far darker than it appeared in 1829. This was personal for Delany: he was denied admission to medical schools and Harvard effectively rescinded their offer after a semester. It directly affected his fellow African Americans in the form of the draconian Fugitive Slave Act of 1850—an act that strengthened the previous Fugitive Slave Act of 1793. Emerging out of the Compromise of 1850, the Fugitive Slave Act required that captured slaves who had found their way to free states be returned to their presumptive masters. The law went further. In response to the 1793 law, states such as Indiana and Connecticut made the right of jury trial upon appeal possible for escaped slaves, while states such as Vermont and New York provided escaped slaves with attorneys as well as making the jury trial a legal right. The 1850 law virtually destroyed all such possibilities, effectively denying the standing of slaves even in free states, while also adding harsh penalties for those who either failed to enforce the law or helped slaves escape. Delany's text addresses both his situation and more significantly the Compromise and the Fugitive Slave Law, prompting him to argue for emigration. To his mind, his dismissal and the Fugitive Slave Law shared the same logic of seeing African Americans as an inferior race.

Delany's interest in the Fugitive Slave Law, not his first reflection on it,[46] brings into focus his sophisticated understanding of the relationship between law and ethical life. He views the passage of the law as effectively settling all appeals one might make to the polity for inclusion.[47] Hence he says, "To imagine our selves to be included in the body politic, except by express legislation, is at war with common sense, and contrary to fact."[48] The reason is that both the passage and maintenance of the law reveal the ethical norms that guide the polity and underwrite the unequal status of African Americans in the United States.

This does not reveal a society that has betrayed itself, as suggested by Walker and Easton, but a social and political community that fundamentally denies the dignity of black folks. Walker, Easton, and Delany disagree about the internal normative coherence of American society as it relates to the standing of black persons. This much Delany says, marking a difference between himself and the earlier thinkers: "We are politically, not of them, but aliens to the laws and political privileges of the country. These are truths—fixed facts, that quaint theory and exhausted moralizing, are impregnable to, and fall harmlessly before."[49] He was, of course, not alone. One newspaper, the first black newspaper of Cleveland, Ohio, captured the status of black Americans in the title they selected: the *Aliened American*. The United States, they said in their first issue, has made black Americans into "aliens—through their Law, their Public Opinion and their Community-Regulations."[50]

Delany's criticism of moral philosophizing targets not only thinkers such as Walker and Easton but most immediately Frederick Douglass, with whom Delany served as a coeditor on Douglass's newspaper, the *North Star*. We will return to Delany and Douglass's disagreement in the next chapter, but it is worth marking their divide since it helps secure Douglass's proximity to Walker, Stewart, and Easton. In a letter, Delany expresses his disappointment that Douglass did not take notice of his 1852 book in his newspaper, now called *Frederick Douglass' Papers*: "I care but little, what white men think of what I say, write, or do; my sole desire is, to benefit the colored people; this being done, I am satisfied."[51] The implication, of course, was that in taking notice of the work of white Americans, as Douglass did with Harriet Beecher Stowe's *Uncle Tom's Cabin* (published in March 1852), he was committed to the goal of transforming white Americans, and thought such a goal possible. Delany had good reasons to hold this belief. As literary historian Robert Levine notes, "What is appealing about Douglass's interactions with Stowe is his working assumption that he could shape her politics and actions. With Delany, however, he remains censorious and dismissive."[52]

Similar to thinkers only a decade earlier, Douglass agrees in 1848 that the main work for black improvement must be "commenced, carried on, and concluded by ourselves."[53] Several months earlier, Douglass powerfully connected the past, present, and future of black Northerners to those enslaved. He pointed to a background culture that binds the enslaved with the nominally free:

> Remember that we are one, that our cause is one, and that we must help each other, if we would succeed. We have drunk to the dregs the bitter cup of slavery; we have worn the heavy yoke; we have sighed beneath our bonds, and writhed beneath the bloody lash;—cruel mementoes of our oneness are indelibly marked in our living flesh. We are one with you under the ban of prejudice and proscription—one with you under the slander of inferiority—one with you in social and political disfranchisement. What you suffer, we suffer; what you endure, we endure. We are indissolubly united, and must fall or flourish together.[54]

Douglass's call for solidarity has in mind not only nominally free and enslaved but also those within the African American community who seem to be divided politically about how to proceed. Less than a decade later in her 1854 "The Colored People of America," prominent lecturer, poet, and abolitionist Frances Ellen Watkins Harper remarks in agreement with Douglass: "nominally free feel that they have only exchanged the iron yoke of oppression for the galling fetters of a vitiated public opinion."[55] For the two, the experiential condition of being black in the United States (i.e., the "cruel mementoes of our oneness") and the evaluative structure responsible for one's domination (i.e., the "ban of prejudice and proscription" and the "vitiated public opinion") require racial solidarity.

This, however, does not require one to reject the possibility of transforming white Americans and forming a good in which both they and blacks share. And it most certainly, Douglass argues, does not require emi-gration. He thus rejects emigration plans because he believes both that black Americans have a rightful claim on the polity and that the beliefs and habits of white Americans are potentially susceptible to transforma-tion. As he explains in his 1851 essay, "Is Civil Government Right?" "while man is constantly liable to do evil, he is still capable of apprehending and pursuing that which is good."[56] This second line of thinking is clearly on display in 1853 as a staple of his view of human nature, albeit now framed as an indictment, when he engages Delany's book and proposal for emigration:

> We don't object to colonizationists because they express a lively inter-est in the civilization and Christianization of Africa; nor because they desire the prosperity of Liberia; but it is because, like brother Delany, *they have not sufficient faith in the people of the United States to believe that the black man can ever get justice at their hands on American soil.*[57]

This passage has deep problems, among which is Douglass's endorsement of "civilizing" Africans. All the same, his language of "faith in the people," which I take up in part 2, is important for understanding the founda-tion of Douglass's outlook.[58] It helps us to understand what we might call Delany and Douglass's divergent discourses of pessimism and faith and their connection to two different understandings of the political identity of the American polity. For Delany, Douglass's position denies the facts on the ground that reflect the alien status of black people in the American context.

Delany's insistence on strictly following the facts—addressing what fundamentally organizes the United States—informs his analysis of the Fugitive Slave Law and fuels his argument for emigration. Emigration-ist arguments were not all of the same kind among African Americans in the nineteenth century. Mary Ann Shadd and James Theodore Holly, for example, worried about the powerlessness of black people in the United States and thus encouraged emigration.[59] As Shadd puts the point about African Americans in her 1852 *A Plea for Emigration*, published the same year as Delany's *Condition*: "The odious Fugitive Slave Law has made a residence in the United States to many of them dangerous in the extreme."[60] Alexander Crummell insisted that black people had a religious duty to restore or redeem the continent of Africa.[61] But with Delany we receive the richest articulation of the need for emigration that turns on a profound criticism of the political and ethical culture of the United States.

His engagement with the Fugitive Slave Law is his attempt to distill the "condition," as indicated by the title of his book, of African Americans. What, in other words, is the social state (to invoke Alexis de Tocqueville)[62] or condition in which they exist? What, he asks, does that condition indicate about one's ethical and political status?

He focuses on the Fugitive Slave Law not because he believes positive law is the primary site of justice but because he takes the idea of law to express the underlying ethos or spirit of the people. Similar to Tocqueville or Montesquieu (whom Delany read),[63] Delany is after the essential characteristic of the United States, but one that explains the status of African Americans. Delany's analysis turns on a distinction he makes in the early part of *Condition*. There he says that the domain of moral law, the sphere where one's "sense and feeling of right and justice" lies, is to be distinguished from physical law, or the law of the political state, that, in the case of the United States, is the result of a cooperative enterprise.[64] The former, moral law, need not necessarily determine and guide the latter. It is possible for the polity to voluntarily construct laws that express their underlying commitments and be legitimate to that extent, even as they swing free of right and justice.

This account leads Delany to describe the Fugitive Slave Law as both a legitimate expression of America and a political monstrosity:

> This is the law of the land and must be obeyed. . . . To suppose its repeal, is to anticipate an overthrow of the Confederate Union; and . . . candidly we believe, the existence of the Fugitive Slave Law *necessary* to the continuance of the National Compact. This Law is the foundation of the Compromise—remove it, and the consequences are easily determined. We say necessary to the continuance of the National Compact: certainly we will not be understood as meaning that the enactment of such a Law was really necessary, or as favoring in the least this political monstrosity . . . but we speak logically and politically, leaving morality and right out of the question—taking our position on the acknowledged popular basis of American Policy.[65]

In its physical or positive character, the law crystallizes the background attitudinal orientation of the citizenry. The law is the material expression of the normative identity of the people, but it stands independent of questions such as "Is this right?" and "Is this just?" For Delany, there is a difference between the *source* or *origin* from which law issues and its *content*. If a law emerges from the polity's decision procedure, say, through the support of the requisite number of those appointed to Congress, it is legitimate to that extent. Legitimacy, as he sees it, is about the proper relationship between the actual law and those on whose behalf the law is issued and over whom.

To be sure, if one treats the Fugitive Slave Law under the category of morality, it turns out to be a monstrosity, a violation of a society that claims to recognize the equal dignity of persons. Unsurprisingly, this is the only basis on which someone like Douglass assesses the Fugitive Slave Law. Speaking several months after the publication of Delany's text to the National Free Soil Convention in Pittsburgh, Douglass explains, "The binding quality of law is its reasonableness. I am safe, therefore, in saying, that slavery cannot be legalized at all."[66] Or again, "Slavery is such a piracy that it is known neither to law nor gospel—it is neither human nor divine—a monstrosity that cannot be legalized."[67] To this, we should add Douglass's other, no less significant point—namely, his vision of human nature as being susceptible to apprehending the good. Douglass thus refuses to disconnect the political foundation of society from its basis in moral or natural law precisely because he believes we may come to hear its call.

In contrast, Delany connects the political foundations of American society to its white male voting population, and then uses the outcome of their decisions as communicating who the citizenry is and in what their commitments consist. This is why he says the Fugitive Law *is* the law of the land and must be obeyed. In a republican polity, the *only* political actors are those described by its constitutional order or physical laws. If the Constitution expresses the concrete existence of the people and is the only source of power, then there can be no conception of the people not fixed by the political instruments that claim to speak in its name. The constituent power of the people—the power of making and remaking the polity—is only ever constituted legal power. "The political basis," he says, "upon which rests the establishment of all free nations, as the first act in their organization, is the security by constitutional provisions, of the fundamental claims of citizenship."[68] Configured this way, efforts by black people to transform white Americans turn out to be futile. In fairness, Delany is not claiming that black Americans do not have a claim on the country. For him they do, and so he agrees with many of the thinkers discussed. "We are Americans," he maintains, "having a birthright citizenship—claims common to all other fellow citizens." Given the constitutional structure of the polity, he continues, those moral claims "may, by virtue of unjust laws, be obstructed."[69] For this very reason, he concludes, "a people capable of originating and sustaining such a law as this, are not the people to whom we are willing to entrust our liberty at discretion."[70]

White Americans are not only capable of bringing into existence a law of domination, Delany reasons, but also capable of sustaining their commitment to it over time; this marks not only African Americans as alien to the polity but the polity as alien to them. It was precisely the connection between racial prejudice and the ethical life of American society that famously prompted Tocqueville to remark, "It can happen that a man will rise above prejudices of religion, country, and race, and if that man is a king, he can bring about astonishing transformations in society; but it is not possible for a whole people to rise, as it were, above itself."[71] In his keynote address delivered to the National Emigration Convention of Colored Men in Cleveland in 1854, Delany explains the radical transformation required to change the status of black Americans:

> In the United States, among the whites, their color is made, by law and custom, the mark of distinction and superiority; while the color of the blacks is a badge of degradation, acknowledged by statute, organic law, and the common consent of the people.
>
> With this view of the case—which we hold to be correct—to elevate to equality the degraded subject of law and custom, it can only be done ... by an entire destruction of the identity of the former condition of the applicant.[72]

By "identity" here, Delany has in mind the identity ascribed to African Americans by virtue of their race, what he calls the badge of degradation instantiated in the political, legal, and cultural life of American society. The identity of white Americans emerges, or so Delany suggests, by virtue of this contrast with their darker counterparts. To overcome this condition requires that one destroy the badge of degradation, but this also involves, significantly, a willingness by white Americans to destroy the legal and customary badge of superiority they now flaunt. This would mean the overthrow of the confederative union to which he referred. White Americans would need, in Tocqueville's herculean imagery, to quite literally transcend themselves. Delany doubts this possibility not because he thinks it unimaginable but because he believes "ages incalculable" would need to pass in order to claim victory.[73] What untold sacrifices, Delany asks, would need to be made by blacks as they wait for whites to become something other than what their conduct suggests and institutions embody?

In many ways, it is this background understanding of the American polity that frames his account of solidarity.[74] Delany is asking African Americans to treat the practices of American society as an indication of what it values and who it is and to confront it head-on. When they do this, he argues, they will see that the problem requires not only cooperation among blacks to resist domination (à la Walker, Stewart, Easton, and Douglass) but a more significant form of racial unity that leads to the founding of an independent state. This explains the title of his book: *The Condition, Elevation, Emigration, and Destiny of the Colored People of the United States*. Because the *condition* of the American polity obstructs the *elevation* of black people, it only follows that *emigration* is necessary if black people are going to provide for their *destiny*. "To advocate," he writes, "the emigration of the colored people of the United States from their native homes, is a new feature in our history, and at first view, may be considered objectionable, as pernicious to our interests. This objection is at once removed, when reflecting on our condition."[75] Of course, Delany does not seem to connect the local issue of white supremacy, from which he is trying to save black Americans, to the equally significant problem of colonialism. Despite any naiveté that attends the recommendation, for surely it can be forgiven in light of the immediacy of the problem, his proposal is nonetheless the result of considering the deeper and darker recesses of America's identity that seemingly resist transformation. To frame the issue starkly: should African Americans pay the price for a change that may never come?

Delany's position sends us back to a comparison discussed in the last chapter between Walker's *Appeal* and the Declaration of Independence. In that context, I argued that for all his insurrectionist language, Walker's invocation of the Declaration did not involve him in following the logic of that divorce document to its conclusion. Delany, in contrast, does not invoke the Declaration in any substantive sense, and yet he seems to say of white Americans what the colonists said of the king: "A Prince whose character is thus marked by every act which may define a Tyrant, is unfit to be the ruler of a free people." This should not be surprising. Speaking at an antislavery meeting in 1850, Delany says to the mayor of Allegheny City and his audience, "Honorable Mayor, whatever ideas of liberty I may have, have been received from reading the lives of your revolutionary fathers."[76] The logic of liberty, given the intractable nature of racialized domination, necessitates that black people move beyond the shores of the American polity. In this, perhaps, Delany was far more consistent with the American Founders than Walker, despite the latter's substantive use of the Declaration.

Two ideas mark Delany's analysis. First, the nation is effectively beyond transformation because the origination and maintenance of exclusion reveal the underlying character of the people that stands at odds with

African American equality and freedom. Second, the depth of the problem calls into doubt the success of any appeals to whites and, instead, requires a radical affirmation of racial solidarity in the form of emigration. As with others, Delany racializes civic virtue, but against the backdrop of his analysis, it points beyond the United States. Emigration turns out to be not an affront to republicanism but an outgrowth of its logic.

Freedom as Racialized Nondomination

Thus far, I have laid out the importance of civic virtue to republicanism and elucidated how civic virtue is racialized in the hands of several black thinkers. In light of white supremacy, civic virtue does not function as a mechanism for stabilizing the community as a whole but rather as a way to underwrite and fortify African Americans. When we place republicanism in the context of racial domination, civic virtue translates into racial solidarity. The weak version of this account turns out to be an endorsement of racial unity as the condition for transforming the polity as such. It thus takes the centrality of character seriously but does not yet imagine the character of white Americans to be unresponsive to the claims of nonwhites, in this case African Americans. The stronger version of this account also endorses racial unity but as a precondition for constituting a new polity altogether. This stronger version also takes character seriously, but it treats white supremacy as so thoroughly constitutive of American identity that appeals for transformation are nearly impossible. Exit, in Delany's hands, becomes the necessary expression of republican commitments.

If the last section allowed us to resituate republicanism within the experiential horizon of black life in nineteenth-century America, this section seeks to supplement contemporary readings of republicanism's notion of freedom as nondomination so that it can bring into view the specific implications of chattel slavery. Philip Pettit has provided a masterful interpretation of this tradition. But when placed against the backdrop of the condition of early black life, it proves inadequate owing to the emphasis he places on political institutions and his failure to address the cultural background of white supremacy to which the thinkers discussed sought to alert us. Indeed, this cultural background distorts the ability to see blacks as fit subjects of republican principles—an idea that continues to haunt us today. Republicanism need not be displaced, but it needs theoretical supplementation in order to properly align freedom as nondomination with the specificity of the conditions confronted by black Americans. This will also involve disconnecting domination from its primary indicator, namely, that of a *dominus* or master, and connecting it more broadly to culture as such than we see in Pettit. Let us get a handle on Pettit's thinking before turning to my worry.

PETTIT AND REPUBLICANISM

In his writings *Republicanism: A Theory of Freedom and Government* and *On the People's Terms: A Republican Theory and Model of Democracy*, Pettit defends a variant of republicanism that draws from Greek and Roman sources. This version argues that "people could enjoy liberty both in relation to one another and to the collectivity, only by being invested with the power and status of the *civis*, or 'citizen.'"[77] To be a citizen comes with a distinct kind of power—a power to hold at bay those who would privately or publicly have you at their arbitrary mercy. In the absence of said power, one is under a condition of domination.

To be dominated, Pettit tells us, involves a relationship in which one person has "(1) the capacity to interfere; (2) on an arbitrary basis; (3) in certain choices that the other is in a position to make."[78] What is significant here is that the dominating party need not use his or her power; he or she need only have the capacity to deploy his or her power over you if he or she so chooses. This is what it means to be at the arbitrary mercy of another—you never know when the dominating party will act. As Cicero (from whom Pettit draws intellectual energy) puts it, "freedom . . . is not a matter of having a just master, but of having none at all." John Locke states the point more forcefully when he observes that "nobody can desire to have me in his absolute power, unless it be to compel me by force to that which is against the right of my freedom, *i.e.* make me a slave."[79] The primary counterexample republicans use, as indicated by Locke's language, is the master-slave relationship. To be a slave is to be at the arbitrary mercy of a master, even if the master is benevolent.

Notice that this account of domination is not merely about actual interference. On this view, Pettit believes republicanism is far more robust when compared to its liberal alternative. Whereas the tradition of liberalism focuses on actual interference as the test for when freedom is threatened or eclipsed, republicanism, argues Pettit, looks to structural conditions in which your actions are dependent on another (be it a private individual or a state official) staying his or her hand. Although the master-slave relationship is the signature example, it reverberates across time in other relationships such as the wife who lives at the whim of her abusive husband or a worker whose job is always in danger.

Republicanism counters the danger of domination with three of its definitive elements. The first is the vision of freedom as nondomination. But how is this realized? It is realized through the second feature: a body of laws that track the interests and concerns of the citizenry and that "satisfy a range of constitutional constraints associated broadly with the mixed constitution." In the event there is the need to realign state and society with the first two points above, point (3) argues that space must be open for citizens to "contest public policies and initiatives."[80]

FROM FREEDOM AS NONDOMINATION
TO RACIALIZED NONDOMINATION

This is a very brief sketch of Pettit's argument. However, it is not clear that this rendering of domination or the response to it adequately addresses the concerns of African Americans. Nor do I think this is peculiar to Pettit's interpretation of the tradition. The reason has to do with the specific account of slavery to which republicanism is a response—namely, political slavery, not chattel slavery.[81] Recall, Pettit explains freedom as an opposition between citizenship and slavery. The historical presumption—and this was at work in Aristotle, Harrington, and the American Framers—was that a status that one enjoyed was now denied. In Aristotle, for example, explains Mary Nyquist, political slavery derived its meaning "from an opposition between those for whom it would represent a demeaning, traumatic loss and those for whom it was supposed to be natural."[82] This idea continued well into seventeenth-century England, under monarchical rule. While it was true that the English monarch was supreme over his subjects, it did not follow that he could do with them as he pleased. Something protected those subjects from the king's domination. That something was cultural views of the worth of even those lowly subjects, an acknowledgment of their fundamental dignity.

During the time of the American Revolution, for example, the idea was not that the colonists were seeking rights they did not have but that they were seeking to reclaim their rightful status as British subjects. For example, in 1774 Jefferson criticizes "the wanton exercise of [the king's] power" against the rights of British America.[83] The king's refusal to respond appropriately, to quote a line from earlier, led the colonists to address him accordingly in the Declaration of Independence: "A Prince whose character is thus marked by every act which may define a Tyrant, is unfit to be the ruler of a free people." The idea, of course, was that monarchy and the idea of a free people could fit seamlessly together and that the king had now acted illegitimately, thus making him a tyrant or master. From Aristotle, to the British monarchy, to the American Founders, political slavery involved a denial of one's rightful standing. A dominating figure was one who acted against standing laws and customs or outside the boundaries of constitutional norms. Addressing this situation merely involved proper alignment with standing laws and customs or ensuring the proper functioning of constitutional norms. Hence Jefferson in 1775 longed for "a restoration of our just rights."[84] The Americans did not create a polity de novo; rather, they established a polity that better aligned with norms with which they were familiar.[85] Pettit's republicanism develops out of this thread of thinking and explains his emphasis on the proper establishment of positive laws and a constitutional order to remove the threat of tyranny.[86]

But if the central problem is chattel slavery rather than political slavery in the way I am tracking it, then Pettit's configuration of republicanism will prove inadequate. Chattel slavery is of a different kind. In the American context, it involves normative claims about white superiority that exceed the response political slavery demands. The problem is not the denial of a status within a political community already recognized as one's due but denial of the very idea that any political status at all might be due to one. For African Americans, the protection of their fundamental worth or human dignity did not form part of the cultural grammar of American life.

In understanding what it means to redirect republicanism from a concern merely with political slavery to one that includes chattel slavery, we should focus less on the figure of the master or *dominus* that political and chattel slavery share and more on the idea that, in the first case (political slavery), one's status as a slave is a violation of recognized standing, and in the second case (chattel slavery), one's status as a slave is perceived to be natural. One cannot reclaim a status in a community that one never had, prompting Delany to describe the American polity as alien to blacks as they are alien to it.[87] It is this second configuration that extends well beyond the figure of the master to the domain of culture itself. This is what Douglass has in mind in his 1848 address when he says of nominally free blacks: "In Northern States, we are not slaves to individuals, not personal slaves, yet in many respects we are the slaves of the community."[88] This is also what Harper is getting at in 1857 when she refers to the "galling fetters of a vitiated public opinion."[89]

How ought we to understand this idea of being a slave of the community or the impaired public opinion of which Harper speaks? For it is this that unites the nominally free blacks in Northern states with their physically enslaved fellows in the South. To get a handle on this, we need to return to an example used by Walker, and we need to explain it with explicit insights from Easton. Douglass and Harper are, in other words, pointing to something that these thinkers had already fleshed out. We begin first by recalling a passage from Walker: "If any of you wish to know how FREE you are, let one of you start and go through the southern and western States of this country, and unless . . . you have your free papers, (which if you are not careful they will get from you) . . . [they will] sell you into eternal slavery."[90] Part of what Walker is doing is trying to capture the way race works. It has internal content that functions as a universal category to eclipse the subjectivity or contextual specificity of the lives of individual blacks.

Something more is at work here, the elements of which tragically reverberate across time, making the imprecision of contemporary republicanism all the more troubling. No thinker better understands the functioning of race than Easton; his reflections are strangely familiar if only because they tap into a way of thinking that continues to haunt the American imaginary. His *Treatise* represents the "first . . . systematic theory of race" by an African American that distills the insidious logic of racial classification.[91] Although in his own time Easton did not occupy center stage in ways that Walker or Stewart or later Harper did, his analysis is so insightful that it can scarcely be ignored as an elucidation of the social and psychological logic of white supremacy.

Armed with his philosophical idealism of "mind making matter," Easton explains that the substantive meaning of one's racial designation is an "auxiliary" to slavery and legal codes of exclusion, following "its victims in every avenue of life."[92] Today we refer to this as racial stigma because it shapes the social epistemic context that we rely on to make judgments about our fellows.[93] The negative connotations associated with African Americans, Easton argues, are located in "public sentiment" (what Harper later calls public opinion) and bias the observing agent. Focusing specifically, and importantly, on black men, Easton explains that if a black man is "found in any other sphere of action than that of a slave, he magnifies to a monster of wonderful dimensions, so large that [whites] cannot be made to believe that he is a man and a brother." More dramatically, "neither can [whites] be made to believe it would be safe to admit [blacks] into stages, steam-boat cabins, and tavern dining rooms; and not even into meeting-houses, unless he have a place prepared on purpose."[94] Of course, Du Bois describes this much later in the form of how does it feel to be a problem, but Easton in the 1830s, asks his audience to wonder "what does it feel like to be a myth"—a monstrous myth.[95]

For this reason, Easton distinguishes in his *Treatise* between the legalized institution of slavery and the practices of racial prejudice to which it is tied, underscoring the way the latter lives well beyond the means of the former. The auxiliary to slavery, he explains, "is . . . capable of accommodating itself to local circumstances and conditions, and appearing with all the nature of the old beast, slavery."[96] The point is that the demeaning qualities attached to blacks persist through institutional transformations and as such retain ideas of hierarchy and domination. This, after all, is the nature of slavery in the United States. Hence chattel slavery can disappear, he reasons, and yet continue to cast a long shadow that leaves one's civic and ethical existence precarious. The danger of this is precisely why Charles Reason, an abolitionist and a figure central to the Negro Convention movement, argues in 1854 that the aim is "to abolish not only slavery, but [also] that other kind of slavery, which for generation after generation, dooms an oppressed people."[97] Here, Reason has in mind how ideas of black people's natural subordinate status shape their economic opportunities. Douglass extends the point in 1862: "Verily, the work does not end with the abolition of slavery but only begins."[98]

Easton is describing the logic of white supremacy; it permeates the cultural sphere (coextensive, we should say, with civil society) and therefore extends beyond any specific institutional instantiation, permitting constant reinvention and reintroduction across evolving institutional forms. This also explains why, in the nineteenth century, blacks traveling in specific states carried free papers. Traveling with free papers was meant to render one exempt from the "natural" or "normal" status of blacks as inferior (per the classification) and therefore from the stigma of race (i.e., what follows them into every avenue of life). It is difficult to deny that in our own time a similar logic creates a condition wherein the "natural" or "normal" status of blacks easily mingles with traits of criminality in the minds of observing citizens and conditions their comportment toward black people, regardless of the observable conduct on display. This will function as the background logic of Ida B. Wells's thinking later in the century. As Easton's argument implies, this social epistemic context renders the status of blacks—the lives they lead and the activities they undertake—precarious, subject to arbitrary domination at best and death at worst. The enormity of this insidious framework is what caused Delany to abandon faith in transformation.

Given the logic of white supremacy, Easton places less weight on the legal endorsement of slavery and more on its cultural status.

> The system of slavery in its effects, is imposed on the injured party in two forms, or by two methods. The first method is, by a code of laws, originating in public sentiment, as in slave states. The other is, prejudice originating in the same [public sentiment], as it exists in free states. The first method is prejudicial, and partakes of the corruptions of public sentiment, which is corrupted by prejudice; but prejudice, in that case, assumes the form of law, and therefore, is not capable of inflicting such deep injuries, as when it exists without the law.[99]

Easton recognizes that chattel slavery is evil and that it inflicts profound harm on those subjected to it. He is not dismissing institutional structures that perpetuate slavery and domination. Rather, he wants to alert his reader to something else. In the context of chattel slavery, prejudice is displaced from public sentiment to codes of law. Prejudice in the law, Easton reasons, is susceptible to removal by the law. "The real monster slavery," he explains, "cannot long exist, where it is sustained by legal codes only."[100] In the absence of codes of law, how does one maintain the distinction between blacks and whites, between the servility of the one and the supposed superiority of the other? Easton answers that public sentiment sustains the distinction. "When public sentiment, therefore, has become so morally, civilly, and politically corrupted by the principles of slavery, as to be determined in crushing the objects of its malignity, it is under the necessity of calling prejudice to its aid."[101] The distinction finds its daily support through the conduct, norms, and practices of white Americans in order to police the boundaries between themselves and blacks.

This logic is part of one's acculturation into American life—the "rituals of race," to invoke Ralph Ellison's much later formulation.[102] These rituals externalize the meaning of white supremacy and distribute its corresponding habits throughout the community, among which include the institutions that administer and facilitate the functioning of the community. Focusing more narrowly, Easton tells us that this acculturation forms the most dangerous kind of education from which habits of conduct emerge. In the 1830s, Easton argues, we find its most insidious form communicated to children: "The first lessons given are, Johnny, Billy, Mary, Sally, (or whatever the name may be), go to sleep, if you don't the old *nigger* will carry you off; don't you cry—Hark; the old *nigger's* coming—how ugly you are, you are worse than a little *nigger*." The second mode of instruction, he says, is to describe personal improvement as the avoidance of becoming "poor or ignorant as a *nigger*." The final instruction, located squarely in comportment, is to induce fear in whites of being made to mingle and "sit with the niggers."[103] Is this not what those students at Harvard communicated to Dean Holmes—a fear by whites that associating with blacks would diminish them and their degree? To avoid this, the symbolic rituals of distinction become necessary. "Anti-Negro stereotypes," writes Ellison much later, "were the currency through which the myth of white supremacy was kept alive."[104] For Easton, the ubiquity of prejudice and its stereotypes mingles with the culture of American life so much so that it gives the impression that it constitutes the nation's first nature, rather than being its acquired second nature. "These impressions received by the young, grow with their growth, and strengthen with their strength. . . . It is this baneful seed which is sown in the tender soil of youthful minds, and there cultivated by the hand of a corrupt immoral policy."[105]

Although Easton gives prejudice systematic attention, he was not alone in underscoring the importance of this in restraining black life, and even shaping institutions supposedly committed to the freedom and equality of black people. Indeed, invocations of the problem of prejudice and its relationship to public sentiment were common during the period. In 1836, before Easton publishes his *Treatise*, clergyman Theodore S. Wright explains in a speech delivered at the New York antislavery society meeting, "It is true that we may walk abroad; we may enjoy our domestic comforts, our families. . . . But, sir, still we are slaves—everywhere we feel the chain galling us. It is by that prejudice which the resolution condemns." In 1838, Samuel Cornish argues that the "the real battleground between liberty and slavery is prejudice against color." "Now we ask," writes Stephen A. Myers in 1842, "if the prejudice which exists at the north is not akin to the slavery of the south? *We* firmly believe it to be so." "To what," ask members of the National Convention of Colored Citizens in 1843, "do the disabilities of the colored people and the slavery of this country owe their existence, more than to public opinion?" Racial prejudice circulates among the masses, and when those prejudices have their play in the world, Douglass insists in 1848, black people become "victims of a deplorable habit." In his criticism of the American Anti-Slavery Society, James McCune Smith writes in an 1855 letter to his friend Gerrit Smith: "It is a strange omission in the Constitution of the American anti-slavery Society that no mention is made of Social Equality, either of slaves or Free Blacks, as the aim of that Society."[106] All recognize prejudice to be of utmost importance precisely because it shapes the social-psychological and institutional horizon of American life.

Easton, in particular, directs his readers to the cultural status of blacks as subordinates that is the foundation upon which codified laws and institutions rest. He does so, however, to alert his reader to what is required to transform the polity. The degrading views of black people form the epistemic context from which individuals derive norms of disregard. As with others, Easton's emphasis is not on political power but the reach of social power that endangers black life. The difference between the two is that the first refers to those wielding institutionally recognized power. In contrast, the second refers to a form of power that accrues to one's identity by virtue of one's social positionality. Addressing the problem, then, is not merely about attending to the existing political-juridical framework; rather, one must seek to disrupt the cultural force of prejudice that disciplines both blacks and whites. "Merely to cease beating the colored people," says Easton, "and leave them in their gore, and call it emancipation, is non-sense. . . . Nothing short of an entire reversal of the slave system in theory and practice" will redeem whites and blacks.[107]

Part of this entire reversal means no longer seeing one's identity as dependent on dominating others. Walker's appeal to the sentimental basis of human life discussed in the last chapter and the redeployment of this approach by Du Bois, Wells, and Billie Holiday in different ways in the next set of chapters presuppose Easton's logic. And yet those who are closer to Walker are also sensitive to the necessity of disaggregating white identity from normative judgments regarding superiority—the problem that strikes Delany as a challenge that we are unlikely to overcome.

However we understand the differences among these thinkers, they advance their arguments about the logic of white supremacy to make a more pointed claim to their black counterparts. Those who take themselves to be free, let us say, in the Northern states in contrast to the Southern states, are profoundly confused. The reason is simple. To the extent that one cannot travel freely across all the states, freedom experienced in any one of the states is an illusion. But notice what is going on here: this is not merely a claim about the laws on the books. All of the nineteenth-century African Americans discussed take seriously not merely the practice of slavery (in which one has a master) but the memory of servitude and dominance; it emerges from and simultaneously conditions the cultural sphere of American life that reaches beyond physical chains. This is why blacks in the North can also be slaves, albeit of the community. The position of African Americans as subordinates is naturalized. Thus, servility is rendered as their normal comportment, and their freedom is seen as a violation of the natural order. More significantly, freedom turns out to be ephemeral, a temporary break from reality that leaves African American liberty without cultural support. In lacking such support, freedom cannot remain resilient, and for that reason it can hardly be called freedom at all. But the response to this, if confined to the domain of legality, will obscure the deeper sense of standing these thinkers are after.

———————

As we will see in part 2, no thinker engaged this problem better than W.E.B. Du Bois. Still, the calibration of republicanism to the problem of racial domination leaves us with an important set of questions. Is the choice between Walker, Stewart, Easton, Douglass, and Harper on the one side and Delany on the other merely arbitrary? Is there something internal to republicanism that can support one choice rather than another? How should we understand ethical and political life in order to make sense of African Americans' commitment to the polity amid racial domination? When Douglass says of Delany that he does not have "sufficient faith in the people of the United States to believe that the black man can ever get justice at their hands on American soil," on what can Douglass stand to advance this striking claim?

In chapter 4, I argue more explicitly that there is a basis within republican thinking to support Douglass's utterance. We see some of it in Walker's reliance on our capacity to judge as a way of situating ourselves in the political world. But that was primarily treated as a capacity of the self, contained in what I called the principle of demotic rationality that Walker's *Appeal* sought to elicit, independent of legal recognition. Is there, however, a way of understanding the legitimacy of republicanism that might support and nurture that principle? How do we connect the malleability of the self—the belief that black and white people can become something other than what they seem to be as a result of white supremacy and racial domination—to the normative structure of republicanism? Legitimacy, in this sense, is not a way of talking about adherence to a de facto polity (the approach Delany took) but about the principle of revision and invention that can connect what the polity *is* to what *it may be* and do so within the very boundary of the background norms with which the polity is familiar. Legitimacy is what prompts one to accept a republican polity as right and see it as having a claim on one's allegiance.

I will not answer these questions in the form of a chronological contribution within African American political thought. Rather, I intend to make explicit a presupposition already at work in the nineteenth-century figures we have thus far considered and that continues after them. Relying on Thomas Jefferson's thinking before Walker and Douglass's thinking after, we can discern the normative foundation of the United States by illuminating the aspirational view of the people that renders America's political and ethical life as a space of contestation and development. This at once retains Jefferson's incipient cosmopolitanism—a way of thinking about the polity as an "imagined community" or "dream country"—while dispensing with his tendency to offer a determinate and fixed view of the polity that was the subject of Walker's critique.[108] The reader should detect, and I will make good on this, an odd symmetry between the unsavory portions of Jefferson's thinking and Delany's specific proposal. In contrast to Jefferson and Delany, by seeking to call into existence a people not yet, Douglass, I argue, enables us to reject treating the descriptive people—those with rights and privileges of the Constitution—as the primary site of political legitimacy. This means that the aspirational view of the people—a people that may yet be—functions as a practical symbol of political action. It is a presupposition of participating in democratic life, but its corresponding dispositional orientation, as Douglass and someone like Anna Julia Cooper understand, is faith. What Douglass intimates in his engagement with Delany, Cooper powerfully lays out in the last chapter of her 1892 text, *A Voice from the South*.

This raises the question: How do you get the descriptive people to embrace new visions of themselves that address white supremacy and racial domination? The answer returns us to the themes of rhetoric, sentiment, and, more explicitly, treating self and society as aesthetic constructions that run not only through Wells and the soul-stirring rendition of "Strange Fruit" by Holiday but also and critically Du Bois (chapters 5, 6, and 7). In Du Bois specifically, these themes will come to form part of the very logic of democracy's dynamic and transformational quality that he deploys in *The Souls of Black Folk*. It is to these themes we must now turn.

PART II

A Society That Never Was but May Yet Be

———◆———

THREE CLAIMS CONNECTED the chapters of part 1. The first was that the cognitive-affective capacity of black and white Americans was a site for remaking self and society. One's ability to judge, as both an epistemic and affective capacity, marked one's citizenly standing—that is, as a member who participates in assessing and shaping the community. For David Walker, African Americans have political standing not because they are legally recognized but because they can render judgments about the quality of their life and the shape of their society. He at once returns his audience to a power that precedes the Constitution—that is, constituent power—and deploys it to think about the ability of black and white Americans to reimagine their social and political community.

Second, the cognitive-affective capacity gained normative direction from the idea of freedom. Freedom demands that individuals resist domination as much as it calls them to oppose being the perpetrators of domination. Walker's criticism of both whites and blacks was really asking them to think of freedom as a social phenomenon; its realization requires affirmation by the community at large. In other words, the meaning and stability of freedom for members of political society require that they be seen or taken in a certain way by other members of society—that is, to be regarded as an equal. On the side of black Americans, this required that they take themselves as free individuals so as to see the demand freedom placed on them under conditions of domination. On the side of white Americans, it required them to see that they now stand as betrayers of that which they otherwise take themselves to be *committed to* and for this reason should be ashamed. I italicize "committed to" because it would be a mistake to read Walker as retrieving a latent commitment on the part of white Americans; rather, he is filling out and enriching the discourse of freedom in circulation and then using this as a framework for calling white Americans to account for their actions. He thus works within familiar terms, even as he expands their meaning beyond what is currently in view for the audience.

Third, and finally, to understand freedom in this way required seeing domination in its racialized form. This last claim involved a recalibration of the philosophy of republican liberty to match the ethical and political conditions of African Americans. Liberty is denied not merely when one does not enjoy political standing but also when one is, as Frederick Douglass said, a slave of the community in which one's status as a subordinate is perceived to be natural. The latter view, as I argued, could not be rectified by constitutional or procedural modifications alone but required a transformation of the ethical life of the community—the culture of society. Hosea Easton's emphasis, for example, on the centrality of public sentiment and the status of racial prejudice therein was his attempt to get behind the laws and go underneath the institutional structures to reveal the unequal status of blacks in the eyes of their white counterparts.

All of the thinkers of part 1 had in mind the way racial domination informed the cultural life of America. White supremacy and the domination it created shaped both self and society, determining from above and below norms of regard and disregard. These thinkers are a piece of a broader way of thinking that informed African American political reflection and activism in the nineteenth century as well as the abolitionist movement of the same period. But there was no consensus on the conclusions one should draw from the cultural life of America. In the 1850s, Martin Delany doubted that white Americans were up to the task of responding appropriately to black Americans. He doubted that the culture of America could get beyond white supremacy, and he came to believe that it was wholly defined by it and to that extent at odds with any attempt by African Americans to make the United States their home. Notwithstanding this significant difference, the crucial point of convergence between Delany on the one hand and Walker, Stewart, Easton, and Douglass on the other is in thinking about the problem of racial domination and white supremacy in cultural terms, in recognizing that the greatest obstacle to freedom and equality is a society in which its citizens are habituated to recognize some as worthy of care and concern while at the same time believing they should withhold them from others. As Iris Marion Young rightly puts it: "To experience cultural imperialism means to experience how the dominant meanings of a society render the particular perspective of one's own group invisible at the same time as they stereotype one's group and mark it out as the Other."[1]

Culture is the symbolic field in which norms of regard and disregard for our fellows circulate; it expresses the underlying ethos of society that shapes the character of the citizenry. "Ethos," writes Sophia Hatzisavvidou, "in its individual aspect may refer to the individual, yet it still reflects what already belongs to the collective, to the compact social realm." What is important here is that ethos does not refer to the private behavioral traits of an individual but is expressive of the life of the social and political community. Politics and ethos are mutually implicated.[2]

To speak in the idiom of character as it relates to practices of racial domination and injustice is always to speak about the relationship between self and society that makes such practices possible. The emphasis here is on the tie between self and society and the way it cultivates and encourages a demeaning orientation toward black people—an orientation captured in words, deeds, and bodily comportment. The citizenry functions as the primary unit of analysis, but not to obscure institutions or to focus on individual behavior. Rather, the point underscores that citizens qua citizens are ultimately responsible for the life they hold in common. This explains why the thinkers of part 1 (and those in part 2) never exclusively discussed the problem in procedural or legalistic terms but directed their energies to the characterological basis of American life.

This points to an issue suggested by Delany's critical intervention. If ethical and political transformation is possible, then it must be because blacks and whites belong to a political community for which the possibility of *radical change* is part of its normative infrastructure. The plasticity of one's cognitive-affective capacities is of little meaning if it cannot *be realized* within the ethical and political framework of legitimacy—that is, what sustains authority and allegiance to political society.

We should stay with this point a bit longer. Legitimation implies that the discursive and political moves one makes must be recognized by those one aspires to transform. The discursive and political moves must belong to a familiar horizon. We might think of the way African Americans often deploy familiar symbols such as the Declaration of Independence or the American Founders. Lacking this familiar horizon, the transformation of individuals will always seem at odds with the culture at large, and political and ethical actors will forever be frustrated in their attempt to reweave the community's web of beliefs and desires regarding who is worthy of care and concern. In this, the crucial point emerges: African Americans must be able to connect the description of the self to which they direct their appeals to the basis of what makes society legitimate in the first instance.[3] As I said in the final pages of chapter 3, legitimacy is not a way of talking about adherence to a de facto polity but refers to the principle of revision and invention that can connect what the polity *is* to what *it may be* and do so within the very boundary of the background norms central to American society.

It might seem reasonable to provide a strictly normative-ideal account as found in the writings of the figures thus far discussed—an account that just lays out their vision of a just society. This will ultimately be unsatisfactory for at least two reasons. First, a strictly normative account would provide theoretical purification that does not respond to Delany so much as ignore his criticism. This would effectively function as a retreat into normative theory.[4] Insofar as Americans continue to combat white supremacy, the traces of a Delanian criticism would persist unabated. Second, a purely normative account would beg the question of how Americans connect their norms to their social conditions. In the absence of a stable bridge, we will be left with a vision of an American society as it is and an account of American life as it ought to be, and no good reason to believe the two are or can be connected.

We can only overcome these problems by articulating a normative point of view from within the cultural-historical horizon of American democratic life. What does this mean, even at this abstract level? We must make *explicit* the normative point of view already *implicit* in democratic life, and that functions as the presupposition of those who participate in that life. We must also explain how African American thinkers sought to enliven that normative point of view such that it might take hold of the citizenry. None of this implies certainty of success.

This point must be understood with care. Antebellum and postbellum struggles by African Americans were always bound to grassroots organizations and institution building. Here we think of the Negro Convention movement, antislavery societies, black churches, fraternal organizations, and semiformal political and economic organizations such as the National Association of Colored Women, Negro-American League, National Association for the Advancement of Colored People, and National Urban League, just to name a few. These are mid-level informal political institutions, distinguished from formal governmental bureaucracies, electoral politics, and political parties. But as with formal political institutions, these mid-level efforts depended on a background political philosophical view about democracy as a practice for organizing human affairs and the people who are part of that practice. It is this background view that

I am after. This takes us to how African Americans imagined the people whom they addressed and the conceptual resources deployed to enable the people to imagine themselves anew. In doing so, we discover not only the significance of the idea of the people that is central to democratic theory and practice (chapter 4) but also the role of imagining self and society as sites of rhetorical, aesthetic, and emotional appeals (chapters 5–7). These last three features—rhetoric, aesthetics, and emotions—function as the vehicles by which these thinkers believe their white counterparts and the nation must travel to reach a new and expanded vision of society.

CHAPTER FOUR

The People's Two Bodies

Faith makes us, and not we it, and faith makes its own forms.
—RALPH WALDO EMERSON, "DIVINITY SCHOOL ADDRESS"

There is a prophet within us, forever whispering that behind the seen lies the immeasurable unseen.
—FREDERICK DOUGLASS, "AGES OF PICTURES"

THE CONCEPT OF the people is central to our political and philosophical discourse. At issue is the proper understanding of the category, who comprises it, how it expands, and its boundaries in the context of globalization.[1] Unfortunately, political theorists have said very little about its explicit or implied use in reimagining the polity's racial boundaries.[2] How, for instance, were African Americans able to invoke the language of the people even as they stood outside the boundaries of the nation's political and affective concerns? How, for example, did David Walker, Maria Stewart, Hosea Easton, Frederick Douglass, and others proceed as if who comprises the people *is* unsettled, despite being formally excluded?

Two forms present themselves. "The people" refers to those individuals with rights and privileges of citizenship as enshrined in a constitutional structure. But the idea of the people also serves as a space for refounding the polity to be more inclusive, destabilizing the idea of homogeneity as a prerequisite for democratic stability. The two forms of the people enable us to think clearly about the sense of uncertainty underwriting political life. This also requires us to attend carefully to the various mechanisms employed to bridge the divide—to call the people to a higher vision.

The attempt to move from description to aspiration highlights the space of contestation and uncertainty that the politically dispossessed have occupied. Reformers have articulated transcendent ethical visions of what kind of community America ought to be and the virtues needed to realize and sustain that way of life. The doubled quality of the people allowed African Americans to appeal to the polity amid exclusion—to call their fellows, in Langston Hughes's words, to "the land that never has been yet"—but without any certainty that those descriptions would come to fruition.

To make good on this argument, I will proceed along an unorthodox path. I turn to a figure who stands in a problematic relationship to black pain: Thomas Jefferson. In doing so, I am making two moves. First, I am breaking the chronological order that characterized part 1. Second, I am focusing primarily on a figure who was himself animated by the logic of white supremacy, and I am doing this to secure the normative logic on which African Americans relied. To the first issue, up until this point the goal was to leave untheorized the presupposition informing the thinkers of part 1 to dramatize a problem—namely, that in the absence of specifying the normative logic of republicanism, it is not clear how to choose between Walker, Stewart, Easton, and Douglass on the one side and Delany on the other.

To the second issue, my claim is not that Jefferson was concerned with the suffering of black folks or their subordination. Instead, I appeal to the normative infrastructure of democracy he elucidates. On his account, this makes possible America's ethical and political transformation. I treat Jefferson as a proxy for a way of thinking immanent to early American political life. In his diverse writings, we find a dynamic and open process for understanding democratic development. Development is an emergent property of viewing the people as an aspirational category, where new configurations of self, society, and the character of both might be reimagined. Instability sits at the core of the idea of the people central to popular sovereignty. This undermines determinant descriptions of who constitutes the civic "we" of political life.

"The 'we,'" writes Jason Frank, "of Jefferson's 'We hold these truths to be self-evident' . . . brings us to the heart of the dilemmas surrounding popular sovereignty in the revolutionary and postrevolutionary years."[3] My reading of Jefferson is inspired by Frank's insightful claim that invocations of the "people are a political claim, an act of political subjectivization, not pregiven," and Angelica Bernal's important observation that "Jefferson outlines a conception of democratic self-constitution that is attentive to societal conflict and temporal change."[4] Applied more broadly, the legitimacy of republicanism is bound to an account of the people that is open. Or to put it differently, the fact that the polity is unsettled, and thus open to new configurations of itself, makes it a fit candidate for allegiance and obedience. This idea of the people is precisely what allowed Walker to resist thinking of citizenship exclusively in constitutional terms and what led him, along with Stewart, Easton, and Douglass, to think the polity susceptible to improvement. All express a culturally recognized understanding of the people in its aspirational register that provides for the legitimacy of society.

The aspirational form of the people is not without issues. The central problem relates to tying legitimacy to the citizenry's openness to the future. In orienting us to a future that may never arrive, we may unwittingly become reconciled to the condition in which we find ourselves. In the second section, I take up this issue and argue that there is no forthcoming resolution—there is no way to escape the uncertainty that defines political life. Instead, we manage this uncertainty by the principle of *faith*. Faith, on my reading, is intrinsic to political life.

Introducing the concept of faith allows us to revisit the disagreement between Delany and Douglass that characterized their relationship of the 1850s. Whereas Delany's pessimism regarding the likelihood of political transformation follows directly from his empiricism—his reliance on the "facts," as he says—Douglass's faith in the American polity exceeds the facts that he needs to justify the stance he commends. This is because formally, as Anna Julia Cooper argues in *A Voice from the South*, faith refers to a conviction that some end ought to command allegiance, whose content is at variance with the actual workings of society, and for which one is willing to struggle. What is intimated in Douglass's thinking of the 1850s is carefully laid out by Cooper in that signature 1892 text.

The discourses of pessimism and faith thus map onto the discourses of the descriptive and aspirational people. The latter serves as the condition of possibility that animates not only Douglass's thinking specifically but the entirety of the tradition with which we are concerned. To be clear, the aspirational people and faith in its realization do not lead to a denial of the horror that often characterizes black life. Rather, the facts of white supremacy, racial domination, and disregard do not exhaust the meaning of what the people can become.

The second problem with the aspirational view of the people that I take up in the third section of the chapter has to do with the way contemporary scholars construe the power of the people through the framework of constitutionalism. Constitutionalism and legality function as shorthand for discussing constituent power. In so doing, scholars exclusively interpret democratic power through the workings of recognized institutions. With this approach, they obscure the claims that citizens make on each other and the appeals they place in public circulation that are formed outside the institutional and legal practices often responsible for their domination. In providing a strict legal interpretation of the people's power, scholars unwittingly exclude a range of voices that did not think of refounding through the framework of law precisely because they were not constitutional theorists but writers and activists of culture. Seeing the matter this way also disrupts the presumed line of continuity between political actors in the present and the founding generation of the past. We no longer find ourselves thinking about African American activists and intellectuals as realizing the untapped potential articulated by the Founders. Instead, we confront the reality that their interventions represent a rupture between the past and imagined future.

Thinking through and beyond Thomas Jefferson

Since its modern incarnation in the eighteenth century, the idea of the people has worked to dissolve the line of demarcation between rulers and ruled central to monarchical and aristocratic regimes. For if the rulers and the ruled shared a political identity—that is, were members of the same citizenry, equal before the law—the power held by the former was merely fiduciary and so meant the latter was never alienated once and for all from the source of authority. The idea of the people served as the solution to the problem modern representative government posed to the status of the minority, who might otherwise be at the mercy of a tyrannical majority. The people, understood as the ultimate source for conferring legitimacy, rendered the position of power holders changeable. But the changeable character of power holders rested on a deeper descriptive designation—it referred to those with rights and privileges of citizenship, enshrined in a constitutional structure and often on visible display during electoral cycles. As John Locke maintained in his *Second Treatise of Government* (1690), political representatives hold power in "trust," and the logic of this followed, as Thomas Paine aptly argued in *The Rights of Man* (1792), from "ingrafting representation upon democracy."[5] This is the body of the people in its most active sense, whose contours are defined by the constitutional order.

The idea of the people also has a radical meaning. This idea calls to mind an "imagined community," "dream country," or "democratic wish" to which political reformers appealed and in which they redescribed the boundaries of the polity.[6] In this radical account, we can only make out the silhouette of a body politic, whose content resists final specification. This sense of the people—a people always becoming—is marked by political visions not yet in existence and informed by a perfectionist impulse. In lacking specification, the people is a site for aspirational visions. The political goals it champions, the ethical outlook it proffers, and the emotions it seeks to rouse aspire to engender a new societal order. In its aspirational mode, the concept of the people inspires faith and provokes action. This is a fundamental feature of the American worldview (not without historical precedent, however) in which it often describes and redescribes, makes and unmakes its political and cultural identity. Priscilla Wald refers to this as the nation's "fashioning and endless refashioning of 'a people,'" and Daniel Howe identifies it as a preoccupation with "making the American self."[7]

This dualistic account is not without its problems, not the least of which is its susceptibility to constrained notions that tie identity to descent as the basis for understanding the people. In Thomas Jefferson, we find both the possibilities and limitations of the discourse of the people. I will return to the limitations later. For much of this section, I argue that the idea of the people provides the background for understanding America— an ethical-political project—as a site of symbolic action. Jefferson ties this twofold idea of the people to the very legitimacy of republicanism.

In invoking the language of symbolic action, I mean to say that for Jefferson the people is a symbol whose discursive and practical content is always in development. My use of the term "symbolic action" comes from Ralph Ellison's famous 1978 essay "The Little Man at Chehaw Station," and he, in turn, borrowed it from Kenneth Burke. Referencing Ellison at this juncture is shorthand for noting the historical vitality of the aspirational idea of the people. Writing almost two centuries after Jefferson, Ellison relies on the normative infrastructure of American life to unsettle self-descriptions of the United States. To treat Jefferson's understanding of the people as a site of symbolic action is to say that it opens space for "negating nature as a given and amoral condition, creating endless series of man-made and man-imagined positives. By so doing, [it] nudges us toward that state of human rectitude for which, ideally, we strive."[8] So conceived, the idea of the people reflexively encodes openness as part of the legitimating logic of republicanism, and thus creates a productive tension between the governmental apparatus and those in whose name that apparatus claims to speak. Here, in nuce, we have a framework through which the transformation of the polity is imagined, apprehended, and reshaped, and without which struggle against the forces of domination and oppression would make little sense.

The aspirational people is thus a presupposition of democratic life. As such, it stimulates action and allegiance even as its content resists being understood as a *fact* of political reality. Notice, there is a distinction between the aspirational people as a presupposition and the content of any specific aspiration offered. Crucially, the aspirational people has a performative quality to it because it produces effects in the citizenry. We criticize the government that acts in our name with the presumption (although not only this presumption) it will work, we protest policies deemed inappropriate with the presumption it will produce better policies, we organize against reigning political administrations at the local, state, and federal level, presuming it will either change the administrations or create a context for better administrations. All these things create and consolidate the impression that a space of contestation exists to redirect or reimagine society. The idea of the aspirational people thus produces significance across time because it opens the possibility to resist the cruelty and indifference of our fellows, becomes a means through which groups potentially share a political vision, and functions to address their political grievances.

In speaking this way, we can make explicit the principle guiding Walker, Stewart, Easton, and Douglass in their appeals to the American polity.[9] When Douglass invoked (in chapter 3) the necessity of faith against Delany's pessimism,[10] he was not merely relying on the fact that the citizenry can change and improve (i.e., a factual claim about the unfinished quality of selves). Rather, he understood the possibility of political and ethical transformation as central to the very legitimating logic of American life (i.e., a normative claim regarding the principle that underwrites republicanism and secures allegiance). In this, he relied on the logic of American normative life, which was powerfully defended by Jefferson.

JEFFERSON AND THE CONDITION OF ETHICAL AND POLITICAL POSSIBILITY

In his classic 1789 letter to James Madison, Jefferson articulates his vision of the unboundedness of the people. "I set out on this ground which I suppose to be self-evident," he explains, *"that the earth belongs in usufruct to the living*; that the dead have neither powers nor rights over it."[11] Although Jefferson advances this thought in the context of undercutting the idea of generational debt, his reflections are not limited to economic matters. His thinking is far more radical. "No society," he writes, "can make a perpetual constitution, or even a perpetual law."[12] He applies this idea to the relationship among citizens and their connection to political authority so as not to permanently bind later and even present generations to prior laws, unresponsive to emerging grievances.[13]

In Jefferson, we find a close connection between democratic sovereignty and the idea of ethical and political development; it foregrounds the importance of understanding the aspirational form of the people. For him, the concept of the people serves as the legitimating core of democracy and does so precisely because it transcends America's political present and includes its past and future. This view informs his thinking when in his 1816 letter to historian Samuel Kercheval he connects the meaning of law and the Constitution to an unfolding vision of political life:

> Some men look at constitutions with sanctimonious reverence, and deem them like the ark of the covenant, too sacred to be touched. They ascribe to the men of the preceding age a wisdom more than human, and suppose what they did to be beyond amendment. . . . But I know, that laws and institutions must go hand in hand with the progress of the human mind. As that becomes more developed, more enlightened, as new discoveries are made, new truths disclosed, and manners and opinions change with the circumstances, institutions must advance also, and keep pace with the times. We might as well require a man to wear still the coat which fitted him when a boy, as civilized society to remain ever under the regimen of their barbarous ancestors.[14]

Jefferson's sensitivity to the developmental character of the natural and social world is part of his political ontology. The features that comprise political life—communities, individuals, institutions, and laws—are themselves assumed to be those parts of reality susceptible to and capable of experiencing change. His view of the natural and social world is part of his idea of the people; it allows him to acknowledge the Constitution as speaking in the name of *a* people and to also recognize the Constitution's failure to capture the polyvocal character of an ever-changing society. But take note: such a description extends not only to the Constitution (guarding against veneration) but ipso facto to its writers as well. Refounding is necessary to prevent the "barbarous ancestors" from stretching their dead hands over the future.

Precisely for this reason, he argues, it is a mistake to think solutions articulated in the past will *necessarily* be effectual in the future. Jefferson does not, as Judith Shklar argues, affirm a "politics of perpetual newness" that commits him to a metaphysics of progress.[15] His work does, however, defend a politics in which evolutionary development is possible. For him, as for Ralph Waldo Emerson and John Dewey, the test of our beliefs is their ability to redeem their worth in the face of experience; they become verified and reverified to the extent they continue to produce satisfactory results in managing the world we inhabit. Jefferson understands the meaning and agency of the people through their ability to construct and reconstruct their social and political world, and he therefore counsels a pragmatically inflected and historically sensitive hope. "His idealism," Dewey aptly remarks, "was a moral idealism, not a dreamy Utopianism."[16]

An important political implication follows from this line of reasoning: the people—understood at an intergenerational level—can never be represented in their entirety in any specific expression of the people's will. This also means that we must never *wholly* identify the soverцign people with the legal and institutional apparatus (i.e., the Constitution and its government) that claims to articulate its aspirations. In Margaret Canovan's words, the gap between description and aspiration leaves "room for appeals to the people against the people's government," and this appeal process necessarily extends beyond formal proceduralism.[17] The appeal process, as Frank underscores, thus reveals a "people that are productively never at one with themselves."[18] Here, we should understand "never at one with themselves" expansively; it denotes not only the absence of agreement (what Frank refers to as "dissensus" in his reading of Douglass's famous Fourth of July address)[19] but also disunity in thought and feeling.

This disidentification—between the people and that which speaks in its name—opens an ongoing, iterative, and contestable vision of political life (the source of Jefferson's radicalism). In this view, citizens can claim, tentatively occupy, and reclaim the space of democratic politics. Although in 1775 Jefferson, speaking in the name of the colonists, seemingly longed for "a restoration of our just rights," he nonetheless offered a theoretical account of the sovereign people that pointed not toward the past but to a future not yet resolved.[20] "What actually happened," Hannah Arendt astutely observes, "at the end of the eighteenth century was that an attempt at restoration and recovery of old rights and privileges resulted in its exact opposite: a progressing and development and the opening up of a future which defied all further attempts at acting or thinking of a circular or revolving motion."[21] This marked a productive tension at the heart of the American founding that modeled the two ideas of the people—a way of thinking of the American people as realizing the rights of the past under properly administered constitutional conditions and a vision of the American people that exceeded its specific constitutional and ethical expression.

The workings of the descriptive people are always conditional. For the people in this sense, primarily when understood through its representational paradigm, implies a remainder that can never be completely absorbed. This remainder forms the morally appealing core of republicanism precisely because it is a site of aspirations that have yet to be articulated. It is constituent power—the power for judging, acting, instituting, and establishing.[22] Government derives its existence from that power; it forms the channel through which agential energy moves. Walker relied on this power in his *Appeal* as he called into existence the citizenly standing of African Americans, independent of constitutional recognition (chapter 1). Depending, as he did, on the capacity to judge, Walker returned his audience to the foundation of American citizenship. But in so doing, he was merely enacting a truth so nicely captured by Sheldon Wolin in our own time—namely, that "democratic action, or the demos as autonomous agent, might be defined as collective action that initially gathers its power from outside the system."[23]

Constituent power is never relinquished even within the representational paradigm; it functions as a normative presupposition of democratic life. This is the power that legitimized the Declaration of Independence in 1776 and the U.S. Constitution in 1787. From the people's "authority," explains James Wilson in the 1790s, "the constitution originates: for their safety and felicity it is established: in their hands it is as clay in the hands of the potter: they have the right to mould, to preserve, to improve, to refine, and to finish it as they please."[24] For this reason, Canovan rightly notes the transcendent and mythical quality that attends this culturally immanent account of the people: "Alongside this everyday people, the western political imagination is haunted by a quite different 'People': the population transformed into a mythic being that is not only the source of political legitimacy, but can sometimes appear to redeem politics from oppression, corruption and banality."[25]

If we keep the history of racial domination and white supremacy in mind, redemption is not the best way to characterize the goal of the aspirational idea of the people. We readily interpret redemption as compensation for the faults of the past—a form of compensation that mitigates the remainders of loss and pain. And yet, it is precisely the traces of loss and pain with which we are often contending.[26] The quest for redemption may ironically obscure our attempts to address the persistence of trauma.

Notwithstanding Canovan's use of redemption language, she strikes me as right in thinking of the notion of the aspirational people as haunting the Western political imagination. Hauntings are often about what we, in the material world, have left unsettled. The collapse of the past and present creates the context for which the present is asked to take responsibility. Taking responsibility is what may allow the people in the present to imagine themselves anew. This is the productive power of the idea of the people.

Historically, political reformers generally and African Americans specifically appealed to this power, and through it they redescribed the content and boundaries of the polity. In 1844, Emerson describes this power as the inexhaustible site for remaking America, what he calls "a new yet unapproachable America."[27] Douglass famously treats the people as not only a collectivity finally specified by the Constitution but also an aspiration struggling to inhabit the world. "It is not," he explains in 1857, "in changing the dead form of the Union, that slavery is to be abolished in the country." Echoing Jefferson: "We have to do not with the dead, but the living; not with the past, but the living present." "Slavery lives in this country," he continues, "not because of any paper Constitution, but in the moral blindness of the American people, who persuade themselves that they are safe though the rights of others may be struck down."[28] Invoking the people by name and noting its infinite power, Whitman exclaims in 1871, "The people! . . . The rare cosmical artist-mind, lit with the Infinite, alone confronts his manifold and oceanic qualities. . . . Their measureless wealth of latent power and capacity."[29] For this reason, Du Bois concludes in 1920 that the "foundation of the argument for democracy" is that "the argument must be continually restated and emphasized."[30] From the eighteenth, nineteenth, and twentieth centuries, the aspirational category consistently denoted (albeit controversially) the power of the people to give direction to their lives, quite apart from its constitutional embodiment, and even that new direction could never describe unexpressed aspiration. In this role, the people did not merely spectate on but could breathe new life into society.

The notion of the people's two bodies is central to Jefferson's political philosophy; indeed, he pushes it to its conclusion. "Cherish, therefore, the spirit of our people," he recommends in his letter to Edward Carrington in 1787, "and keep alive their attention. Do not be too severe upon their errors, but reclaim them by enlightening them."[31] We hear echoes of this in 1820: "I know no safe depository of the ultimate powers of the society, but the people themselves: and if we think them not enlightened enough to exercise their control with a wholesome discretion, the remedy is, not to take it from them, but to inform their discretion by education."[32] Jefferson's use of the term "spirit" in the first quoted line is more than ornamental. As Samuel Johnson observes in his 1755 *Dictionary*—the most commonly used dictionary in the eighteenth century and one Jefferson owned and recommended—the word "spirit" denotes "temper" or "habitual disposition of mind."[33] Applied to the citizenry, it refers to a characteristic orientation underwriting American democracy ("the mainspring," as Jefferson calls it).[34] Appeal to the people's "good sense" when they are in error, Jefferson counsels, for it *may* yet, he believes, contain the source of their enlightenment.[35] Similarly, Walker, Stewart, Easton, and Douglass advanced appeals under the presumption that the people could be reclaimed and improved and that the logic of democratic legitimacy depended on this possibility.

Precisely because of the need to make the citizenry responsive, Jefferson (and later generations) emphasized the importance of character in theorizing the democratic self, and the language of "sense" and "sensibility" achieved primacy in American political discourse because it accentuated the malleability of the cognitive and affective dimensions of the self. Sensibility, in particular, referred to one's capacity to be sensitive to a morally and aesthetically charged world and, to that extent, could be "strengthened by exercise."[36] A great many African Americans, as suggested by earlier chapters, presupposed this capacity of sensitivity in their appeals to the polity. And thinkers as diverse as Whitman, Du Bois, and Baldwin are often united in their shared concern to force Americans to consider the following question: *How must we understand ourselves such that we can make and remake American society in response to its changing circumstances?* Whitman put it best in the form of a challenge to American democracy in *Democratic Vistas*:

> For not only is it not enough that the new blood, new frame of democracy shall be vivified and held together merely by political means, superficial suffrage, legislation, &c., but it is clear to me that, unless it goes deeper, gets at least as firm and as warm a hold in men's hearts, emotions and belief, as, in their days, feudalism or ecclesiasticism, and inaugurates its own perennial sources, welling from the centre forever, its strength will be defective, its growth doubtful, and its main charm wanting.[37]

Here democracy is a stand-in for the principles of openness and equal standing. These principles not only must find expression through the machinery of democracy (what Whitman calls political means) but more significantly must shape the very outlook of the citizenry (taking a firm and warm hold in men's hearts, as he says). How this would be done involved thinking of the polity, in the idiom of the Romantics, as a work of art—a performance that aims to enact proper responsiveness to and regard for one's fellows. I will say more about this in the next couple of chapters.

What all of this suggests is that the spirit of openness pervades the descriptive view of the people. It is the inherent rebelliousness of political life. Constitutionalism draws its authorizing power from this spirit and can never (theoretically) extinguish it without compromising the very legitimacy of democracy. Jefferson applies the logic of holding power in trust otherwise associated with the relationship between political representatives and their extant constituency to the wider temporal framework of past, present, and future generations. What the Greeks called *demokratia*—literally, the power of the people—is, in Jefferson's hands, temporalized. To his mind, we can now speak of past, present, and future generations holding power in trust (or "in usufruct," to use his language) for a people not yet in existence.

All these references to "a people not yet" may seem unusual, especially given the importance we place on those with rights and privileges as stipulated by a constitutional order. But this account only seems unusual if we deny that the idea of order itself is made and remade, often breaking with the specificity of the constitutional form we find at the founding moment. This is why Jefferson asks us to see our relationship to the Constitution in developmental terms. After all, Americans have often contested the boundary and composition of "We the People" by offering competing constitutional projects. From settler activists to abolitionists to indigenous communities to black nationalists, we consistently see a polity struggling to reclaim its moral authority in the face of new demands and grievances.[38] Understood in this way, the descriptive people is always "legitimized from the standpoint of the future."[39] And we often use the dangers of closure and unresponsiveness as tools of critical assessment—to hold the nation to account for wrongs committed in the name of the people. The mistake we often make, I think, is in believing that allegiance is attached to the *institutional or juridical form* of authority, and this, in part, is because of the materiality of representative institutions and constitutional laws when compared with the elusive idea of a people not yet. But it seems more accurate to say that our allegiance is partly attached to the *norm* of openness, to the possibility of articulating aspirations, upon which *institutional or juridical form* is loosely based. As Sofia Nasstrom explains, the "constitution of the [descriptive] people is not a historic event," fixed in time once and for all. Rather, the people "is an ongoing claim that we make,"[40] and this underwrites the specific appeals we find historically excluded groups advancing throughout American history. This troubles the ease with which we treat those recognized by the Constitution as settled and instead allows us to bring those at the margins to the center of analysis in America's unfolding, but contested, ethical and political narrative. This gives us now a recharacterization of the thinkers we considered in earlier chapters. When Walker, Stewart, Easton, Douglass, and others orient themselves to the polity, calling it to embrace new configurations of itself, they do so precisely under this specific logic of legitimacy.

I do not want to take this reading of Jefferson too far. After all, Walker rightly criticizes Jefferson's ideas about black Americans and the ways in which he constrained the vision of who could count as a citizen. We should not confuse the use of Jefferson here with unvarnished acceptance. His nationalism and its connection to his defense of racial homogeneity must remain a source of grave concern, especially given its subsequent repackaging throughout American history. The idea of the nation has often been based on two forms, that of "race" ("descent," a community of heredity and ancestry) and that of "consent" (a community of "mature free agents").[41] The very identity of the American polity has often revolved around these two warring and contested visions.

This is partly, although not exclusively, because the idea of the people contains an ambiguity. Although the aspirational core of the people is used by Jefferson to disrupt binding the present and future of America, the definite article (*the*) implies a unitary view of political society that, when combined with Jefferson's racism, is often harnessed for exclusionary ends.[42] Jefferson translates this unitary quality into a vision of national particularism—a vision of a racially homogeneous political community—that is the *specific* content of his aspiration for America. We need only think of his emphasis on the Anglo-Saxon heritage of the American polity in 1774 and his demeaning description of blacks, already discussed in part 1, from his *Notes on the State of Virginia*.[43] This particularism haunted the American imaginary, threatening to permanently limit its reach and close the political and affective borders of the nation. Later thinkers sought to disconnect the people as an aspirational category from specific visions of homogeneity to which it was often tied. That is, they hoped the people would *choose* to be other than what their treatment of black people suggested. In this, they sided with the idea of a nation—a people—founded on a choice. "To belong to a nation," Tzvetan Todorov writes of the consensual model, "is above all to accomplish an act of will, to make a commitment to live together by adopting common rules, thus by envisioning a common future."[44]

The particularism, for example, we see in Jefferson and its connection to politics functioned in Delany's thinking, as we examined in the last chapter, to settle the meaning of the people. This odd overlap between Jefferson and Delany is worth noting, even if the motivations of each are vastly different. Recalling an observation from the last chapter, the disagreement between Delany on the one hand and Walker, Stewart, Easton, and Douglass on the other turned on the weight they accorded the descriptive form of the people in thinking about the dynamism of the American polity. Putting aside ethical appeals, as Delany did in *Condition, Elevation, Emigration, and Destiny of the Colored People of the United States*, leads to privileging the descriptive people. Delany used the descriptive people as the only basis for understanding the source of America's political legitimacy.

> Heretofore, it ever had been denied, that the United States recognized or knew any difference between the people—that the Constitution makes no distinction, but includes in its provisions, all the people alike. This is not true, and certainly is blind absurdity in us at least, who have suffered the dread consequences of this delusion, not now to see it.[45]

Strikingly, Delany's outlook received confirmation in 1857 in *Dred Scott v. Sanford*.[46] The opinion of the Supreme Court (rather than the rationales of the individual justices) focused on the language of the people to assess the legal standing of a black man (Dred Scott) to bring suit in a federal court. The issue at hand turned on whether those of African ancestry were included in the category of the people as specified in "We the people" of the Constitution. The Court was clear that the people referred to a limited—descriptive—class of persons as understood by the Founders. For the Court, the "question before us is, whether the class of persons described in the plea in abatement compose a portion of this people, and are constituent members of this sovereignty? We think they are not."[47] As with Delany, albeit for radically different reasons, the Court collapsed the descriptive people and constituent sovereignty, removing any hints of the aspirational body of the people.

But Delany's account involves a conflict that resists resolution on his terms. His decision to exclusively rely on the descriptive people as they appeared in the present rendered the polity static, unchanging, and unresponsive to new and emerging grievances, even of those recognized by America's constitutional order. In collapsing constituent and established power, Delany leaves the polity without a means to explain its developmental character—indeed, its very origins. In dropping the aspirational form of the people, Delany also abandoned that very feature that brought the American polity into normative existence in the first instance—that is, the reliance by the colonists on the empty place of power to establish their political community over and against the monarch.

The irony of Jefferson's view (and why Delany's position seems questionable to someone like Frederick Douglass) is that most reformers challenged homogeneity by appealing to the aspirational view of the people Jefferson defended in the first instance. His hypocrisy may well have been damaging, but it did not need to constrain the nation's future. Cherish the spirit of openness, to recall his idea. How far one could push openness on matters of race was a source of skepticism, undoubtedly owing to his racism. As Jefferson reflected on the inclusion of African Americans, for instance, he concluded that "deep-rooted prejudices entertained by the whites; ten thousand recollections, by the blacks, of the injuries they have sustained" made it difficult, if not impossible, to persuade each race that inclusion was genuinely possible.[48]

The central question is, how does one make the descriptive form of the people receptive to modification? This question is another way of focusing on public sentiment, to use Hosea Easton's language, or public opinion, to recall Frances Harper's thinking. Jefferson's invocation of persuasion and the importance he accords aesthetics to ethical life provide an important clue (even if he did not make use of it). This was the ground on which citizens often fought for America's soul. "In a republican nation," Jefferson wrote to David Harding in 1824, "whose citizens are to be led by persuasion and not by force, the art of reasoning becomes of first importance."[49] Persuasion requires speakers and writers to confront communities through speech with experiences—that is, rich accounts of dreams unrealized, horrors encountered, possibilities that may yet be, and promises that seek fulfillment. When Jefferson refers to persuasion, he has in mind not sophistry but a form of appeal that directs and guides its auditors to intimations of the truth that, if acted upon, he believes, will produce a better way of life. Persuasion, in this second form, appeals to the audience's capacity for judgment—that is, attempting to transform both their sense and sensibility.

Persuasion helps transform sense and sensibility, but what stabilizes it over time, Jefferson insists, is the imagination. This may seem odd, since the content of the imagination is precisely what does not exist in the world or in us. But Jefferson's thinking is that the imagination helps vivify what stands in the future and what seems remote, and reflexively conditions comportment. Here is how Jefferson puts it:

> Every thing is useful which contributes to fix in us the principles and practice of virtue. When any signal act of charity or of gratitude, for instance, is presented either to our sight or imagination, we are deeply impressed with its beauty and feel a strong desire in ourselves of doing charitable and grateful acts also. On the contrary when we see or read of any atrocious deed, we are disgusted with its deformity and conceive an abhorrence of vice.[50]

This is a familiar cognitive-affective framing of the sentimental mode of thinking, but it is one central to how rhetorical appeals are filled out. Rhetoric is directed to and presupposes the transformative power of the self, seeking to elicit from one's listeners or readers feelings of attraction or revulsion. Attraction, what Jefferson refers to as a strong desire, highlights the way the objects of the imagination pull us toward them, shaping belief and action. Indeed, this view comes to characterize the aesthetic vision of democracy in Walt Whitman, the rhetorical appeals of W.E.B. Du Bois's *The Souls of Black Folk*, the political aestheticism of the Harlem Renaissance, and the antilynching interventions of groups and figures as diverse as Ida B. Wells, the NAACP, and Billie Holiday. All recognize that rhetorical projections in the world depend on those engaged, pulling them toward or pushing them away from the imagined object. In either case, the aim is to create a feeling of ownership by the one on the receiving end of persuasion; auditors, as we say, turn things over to reject, endorse, or amend the beliefs under consideration.[51] In being a participant in the process, the auditors retain and employ their reflective and emotional agency. In a community where rhetoric and aesthetics mix as part of securing the moral rectitude of the polity, democracy turns out to be a project of art. But before turning to this issue in the next few chapters, other concerns require attention.

On Political Legitimacy and Faith: Delany, Douglass, and Cooper

Two problems attend the account I have thus far provided. The first is internal to the aspirational form of the people. Political actors, the worry might go, seem inescapably caught in a situation in which they give allegiance to a polity based on its openness to a future that may never come. They reach for an aspiration that may forever elude their grasp, as they nonetheless work within a polity that denies or frustrates their standing as citizens. My claim is that this is unavoidable and it is what necessitates faith.

The second problem, discussed in the next section, is external to the account provided above but relates to how scholars describe constituent power. This problem threatens to connect constituent power to formal constitutionalism that renders the actions and writings of the thinkers we have thus far considered (and will consider) meaningless. The secondary feature of this problem emerges out of a desire to see continuity between the founders of political society and later generations that obscures the disruptive workings of the latter.

I have argued in my reading of Jefferson that the legitimacy of democratic rule is found not in the past or present but in a community's responsiveness to the future. For this reason, many of those in the tradition of American and African American political thought often emphasize the dispositions needed to sustain a free and self-governing polity. Emphasizing the dispositional quality of the citizenry is fundamentally about what might make the people sensitive and attuned to the demands time, change, and the needs therein make on them. So what commands allegiance—that is, acceptance of authority and the legitimate right of that authority—is belief in society's openness to an iteration of itself not yet realized, even as political actors (those informed and guided by that figuration) struggle to convince their fellows to make that vision of society a reality.

But on this account, our allegiance is uncomfortably attached to a form of responsiveness that has not yet been provided. This immediately raises the question of why one would assent to such a form of political life. This is especially troubling in the context of racial domination, given how frequently the United States has willingly ignored the grievances of African Americans. Engaging this question via Delany, Douglass, and Cooper will help us understand the relationship of faith to the aspirational idea of the people.

DELANY'S PESSIMISM ONCE MORE

In a short May 1852 letter to William Lloyd Garrison's newspaper *The Liberator*—one month after the publication of *Condition*—Delany writes the following:

> I am not in favor of caste, nor a separation of the brotherhood of mankind, and would as willingly live among white men as black, if I had

an *equal possession and enjoyment* of privileges. . . . If there were any probability, I should be willing to remain in the country, fighting and struggling on, the good fight of faith. But I must admit, that I have no hopes in this country—no confidence in the American people—with a few excellent exceptions—therefore, I have written as I have done.[52]

Douglass responds a year later in May 1853. The immediate context for Douglass's response was not Delany's public letter (although Douglass likely read it) but Delany's reflections on Harriet Beecher Stowe. Delany, you will recall, was disappointed that Douglass paid attention to Stowe's *Uncle Tom's Cabin* but so little to *Condition*.[53] At a crucial juncture in Douglass's response, where he discusses the colonizationists' plans versus committing oneself to transforming the United States into a home for black people, he contends:

> We don't object to colonizationists because . . . they desire the prosperity of Liberia; but it is because, like brother Delany, they have not sufficient faith in the people of the United States to believe that the black man can ever get justice at their hands on American soil. It is because they have systematically, and almost universally, sought to spread their hopelessness among the free colored people themselves; and thereby rendered them, if not contented with, at least resigned to the degradation which they have been taught to believe must be perpetual and immutable, while they remain where they are.[54]

The reader should take note of the language of hope and faith in these passages. We should not read this casually but as something that bears on Delany's and Douglass's different understandings of the epistemic context of the struggle by black Americans for freedom and equality in the United States.

Hope, as Patrick Shade notes, is an "active commitment to the desirability and realizability of a certain end."[55] Delany, it appears, ties hope to confidence in bringing to fruition what one desires. As he suggests in the letter and argues more forcefully in *Condition*, hope stands within a world of probabilities informed by facts that provide indications of what is possible. To recall a line from Delany: "We must abandon all vague theory, and look at facts as they really are; viewing ourselves in our true political position in the body politic."[56] Earlier in *Condition*, where he discusses the comparative status of black people "in relation to our Anti-Slavery friends," he explains that "we are nevertheless occupying a miserable position in the community . . . and what we most desire is, to draw the attention of our people to this fact."[57]

His interest in drawing his readers to the facts is unsurprising. Delany stands within a milieu that includes not only the critical idealism of the transcendentalists but the empiricism of African American thinkers and activists such as Sarah Mapps Douglass, J.W.C. Pennington, and James McCune Smith. For them, the facts are thought to disclose an objective, unbiased reality—a reality they often used to call into question false views about black people.[58] Delany's empiricism moves in a different but no less important direction. He takes the facts of black subordination and white supremacy, at least in 1852, as exhausting not only what is but what is possible.

In contrast to hope, faith is a passionate conviction, coterminous with a vision of life or object not in existence. Both hope and faith share an attachment to something not present. The source of difference between the two is that hope marks levels of confidence in achieving what is desired, while faith is the expression of a loving, even if difficult, commitment precisely because there is no confidence to be had—at least based on some facts of the matter—in its realization.[59] This seems to capture Douglass's position; he is clear that we should not take the facts of the degradation of black people as settling the matter of their future condition in the United States. In contrast, Delany ties hope and faith together in a specific way. He not only dispenses with hope because there is no evidence to sustain it, but more significantly he is without faith that there is a narrative of American and African American life that can provoke whites to change.

But why precisely does Delany appear to be without faith? Some of this has already been laid out, but it is worth expanding and systematizing those reflections under the heading of what we might call the three markers of Delany's pessimism. The first is his belief in the *general burden of historical inegalitarianism*. This is how Delany captures it in chapter 1 of *Condition*, "Condition of Many Classes in Europe Considered": "That there have been in all ages and in all countries . . . classes of people who have been deprived of equal privileges. . . . These are historical facts that cannot be controverted."[60]

Delany might be offering us a descriptive claim about the past. But I am not sure that is exactly what he is doing. This is because his claim about inegalitarianism comes in a chapter that bears the first substantive word of the book's title: condition. For him, "condition" denotes the particular mode or manner of a person or a thing. Since Delany speaks of inegalitarianism as a condition of all ages and all countries, and given how the term functions in his text, there seems to be no good reason to believe this "condition" will disappear any time soon—or at all. Hence his classic line in defense of nationalism: "That there have in all ages . . . existed a nation within a nation—a people who although forming a part and parcel of the population, yet were from force of circumstances, known by the peculiar position they occupied, forming in fact . . . but a restricted part of the body politic of such nations, is also true."[61]

If the interpretation offered thus far is correct, or minimally plausible, what Delany is doing is reifying historical facts as the immovable markers of human nature. Or, to put it differently, history is how we bear witness to the workings of humanity's immovable nature. In fairness, he seems not to deny that political and historical transformations have taken place. After all, he acknowledges the development from monarchies to republics. He also observes that "the colored people of today are not the colored people of a quarter of a century ago." They rightfully, he believes, long for privileges they did not seek twenty-five years earlier.[62] But Delany also sees those developments as ironically laced with the persistent markers of hierarchies based on inclusion and exclusion, equality and inequality.[63] Invoking inequality in Europe principally (although not exclusively), he explains that "it is . . . our intention . . . *simply to set forth the undeniable facts, which are as glaring as the rays of a noon-day's sun*, thereby to impress them indelibly on the mind of every reader of this pamphlet."[64] It is not that the facts "cannot be controverted"—they *are* the past—but because they define the temporal fields of the past, present, and future that humans have occupied, currently occupy, and likely will occupy. That is, human nature is the kind of nature when understood socially that generally produces political and ethical hierarchies to organize human relations. This is the human condition; it is the manner or mode of humanity's nature.

This leads to the second and third markers of Delany's pessimism. He understands the practice of racial domination as defining what American society *in itself really is*. Racial domination in the United States is thus a localized manifestation of the general burden of historical inegalitarianism. The intrinsic propensity toward hierarchy that defines human nature expresses itself through racial difference, shaping the modern world generally but serving as the foundation for the American polity specifically. Finally, the burden of historical inegalitarianism and its specific manifestation in the facts of racial domination in the United States appear to be effectively institutionalized via Delany's *positivism*. This partly explains why, in his 1854 speech to the National Emigration Convention of Colored Men, he addresses the audience as "fellow-countrymen," in contrast to "citizen," as David Walker had done in his *Appeal*. "We have not addressed you as citizens," he explains, "a term desired and even cherished by us—because such you have never been."[65] For Delany, the only individuals who are legitimate political actors are those descriptively defined by the Constitution, for they constitute "an essential part of the ruling element of the country in which they live." That is, since the Constitution expresses the concrete existence of the people and is the only source of legitimate power (the embodiment of what Delany calls the "sovereign principle"), it follows that there can be no other conception of the people that is not already determined by the Constitution.[66] These are, as he says, the facts that we must squarely confront.

DOUGLASS AND THE PRINCIPLE OF FAITH

Douglass's thinking contrasts sharply with Delany's, but especially what he lays out in his famous Fourth of July address. Douglass delivers the address only several months after the publication of *Condition*. This is his signature speech precisely because it so powerfully captures both his critical relationship to the American polity and his profound sense of faith in it. Let me briefly sketch some of the relevant elements of the address before turning to an analysis of it.

Three features mark the first portion of the address: a meditation on the revolutionary spirit of 1776; an understanding of the uncertainty surrounding the Founders' political vision; and a characterization of that vision. All these elements, quite importantly, are part of Douglass's efforts to ingratiate himself with his audience so as to put them in a receptive frame of mind. To the first, he tells his mostly white audience, "This, for the purpose of this celebration, is the 4th of July. It is the birthday of your National Independence, and of your political freedom. This, to you, is what the Passover was to the emancipated people of God. It carries your minds back to that day, and to the act of your great deliverance." There is, he says, "hope in the thought" of America's youth—in its potential to grow into a nation worthy of the Founders' sacrifice.[67] To the second, Douglass insists that his audience orient themselves properly to the ground of uncertainty upon which the Founders stood. He distinguishes between the outlook of the Founders and the presumptions of his own time: "But your fathers, who had not adopted the fashionable idea of this day, of the infallibility of government, and the absolute character of its acts, presumed to differ from the home government in respect to the wisdom and the justice of some of those burdens and restraints." There was no good reason to believe that they were right or would win the day. "To say *now*," Douglass continues, "that America was right, and England wrong, is exceedingly easy. . . . It is fashionable to do so; but there was a time when to pronounce against England, and in favor of the cause of the colonies, tired men's souls."[68] Third, they were animated by a cause expressed in the Declaration of Independence that Douglass refers to as the "RING-BOLT to the chain of your nation's destiny."[69]

With those tributes of the past in place, Douglass shifts to the second portion of his address: "My business, if I have any here to-day, is with the present. . . . We have to do with the past only as we can make it useful to the present and to the future." He invokes Henry Longfellow's romantic poem of 1839, "A Psalm of Life"—"Trust no future, however pleasant, / Let the dead past bury its dead; / Act, act in the living present, / Heart within, and god overhead."[70] But we might also hear the echo of Jefferson: the "earth belongs in usufruct to the living." In this section of his address, Douglass famously underscores the "hypocrisy" at the heart of the American polity. The second-person pronoun stands in sharp contrast to its first-person counterpart: "This Fourth of July is *yours*, not *mine*. *You* may rejoice, *I* must mourn."[71] His staging of a national independence that his white fellows enjoy, but from which his people are excluded, reveals a nation divided within itself. This stands as a testament to the ignoble character of the polity. The fact of slavery not only defines the past and present but will deform the future: "Whether we turn to the declarations of the past, or to the profession of the present, the conduct of the nation seems equally hideous and revolting. America is false to the past, false to the present, and solemnly binds herself to be false to the future."[72] Here Douglass recalls ideas from an earlier time—thoughts that often darkened his spirit and troubled his outlook. Writing from Ireland in 1846, Douglass remarks in his letter to William Lloyd Garrison: "In thinking of America, I sometimes find myself admiring her bright blue sky—her grand old woods—her fertile fields— her beautiful rivers—her mighty lakes, and star-crowned mountains. But my rapture is soon checked, my joy is soon turned to mourning. When I remember that *all* is cursed with the infernal spirit of slaveholding."[73]

Douglass concludes his Fourth of July address on a very different note. "I do not despair of this country. . . . I, therefore, leave off where I began, with hope. Drawing encouragement from the Declaration of Independence, the great principles it contains, and the genius of American Institutions, my spirit is also cheered by the obvious tendencies of the age."[74] Given his understanding of the American polity—its character and culture as they relate to the standing of black people—why conclude in this way?

The reason is that Douglass holds fast to the idea that he can put the revolutionary spirit of 1776 in the service of a racially just society that has

never before defined American life. In this, Douglass's invocation of Longfellow's poem is far more significant than we might first think. The young
man of the poem seeks help from neither God nor the psalmist to whom
he speaks; rather, it is in himself he finds his great and creative powers for
living, reminded only by the "lives of great men." From them, Longfellow's
young man discovers that "we can make our lives sublime" and create in its
wake "footprints" in which others, tempted by life's disappointments, may
nonetheless "take heart again."[75]

This is the model Douglass appropriates as he redeploys the revolutionary spirit of 1776. The Founders, Douglass says, "have lived, died, and
have done their work, and have done much of it well," but their children
have not. "You live and must die," Douglass says, "and you must do your
work."[76] He distinguishes between the Founders and those in the present.
He does so to insist that white Americans earn their claim to the valuable
past (i.e., the revolutionary legacy of the Founders and the freedom it made
possible) by how well they respond to the present. For Douglass, the revolutionary spirit is the power for making and remaking society. He draws
on the people as aspiration, grounding his view of the plasticity of human
nature in the normative infrastructure of American ethical and political
life (the footprint, we might say, of those who came before). Together,
these two features open out on to the creative possibility for reimagining America, as the Founders once imagined their future. Douglass thinks
that inhabiting that revolutionary spirit and putting it in the service of a
racially just society will be so compelling that his fellows will want to take
it up. Similar to the Founders of old, he too does not know if it will work,
and he has good reason to believe that it will not. And yet, he has faith the
nation will become something other than what it is.

Admittedly, sometimes it is Douglass's religious commitments at work
informing his faith. Writing, for example, in the wake of the *Dred Scott*
decision, he tells us that Justice Taney "may decide, and decide again; but
he cannot reverse the decision of the Most High. He cannot change the
essential nature of things—making evil good, and good evil."[77] Similar to
David Walker, Douglass speaks, as he often does, in his prophetic voice,
pronouncing truths, providing warnings, and imagining anew. Other
times it is Douglass's vision of human nature that underwrites his faith.
"While man is constantly liable to do evil," he tells us in 1851, "he is still
capable of apprehending and pursuing that which is good."[78] This is Douglass's belief in the malleability of human nature that supports its growth
and development. On this point, he also insists that the mere fact of our
elasticity does not mean we will develop in a direction that unifies and

harmonizes humanity. Proper development often requires appropriate cultivation.

In this sense, and more consistently, it is Douglass's specific idea of America that is the source of his faith. Whatever he hopes for seems to have no other ground than this idea itself. Hope draws encouragement from the ideas of the Declaration of Independence—the dominant symbol of the American imaginary—but this is wholly normative in character rather than empirical in Delany's sense of things. For Douglass, then, hope and faith come together in a way that contrasts with how it came together for Delany, and mirrors Hebrews 11:1: "Now faith is the substance of things hoped for, the evidence of things not seen." The Declaration is the great "ring-bolt" of the nation's destiny, but its lived meaning anchors itself in a vision of the United States that does not yet exist. This is why the Declaration, for Douglass, serves as a guide.

We must read these last two sentences with care. Douglass does not assimilate his thinking to the Founders, which he is now claiming to be incomplete in its expression.[79] This is the story (some will call it a lie) Americans often tell about the nation, its unfolding quest to inhabit that perfectly stated vision—its creed—that the nation has only imperfectly realized. This is the story to which someone like James Baldwin comes to direct his sharpest criticisms.

The assimilationist reading of Douglass, I think, wrongly attributes a naiveté to him regarding the centrality of racial disregard to American life and ultimately obscures the rhetorical framework in which he often works.[80] Recall, in the second section of Douglass's speech where he tells us he will deal with the present he criticizes the Founders of the past: *"Whether we turn to the declarations of the past, or to the profession of the present, the conduct of the nation seems equally hideous and revolting."*[81] The past for him is only as useful as those portions of it that can be made to serve the present, and he encourages his audience to take note that the political actors of the past are not without fault. This should bring to mind Longfellow's poem once again: we take heart as we consider the footprints of the past, but we are not meant to walk in the shoes of our ancestors. Or, we might recall Jefferson's language of the barbarous ancestors, whose regimen we must escape if we mean to do right by the claims of our own time.

What, then, is Douglass doing? How ought we to understand his relationship to the Founders? As I read him, imagining a racially just polity, as he did, reflexively shapes his faith into an articulation of claims that stand outside because they exceed the political and ethical configuration of the descriptive people. This much Douglass suggests about his relationship to the principles of the nation in an address of 1853: "But for my poor people enslaved—blasted and ruined—it would appear that America had neither justice, mercy nor religion. She has no scales in which to weigh our wrongs—she has no standard by which to measure our rights. Just here lies the difficulty of my cause. It is found in the fact that we may not avail ourselves of admitted American principles."[82]

Relying on the Declaration and the Founders creates a common context of concern between Douglass and his audience. This is his "rhetorical and communicative settings" and the context of legitimation.[83] We have seen this before in Walker, and Du Bois in chapters 6 and 7 will provide us with a more formalized understanding of the workings of rhetoric. This rhetorical context is what gives his speech the *appearance* of a narrative of decline—the Founders were great because of their principles, but you in the present are not because you have strayed from the path of righteousness. But he deploys the Declaration not as white Americans understand it (what they *admit* those principles to mean in both the past and present and of which black people cannot avail themselves) but rather to recast the citizenry's understanding of those principles altogether to reshape what the polity might become. Douglass is demanding that white Americans in the present earn their "rich inheritance of . . . liberty,"[84] but he reinterprets the ethical content of liberty so that its proper workings benefit both white and black people.[85]

This reimagining of freedom will be familiar. This is what Douglass is after when he discusses black *unfreedom* as being a "slave of the community" (in 1848) or the "slave of society at large" (in 1855).[86] He is not principally interested in seeing freedom as a response to institutional practices of arbitrary power that denies to persons the standing they otherwise had (think, for example, of the Founders' reasons for revolting from the British Crown and why they are to be applauded). Rather, he demands that freedom address a form of arbitrary power that denies that persons were fit to have standing at all in the community. As Sharon Krause powerfully puts the point of Douglass: the efficacy of individual initiative "is always contingent both on material conditions and on social reception, on how other people understand and respond to the initiatives that individuals begin."[87] This, of course, is bound to the standing of persons—to showing proper regard for them. In other words, Douglass is concerned about the cultural life of the polity and the centrality of racial disregard to it. Douglass's faith-based claim is one that imagines, to use Gooding-Williams's language, a "radical reconstruction" of the ethical basis of American life as it relates to the standing of black people.[88]

COOPER AND THE STRUCTURE OF FAITH

Only a few short decades later, we see a more formal account of the earlier Douglass-esque version of faith that sharpens its relationship to political life. Anna Julia Cooper—former slave, activist, and historian by training—sees faith as neither a proper interpretative enterprise of scripture nor a process of stabilizing theological certainties. She provides us with a formal structure to faith that I am suggesting is latent in Douglass's thinking.

Cooper is significant because her writings develop during two parallel crises that defined the late nineteenth and early twentieth centuries. In the Gilded Age, Americans' commitment to progress was laced with feelings of spiritual malaise and the cold realization of the growing development of economic inequality. The erosion of religious authority led to a kind of spiritual sickness—not merely an estrangement from a stable theological order containing moral direction but a sense that no such order existed in the Gilded Age. In one sense, this stimulated the Social Gospel movement in the last three decades of the nineteenth century and its aim to tie Christianity to social reform and institutional transformation. It also explains the drift of writings in the 1870s and 1880s from other American theologians seeking to reconcile evolution of the species with some brand of moral progressivism.[89] But Cooper is also important because her writings develop during one of the darker periods of black life in America—what we call the nadir of American race relations as white men (mostly) grappled with what they perceived as the weakening of their standing and as black people lived at the arbitrary mercy of white resentment. Standing well on the other side of the Civil War, Cooper confronts a period, not unlike Delany and Douglass, in which the nation affirmed the unequal standing of black people.

This produced different responses by African Americans. Some, like prominent black journalist T. Thomas Fortune, paid careful attention to the imbrication of racial domination and economic exploitation. This, Fortune maintained in his 1884 work, *Black and White: Land, Labor, and Politics in the South*, required more focused attention on the class position of black people. "The future struggle in the South," he argued, "will be, not between white men and black men, but between capital and labor, landlord and tenant."[90] This would not be his final position, but at this moment, he prefigured the full-throated socialism of A. Philip Randolph and Chandler Owen, even if they ultimately offered far more radical reforms. In others, say minister Henry McNeal Turner, you get a brand of pessimism that recalls Delany and prefigures Marcus Garvey. Writing in

1895, he argues: "I believe that the Negroid race has been free long enough now to begin to think for himself and plan for better conditions than he can lay claim to in this country or ever will. *There is no manhood future in the United States for the Negro.*"[91]

Despite the different approaches, American citizens (white and black) were running on two parallel tracks, each terminating in a crisis of faith. White Americans struggled to stabilize meaning and an ethic of care against the encroachments of capitalism, leading American philosopher John Dewey to say in 1904: "If our civilization is to be directed, we must have such a concrete and working knowledge of the individual as will enable us to furnish on the basis of the individual. . . . substitutes for those modes of nurture, of restraint and of control which in the past have been supplied from authorization supposedly fixed outside of and beyond individuality."[92] Black Americans struggled to survive amid the ruins of Reconstruction and the forceful reassertion of racial disregard and violence. While some turned inward, others searched for the light of care in the eyes of their fellows.[93] In the 1880s, even Douglass found it difficult to hold on to the faith that steeled him in the 1850s. Hence W.E.B. Du Bois could say in 1903: "Merely a concrete test of the underlying principles of the great republic is the Negro Problem, and the spiritual striving of the freed-men's sons is the travail of souls whose burden is almost beyond the measure of their strength."[94] The first group struggled to provide itself with its own inner strength and ethical vision, and one choice by African Americans was to use faith to fortify their souls and imagine beyond the horror of the present.

The response to this shared plight—a crisis of faith—even if stimulated by different reasons, is best captured in the philosophical pragmatism of the late nineteenth century. I do not have in mind what passes for the traditional figures—Williams James or John Dewey—but that of Cooper. In her magisterial text *A Voice from the South* of 1892, Cooper focuses on the lives of black people, but especially of black women. The philosophical infrastructure of her text—indeed her thinking—can be distilled into several components that later pragmatists make central to their own thinking, even if not by way of Cooper: (1) anti-foundationalism, (2) contextualism, and (3) faith.[95] Cooper rejects a form of knowledge that places its foundations beyond critique and evaluation. She sees knowledge as a function of our interactions with the wider environments in which we are located and she thus privileges contextualism. Contextualism is a means by which we take a broad survey of the landscape in our quest to claim our beliefs as candidates for being true. Contextualism thus intensifies the necessity of perceptual responsiveness. Her anti-foundationalism and contextualism come together in a striking way. As she writes in the preface, reflecting on the failure to listen to black women, if we are to have a clear understanding, the "truth from *each* standpoint [should] be presented at the bar. . . . The 'other side' has not been represented by one who 'lives there.' And not many can more sensibly realize and more accurately tell the weight and the fret of the 'long dull pain' than the open-eyed but hitherto voiceless Black Woman of America."[96] Black women are an important case study by which Cooper advances the need to take one's embodied existence and experiences seriously as we quest after knowledge and advance truth claims about our communities and the people who inhabit them.

These features are important to how Cooper thinks about the resources of faith. Our vision of a good that does not yet exist will often be drawn from who we take ourselves to be and the resources of our community. But they do not finally provide faith with empirical warrant, she argues in her last chapter, "The Gain from a Belief." There Cooper lays out a vision of faith that not only captures Douglass's thinking of an earlier time but prefigures much of what comes later both in African American political thought and the tradition of philosophical pragmatism. "I do not mean by faith," she writes, "the holding of correct views and unimpeachable opinions on mooted questions, merely; nor do I understand it to be the ability to forge cast-iron formulas and dub them TRUTH."[97] Rather, faith involves submitting oneself to a vision of life that one projects into a world at variance with that vision and for which one is willing to act. In this regard, faith *is* a reality for its holders, for it orients them in space and moves them through time, influencing their ethical and political choices. This is what Cooper has in mind when she says, "faith means *treating the truth as true*."[98]

There are three points to observe about this gnomic line that recall my earlier comments about the philosophical infrastructure of her thinking. First, "truth" here is not capitalized as it was previously and therefore is not, on Cooper's view, unassailable. Second, for that reason treating the truth of one's faith as true means that it stands within our practices of inquiry and therefore is susceptible to doubt and error.[99] Third, treating the truth of one's faith as true entails a commitment to and investment in one's faith; these features (i.e., commitment and investment) potentially create the conditions for faith's realization. This last point disciplines the first two in order to guard against insisting on a strict evidentiary standard for grounding one's faith (more on this below).

Some of what Cooper is doing in that final chapter of her book—a text that is ostensibly concerned with addressing the themes of patriarchy, white supremacy, and racial uplift in the era of Jim Crow—is arguing against philosophical skepticism. But she is also trying, and here now is the connection to Delany and Douglass, to make sense of the necessity of holding a belief as true as a precondition for securing its place in the world. Here, she has in mind most immediately the orientation of former slaves. We can say she has in mind someone like Douglass:

> The slave brother, however, from the land of oppression once saw the celestial beacon and dreamed not that it ever deviated from due North. He *believed* that *somewhere* under its beckoning light, lay a far away country where a man's a man. He sets out with his heavenly guide before his face—would you tell him he is pursuing a wandering light? Is he the poorer for his ignorant hope? Are you the richer for your enlightened suspicion?[100]

There is no way to speak of the slave brother's belief, to borrow Robert Adams's language, as "proportionate to the strength of the evidence" supporting it.[101] As such, Cooper's use of "ignorant" denotes the fact that "the slave brother" is without the knowledge to secure his hope. Her point is that in a world where holding a belief depended on whether the strength of the evidence was favorable, we would find a great many things unrealized, including, perhaps, living in a society that affirms rather than denies one's standing. Per the title of the essay, this is what Cooper calls "the gain from a belief."

We hear the echo of this account of faith when James says of the term in 1897, "Faith is the readiness to act in a cause the prosperous issue of which is not certified to us in advance."[102] There is a difference, then, between what John Dewey (and Douglass, Cooper, and James before him) refers to as "belief that is a conviction that some end *should* be supreme over conduct and belief that some object . . . exists as truth for the intellect."[103] By this, Dewey explicitly intended to treat certain kinds of belief as imaginative possibilities (i.e., aspirations) that political actors believe ought to organize the lives of their fellows and in which they invest their energies.

We can make two observations based on Douglass's thinking and the structure of faith articulated by Cooper and others. Douglass rejects Delany's idea of the burden of historical inegalitarianism. He refuses to remove the human element from the facts of American history. He thinks that since the human element is not the sort of thing that is fixed once and for all, there is no reason to think that the future need only repeat the past. As a result, Douglass rejects the presumptive propensity for illegitimate hierarchy as a necessary feature of human nature and so, in turn, its immovable expression in racial hierarchy as the foundation of American society. He refuses to accept the foundation of Delany's hopelessness by raising doubts about how he characterizes the context of those capable of hoping in the first place.

The second and more important observation relates to the epistemic differences between Delany and Douglass's views regarding the struggle of African Americans. This connects to the formal character of faith that explicitly animates Cooper, James, and Dewey. There is a difference between a belief that is a conviction that some end should guide conduct (Dewey's language), say, for example, belief in the realizability of a racially just polity, and a belief that exists as truth for the intellect, say, for example, that the Sun will rise in the East and set in the West, where that claim depends on a constellation of facts about the rotational axis of the Earth. For Douglass, the first kind of belief, the one he holds given the problem of white supremacy, must function as a precondition for political engagement. This is what he thinks Delany misses about the logic of struggle in which black people find themselves. In other words, Douglass's belief must run ahead of the evidence needed to sustain it in a way that will never square itself with Delany's strict evidentiary demand. This is not a rejection of empiricism by Douglass; rather, he does not accord it imperial standing in ethical and political matters. As Cooper might put it: Is Douglass the poorer for holding the belief that he does? Is Delany the richer for his pessimism?

Here, then, is Douglass and Cooper's point. In seeking to convert one's belief into a matter of intellectual assent—a feature of political reality that is "as glaring as the rays of a noon-day's sun" to use Delany's metaphorical standard—we often reject faith as a condition for political engagement. And yet the latter more accurately reflects the fact that we do not exercise ultimate control over those to whom we appeal and on whose responses we often depend. So, for Douglass and Cooper, the illusion is not in thinking that one must rely on faith in political life but in believing that one can get on living in a democratic society without it.

The People and Constituent Power
beyond Constitutionalism

The idea of faith discussed in the last section helps us understand the connection that obtains between political legitimacy and the aspirational view of the people. The worry was that our commitment is bound to a future that may never come. The exchange between Delany and Douglass shows that there is no way to escape this danger but that it is nonetheless necessary to realize a vision of political and social life that does not yet exist. In other words, the companion dispositional orientation toward the aspirational view of the people is faith in its realization.

The other problem with invocations of the people has to do with confusion about the meaning of constituent power that obscures its ethical character and, instead, focuses on its formal constitutional dimension. The problem is best captured in Andreas Kalyvas's otherwise insightful essay, "Popular Sovereignty, Democracy, and the Constituent Power." There Kalyvas argues for an alternative form of sovereignty that rejects identifying it with command and coercion as bound up in, let us say, the figure of the king, and rather associates it with the collective process of production and creation.[104] The former remains trapped in the domain of unconditional power, while the latter moves us into the sphere of conditionality that reflects the process of contestation informing the internal dynamics of "the multitude," "the Community," "the People," "the Nation."[105] The first fundamental trait of constituent power, Kalyvas explains, is located in its "positing aspect."

> From the perspective of the constitutive act, the sovereign is the one who makes the constitution and establishes a new political and legal order. . . . The sovereign is the original author of a new constitutional order and sovereignty *qua* constituting power manifests itself in a genuine process of constitutional making as supra-legislative power enacting fundamental laws.[106]

As I read him, we see the materiality of constituent power in the process by which the sovereign creates new political and legal norms. It is the process of "legislating," says Kalyvas, that expresses constituent power.[107]

The problem with this account is that it too narrowly construes constituent power's expression. More precisely, this account threatens to render meaningless the actions of those marginalized groups who rely on constituent power to reconfigure the ethical life of the community. How, on Kalyvas's account, do we make sense of the appeals made by Walker, Easton, and Douglass? On what does someone like James Baldwin, as we will see much later, rely in order to resist collapsing the meaning of America with its racist legal and political practices? If we accept Kalyvas's account of constituent power as it is, we will be denied a means to explain the extra- but nonlegal approaches often taken by these thinkers that intend to reconstitute society on a deeper level than can be expressed in constitutional norms. As Jonathan White and Lea Ypi explain, "Conceiving the people as a practical enactment is instructive in empirical terms because it helps us to make sense of the many everyday political contexts in which ideas of 'the people' are invoked as a rallying cry."[108] I do not mean to deny that American history, for example, is punctured by critical moments of radical change at the level of constitutional development. From the Founding to Reconstruction to the New Deal to the civil rights movement, each of these moments launched a new regime, with transformed baseline values.[109] Nonetheless, we would do well not to identify those moments as the exclusive expression of constituent power.[110] We need only, then, expand our understanding of the workings of constituent power—an expansion that finds historical support in the thinkers we have thus far considered—in order to do justice to the hidden voices that seek to imagine society anew.

The additional effect of doing this is that it allows us to take seriously substantive ruptures between the past and present that defenders of constituent power seem unable to address. After all, how should we understand the ethical visions offered in the name of the people? Do they refer, in Jürgen Habermas's language, to an "untapped normative substance of the system of rights laid down in the original document of the constitution"?[111] Or do they entail a more profound transformation, whose aim is to reshape the ethical character of the polity itself that is discontinuous with the intentions of constitutional framers?

Habermas's language emerges in the context of addressing the paradox of founding at the heart of democratic theory, the belief that a constitutional assembly, for instance, "cannot itself vouch for the legitimacy of the rules according to which it was constituted."[112] This paradox leads, in Habermas's understanding, to an "infinite regress" in trying to ascertain legitimate foundations. I am less interested in the paradox itself that democratic theorists delight in and more concerned with the solution Habermas offers and what this proposal means for understanding the thinkers discussed in this book. It is worth citing him at length, to put on full display the philosophical slippage at the core of his thinking:

> I prefer not to meet this objection [that is, the paradox of founding] by recourse to the transparent objectivity of ultimate moral insights that are supposed to bring the regress to a halt. Rather than appeal to moral realism that would be hard to defend, I propose that we understand the regress itself as the understandable expression of the future-oriented character, or openness, of the democratic constitution: in my view, a

constitution that is democratic—not just in its content but also according to its source of legitimation—is a tradition-building project with
a clearly marked beginning in time. All the later generations have the
task of actualizing the still-untapped normative substance of the system
of rights laid down in the original document of the constitution. . . . To
be sure, this fallible continuation of the founding event can break out
of the circle of a polity's groundless discursive self-constitution only if
this process . . . can be understood in the long run as a self-correcting
learning process.[113]

Observe that Habermas opens the passage by rejecting moral realism but
then concludes by interpreting the transcendent ethical vision of later
generations as actualizing a latent, untapped normative substance. The
ethical visions on offer do not put in place something absent; rather, they
bring what is there, at a morally primitive level, to fruition. The learning process Habermas references at the end of the passage denotes the
acquisition of an ethical vision that is implicit. This most certainly sounds
like the position of a moral realist. We can allay any doubts regarding
my reading by attending to the line of consistency that Habermas draws
through history, uniting both constitutional founders and reformers: "All
participants must be able to recognize the project as *the same* throughout
history and to judge it from *the same perspective*."[114] Hence the historical
grounding of the moment of progress, at least for Americans, turns out to
be the 1787 constitutional convention in Philadelphia.

If Kalyvas's account seems to sideline the thinkers with which we are
concerned, Habermas muddles the descriptive and aspirational dimensions of the people and, in turn, leaves us unable to confront the ethical
rupture at the core of the American polity.[115] What, for instance, would it
mean for Walker or Douglass or Du Bois to "start with the same standards
as the founders" or to judge the American project from "the same perspective"? After all, and as we have seen in Walker and Douglass specifically,
it was precisely the ethical basis of social life that these thinkers hoped
to redescribe. The aim was to make the polity inclusive in two related
domains: the juridical and ethical spheres of American life.

There is an important observation here to track. Making American
society inclusive did not amount to bringing to fruition the "untapped normative substance of the system of rights laid down in the original document of the constitution"; rather, it involved a reconfiguration of who was
taken or seen as subjects of rights in the first place. This reconfiguration
involved creating relationships among persons—blacks and whites—not

previously permitted and talking about and living those relationships in different ways. We abandon the idea that a system of rights is maturing and we also avoid valorizing the Founders, while treating subsequent political actors as struggling to move into closer proximity to them. We avoid the odd characterization in which progress is measured by our proximity to political actors of the past. Instead, we come to think of the polity as transforming, and this transformation involves new semantic and experiential content for understanding who are the subjects of rights.[116] On this reading, we no longer draw a line of historical consistency that ties the descriptive and aspirational views of the people together. Rather, we acknowledge that the political-ethical world that someone like Walker, Douglass, or Du Bois envisioned is radically different from the one on offer by the Founders.[117] This does not mean breaking with history, as James Baldwin will tell us; rather, it means "one enters into battle with that historical creation, Oneself, and attempts to recreate oneself according to a principle more humane and more liberating; one begins the attempt to achieve a level of personal maturity and freedom which robs history of its tyrannical power, and also changes history."[118]

This is the moment of rupture. It allows us to do proper justice to the distinctive voice of African Americans that is more than a reiteration of what the Founders desired. It also allows us to take seriously the scars of mistreatment and disregard—the trauma—that haunt the present. Writing in the wake of the Civil War and the collapse of Reconstruction, Douglass describes this haunting as the "left behind influences" of slavery and rebellion, and Du Bois refers to it as the "shadow of deep disappointment [that] rests upon the Negro people."[119] Both insist that we must act in the present in light of the past. But both ask us to recognize that the present will always contain the unaltered memory of pain and disregard; the present bears the imprimatur of the irrevocable character of past wrongs. The fate of the future, then, will largely depend on society's ability to reckon with the past, without insisting on absolution. In such a society, living a shared life *is* imaginable and progress *is* possible. However, they both may depend on America abandoning its long sought-after quest of achieving redemption from its sins.

———◆———

I have argued that two related accounts of the people underwrite the political and ethical appeals for a racially just society. The thinkers we have thus far considered recognize those described by the Constitution.

They also insist that we see the legitimacy of the polity as always standing in excess of those who claim to speak in its name. For unless the polity is always perfectly structured, they demand that we think about our allegiance as attached to a figuration of society that does not yet exist. This is the two bodies of the people—its descriptive and aspirational forms.

This presupposition structured the outlook of those of part 1 of this book but was not arbitrary. It formed part of the central normative logic of the American polity whose greatest defender was Thomas Jefferson. The nineteenth-century African American thinkers we have considered were not merely relying on a rich conception of human nature to justify their appeals to their white counterparts but rightly believed that their understanding of the malleability of their fellows fit within the normative infrastructure of republicanism. On this view, white supremacy and racial domination may well be part of the cultural life of American society, but they need not exhaust what the polity may become.

If we retrace our steps, the aspirational idea of the people was not without problems. The principal issue was the tendency to think about the workings of constituent power through the narrow lens of constitutionalism. This view failed to take seriously how constituent power is deployed outside the horizon of the institutional forms of republicanism and often by those seeking to remake the cultural life of a community. By focusing narrowly on constitutionalism as the site of constituent power, we obscure altogether the wider use of the aspirational idea of the people. In our quest to see the iterative process of political life as coming closer to the founding vision, we also risk ignoring altogether the rupture that exists between the past and those seeking to reimagine the future.

The other problem with the aspirational view of the people is the uncertainty that attends it. This is the sense in which our allegiance seems attached to a figuration of the people that may never arrive. In taking up this issue, I focused on the importance of faith. Faith involves committing oneself to a vision of life that is at odds with the empirical reality of society but for which one is willing to struggle to realize. Faith exists in excess of the facts needed to sustain it. Faith is the comportment one assumes toward the aspirational idea of the people.

To draw us back to Delany and Douglass, you might think, "Douglass's position is just nonsense. If you follow Douglass, it involves black people holding beliefs that are simply unreasonable for them to hold about their white counterparts. If black people use faith-based beliefs to structure and organize their ethical and political dealings with the polity, they will unwittingly tether themselves to an irredeemably unjust polity." From this perspective, black people will find themselves holding ideas of an imaginary society—a society to come—while the real American society leaves them open to disregard at best and premature death at worst.

There is much sense in this worry. It was part of Delany's thinking and informs a complicated thread of African American political and literary thought, from Henry McNeal Turner to Marcus Garvey and Ann Petry to Mittie Maude Lena Gordon to Malcolm X to Stokely Carmichael and contemporary defenders of Afro-pessimism. As Carmichael remarked in his famous Black Power speech at Berkeley in 1966, representing a shift in vision and leadership of the Student Nonviolent Coordinating Committee, and sounding very much like Delany more than a century earlier: "we've always moved in the field of morality and love while people have been politically jiving with our lives. And the question is how do we move politically and stop trying to move morally?"[120] Of course, Carmichael was to King (in one sense) what Delany was to Douglass.

I will not claim that the faith-holders can finally alleviate this worry. This, of course, is the issue; it continues to haunt us. Living in the reconstructed image of Matthew Arnold's *Stanzas from the Grande Chartreuse*, the faith-holders often wander between two societies. One is the evidence of a racially unjust society that they believe cannot long live. The other is the disparate and incoherent pieces of a racially just society that struggles to be fully rendered into a coherent pattern of life. The claims of the faith-holders will always appear to be on shaky ground to those who seemingly believe that the motivation for political struggle and transformation is settled by the facts at hand. This is also why doubt tempts the faith-holders; it tries their souls and thus requires courage as its executive virtue.[121] To say faith-based claims are beliefs is to say the danger of being mistaken is always present. But beliefs held in the absence of a full grounding in facts—the full-throated empiricism of Delany—will always appear unreasonable to those who think they hold the facts.

An observation presents itself at precisely this moment. I do not think faith-holders are naïve. Douglass, for example, seemed just as realistic about America's past and present, although he did not engage in the ontologizing of history that we observed in Delany. Douglass might be thought to hold a true realism for just this reason. He was clear that America's past was bleak and seemed quite clear that the prospect for the future was dim; he was no optimist. "America," he said in the Fourth of July address, "is false to the past, false to the present, and solemnly binds herself to be false to the future." Here, this binding of itself—this falsity that persists into America's future—is Douglass way of talking about the irrevocable deed of white supremacy and human enslavement that will run alongside any deed done to redress it. Given this way of seeing things, his faith was not reasonable at all. Perhaps this is the often-unstated point about political struggle. "A reasonable man," Toni Morrison tells us in her essay "Moral Inhabitants," "adjusts to his environment. And [sic] unreasonable man does not."[122] Or to avoid the declarative, we might ask, when has a radical change in the political and ethical life of a community ever come about because of reasonable people?

This allows us to entertain another observation. I am often struck by claims that white supremacy is fundamental to the polity and that anti-blackness defines America. I am struck not because these things are not true—they are—but because they are often presented as exhausting the normative logic of American life. This was Delany's way of thinking. But the question of what America "really" is, the aspirational idea of the people suggests, defies articulation, even as we struggle to say something substantive about our ethical and political identity. When Delany framed his inquiry as having figured out what America really is—that is, its condition—the struggle against racial domination could only appear as external to or alien to America's ethical and political life. Struggle could not appear, as Douglass hoped it would, as those parts of the richness and beauty of American life trying to win the day. Douglass's position was not wholly unhinged from the ethos of American life, even if it located itself within the normative foundation that underwrites the polity. Those who follow Douglass are less interested in figuring out what America really is and are rather concerned with how to get the people to embrace a higher view of itself as it relates to the ethical and political standing of black people. One such possibility is to confront the nation with the horrors it has created.

CHAPTER FIVE

Lynching and the Horrific

FROM IDA B. WELLS TO BILLIE HOLIDAY

They [citizens of Wisconsin and Missouri] had never heard of Billie
Holiday, let alone "Strange Fruit."... They had never heard anything
remotely like this.... I remember one girl just broke down and started
sobbing. I was propagandizing, spreading the word. It made an impact
on people. For the first time in their lives it made them think about the
lynching victims as humans, as people.

—WARREN MORSE, QUOTED IN *STRANGE FRUIT:*
THE BIOGRAPHY OF A SONG

ONE OF THE HORRIFIC IMAGES in American history is of a "black body
swinging in the southern breeze." Abel Meeropol—a Jewish American—
first wrote the line in his 1937 published poem, "Bitter Fruit,"[1] after viewing Lawrence Beitler's graphic and horrific photo depicting the lynching
of J. Thomas Shipp and Abram Smith (fig. 1). Although Meeropol eventually put the words to music, jazz singer Billie Holiday's haunting rendition
of the song, now titled "Strange Fruit," first recorded in 1939, made it a
classic.[2]

The shift from *bitter* to *strange*—it is not clear why the title changed—
marks an important transition in understanding the meaning of lynching in
America. Meeropol's initial use of "bitter" captures the image's unsavory quality. "Bitter" brings to mind a harsh, disagreeably acrid taste.[3] And yet, the com-
monness of black bodies hanging from trees between the late nineteenth and
first third of the twentieth century explains, perhaps implicitly, the necessity
of changing the title.[4] We might ask how *strange* that white Americans did
not find the visual spectacle of black suffering *bitter*. From the perspective

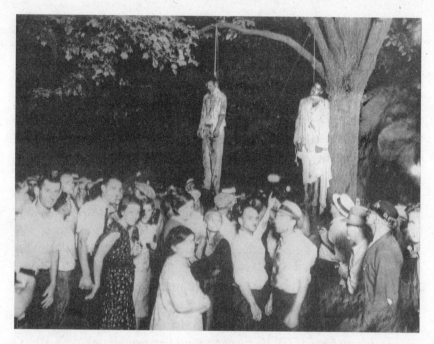

FIGURE 1. The lynching of J. Thomas Shipp and Abram Smith, Marion, Indiana, 1930. Photo courtesy of Indiana Historical Society, P0411.

of African Americans, the question itself marks the crisis at the heart of American ethical life—a form of distance between the races that permits white Americans to cannibalize their fellows as part of some twisted idea of ethical and political sustenance.

Lynching in America was not merely a violation of natural rights and human dignity. It was coextensive with and troubled the meaning of a democratic ethos. The swinging of black bodies in post-Reconstruction America was emblematic of an aesthetically charged spectacle much like we see in Beitler's photo that underscored the vulnerability of black life.[5] White Americans were socially habituated to the permissibility of black suffering. This raised a critical but familiar question: How does one practically and conceptually address the simultaneous existence of a professed commitment to equality and liberty alongside the fact that white Americans visually digested those with whom they otherwise shared the same space?

The horror of lynching, I want to suggest, provides insight into how African Americans sought to engage racial disregard and envision a healthy democratic ethos. I do not deploy horror as a literary genre. Horror refers to an emotional state that tracks, in different degrees, a mixture of fear, disgust, and our apparent powerlessness in the face of the object of our horror. I make no distinction between what Noel Carroll refers to as art-horror (say, the fictional and fantastical confrontations with vampires or zombies that stand outside reality) and natural-horror (say, the encounter with lynching and mutilation of human bodies that stand within the orbit of reality).[6] Sometimes the two correspond. In these cases, the aim is not to place perpetrators outside the sphere of humanity. The point is to indicate how the quest to maim and extinguish life transforms people. They are fantastical monsters, not of some fictionalized world but of our own—they live in us and next to us.

This was precisely what Ida B. Wells had in mind at the end of the nineteenth century as she investigated lynchings. In response to those who sought to diminish the centrality of racial hatred by pointing to the higher rates of white lynching versus black lynching, she writes the following: "The beast of prey [white people] which turns to destroy its own is not considered less, but more bloodthirsty and ferocious than when it preys on other animals. The taste for blood grows with indulgence, and when other means of satisfying it fail he turns to rend his own household."[7] Wells's goal, not unlike that of the antilynching campaign of the National Association for the Advancement of Colored People (NAACP) a decade or so later,[8] is to horrify the reader: white Americans who engage in lynching are bloodthirsty and ferocious. The ultimate aim of her mode of presentation, she says a year later, is transformation—"the creation of a healthy public sentiment."[9] Wells and others harnessed horror to remind people of their agency rather than treating it as something over which Americans exercise no control. They often did so by appealing to America's self-image—its sense of itself as a civilized and free society.

Using horror as a lens allows us to see the normative character of Holiday's performative rendition of Meeropol's song. The song aspires to capture America's imagination by deploying the very method that sustained and sanctioned black suffering—namely, the horrific spectacle. As Amy Wood notes of antilynching activity, "lynching opponents trusted the same assumptions about spectatorship that bolstered prolynching thought—that to see an event was to understand its truth."[10] Just as the lynching of black Americans was an event in which a sense of community formed, as white Americans joined together in a carnivalesque cultural experience to disregard the very notion of black security, Holiday attempts to foreground the spectacle of pain through a rhythmic counterweight.

In reading the song this way, I argue that Meeropol and Holiday attempt to reeducate the American public through the horrific. Reeducation foregrounds both process (i.e., method or approach deployed) and a normative presupposition. On the side of process, I make three points. First, it is an artistic and performative context that shapes the process of reeducating the audience. We see this in the words of the song and Holiday's performance of it. Second, when we combine the words with Holiday's dramaturgical displays, the entire enactment restages the lynching of black people as a form of suffering. It seeks to use the fact of consumed suffering (i.e., what marks the fruit's strangeness and therefore its horror) as a means for transforming the sensibilities of the public. Third, the aim—that is, the content of reeducation—is to properly align the public's intellectual and emotional senses with reality's demand. On the side of normative presupposition, the process cast into relief the proper conceptual register on which the song functions; it is a form of democratic protest in response to the summary murder of black people. Akin to Wells and the NAACP, Holiday reorders the hierarchy of value and black people's place therein. At the base of her appeal is a vision of a people not yet realized.

To help my interpretation of the song gain normative traction, I turn to a figure that, like Thomas Jefferson in the previous chapter, stands in a problematic relationship to black inequality: Walt Whitman. At times, black people function in his writings as dangers to the republic. His thinking oscillates between articulating an ambitious vision of an inclusive democracy and seeing black people as inescapably unfit for self-governance.[11] I do not deny his racism or argue that he explicitly or implicitly concerns himself with black people's suffering.

And yet, no thinker insisted as intensely as Whitman on binding aesthetics and democracy and seeing in the former a means to re-create the citizenry. In his edited 1876 *Democratic Vistas*, I argue, aspirations become possibilities insofar as they capture the people.[12] Whitman gives this point a formal character that places him within the horizon of earlier figures that accord aesthetics a central role in democratic development and prepares the way for understanding those that follow. Similar to my reading of Jefferson, Whitman functions as a proxy for a general way of thinking. To capture the people requires more than propositional reasoning. Instead, it involves an aesthetically limned engagement that paints a picture of self and society to which we become emotionally drawn or, as we will see, from which we might recoil.[13]

In the second section of the chapter, I turn to Wells and the NAACP to elucidate the textual and visual politics of antilynching activism of the late nineteenth and early twentieth centuries. Here we see horror deployed as part of a tactic of ethical transposition to redirect the gaze of criminality from black people toward their white counterparts. Against this backdrop, the power of "Strange Fruit" shines through. We can best understand the hope of the song through the aesthetic framework stipulated by Whitman. On the one hand, the song presupposes that the meaning of the people is unsettled and this bespeaks the openness of democracy; on the other, the piece and what Meerepol referred to as Holiday's "styling" of it aspire to engender aversion to black suffering by white Americans that continues the work of Wells and the NAACP.[14] Holiday claims for herself, her black fellows, and America the essential framing elements that many African Americans used for thinking about democratic development. The song's economy balances the horrific that necessitated the song's construction and the sense of hope that points toward the auditors' possible transformation.

Walt Whitman and the Democratic Aesthetic

Thomas Jefferson understood persuasion as essential to the aspirational view of the people. Walt Whitman provides persuasion with aesthetically charged content. This approach was not lost on Jefferson. "We are," explains Jefferson a century before *Democratic Vistas*, "wisely framed to be as warmly interested for a fictitious as for real personage. The field of imagination is thus laid open to our use and lessons may be formed to illustrate and carry home to the heart every moral rule of life."[15]

Neither Jefferson nor Whitman was alone in this regard. Thinkers used the image of enslaved people to move viewers to a position of ethical rectitude. We are, for example, reminded of David Walker or the slogan of the American Anti-Slavery Society: "KEEP IT BEFORE THE PEOPLE."[16] In his lectures on pictures of the 1860s, Frederick Douglass—the most photographed man in the nineteenth century—emphasized and insisted on the power of the image. He accords our "picture-making and picture-appreciating" capacities a central role in ethical and political development. As he says in a lecture delivered at Boston's Tremont Temple:

> As the moral and social influence of pictures, it would hardly be extravagant to say of it, what Moore has said of ballads, give me the making of a nation's ballads and I care not who has the making of its laws. The picture and the ballad are alike, if not equally social forces—the one reaching and swaying the heart by the eye, and the other by the ear.[17]

Douglass's point is extravagant (he never lost sight of the significance of laws and institutions), even if not wildly off the mark given the iconography of abolitionism and the importance of narrative form to the struggle for racial justice.[18] Whitman is thus symbolic of a period of American life in which aesthetics and the meaning of politics ran together.

As with Jefferson and Douglass, Whitman believes that our ethical and political reasoning is most potent when it ties the self's affective and reflective dimensions in one process. For all these thinkers, our affective states are value judgments about the world. This much Whitman suggests: "Long enough have the People been listening to poems in which common Humanity, deferential, bends low, humiliated, acknowledging superiors. But America listens to no such poems. Erect, inflated, and fully self-esteeming be the chant; and then America will listen with *pleased ears*."[19]

The human sensorium figures prominently in Whitman's writings: "I believe in the flesh and the appetites, / Seeing, hearing, feeling."[20] In the passage above, pleased ears express a latent possibility made manifest. The American self, in other words, is capable of responding affirmatively to practices that reject domination because that *is* America.

Whitman is extravagant in his characterization of the public philosophy of the United States. The domination of women, black people, and Native Americans was on full display. But his claim is overdrawn in another sense. His reflections too quickly encourage the belief in a coherent vision of the good already latent in American life. His social theory often veers off into a hazy commitment to some active mind that works in the background. All of this too easily slides into a story about American exceptionalism—an absorptive nationalism that imperializes America.[21]

More often, however, he is trying to elicit what he claims to be the case. In this regard, he and Douglass inhabit a similar rhetorical context. In this second sense, pleased ears presuppose an active process by the listener, what Whitman calls "supple and athletic minds" that meet the poet's, vocalist's, and orator's sound.[22] "The reader will always have his or her part to do," he says, "just as much as I have had mine."[23] This is both an ethical and a political position. The values of democracy stick, Whitman believes, when their endorsement emerges from within rather than being coerced.

A central question emerges in Whitman's deployment of aesthetics for political-philosophical ends. If a powerful picture of self and society can elicit a longing to be that self and inhabit that society, might the same logic generate aversion?

WHITMAN AND THE DEMOCRATIC SEER

In his classic 1927 work of political theory, *The Public and Its Problems*, John Dewey famously refers to Whitman as democracy's seer: "Democracy will come into its own for democracy is a name for a life of free and enriching communion. It had its seer in Walt Whitman."[24] Dewey's thinking and invocation of Whitman place them both in a tradition that emphasizes democracy's constitutive openness, what Whitman calls the "trying [of] continually new experiments."[25] This 1927 invocation of Whitman fits within the broader period of the 1920s, especially the artistic experimentalism of the Harlem Renaissance. As George Hutchinson has explained, thinkers such as Alain Locke, James Weldon Johnson, and Langston Hughes viewed Whitman as a harbinger of a new world—an aesthetic democracy to come.[26] Of course, Whitman's language lends support to thinking of him in this way:

> We have frequently printed the word Democracy. Yet I cannot too often repeat that it is a word the real gist of which still sleeps, quite unawakened, notwithstanding the resonance and the many angry tempests, out of which its syllables have come, from pen or tongue. It is a great word, whose history, I suppose, remains unwritten, because, that history has yet to be enacted.[27]

For Dewey, seer signifies a person possessing profound ethical or spiritual insight, the kind of perception distilled from one's experiential engagement with the world. The African American literary critic William Stanley Braithwaite refers to Whitman as "a spiritual artist and mystic."[28] Elsewhere, Dewey uses a word often deployed to describe the seer's activity—that is, as being *prophetic*. As he explains, "There is a prophetic aspect to all observation; we can perceive the meaning of what exists only as we forecast the consequences it entails."[29] Hence faith in the people, Whitman explains, depends not on "churches and creeds" if they turn our gaze away from the experience and demand of life but on the development of the "identified soul."[30]

In Whitman's case, the notion of prophetic (the workings of a bounded imagination) as well as the meaning of the soul (as that which is present but indeterminate) lead him to cast his democratic vistas as "speculations" or "suggestions"[31] about the future. "Democracy too," he explains, "is law, and of the strictest, amplest kind. . . . the law over all, and law of laws, is the law of successions; that of the superior law, in time, gradually supplanting and overwhelming the inferior one."[32] Because the law of succession points

LYNCHING AND THE HORRIFIC [183]

to what is unrealized, Whitman's writings function in a hortatory mode. It is philosophy as poetic ministry aimed at what George Kateb calls the soul's "potentiality."[33]

This should be familiar to us; it captures the vision of the soul we encountered in part 1. It will return in our reflections on W.E.B. Du Bois in the next two chapters. The language of "faith" and "soul" casts a wide historical net. From the 1830s to the 1870s to the 1920s, white and black thinkers and activists sought to articulate a non-transcendental account of faith that emphasized the imagination's prophetic power. However, they did so by tying the imaginative projection suggested by faith to the cultivation of the soul and both to democratic ends. Notably, this heightened the urgency for African Americans given the stakes—not merely of their flourishing but their very lives. But what both white and black thinkers often shared is the belief that political life is about tending to souls and thus forecasting—to use Dewey's language—a vision of American life that affirms both freedom and equal regard.

The question that is prominent in Whitman's writings (what prompts Braithwaite to see him as a mystic and Dewey to dub him as democracy's seer) is the following: How must we understand democracy to realize freedom and equality? Here is how Whitman answers:

> What I say in these Vistas has its main bearings on Imaginative Literature, especially Poetry, the stock of all. But in the region of imaginative spinal and essential attributes, something equivalent to creation is imperatively demanded. For not only is it not enough that the new blood, new frame of Democracy shall be vivified and held together merely by political means, superficial suffrage, legislation, etc., but it is clear to me that, unless it goes deeper, gets at least as firm and as warm a hold in men's hearts, emotions and belief, as, in those days of Feudalism or Ecclesiasticism, and inaugurates its own perennial sources, welling from the center forever, its strength will be defective, its growth doubtful, and its charm wanting.[34]

This passage occurs in the early portion of *Democratic Vistas* that sets the stage for the rest of the text. First, Whitman identifies democracy as extending beyond its legal and political apparatus. Second, he identifies art as the basis for eliciting a way of being democratic. Finally, he sees art as containing the possibility of informing our sensibilities—those associated with our cognitive and affective faculties—thus giving life to a new character.[35] Let us attend to the meaning of this passage.

ART AND INTERIORITY

In *Democratic Vistas*, aesthetics is a cooperative project in rearranging sense and sensibility and remaking character.[36] Why does Whitman understand art in this way? His answer relates directly to his understanding of democracy as something that enables agency and does so in the service of freedom and equality. These are, we might say for Whitman, the primary goods of democracy. But these goods are not strictly political, say in the sense that one might think of the right to vote and thus the good of sharing in power. He also has in mind something like our affections for and beliefs about social life that bind the citizenry to the values of liberty and equality. This is the sense in which Whitman speaks, as in the extended passage above, of a form of democracy that goes deeper and animates the citizenry's hearts and minds. He seems to think that unless we have this identitarian attachment to democracy, its political infrastructure will be insufficient.

Another way of putting the point of the previous paragraph is to say the following: Whitman wonders about Americans' ability to affirm the principles of freedom and equality when the law is silent and when government intervention is stilled. Behind this—indeed the motivation for writing *Democratic Vistas*—is Thomas Carlyle's 1867 *Shooting Niagara and After*. Carlyle wrote that essay in response to Britain's passage of the Reform Act of 1867 that expanded suffrage to working-class men.[37] For Carlyle, universal suffrage marked a decline and left society vulnerable to the masses.

In his response to Carlyle, Whitman reflects on the vitality of self-governance in the broadest sense. Whereas Carlyle dismisses the masses in favor of the aristocracy, Whitman concerns himself with engaging their capacities. This leads him to think about democracy beyond political and legal institutions and, instead, think about it on the level of habit. This is democracy understood at the level of ethos or what Whitman calls "culture." Consistent with the principle of equality, he explains that a democratic culture is not for "a single class alone." How far must it reach? "I should demand," he says, "of this programme or theory [of Culture] a scope generous enough to include the widest human area."[38]

In making culture central, Whitman is doing two things. First, he means for us to see democracy as a way of living (covering the widest human area). It is reproduced (or deformed) in a community's social learning. Second, crafting a culture of this kind is intended to remind the citizenry of its power in shaping their community and reshaping themselves. Like Jefferson or Douglass, for Whitman a democratic ethos involves an attitude of openness (a characterological orientation), which gives life to new aspirations. The norm of openness points outward toward the world and, even if only potentially, it reflexively works on the self that authorizes power.

Reflexive engagement with oneself is subject to being guided and developed and this requires, Whitman believes, models of living. Law is unsatisfactory as an external imposition, and mere rational appeal that does not simultaneously inspire the soul will suffer from a motivational deficit. We will lack the resources to understand why we are motivated to live one life rather than another. Hence he famously says in *Leaves of Grass*: "I and mine do not convince by arguments, similes, rhymes. We convince by our presence."[39] That one persuades by mere presence underscores the power of the image that stands out, and from which one can read off a form of conduct that captures and captivates, and is generative of ways of living.

Given the importance he accords models of living and presence, art emerges as the central candidate to support and bind us to a democratic ethos. In the section of *Democratic Vistas* where he mentions "pleased ears," he approvingly quotes Ainsworth Rand Spofford, the Librarian of Congress: "The true question to ask respecting a book, is, *Has it helped any human soul?*" Whitman explains that this "is the hint, statement, not only of the Great Literatus, his book, but of every great Artist."[40] What, we should ask, are the criteria of helping a human soul?

GUIDING THE DEMOCRATIC SOUL

Whitman tends to think of the role of art along the lines of improving the interior self; in fact, he calls artistic interventions the "mother of the true revolution"; it transforms "the interior life."[41] Art, then, is part of the perfectionist goals he attributes to democracy, what Emerson calls in his essay "The Poet" "*ascension*, or the passage of the soul into higher forms."[42] Douglass sees in art (specifically the photograph) the possibility for "a new birth" in which the "soul is raised to a higher level of wisdom."[43] Whitman does not deny that one may be interested in art for its own sake. As he explains, "it may be that all works of art are to be first tried by the art qualities, their image-forming talents, and their dramatic, pictorial, plot-constructing, euphonious and other talents."[44] But he is clear, and Du Bois will echo this point in his "Criteria of Negro Art" of 1926, that this is not where its import lies in a democratic society. The role of art is to offer suggestions for ways of living democratically. Art, he explains, is to be "strictly and sternly tried by their foundation in, and radiation, in the highest sense, and always indirectly, of the ethic principles, and eligibility to free, arouse, dilate."[45] Notice that art is tried indirectly by "the ethic principles" because adherence to them must be non-coercive and voluntary if they are to become habitual.

The role Whitman accords habit should not obscure the status of reflective agency. To voluntarily embrace what is on display is to say with heart and mind that I am persuaded of its truth. "You shall learn to listen to all sides," he says in *Leaves of Grass*, "and filter them from yourself."[46] Notice, individuals are learning to *listen to* and *filter from*. These two refer to different abilities—one's receptive capacities, on the one hand, and one's ability for communicative dispersal, on the other. He repeats the claim later, but now emphasizing the perfectionist role played by attending to the voices of others: "I think I will do nothing for a long time but listen, And accrue what I hear into myself. . . . and let sounds contribute toward me."[47] We get a preview of what is to come. Letting sounds contribute toward me is precisely what is at work in Holiday's performance of "Strange Fruit."

Here, I think, we begin to see that the value of art lies with the epistemic and social habits it cultivates. The persuading presence refers to art that arouses (as in awaken) or dilates (as in expand) the self. Thus artistic intervention is a device for developing what we might call ethical attentiveness (the idea of arousal of our receptive capacities). Ethical attentiveness makes sympathetic identification with others possible (the idea of dilation or our communicative dispersal ability directed within the self). Ethical attentiveness and sympathetic identification do not merely point outward, functioning like sensory nodes to alert us to the pain of others. They also point inward, guiding the self and enabling repair and improvement.

Here, we return to the language of "pleased ears." The term signifies hearing appropriately as when one is drawn, almost without reflection, to beautiful sounds. Or in its ethical register, it is listening appropriately, almost without reflection, to the claims of right, justice, and truth, as when the sounds of freedom rather than domination move the citizenry because these are the sounds of the democratic self. I say *almost without reflection* because for Whitman such sounds tap into an "intuitional sense" coterminous with democracy.[48] Artistic intervention does not provide what is absent; rather, for him, it makes manifest what lies below the surface, helping to give it form and shape in the everyday world. Because Whitman means to include not only what is heard but what may be seen or felt, his ideas include the vast array of impressions that may stimulate the body.

This way of thinking about the human sensorium is tricky because it may very well be the case that artistic productions put us in touch with truths about ourselves and our community that are far from pleasurable. Ida B. Wells's work on lynching only a few years later, for instance, is animated by the great Socratic question: Must truth be beautiful before the democratic masses accept it? This question and how Wells puts it to her readers dispense with Whitman's gentle sentimentalism in *Democratic Vistas*. The words she reaches for and the images she conjures cut at the malignancy of the soul. She is concerned with moving her readers affectively, to be sure. But what informs her prose is the chill of horror that Americans are a monstrous people rather than a civilized society. "A large portion of the American people," she writes in *Red Record*, "avow anarchy, condone murder and defy the contempt of civilization."[49] Du Bois and his editorial work at *The Crisis*—the NAACP's journalistic arm—follow Wells in this regard.[50] Meeropol and Holiday are continuous with a literary and dramatic effort that uses lynching rituals in plays and novels to underscore whites' demeaning attitudes toward blacks, consolidate and direct the energy of black people in the service of racial justice, and shame the white community.[51]

This darker character to the aesthetic basis of life is not lost on Whitman. He acknowledges that to "fend off ruin and defection" the citizenry needs "newer, larger, stronger . . . compellers."[52] Accepting truths about oneself and one's community may involve embracing displeasure. "It may be," he explains, "a single new thought, imagination, principle, even literary style . . . put in shape by some great Literatus . . . '*may duly cause changes, growths, removals, greater than the longest and bloodiest war.*'"[53] We need poets, he says, that "make great poems of Death," not only of life but "beyond" life.[54] Whitman does not mean to suggest that the transformation potentially produced by artistic intervention is equal to the pain of war but the form of death (removals, to use his phrase) that potentially occurs because of art's intervention is one of the soul and this involves growing pains. To be sure, he means physical death; keep in mind the horror of the Civil War lingers for Whitman. But what is philosophically interesting is that he also means death metaphorically. We must let go of older selves as we quest after selves larger and more expansive. This way of thinking—one that we will see is at the heart of Wells's writing and is most certainly central to James Baldwin's thinking much later—refuses nostalgia and embraces Whitman's claim: "Democracy . . . is a word the real gist of which still sleeps, quite unawakened."[55]

This reading of Whitman must not go too far. I mean this in two senses. In the first sense, Whitman avoids a naive endorsement of democracy and his perfectionism is wedded to a kind of realism.[56] Although a poet, Whitman was also a reporter and editor for the *Brooklyn Edge*, a newspaper in Brooklyn, New York. His journalistic realism informed his aestheticism. "I am the poet of reality," he wrote in the 1840s.[57] The passage cited earlier from *Leaves of Grass*, in which Whitman says you shall learn to listen to all sides and filter them from yourself, is preceded by the following: "You shall no longer take things at second or third hand. . . . You shall not look through my eyes either, or take things from me."[58] Whitman is not here rejecting sympathetic identification. He intends for us to inhabit the space of another, not because we have appropriated their view but because we have learned to see, genuinely hear, and feel. This is Whitman attempting to train our perceptual capacities as much as it is him suggesting that art ought to accurately record the world so that we may adequately respond. We can detect some of the repetition of this point in *Democratic Vistas*, but now as he chastises Americans:

> I say we had best look our times and lands searchingly in the face, like a physician diagnosing some deep disease. Never was there, perhaps, more hollowness at heart than at present, and here in the United States. . . . What penetrating eye does not everywhere see through the mask. The spectacle is appalling. We live in an atmosphere of hypocrisy throughout.[59]

We should not go too far in a second sense. Whitman does not escape falling prey to America's ills. He did not consistently look his times in the face and confront the horror of black suffering that ran alongside his ideas about democratic community. After all, the identitarian attachment to democracy often gains importance because it provides white Americans with economic and psychological comforts that rely on exploiting black people or rendering them invisible. As Eddie Glaude tells us, if Carlyle compelled a robust defense of democracy by Whitman, "he felt no need to address one of the underpinnings of Carlyle's essay. 'Niggers' are everywhere in the beginning of Carlyle's piece."[60] Whitman takes us some distance but not far enough.[61] We find in him a framework for democratic development that he ultimately fails to exploit and one that is put to better use by those with a more penetrating eye and discerning sound. Ironically, his approach suggests that we keep an eye out for better models.

Words and Pictures: Ida B. Wells, the NAACP, and Horror as Antilynching Activism

Whitman's understanding of art is preparatory work for what Holiday puts on display, attempting to awaken society to the horror of lynching. As Whitman explains, "Literature, Songs, Esthetics, &c, of a country are of importance principally because they furnish the materials and suggestions of Personality for the women and men of that country, and enforce them in a thousand effective ways."[62] To say that they are effective is an overstatement, given the dependence of the orator, poet, visual artist, or vocalist on the audience standing in right relationship to what is being presented.

But enforcement strikes a more critical note, for it does not bespeak a legalistic engagement but an ethical one. As Whitman noted earlier, and Holiday seeks to do, song aims to bring about not only "growths" but "removals" as well. Holiday's version of Meeropol's song and her stylized performance of it seeks to evoke in the listener a self-imposed mode of conduct toward black life, inviting the spectator to identify the "fruit" of human suffering hanging from trees as "strange." Whereas Jefferson's notion of democracy presupposes the people as an aspirational category, and Whitman renders those aspirations efficacious through aesthetic appeals, it is in Holiday that we find these implicit theoretical frameworks but the content she provides extends their reach to serve racial justice.

I want to insist that the song is part of a more general orientation consistent with the antilynching activism that closed the nineteenth century and opened the twentieth. Wells's writings so thoroughly capture one of the central preoccupations of African American thinkers at the time. As she put it in 1892, we must dip ourselves in the "corruption" of American life.[63] Here, she is referring to the lynching of black people. In doing so, we must, Du Bois tells us in 1916, give lynching the "widest publicity"—an attempt to get society to look its times searchingly in the face.[64] Another way of saying this is that we must give America's horror the widest publicity. This approach binds Wells, the NAACP, and Holiday together in one project of critically reimagining the American polity.

AMERICAN HORROR: WELLS AND
ETHICAL TRANSPOSITION

In his 1940 semi-autobiographical reflection *Dusk of Dawn*, Du Bois retrospectively recounts his "break" from his social scientific work of the 1890s: "Two considerations broke in upon my work and eventually disrupted it: first, one could not be a calm, cool, and detached scientist while Negroes were lynched, murdered and starved; and secondly, there was no such definite demand for scientific work of the sort I was doing, as I had confidently assumed."[65]

Du Bois has in mind the horrific lynching of Sam Hose in 1899. An itinerant black worker, Hose was accused of killing his white employer and raping his employer's wife. After a ten-day search, he was captured, tortured by body dismemberment, and burned, and all this reportedly before a crowd of two thousand people in Newnan, Georgia.[66] Du Bois recalls that during his trip to the offices of the newspaper *Constitution*, where he planned to publish a statement regarding the "evident facts" of the matter, he discovered that Hose had been lynched and "his knuckles were on exhibition at the grocery store farther down" the street on which he was traveling.[67]

Although Hose's lynching received widespread news coverage, it was part of a broader system of cruelty backed by de jure and de facto segregation. Reconstruction left the memory of interracial cooperation, but it did not radically transform America's ethical life—its culture of racial disregard. This was mainly due to the unstable commitment to affirming the equal standing of black people. "It was quite common," explains C. Vann Woodward in his classic study *The Strange Career of Jim Crow*, "in the eighties and nineties to find in the *Nation*, *Harper's Weekly*, the *North American Review*, or the *Atlantic Monthly* Northern liberals and former abolitionists mouth the shibboleths of white supremacy regarding the Negro's innate inferiority, shiftlessness, and hopeless unfitness for full participation in the white man's civilization."[68]

This way of thinking—not novel—found continued legal support. A series of Supreme Court cases, for example, challenged the equal access to public accommodation feature of the Civil Rights Act of 1875. The Supreme Court maintained in 1883 that neither the Thirteenth nor Fourteenth Amendment empowered Congress to outlaw racial segregation by private individuals. The result weakened the Civil Rights Act. African Americans were (as was the case before) at the arbitrary mercy of southern legislatures and courts. The Court also upheld the constitutionality of segregation in *Plessy v. Ferguson* (1896), augmenting discriminatory practices.[69] Lynching appeared extrajudicial, but in truth it was part of a culture of disregard that found support in the legal infrastructure of American life.[70]

Inequality in the law was the legal manifestation of a culture of violence and terror that black people experienced daily. "The simple word," Wells powerfully explains in 1893, "of any white person against a Negro is sufficient to get a crowd of white men to lynch a negro."[71] We should stay with this line a bit longer. Wells is clear, an agent will ultimately be involved; after all, some white person will be the accuser. She is also clear that every white person holds this power in reserve, and although the power of ending black life is extraordinary it can be used with a "simple word." This is—to put it simply—a condition of domination. Hose's lynching was a dramatic expression of that condition, and Wells put it and many others on powerful display. But to what end?

Born in 1862 and raised during Reconstruction and its collapse, the firebrand Ida B. Wells put African Americans' concerns and the violence they endured at the center of her thinking. We see this in many of her writings, including *Southern Horrors* (1892), *Red Record* (1895), *Lynch Law in Georgia* (1899), "Lynch Law in America" (1900), *Mob Rule in New Orleans* (1900), "Lynching and the Excuse for It" (1901), and "Our Country's Lynching Record" (1913). In these works, Wells is both an investigative journalist and social critic. Her work reveals white Americans' "cruelty and barbarism" by telling what she calls the "whole truth."[72] Her social theoretical analysis of white supremacy, white patriarchy, its sexualized dimension, and the danger posed to black men sits at the heart of her antilynching writings.

These features of her social theory reveal the "unwritten laws" of American life.[73] When Wells uses this term, she has in mind a set of beliefs about black people and their ethical and political standing that is part of one's social learning in the United States. She excavates the underside of American culture—that portion that constantly endangers the vision of democracy for which Whitman calls in *Democratic Vistas*. More specifically, the unwritten laws refer to the network of norms, habits, and symbols that work *defensively* to protect white men's political and sexual identity while *offensively* providing "justification" for taking the lives of black people. Wells locates the "facts" of lynching in detailed stories that at once reveal America's cruelty and does so even as she holds the "belief that there is still a sense of justice in the American people."[74]

Much of the discussion of Wells typically focuses on her revelation of the workings of patriarchy and gender politics as the real justification for lynching, rather than the fabricated reason of white women being raped or being threatened with sexual abuse by black men. This also permitted Americans to ignore the true sexual horror—the abuse and rape of black women by white men. On careful reading, Wells is, as Naomi Murakawa remarks, "a foundational thinker on racial criminalization"—a process that codes crime as black.[75] This focus strikes me as an important one. There are also a set of background themes I want to draw out and that are worthy of attention—Wells's moral psychology, its relationship to her emphasis on fact-telling, and the status of horror in her thinking.

Wells's language of "a sense of justice" referred to earlier is vital for understanding her moral psychology and reliance on the "facts." Two caveats. First, the phrase "a sense of justice" appears twice in her significant works, once in *Red Record* and the other in *Lynch Law in Georgia*.[76] The first appearance is in the voice of a black minister—Reverend King—and the second comes from Wells. The context for the first use of the phrase is when Reverend King protested the 1893 lynching of Henry Smith. Smith was accused of assaulting a four-year-old white girl in Paris, Texas. In that passage where Reverend King reports refusing to leave Smith's side (despite being strongly encouraged by whites to do so), he says: "I opposed the legal measures before the arrival of Henry Smith as a prisoner, and I was warned that I might meet his fate if I was not careful; but the sense of justice made me bold."[77] Second, more often, Wells reaches for the word "conscience" rather than "a sense of justice."

When Wells uses "a sense of justice" what she has in mind is a capacity that helps us understand the rightness or wrongness of an act. This is precisely what Reverend King meant. His was a sense that the act of lynching Smith was wrong and his conviction in the truth of that sense made him bold. More often, Wells captures her meaning of the sense of justice when she refers to "conscience" or "public conscience" or "humane conscience."[78] In many instances, she concerns herself with awakening conscience or with its deformation.

The idea of the sense of justice illuminates why she often relies on the facts. Like her more commonly used term "conscience," "the sense of justice" enables a proper recognition of the facts' meaning—that is, the ability to see the facts as also the deliverances of the wrongness of the acts those facts describe. As she says to the reader in *Red Record*'s conclusion: "1st. You can help disseminate the facts contained in this book by bringing them to the knowledge of everyone with whom you come in contact, to the end that public sentiment may be revolutionized. Let the facts speak for themselves, with you as a medium."[79] This she believes will move the American people—revolutionizing public sentiment in the service of racial justice.

The quest to transform public sentiment runs throughout the nineteenth century. Whitman's concern, for instance, with the cognitive and affective capacities of the American citizenry is about how to train them to support democratic values. The emphasis on public sentiment and training the senses mingles in important ways with the empiricism of the day. In this regard, Wells's perpetual invocation of the facts carries the same markers of Whitman and Martin Delany's empiricism of earlier decades. From the facts, one can understand reality. "The true poem is the daily paper," Whitman writes.[80] "The facts [of lynching]," Wells says in her posthumously published autobiography, "were enough of themselves to arrest and hold the attention."[81] With all this emphasis on the facts, one commentator worried in 1901: "This is a world of reality and romance breaks against many hard facts."[82]

Wells did not go this far. It is true she was not wholly persuaded ethical appeals would or could work. Wells also understood the role of economic interests and often deployed them to unsettle her white counterparts.[83] Here she recognized that the economic success and labor competition of black people often motivated racial violence. From the start, economic relationships between blacks and whites were underwritten and directed by the intensity of racial disregard. But she did not finally settle on the pessimism you find in Delany of the 1850s or its most proximate expression in Henry McNeal Turner's writings of the 1890s. For her, as was the case for the vast majority of African American thinkers, the facts must be housed within a richer account of persons' moral psychology and their capacity for transformation. As such, her truth-telling is a provocation to the nation to engage in a critical examination of itself and its treatment of black people.

Wells's claim that she is merely presenting the facts is somewhat deceptive. She knows all too well that fact-telling, primarily where the killing of black people was concerned, is not a neutral affair. The medium is not passive.[84] After all, the success of lynching did not depend exclusively on the presence of the victims but also on white Americans serving as spectators. In these contexts, they were "socially" habituated to find the displays "aesthetically acceptable."[85]

The perceptual landscape thus mattered a great deal. Newspaper and journalistic accounts of lynching in the late nineteenth and early twentieth centuries often conspired with the mob by portraying them as defenders of the peace. Reports often rendered vigilante violence as expressions of self-governance and shaped public perception. It captured the reading public from the point of view of the lynching mob, reproducing ideas of peacekeepers on the one side and black people deserving of violence on the other. Wells captures this very point in gripping fashion in the 1893 pamphlet (to which Frederick Douglass, Irvine Garland Penn, and Ferdinand L. Barnett also contributed as authors) *The Reason Why the Colored*

American Is Not in the World's Columbian Exposition. In the chapter titled "Lynch Law," she writes:

> The men who make these charges [against black people] encourage or lead the mobs which do the lynching. They belong to the race which holds Negro life cheap, which owns the telegraph wires, newspapers, and all other communication with the outside world. They write the reports which justify lynching by painting the Negro as black as possible, and those reports are accepted by the press association and the world without question or investigation.[86]

Despite the contestatory terrain of fact-telling, Wells accepts journalism even as she deploys it under constrained conditions. We see the first when she tells us she will rely on the statistical gathering of lynching by the reputable *Chicago Tribune*: "compilations made by white men. . . . Out of their own mouths shall the murderers be condemned."[87] The facts are not intrinsically motivating because their epistemic status as trustworthy depends on the deliverer's ethical standing: can the reporter be trusted? Because of the epistemic inequality[88] at the heart of the American polity, Wells tries to guard against accusations of partiality. As Juliet Hooker puts it, Wells faced "heightened constraints" on her "authorial voice" due to her gender and race.[89] Reporting by black people, especially that of a woman, did not have the same standing when it came from whites given the unwritten laws of American society. Despite this, Wells insists that black people put journalism to higher and nobler purposes. For example, in a speech she delivered to the National Press Association, subsequently published in *A.M.E. Zion Church Quarterly* in 1893, she implored African American journalists to tell the stories of the "tortured and outraged," which, she continued, is the "first step toward revolution of every kind."[90]

Her quest to awaken the sense of justice relates to how she and others discuss lynching—what it reveals about the activity and the people who commit it. *The Times* of London referred to Smith's lynching in 1893 as "the most revolting execution."[91] In 1894, undoubtedly influenced by his reading of Wells's work, Douglass refers to the "ghastly horror" and "the blood-chilling horrors" of lynching.[92] In 1904, prominent African American activist Mary Church Terrell—an associate of Wells's—refers to the lynch mob as "fiends" and "bloodthirsty."[93] Not only does Wells herself use "horror" to adorn the title of her book *Southern Horrors*, but you can readily find in her work language that seeks to conjure images of humans deformed by their bloodlust to kill black people. Her language seeks to stimulate feelings of fear and disgust in the reader. Consider some of the words Wells uses in her descriptions of the lynch mobs: "bloodthirsty," "evil," "fiendish," "inhuman."[94] Consider the language she uses to describe the activity of lynching: someone was "barbarously lynched," or lynching reveals the "barbarism" of its perpetrators, or lynching is a "gory campaign," lynching is "dehumanizing," or black people are victims of "savage orgies."[95]

Wells and others consistently deployed this language not to place white people outside the reach of human concern, even as the language easily invites this idea. They did not traffic in the language of dehumanization—that is, seeing white people qua white people as subhuman animals—to justify ill treatment.[96] We must be sensitive to the rhetorical context and the reach of the claim. Their language aims to awaken in the reader the demand of their humanity in the face of black death. So even when Wells deploys the language of "inhuman" it functions as a truth mirror, raising the question: Do you like what you see?

Wells and others hope the horror they describe will do substantive—transformative—work. What Douglass and Terrell learned from Wells is the rhetorical art of what we might call ethical transposition. That is, Wells reverses the subject position of those to whom ethical predicates are attached, thus redirecting the mind's eye. She redirects the signification of criminality from those lynched to the lynch mob. The "stigmatization of crime as 'black,'"[97] to borrow from Khalil Muhammad, and thus as a legitimization of lynching comes under enormous epistemic, ethical, and political pressure by Wells.

What is philosophically interesting here is how the idea of humanity grounds her engagement. She and others understand the background ethical and epistemic context as one in which aversion to the brutalization of human beings has *some* standing in society. As Walter White, the NAACP assistant secretary, put it succinctly decades later in his 1929 work, *Rope and Faggot: A Biography of Judge Lynch*: lynching has become "an *almost integral* part of our national folkways."[98] There is little doubt that Wells held this view—this sense that the folkways have not been wholly deformed. The ethical predicate of "bloodthirsty" or "fiendish" to describe lynchers hooks into a background, or so she believes, specifying limits to human punishment and thereby according human beings some bodily dignity and respect. Wells puts the point powerfully in *Red Record* as she highlights the United States' record of concern for the humanity of different peoples. In a chapter appropriately titled "Remedy," she writes:

Surely the humanitarian spirit of this country which reaches out to denounce the treatment of the Russian Jews, the Armenian Christians, the laboring poor of Europe, the Siberian exiles and the native women of India—will not [*sic*] longer refuse to lift its voice on this subject. If it were known that the cannibals or the savage Indians had burned three human beings alive in the past two years, the whole of Christendom would be roused, to devise ways and means to put a stop to it. Can you remain silent and inactive when such things are done in our community and country? Is your duty to humanity in the United States less binding?[99]

It is a stunning passage. For her, Americans readily acknowledge the humanity of different peoples and do so as a condition of their own self-description as a nation. This fact reveals the country's hypocrisy in falling short of recognizing the humanity of black Americans. She presses this point to secure proper alignment between the citizenry's actions and the full demand of respecting human dignity. Humanity, as Courtney Baker rightly observes of the period in which Wells wrote, "is less of a condition than it is an idea that signals to others how those identified as human beings ought to be treated."[100]

In proceeding this way, Wells put hard questions to the polity. If citizens can lie at will to justify killing people and fabricate stories to gin up a mob, how can democratic rule survive? How can a self-governing society be left to its own devices if it so easily allows its passions and desires to suspend respect for bodily integrity? Is it even possible, she contends, to claim one's society as free and civilized in the face of lynching? "It is," as Wells puts it, "the white man's civilization and the white man's government which are on trial."[101]

In a society that devalues black life, why pursue this approach? Why think it might be successful? Although the practice of fact-telling is contestatory, for Wells the battle takes place against the backdrop of a society that claims to be civilized and insists on this precisely because it projects a commitment to freedom. That is, American nationalism, and even its so-called exceptionalism, provides a standard by which to ask the country to judge itself.

Here, we must move with care, lest we miss how Wells plays with the ethical life of the nation to redirect it toward nobler ends. Americans have often lived in denial about their domestic racial cruelty and its importance to their national self-conception. One of the central reasons is how the United States configures its narrative of exceptionalism. The United States is, or so the argument goes, a beacon of civilization to others. The sincerity of this point is not what matters. What is significant is how the mythos of the United States shapes the national sense of justice to which Wells appeals and the ground on which she proceeds, even as a competing bloodlust for black people's death plagued the United States. This is as much a claim about the United States' sense of itself as much as it is a claim about the polity's image in the minds of other countries. Wells plays on this by internationalizing the horror of lynching. Lynching is not merely the fault of random mobs that flout the law or a few backward states—it reflects something about the nation's identity. "No other civilized nation," she writes in *Red Record*, "stands condemned before the world with a series of crimes so peculiarly national."[102]

Wells often uses the words "barbarism" (and its cognates) and "domination" to mirror back, ironically, what takes place in the American polity. For example, in *Red Record*, after describing the 1892 lynching of three African Americans, Hamp Biscoe, his pregnant wife, and their thirteen-year-old son in Keo, Arkansas, Wells writes:

> Perhaps the civilized world will think, that with all these facts laid before the public, by a writer who signs his name to his communication, in a land where grand juries are sworn to investigate, where judges and juries are sworn to administer the law and sheriffs are paid to execute the decrees of the courts, and where, in fact, every instrument of civilization is supposed to work for the common good of all citizens, that this matter was duly investigated, the criminals apprehended and the punishment meted out to the murders. But this is a mistake; nothing of the kind was done.[103]

Sarcasm drips from the passage as she moves from what should have happened to what actually happened. The United States, she thus claims, does not model civilized development or freedom; it exhibits degeneration and domination and we all should recoil as a result.

The discourse of horror and how it figures in Wells's thinking function less to paralyze the reader and more to awaken their capacities. Her invocation of horror already contains the clue to its redress. In recoiling from the United States' degeneration and domination, she invites the reader to see true civilizational improvement as bound to the status and protection of African Americans.

NAACP'S REDEPLOYMENT OF LYNCHING

Similar to the investigative journalism of Wells, lynching photographs were crucial weapons in the arsenal against white supremacy. Increasingly, from Wells's writings through the 1920s and into the 1930s, both lynching photographs and literary recounting of lynching events found their way into the tactics of antilynching activists, especially the NAACP.[104] The NAACP grew out of the earlier Niagara Movement of 1905, as it insisted on the civil rights of African Americans in the face of intense violation by white Americans and the perceived compromised vision of Booker T. Washington. From its earliest issue of *The Crisis*, the NAACP placed antilynching activism at the center of its work. As Megan Ming Francis writes, from "1911 to 1923, the NAACP focused most of its attention on lynching and mob violence."[105] They did so, as Jenny Woodley argues, as part of their overall "cultural campaign" to shift public sentiment.[106]

The image of lynched black people figured prominently in their efforts. But in one sense, this is an odd occurrence. Why circulate images and propagate descriptions of such horrific acts? As Daisy Lampkin, the first field secretary of the NAACP in 1930, reported in an interview: "We were so ashamed that whites could do that to us, that we hardly wanted to talk about it publicly."[107]

But just as lynching events and photographs tied white participants together in a community organized around norms and practices that involved policing and brutalizing African Americans, antilynching activists increasingly came to see the pictures as a visible testimony to the moral depravity of white Americans that might galvanize the black community. As Amy Louise Wood notes:

> Lynching opponents also sought to challenge the original intention of these photographs by inverting the racist assumptions of black bestiality and propensities for violence that undergirded the defense of lynching. They instead represented white mobs as savage threats to American civilization, a representation that held particular force in light of the United States' international role as a beacon of democracy.[108]

Let us reflect on this point with an example, keeping Wells's approach close at hand. In a 1935 NAACP antilynching pamphlet, one sees a lynched Rubin Stacy surrounded by seven white children who gaze at his lifeless body, with the following caption:

> Do not look at the Negro.
> His earthly problems are ended.
> Instead, look at the seven WHITE children who gaze at this gruesome spectacle.
> Is it horror or gloating on the face of the neatly dressed seven-year-old girl on the right?

Is the tiny four-year-old on the left old enough, one wonders, to
comprehend the barbarism her elders have perpetrated?[109]

The pairing of the Stacy lynching with a caption that overtly provides interpretative guidance stands in stark contrast to what we saw much earlier in
Beitler's photo of Thomas Shipp and Abram Smith (fig. 2). In the NAACP
photo, we see an attempt to reverse the moral lesson of such photographs.
In Beitler's photo, the white man in the foreground stares intently into
the camera and points to the lifeless bodies of Shipp and Smith that hang
above, as if to say to viewers something like the following: "This is how it
ought to be done—how treatment of Negros is supposed to be exacted."[110]
In the NAACP photo, the caption means to undercut the moral legitimacy
of a similar treatment, relocating bestiality from the black subject to the
white agent. We are, once again, on familiar territory. As it was with Wells,
the underlying question at work is the following: Is this becoming of a civilized people, both the violence on display and the subjection of youth to it?

How could this approach have any hope of succeeding? Here we confront the subtlety of the NAACP's strategy, but one that extends what was
on display in Wells's investigative journalism. An obvious representational
realism informed lynching photographs: to see the image entailed accepting the truth of its occurrence, allowing viewers to bear witness to the
event. But without weaving the photographs into the linguistic tapestry
of horror, the image might well become merely a recording of who was
killed, how, and by whom. It might even be a source of pleasure to some.
Both lynching and antilynching activists stood within the same epistemological but contestatory domain, the latter attempting to redescribe the
photo's meaning and deploy horror to transfigure the American public. The
NAACP's caption is thus guided by a critical tripartite assumption, without
which the appeal would scarcely make sense—namely, that a standard of
being civilized is at work within the wider culture (think of Wells's deployment of humanity), that it cannot be theoretically squared with the treatment of African Americans accurately on display, and that the American
demos can be awakened to this fact. The shared epistemological domain
allows for a reframing of similar images in which the power of language
(the NAACP's caption) aspires to release the horrific reality of the photo.
Like Wells's intervention, the aspiration of the NAACP aligns itself with
the theoretical presumption of democratic openness that is a precondition
for reframing the photo in the first place.

Notice that the questions in the caption seem less interested in distill-
ing a description of the participants and more concerned to confront the

FIGURE 2. NAACP antilynching pamphlet, 1935, depicting the lynching of
Rubin Stacy, Fort Lauderdale, Florida. Courtesy of the National Association
for the Advancement of Colored People.

viewer with their thinking. It is a provocation that infuses the photo with
new meaning. Lynching opponents sensationalized lynching events and
photos to capture the entire spectacle and redirect the moral gaze. The
aim was to properly align one's reactions to the cruel reality of the event.
In the hands of the NAACP, lynching now figured, as it had for Wells, as
an act of moral barbarity unbecoming of a civilized society. Whereas the
photos once served as artistic mementos of white superiority, they could
now be used as artifacts of white cruelty in the context of both a textual
and now a new "visual politics."[111]

Toward the People's Reeducation:
Billie Holiday on Strange Fruit

It is precisely this redirection of the moral gaze that informs Meeropol's song and which frames Holiday's 1939 rendition of it. As David Margolick explains, Meeropol wrote the poem and ultimately put it to music apparently in response to seeing the Shipp and Smith lynching photo—a photo that "haunted him for days."[112] The poem originally appeared in the *New York Teacher* in 1937. Although previously sung, it was subsequently given to Holiday by Meeropol at Café Society in New York City where she performed it regularly. Up until that point, no single piece of music made lynching its primary subject matter. The song achieved a remarkable degree of success (given the subject and the singer) by becoming #16 on the U.S. Billboard charts. For Meeropol's part, he explains: "I wrote 'Strange Fruit' because I hate lynching and I hate injustice and I hate the people who perpetuate it."[113] Framed as such, the intention behind the song seems confined merely to the expression of anger. It is a cathartic release that distances Meeropol from those in the photo who approvingly bear witness to the lynching.

However, Holiday's description of the song as her "personal protest"[114] and her reported response to her mother that she believed singing and performing the song may "make things better" seem to capture more accurately what she and Meeropol intended.[115] A personal protest captures the identification between the artist and the message they intend to convey. She prefigures the political turn that we associate with Nina Simone ("Mississippi Goddam" of 1964), Sam Cooke ("A Change Is Gonna Come" of 1964), or James Brown ("Say It Loud—I'm Black and I'm Proud" of 1968). All of them had a moment of personal protest in which they placed art in the service of political resistance. There is, I argue, an analogous relationship between Wells and the NAACP's antilynching activism, on the one hand, and the song and Holiday's rendition of it, on the other. All seek to convey—to call into existence—a new ethical sensibility.

This raises the question: What does the song mean to tell its listener? That it might make things better most certainly places Holiday in the space of aspirational politics. Meeropol and Holiday believe the polity can respond appropriately to the song's claims—a belief that who the people are (as displayed in the cruelty exacted on black bodies) need not determine who they may yet become. The song, then, is more accurately a democratic protest; it articulates grievances directed to an audience that they believe is capable of hearing appropriately. Consistent with the work of activists, the song lays claim to lynching, recontextualizes it, and gives it back to the demos which may yet be reeducated by it. Meeropol and Holiday's orientation makes explicit the presumption that the people may not stand beyond reproach. And Holiday's specific performance models a form of life that seeks to transfigure the social and political world.

Consider the song in its entirety.

Southern trees bear a strange fruit,
Blood on the leaves and blood at the root,
Black Body swinging in the Southern breeze,
Strange fruit hanging from the poplar trees.

Pastoral scene of the gallant South,
The bulging eyes and the twisted mouth,
Scent of magnolia sweet and fresh,
And the sudden smell of burning flesh!

Here is a fruit for the crows to pluck,
For the rain to gather, for the wind to suck,
For the sun to rot, for a tree to drop,
Here is a strange and bitter crop.[116]

The words are simple in their display of the horrific, but they oddly describe the lynched victims as "strange fruit" and, subsequently, "strange and bitter crop." The words alert us not only to the spectatorial dimension of lynching, as evidenced in the photograph that stimulated the song's production, but also to the subtle consumerism at work. The song collapses the senses of sight and taste into one mode of engagement. White Americans are visually consuming and digesting lynched black Americans. The deployment of "strange" and "bitter" now recasts the meaning of "fruit" in its new light—it is unhealthy, a corruption of the soul. The words stage a realignment between the horror of lynching and its adverse effects on the polity that are otherwise denied; in its ethical register, the song tells us that we can never distill value from the harm done to black Americans.

But if the words attempt to convey the consumption of horror, Holiday's performance aspires to stimulate an accurate assessment of lynching in her listeners. She tries to capture her audience and train their moral sensibilities through her vocal and dramaturgical display akin to Wells's use of "horror" or the NAACP's 1935 caption. And what figure better to do this than one whose voice is consistently described as "haunting."[117] Consider two reflections on her performance of the song, one from Meeropol (more appropriately mirroring Holiday's thinking) and the other from artist Albert Hirschfeld:

> She gave a startling, most dramatic and effective interpretation, which could jolt an audience out of its complacency anywhere [*sic*]. This was exactly what I wanted the song to do and why I wrote it. Billie Holiday's styling of the song was incomparable and fulfilled the bitterness and shocking quality I had hoped the song would have. The audience gave her a tremendous ovation.[118]

> It was a beautifully rendered thing, like a great, dramatic moment in the theater. To see Billie Holiday alone was something else, but this particular song made one sit and listen and think.[119]

What is at work in these descriptions but not easily susceptible to textual elucidation is the subtle inflections in Holiday's voice coupled with the somatic indicators (literally, her bodily gestures) that give the song its "shocking quality" and that make one "sit and listen and think."

Consider one of her last performances of the song in 1959 on "Chelsea at Nine," a weekly international cabaret show from a London theater that aired from 1957 to 1960.[120] Of course, we might well imagine some variation between 1959 and her earlier performances (Holiday would die five months later), but perhaps not much.[121] The haunting music, the piano, played in B-flat minor accompanies the entire song. One need not be a musician to hear the arrangement's sad and dark quality—B-flat minor functions as a sinister, "dark" key.[122] Before Holiday begins, the listener is being primed for anguish and loss; the music attempts to fashion and generate an appropriate response to match its grim sound. It is no wonder that upon hearing Holiday perform the song in an apartment in 1938, one guest remarked, "the apartment became a cathedral, the party a funeral."[123] Holiday's regular performance of the song at Café Society involved simple but deliberate staging—the suspension of service, a darkened room, and only a spotlight on Holiday's face—to set the mood and render the entire atmosphere of the café continuous with the claims of the performance. Like the proverbial moment of silence, the staging places the audience into a tragic horizon, the fitting expression to which can only be mournful contemplation. Holiday's voice enters; it is an appropriately stern counterpart to the seriousness of the lyrics. The dominant feelings that saturate the song are both contempt and disappointment; in other words, a lamentation is directed at the nation of which the audience is a part.

By 1959, the civil rights movement was in full swing and lynching was a practice mostly in the past. But to focus here is to obscure the power that inhered in Holiday's haunting voice and to miss that the devaluation of black life on display in the form of lynching was consonant with the disregard that the civil rights movement protested. As Emily Lordi puts it, here appropriating Avery Gordon, Holiday makes the "'the over-and-done with' come alive." To be haunted in this sociopolitical sense is to be plagued by—confronted with—"a repressed or unresolved [form] of social violence [that] is making itself known."[124] If hauntings conjure images of ghosts that horrify and from which we are likely to recoil, they also and perhaps more significantly represent unfinished business. In their ethical-political form, hauntings call us to act, lest our lives be marred by the repressed.

In Holiday's voice, then, contempt and disappointment are coupled with somatic indicators in the "Chelsea at Nine" performance. She stands still; her eyes turned downward. She looks up at her audience, disgust and curiosity flash across her face as she sings "southern trees bear strange fruit." A grimace framing the words "blood at the root" follows as her body sways almost imperceptibly. But it is with "bulging eyes and twisted mouth" that she contorts her mouth as if to mimic the dead, both raising the volume of her voice and singing the line in a strained vocal that closes with a look of contempt. Holiday models for her audience what she deems appropriate responses to lynching. By aiming her performance to the bodily level of democratic practice, Holiday hopes to retell the story of bearing witness to lynching and the reactions it ought to stimulate. It attempts to make present what one would think appropriate—a gasp, a cringe, a look of outrage. What Ralph Ellison said of the novel might well be said of Holiday's antilynching performance: it is "a way of possessing life, of slowing it down, and of giving it the writer's [and singer's] own sense of values in a delicately and subtly structured way. All this, of course, is not simply a matter of entertaining, but is a way of confronting reality, confronting the nature of the soul and the nature of society."[125]

Her performance is not ethically, cognitively, or emotionally neutral; it is informed by a cognitive-affective vision of a barbaric nation that she mirrors back to the public. The mode of delivery is not exclusively concerned with helping us understand lynching (Wells had already laid that out) but to help us feel what should be felt and to display the appropriate emotions to it through a mimetic display of the horrific. The meaning of the song contains a hidden somatic-affective road map that Holiday's gestures make explicit for consideration. In doing so, her words and performance reach out toward the listener, asking them to think and feel the norm being conveyed—that such events should at all times be met with disgust. Or to put it differently, she performs the very thing she hopes to arouse in her listener.

Here Whitman returns, but now transformed by Holiday. What Whitman says in *Leaves*, Holiday more effectively realizes and deepens in her performance: "Your very flesh shall be a great poem and have the riches and fluency not only in its words but in the silent lines of its lips and face and between the lashes of your eyes and in the very motion and joint of your body."[126] Keeping Holiday's performance in mind, the claim is that one can literally read off a mode of conduct and, as a result, place lynching, its victims, and its perpetrators within a new ethical economy. When I say "read off a mode of conduct" I mean that we can articulate norms against lynching and its perpetrators on the one hand, and norms for the protection of would-be victims of such crimes on the other.

This is a transvaluation of the values that sustained lynching, a reordering of blacks' ethical standing in the scheme of America's social and political framework. Holiday's engagement does not articulate a direct argument for the dignity of black life. Because she aspires to persuade by presence, her encounter is subtle as is the emergence of the new ethical economy she proposes. But it is not mysterious for being so. The revelatory dimension of the words is evident in Holiday's gestures. Taken by themselves, the words appear descriptive of lynching, but when the entire performance is considered Holiday's bodily articulation renders a judgment against what the song describes. In confronting the audience with and moving them toward the horrific through her somatic engagement, she attempts to simultaneously orient them differently and positively to the black subject. You cannot consistently be moved at the cognitive-affective level without being drawn to or aroused by the ethical claim being advanced. The ethical request reflexively endows the black body with worth otherwise flagrantly denied by the act of lynching, or so that is the aspiration.

CHAPTER SIX

Propaganda and Rhetoric

ON W.E.B. DU BOIS'S "CRITERIA OF NEGRO ART"

The truth of art tampers.

—W.E.B. DU BOIS, "REVIEW"

IF THE IDEA of the people opens up space for evocative appeals to reimagine and reconstitute society, then W.E.B. Du Bois's intervention sought to give such reconstitution direction. Similar to my reading in the last chapter, his goal was to answer a question: How do you move the people, and here we mean white Americans enjoying the rights and privileges of American democracy, such that they will embrace a reconstituted view of themselves? In reading *The Souls of Black Folk* (hereafter *Souls*) as a response to this question we should see the text as working in the domain of rhetoric. Rhetoric functions to move the audience, but unlike our discussion in part 1, Du Bois theorizes the purpose of rhetoric and its aesthetic power specifically. In this, he makes his art and propaganda one.

Political theorists have explored the similarities and differences between rhetoric and democratic deliberation.[1] As Bryan Garsten notes: "When speakers or writers try to persuade us of something, they are confronting us with a particular situation in speech. . . . [T]hey are . . . drawing upon and reorganizing our existing patterns of thought and emotion—they are appealing to our capacity for judgment."[2] We might easily read this formulation as describing Du Bois's orientation as well, encouraging his readers from the outset of *Souls* to study his words with him so that they may arrive at shared judgments regarding the plight of African Americans.[3] Attesting to the role of rhetoric in *Souls*, Arnold Rampersad explains: "For the first fifty years and more of his life [Du Bois] showed the mark of classical principles of rhetoric . . . *The Souls of Black Folk* is overwhelming evidence" of this fact.[4]

This makes sense. Du Bois's training as a graduate student at Harvard University included the instruction of English professor Barrett Wendell.[5] The central text for the course Du Bois took with Wendell was *The Principles of Rhetoric* (1878), written by Adams Sherman Hill, the Boylston Professor of Rhetoric and Oratory at Harvard (1876–1904). Now, I do not want to take the following analysis too far, especially given that in his teaching and administrative capacities Hill gives greater weight to composition rather than rhetoric. Notwithstanding, in his elucidation of rhetoric, Hill's 1878 work carries the stamp of the older, classical tradition of Aristotle and Cicero. At the very outset, Hill underscores the purpose: rhetoric "uses knowledge, not as knowledge, but as power."[6] Here power is not understood as coercive institutional force; rather, power refers to the capacity of speech to challenge institutional authority and, above all else, to move and transform others. In good classical fashion, one crucial aim rhetoric serves is political and ethical development.[7] This, Du Bois understands.

The theme of rhetoric, its political character, and its relationship to emotional states in *Souls* has received little to no attention. To be sure, I agree with, and in some instances reiterate, the importance Rampersad attaches to Du Bois's training in rhetoric.[8] My argument extends his insights by underscoring the politically transformative possibilities Du Bois accords rhetoric in influencing the soul of white Americans—that is, how they see themselves and what, based on that self-conception, they desire. But if Rampersad does not attend to the political character of rhetoric, the theme of rhetoric has gone equally unnoticed by those interested in the political vision of the text.[9] One of my aims is to correct this picture and in so doing elucidate how Du Bois enacts the relationship between rhetoric and emotional states, *revealing the imminently democratic character of his approach*. We come to appreciate how the art of rhetoric and the political aspiration of the text are constitutively tied together. They form part of a single desire to enrich the judgment of the reader regarding the plight of African Americans. This continues a theme already at work in David Walker. The power of *Souls* is bound up with its aspiration to persuade through an appeal to affirmative and negative emotional states, namely, sympathy and shame. Indeed, it is precisely Du Bois's quest to evoke in the reader sympathy for the suffering of black people and shame in being complicit in their suffering that was the key to involving and directing the judgments of his white counterparts.

Du Bois's enlistment of his audiences' judgment seeks to forge a partnership of discovery and transformation that honors their equal capacity for self and collective transformation. He leaves his audience in a position of self-possession that is the hallmark of reflective agency and democratic engagement. Persuasion that aspires to reach into the soul of the self depends on one's interlocutor finally saying: "I am persuaded." Those concerned with Du Bois's political philosophy and who emphasize the elitist dimension of his thinking miss altogether the democratic quality of rhetoric this chapter pursues. Without diminishing the vexing issue of a vanguard politics in Du Bois, one critically important result of attending to rhetoric is that Du Bois never abandons the belief that the rhetorician must always stand before the citizenry for critical appraisal. The reader for Du Bois is always, as Sheila Lloyd puts it, a "citizen-traveler."[10] A democratic rhetoric is always attempting to combine two different but compatible modes of politics that are obscured by overstating the elite vision of leadership in Du Bois's philosophy—namely, a form of politics that is engaged in showing the way (e.g., the rhetorical posture of speaking to) and a form of politics that is nonetheless dependent on those to whom one speaks (e.g., for assessing, revising, and assenting to the way forward). Rhetoric thus embodies the inescapable features of democratic life—that is, of ruling and being ruled in turn. The central aim of rhetoric, as we will see over this chapter and the next, is to elevate the soul.

———◆———

In this chapter, I travel with Du Bois from his 1926 essay "Criteria of Negro Art" (hereafter "Criteria") and the period of the Harlem Renaissance back to his 1903 work *Souls*. In the later work, we discover the resources for understanding the rhetorical character of the earlier work: "all art is propaganda and ever must be," a mode of persuading the community in the direction of some cause that neither panders nor manipulates but enlists the reflective autonomy of his audience.[11] Specifically, I provide an extended discussion of "Criteria": its context, animating concerns to secure what Du Bois calls "sympathy and human interest" and the intimation of those concerns in *Souls*, and the democratic character of propaganda.

Although this may strike the reader as anachronistic,[12] I insist that his description of propaganda *formalizes* his earlier training in rhetoric, albeit stimulated mainly by the politics of misrepresentation to which black thinkers and artists of the 1920s sought to respond. The formalized character of that training gives us a vantage point from which to see more clearly the aims of his earlier work—namely, to elevate the soul of the nation through a mix of aesthetic and affective appeals. In seeing Du Bois as formalizing his early training, I maintain that he aestheticizes politics as an instrument of cultural transformation.[13]

The Context of Criteria of Negro Art

Why did Du Bois find it necessary to stipulate the criteria of Negro art? At the beginning of his 1924 essay "The Negro in American Literature," prominent literary critic and poet William Stanley Braithwaite provides us with a useful start in answering the question.

> True to his origin on this continent, the Negro was projected into literature by an over-mastering and exploiting hand. In the generations that he has been so voluminously written and talked about he has been accorded as little artistic justice as social justice. Antebellum literature imposed the distortions of moralistic controversy and made the Negro a wax-figure of the market place: post-bellum literature retaliated with the condescending reactions of sentiment and caricature, and made the Negro a *genre* stereotype. Sustained, serious or deep study of Negro life and character has thus been entirely below the horizons of our national art. Only gradually, through the dull purgatory of the Age of Discussion, has Negro life eventually issued forth to an Age of Expression.[14]

Braithwaite has in mind the still looming figures in Harriet Beecher Stowe's *Uncle Tom's Cabin*, the Plantation School writers who nostalgically reimagined the antebellum period, and the graphic age of E. W. Kemble and A. B. Frost—two illustrators who provided distorted images of African Americans.[15] They often, in both prose and illustrations, depicted African Americans as servile or in need of paternal direction or licentious. But if we understand the various representations of African Americans as merely the imaginings for fictionalized worlds, it is not clear why Braithwaite's objections should prove persuasive. What, after all, is wrong with the piety and servility of Uncle Tom? The traits of "loafing, stealing, and effrontery"[16] most certainly seem like traits of human nature and so why be concerned that they find their way into the writings of folklorist Joel Chandler Harris or novelist and playwright Thomas Dixon as part of their depictions of African Americans?

Braithwaite understands that the artistic representations of black people extend beyond the imagination. They shape the cultural life of the community. This is a staple of his thinking and, indeed, the broader

Harlem Renaissance.[17] In "Enter the New Negro" of March 1925—a piece that became the lead essay in *The New Negro: An Interpretation*—Alain Locke, the dean of the Harlem Renaissance, argues that black people have been "a stock figure perpetuated as an historical fiction partly in innocent sentimentalism, partly in deliberate reactionism," a "social bogey or a social burden." In "The Social Origins of American Negro Art" of October 1925, Du Bois maintains that the necessity of black art is a response to the negative depictions of black people that have historically been in public circulation.[18] The caricatures of black people, with their stereotyped mannerisms, habits, and moral permissibility, at once claimed itself to be an accurate representation of who they are, all the while deforming black people into subjects unworthy of equal standing and proper regard. "Stereotype works," explains Martha Nadell, "by containing the pretense of accuracy and hence authority—something the Harlem Renaissance critics saw as particularly problematic."[19]

On Braithwaite's account, these negative representations are troubling both because of how they misrepresent and because such deformations structure the self-understanding of Americans. Importantly, misrepresentation and deformation are themselves expressive of the norm of white supremacy that ipso facto serves as justification for the mistreatment of African Americans. Not unlike the position of earlier thinkers, internalized misrepresentations may lead to a diminishment of one's self-esteem, arresting the soul and constraining the imagination. In both tone and structure, Braithwaite's concern is similar to Hosea Easton's worry a century earlier regarding the representations of black people in the stories read and narrated to children.

Indeed, only two years before Braithwaite's article, Walter Lippmann offered a compelling account of the stereotype: "The subtlest and most pervasive of all influences are those which create and maintain the repertory of stereotypes. We are told about the world before we see it. . . . And those preconceptions, unless education has made us acutely aware, govern the whole process of perception."[20] This is why black people, as Braithwaite says in the quote above, have been accorded as little artistic justice as social justice. The two, he believes, are connected and both point toward abilities and capacities in African Americans that a great many white Americans wished to deny. Here too Lippmann proves insightful: "The system of stereotypes may be the defenses of our position in society. . . . [A]ny disturbance of the stereotypes seems like an attack upon the foundation of the universe. It is an attack upon the foundations of *our* universe, and, where big things are at stake, we do not readily admit that there is any distinction between our universe and the universe."[21] Similar to Lippmann, Braithwaite and the Harlem Renaissance writers knew all too well the authoritative status of stereotypes—the way they seemingly function as biological facts.

Lippmann's understanding of the stereotype was part of his more general socio-psychological analysis of American life—an account that centralized the dynamism of culture in understanding political and social relations. But it was hardly new, if now dressed in a more social scientific garb. This mode of analysis fits within a longer, even if varied tradition of thinking that centralizes culture—from Walt Whitman's *Democratic Vistas* of 1871 to Anna Julia Cooper's *A Voice from the South* of 1892 to Ida B. Wells's attack on the unwritten laws of American life in *Southern Horrors* of the same year to the NAACP's campaign against the racist, but popular film *Birth of a Nation* of 1915 to W.E.B. Du Bois's 1920 *Darkwater* to John Dewey's 1922 *Human Nature and Conduct*. These works share a focus on how meaning in society becomes publicly accessible and socially distributed in shaping the value sphere in which people live. Although they did not focus as Lippmann did on the structure of stereotypes, Cooper, Wells, the NAACP, and Du Bois tie the beliefs about black people to the habits of racial domination and violence. This, of course, is also why for Braithwaite and many in the Harlem Renaissance the stories and depictions of black people are so critical to their ethical and political standing.

Debates about the representation of African Americans circulated throughout the 1920s—what kinds of depictions should be encouraged, who should be responsible for them, and what role black artists had in responding to negative descriptions and uplifting the race. These questions informed a cadre of thinkers from Eric Walrond's short "Art and Propaganda" of 1921 to Locke's *The New Negro* anthology of several years later. These issues structured the unintended debate between George Schuyler in the "The Negro-Art Hokum" of 1926 and Langston Hughes's response in "The Negro Artist and the Racial Mountain" of the same year.[22] These themes served as the subject of Du Bois's 1926 symposium, "The Negro in Art: How Shall He Be Portrayed?" hosted in *The Crisis*. But even a cursory glance at the responses to Du Bois's question reveals that few believed African Americans were duty-bound to direct their art to the cause of social justice. The unencumbered freedom of the artist, many argued, was far too important. As playwright and novelist Heyward DuBose argues, who himself was not an African American, black people must be "treated *artistically*. It destroys itself as soon as it is made a vehicle for propaganda. If it carries a moral or a lesson they should be subordinated to the *artistic* aim"[23]

With more time and a different set of animating questions, we could trace the political-philosophical pressures generated by these issues, Braithwaite's confrontation with his past and present of how African Americans appear in the artistic imagination of white artists, and the quest for artistic freedom that informed many of those associated with the Harlem Renaissance. But what we can say is that the writers and artists of the period were animated by a burning question: How ought we to understand the relationship between art and politics in the quest to secure the standing of black people and transform American society?

Du Bois's "Criteria of Negro Art" (1926) is his answer to this question and to the symposium that he organized. But whereas most read this essay as the dividing line (and there is some truth in this) between Du Bois and many in the Harlem Renaissance, especially Alain Locke, the essay suggests closer proximity between these two figures.[24] Surely they each were seeking to avoid black artists needing to manage the unacceptable demands of what Langston Hughes called the "undertow of sharp criticism and misunderstanding" from black people and "unintentional bribes from whites." The choice must not be between the demand, "Oh, be respectable, write about nice people, show how good we are," and the equally unacceptable request, "Be stereotyped, don't go too far, don't shatter our [white people's] illusions about you, don't amuse us too seriously. We will pay you."[25]

I want to be clear about what I intend in drawing Du Bois and Locke (and by implication Hughes) together on the issue of art and propaganda. To be sure, Du Bois and Locke's articulated disagreement is of historical interest; we want to get it right how each understood what they were doing and how they thought what they were doing stood in relation to the other. But it is a mistake to assume they clearly understood each other; in fact, there was a great deal of misunderstanding between the two. We should therefore guard against using their articulated disagreement as the basis for a political-philosophical difference, especially, as I shall suggest in due course, if they misunderstood each other.

Finally, in treating "Criteria" as I do, I insist it is less of an original statement as much as it serves to crystallize Du Bois's earlier thinking regarding the relationship between art and politics that informs *The Souls of Black Folk*. In 1903 Du Bois is already writing according to the criteria of Negro art and it becomes necessary to formally stipulate it in 1926. I have thus found it necessary at various moments in my discussion of "Criteria" to fold *Souls* into the discussion, delaying a full treatment of that text until the next chapter. But we begin with "Criteria" to help illuminate the less formalized commitments of *Souls*.

Criteria of Negro Art and Its Intimations in the Rhetoric of Souls

Du Bois delivered "Criteria of Negro Art" at the 1926 NAACP's annual meeting in Chicago. He subsequently published the lecture as part of "The Negro in Art" multi-issue series that appeared in *The Crisis*. In "Criteria," an essay that seeks to embolden black artists against the humiliating and exclusionary standards imposed on them by white America, Du Bois offers one of his most oft-repeated statements that explains what he intended much earlier in *Souls*: "Thus all art is propaganda and ever must be . . . I stand in utter shamelessness and say that whatever art I have for writing has been used always for propaganda for gaining the right of black folk to love and enjoy."[26]

In isolation, the first of these sentences might well strike the reader as strange, especially for those of us who see in propaganda the opportunity to manipulate and deceive the public. In the 1920s, there was a great deal of misunderstanding about Du Bois's use of the term. The passage is prefaced, however, by Du Bois's explicit explanation that artists are conveyers of moral and political truth, in possession of tools for bringing truth into view for their fellows:

> First of all, he has used the truth—not for the sake of truth . . . but . . .
> as the one great vehicle of universal understanding. Again artists have
> used goodness—goodness in all its aspects of justice, honor, and right—
> not for [the] sake of an ethical sanction but as the one true method of
> gaining sympathy and human interest.[27]

When Du Bois weds truth and goodness to the artist's work and art to propaganda, he means for the reader to understand art as a vehicle for expanding the horizon of the recipient.

This seems an odd use of propaganda. This is because we typically associate propaganda with manipulation or partial facts masked as truth. This was a prominent view during the interwar period. For example, both Walter Lippmann and Edward Bernays (the father of public relations) served on the Committee for Public Information, an arm of the federal government tasked with influencing public opinion during World War I.[28] In their works of the 1920s, both underscored the public's susceptibility to propaganda, although Bernays clearly believed he could redeem propaganda in the name of democratic governance.

Du Bois is sensitive to this view. But he aims to return his audience to an older use of propaganda—a view in which propaganda meant propagation of faith believed to be true.[29] For Du Bois's part, it is the propagation of a fuller depiction of African Americans that cuts against partial or one-sided portrayals. This is why Du Bois encourages black artists to resist the need to satisfy their white audiences' desire for "literary and pictorial racial prejudgment[s] which deliberately distorts truth and justice, as far as colored races are concerned."[30]

Two questions nonetheless present themselves. How should we understand Du Bois's use of the language of truth and goodness? How do these two terms help illuminate the interior meaning of the work of black artists? I will take each of these questions in turn.

TRUTH AND PROPAGANDA

Du Bois's interest in propaganda emerges in two other places (although not only two) worth considering. The first is his earlier 1921 editorial, "Negro Art." The second, almost a decade after "Criteria," is in his 1935 book *Black Reconstruction*. It is worth saying a word about both of these reflections. They help us understand Du Bois's distinction between what we might call positive and negative propaganda and its relationship to the theme of truth central to "Criteria." These two other works prefigure or amplify claims of his 1926 essay.

In the first—"Negro Art"—Du Bois rejects a one-sided view that African Americans often present of themselves. This turns out to be, on Du Bois's account, the negative description of propaganda. Consider the passage that I quote at length.

> Negro art is today plowing a difficult row chiefly because we shrink at the portrayal of the truth about ourselves. We are so used to seeing the truth distorted . . . that whenever we are portrayed on canvas, in story or on the stage, as simply human with human frailties, we rebel. We want everything that is said about us to tell of the best and highest and noblest in us. We insist that our Art and Propaganda be one.
>
> This is wrong and in the end it is harmful. We have a right, in our effort to get just treatment, to insist that we produce something of the best in human character and that it is unfair to judge us by our criminals and prostitutes. This is justifiable propaganda.

On the other hand we face the Truth of Art. We have criminals and prostitutes, ignorant and debased elements just as all folk have. When the artist paints he has a right to paint us whole and not ignore everything which is not as perfect as we would wish it to be.[31]

Du Bois intends to direct his comments to an African American audience. He rejects those who insist that we ought only to tell of the best and noble in black life. This is harmful, Du Bois believes, because it will undercut expressive autonomy. But notice that he ties justifiable propaganda to a fuller depiction of black life. Just as we should not insist on only painting positive images of black people, we should not exaggerate the more unsavory elements that form part of them and their community. By 1926, Du Bois does not betray his earlier claim that we should not insist on art and propaganda being one. Rather, that unity must be justifiable—that is, it must not be partial in its substance or aims.[32]

Du Bois comes back to this distinction between positive and negative propaganda in his 1935 work, *Black Reconstruction*. This work intends to correct the view that Reconstruction represented the most backward period of the country in large part due to the perceived moral and political elevation of black people over their white counterparts in the South. In his chapter "The Propaganda of History," Du Bois reflects on the uses and abuses to which historians have put history in their telling of Reconstruction:

If, on the other hand, we are going to use history for our pleasure and amusement, for inflating our national ego, and giving us a false but pleasurable sense of accomplishment, then we must give up the idea of history as a science or as an art of using the results of science, and admit frankly that we are using a version of historic fact in order to influence and educate the new generation along the way we wish.[33]

Du Bois's phrase "the way we wish" suggests something contrary to what the facts permit and truth demands. He is essentially tracking the use of "truth" he invokes in "Criteria." In both works, he is concerned with beliefs that come wholly unhinged from the past and present and therefore function as unassailable claims:

It is propaganda like this that has led men in the past to insist that history is "lies agreed upon"; and to point out the danger in such misinformation. It is indeed extremely doubtful if any permanent benefit comes to the world through such action. Nations reel and stagger on their way; they make hideous mistakes; they commit frightful wrongs;

they do great and beautiful things. And shall we not best guide humanity by telling the truth about all this, so far as truth is ascertainable.[34]

The partiality of the historians of Reconstruction distorts the truth and
for just this reason fails to illuminate human life and provide guidance.

Lest we read too much into this, Du Bois is not concerned with reporting what Leonard Harris calls an "objectively real truth" in history.[35] He is
clear that we should tell the truth so far as it is ascertainable, acknowledging in that formulation that truth may elude our grasp. Du Bois is more
interested in one's motivation toward the practice of narrating history.
Similar to Anna Julia Cooper's pragmatic way of understanding the pursuit of truth, we might say Du Bois confronts us with a question: Is one
concern to participate in a practice of giving and asking for reasons for the
beliefs one holds about the past as one engages in historical narration? Is
one tethered, as Paul Taylor says, "to the commitment to getting things
right," and thus disciplined by the various epistemic practices involved in
trying to get things right?[36] Du Bois's claim is that Reconstruction historians have not been interested in participating in this practice any more
than the artists who have told partial stories and offered one-sided depictions of black people. In this way, Du Bois joins Cooper's 1892 longing
for "an authentic portrait, at once aesthetic and true to life, presenting
the black man as a free American citizen, not the humble slave of *Uncle
Tom's Cabin*—but the *man*, divinely struggling and aspiring yet tragically
warped and distorted by the adverse winds of circumstance, has not yet
been painted."[37] To say it is propaganda "like this" that distorts implies
there is some other way to conduct propaganda. This other way is found in
its most explicit form in "Criteria" and intimated in the early essay already
considered, "Negro Art."

Du Bois's description in "Criteria" of art as a vehicle for persuasion provides a perspective on which to understand his broader approach. In "Criteria," but also "Negro Art" and *Black Reconstruction*, he is not merely providing direction to would-be artists; rather, he means to signal something
about his method as a writer. He treats art as a broader category that is
engaged in persuasion. It includes his literary engagements with the public,
and not merely those expressed by his fiction and theatrical productions
such as *The Quest of the Silver Fleece* (1911), *The Star of Ethiopia* (1913), or
Dark Princess (1928). One notices this at the very outset of *Souls*: "study
my words with me. . . . seeking the grain of truth hidden there."[38] *Souls* is
thus the product of an artist of letters; it exemplifies the aims stipulated
decades later in "Criteria." In it Du Bois seeks to expand the horizon of

the recipient—to cultivate a sympathetic imagination. As an artist of letters, what we should call a rhetorician, Du Bois employs propaganda to provide access for African Americans to "love and enjoy," and this consciously informs his work. Or to put it differently, *Souls* is an attempt to persuade his white counterparts to embrace an alternative view of America in which African Americans can experience love and joy unhampered by domination.

GOODNESS AND PROPAGANDA

This alternative view of America allows us to explore the other feature of Du Bois's essay, his emphasis on goodness. I have noted his account of truth, but what of the idea of goodness which, on his view, artists have used not for the "sake of an ethical sanction but as the one true method of gaining sympathy and human interest"? One way of approaching this question is to recall thinkers we have already considered—David Walker, Frederick Douglass, Ida B. Wells, and Billie Holiday—in their own dramatized engagement with black life and the horror of white supremacy. Each of them described the horror of black life, but they often did so by invoking presumptively shared ethical commitments. Each of them relied on the familiar normative language of the American polity while simultaneously seeking to enrich it. Recall when Walker discussed the violently abused slave and what the observer ought to see. Or when Douglass narrated the nobility of the Founders as they quested after freedom, if only to dramatize for his white audience how far they were from their revolutionary parents. Or finally, we might think about the idea of horror in Wells and Holiday as a way not to mark the impotence of spectators but to remind them of their transformative power to reorder the ethical value sphere of American life. In each case, they tapped into an ethical framework (a vision of goodness, sometimes distilled from horror) that was not wholly out of view given the unethical conditions they described. As Taylor puts it, the ethical "constitutes the framework within which we respond" to the scenes on display.[39] The scenes, in other words, do not proscribe as much as they are oriented by an ethical vision (that is itself not wholly foreign) and aspire to elicit from the audience assent to the claims being made by that vision. This is why Du Bois says the artist is not using goodness as a penalty (ethical sanction) but to generate identification and concern (sympathy and human interest).[40] Precisely because he is interested in the interior workings of culture, he realizes there is no mechanism of social control to secure ethical enforcement. In saying that artists do not use goodness as an ethical sanction, he means to capture its noncoercive character; art, in other words, aspires to persuade from within.

Why is the artist engaged in this practice at all? The artist, Du Bois tells us, "becomes the apostle of truth and right not by choice but by inner and outer compulsion."[41] By inner compulsion, he has in mind a desire to proffer grander visions of life—to give content to the image of what self and society may become. This is the aspirational register on which the Du Boisian artist works.[42] The artist, not unlike Douglass or Whitman or Cooper, is a faith-holder—that is, the artist is moved by outer compulsion because those visions of life offered stand in tension with and seek to address the society currently on display.

Early twentieth-century America, with its various forms of exclusions and violence against black people, is one in which the longing of black souls is frustrated and stunted. But it is also a society ethically incoherent, as it quests after a vision that it constantly betrays. For that reason, Du Bois tells us, the United States is literally an ugly society.[43] This is both the power and tragedy of the gifted second-sight that he famously describes in *Souls*, invokes in *Darkwater*, and reiterates in "Criteria": "We who are dark can see America in a way that white Americans can not."[44] The measure of America's ugliness—the wider view of how society is organized institutionally and normatively as it relates to the standing of black people—is based not merely on the private ethical standards of the artists but on standards that should also be familiar to the audience one is seeking to influence. Given the state of ugliness, Du Bois asks: "Who shall right this well-nigh universal failing? Who shall let this world be beautiful?" Inner and outer compulsion is thus a dynamic and creative relationship that brings into view the experiential quality of black life that requires a response. Du Bois uses such experiences as a way to guide the moral and emotional nature of his white fellows.

Here the aim of rhetoric begins to come into view. The point of rhetoric is to take the reader to the experiential source from which appropriate emotions and judgments spring. The dynamic relationship between inner and outer compulsion that Du Bois describes in "Criteria" exemplifies and enacts Hill's claim in *Principles of Rhetoric*: "We are made to feel by being taken to the sources of feeling." The point of this line is that "neither reason nor duty" governs the workings of the heart; rather, it is one's focus on the object itself that may elicit its own affective response.[45] Think of Meeropol and Holiday and the movement of "Strange Fruit": "Pastoral scene of the gallant South, / The bulging eyes and the twisted mouth."[46] This approach fuels the "storied" or "narrativized" structure of *Souls*, the way many of its chapters turn on the detailed depictions of dreams unrealized (chapters 2, 4, 12, and 13), communities destroyed (chapters 4 and 9), and lives lost (chapters 11 and 13). Indeed, Hill emphasizes the important role of narration and argues that its quality is measured by "movement." He ties narration and movement together because a good rhetorician is assessed by how well they can *move*—in heart and mind—the audience.[47]

This emphasis on narration points to yet another important feature of *Souls* that relates to the role "Criteria" accords experience. We have already noticed this in previous thinkers. Consider, very briefly, two passages— the first from "The Forethought" and the second from the conclusion of chapter 1:

> Herein lie buried many things which if read with patience may *show* the strange meaning of being black here in the dawning of the Twentieth Century.

> And now what I have briefly sketched in large outline let me on coming pages tell again in many ways, with loving emphasis and deeper detail, that men may *listen* to the striving in the souls of black folk.[48]

I will return to the modal verb "may" in a moment, but for our purposes although Du Bois uses "listen" in the second of the two passages, more consistently throughout *Souls* he puts before the *eyes* of his audience the horror of American life. To listen entails that the audience will actively seek to comprehend, interpret, and evaluate what they hear. But this is largely because they have also been transformed into spectators. Here Du Bois stands on familiar territory in which visual impressions are a hallmark of both African American appeals and an older classical rhetorical tradition. For him, the reader comes to *see* the "strange meaning of being black," as when we say "I see" or "I see what you mean." Both formulations denote that one understands. Of course, seeing partly explains both the narrative quality of *Souls* as already noted and the ornamentation that famously characterizes Du Bois's language throughout the book.[49]

This process of getting the audience to see helps to elicit from them an emotional response that might generate a desire to alleviate the condition of African Americans specifically and to expand the political-ethical imagination of the broader citizenry. To see, in this context, is to be moved and one is moved by virtue of one's feelings. This is why horror figures so prominently in Ida B. Wells's writings. Similarly, it is the repulsive conditions that African Americans endure under the weight of Jim Crow that serve as the backdrop for Du Bois's reflections. He is thus pursuing the goal he formalizes in "Criteria": "I am one who tells the truth and exposes evil and seeks with Beauty and for Beauty to set the world right."[50]

ART OR PROPAGANDA: LOCKE AND DU BOIS

Of course, Du Bois is sensitive to a view of the artist whose vision of beauty stands above and is not primarily determined by the truth of public atrocities—a vision of the artist that "take[s] their material objectively with detached artistic vision."[51] These are Locke's words. Under conditions of misrecognition, misdescription, and racial domination, Du Bois ultimately thinks this approach is irresponsible. In his otherwise favorable review of Locke's *The New Negro*, he worries:

> With one point alone do I differ with the Editor. Mr. Locke has newly been seized with the idea that Beauty rather than Propaganda should be the object of Negro literature and art. His book proves the falseness of this thesis. This is a book filled and bursting with propaganda but it is propaganda for the most part beautifully and painstakingly done; and it is a grave question if ever in this world in any renaissance there can be a search for disembodied beauty which is not really a passionate effort to do something tangible, accompanied and illumined and made holy by the vision of eternal beauty.[52]

This most certainly created the context for a grand public debate between the two, but this raises a question of whether Locke held the position in the way Du Bois suggests and scholars often insist. In fairness to Locke, there was a great deal of misunderstanding between him and Du Bois over the ultimate role of art in social transformation. They were talking about different types of propaganda. To put it differently and somewhat heretically, semantically they were at odds, but philosophically they shared similar goals.

In such essays as "The New Negro" (1925), "The Negro Youth Speaks" (1925), "To Certain of Our Philistines" (1925), "The Message of the Negro Poets" (1927), and "Art or Propaganda" (1928), Locke defends a vision of black art founded on expressive autonomy that refuses to be determined by the narrow desires of white people. As he says in "The Message of the Negro Poets," for example: "If Negro poetry . . . had addressed primarily its own audience, it would have been good poetry in the sense that the 'Spirituals' are. But for the most part it has been a 'play-up' to the set stereotypes and an extroverted appeal to the amusement complex of the overlords."[53] His reference to overlords, in this context, turns out to be the white consumers of black art. This, of course, is in contrast to directing "Negro poetry" to its black audience. His language of "play-up" and "extroverted appeal" suggests that what he has in mind when he uses propaganda is precisely the one-sided and therefore negative conception of propaganda that Du Bois rejects. Indeed, Locke uses this language again the following year in "Art or Propaganda" when he says propaganda is too "extroverted for balance or poise or inner dignity and self-respect."[54] This use of extroverted as an obstacle to balance and poise suggests that external pressures overdetermine the inner aesthetic light of black people, thus making the art expressively untrue to both the artist and the world the art represents.[55]

This way of seeing Locke gives us a wider perspective from which to understand a critical passage in his essay that opens his edited volume, *The New Negro*:

> The thinking Negro even has been induced to share this same general attitude, to focus his attention on controversial issues, to see himself in the distorted perspective of a social problem. His shadow, so to speak, has been more real to him than his personality. Through having had to appeal from the unjust stereotypes of his oppressors and traducers to those of his liberators, friends and benefactors he has had to subscribe to the traditional positions from which his case has been viewed. Little true social or self-understanding has or could come from such a situation.[56]

What is the general attitude? For him, it is the attitude of the stereotypical view of black Americans that they must either be kept in their place or helped up, for without assistance they would not find their way. Here again, these narrow views, constructed and mostly propagated by white Americans, use shadows as the basis for understanding reality. They fail, and here Locke was very much in keeping with the philosophical pragmatism of his day, to honestly address the experiential conditions of black life. Locke's point is that black people advance their appeals to white Americans, and are often premised on these very same misconceptions. The result is that black people are not transparent to themselves and they make little advancement in constructing a richer landscape of black life that Locke believes is necessary to the social development of the polity.[57]

It is not then the case that Locke is "squeamish about political struggle," as Nancy Fraser argues, and thus renders the Harlem Renaissance an "apolitical movement of the arts," as Henry Louis Gates Jr. maintains.[58] His approach is subtle, but no less political for being so. He sees the image of the New Negro as political by implication rather than intention. For him, the contest over the image *is* the political struggle, even if Locke does not defend the cultural nationalist position found in later figures such as Harold Cruse, Amiri Baraka, and Ron Karenga. Contrary to Fraser's reading, the fight over the black image has long played a central role in African American freedom movements. Locke does not cite Walt Whitman to this effect (although we know he was an influential thinker for Locke),[59] but it is reasonable to say that he is after Whitman's magnetic vision of attraction as the basis for organic ethical and political transformation. To recall Whitman's line in *Leaves of Grass*: "I and mine do not convince by arguments, similes, rhymes. We convince by our presence."[60] For Locke, the mere circulation of new images and descriptions of black people in the public sphere helps shape aesthetic vision of both the artist and the audience. Art, in other words, is about "the proper training of the sensibilities" on which our ethical and political orientation depends.[61] For him, modes of seeing are political.[62]

On this point, Du Bois and Locke are much closer than they believed. Du Bois is clear, and it now appears that Locke can join him, in saying that "here and now and in the world in which I work they [beauty and the truth of life] are for me unseparated and inseparable."[63] "Our espousal of art," says Locke in a line that Du Bois could have written, "becomes not mere idle acceptance of 'art for art's sake,' or cultivation of the last decadences of the over-civilized, but rather a deep realization of the fundamental purpose of art and of its function as a tap root of vigorous, flourishing living."[64] We should not understate this last line; it pulls Locke and Du Bois together. Both are in agreement in thinking of the black artist in ethical rather than aesthetic terms—that is, as seeking the ethical improvement of the polity by expanding the perceptual capacity of white Americans and elevating the standing of black Americans rather than focusing on the form of the art object. In this, and as it relates to the relationship between art and propaganda, they are not after a theory of aesthetics but the aesthetic basis of ethical life.[65]

In describing art as propaganda (in the positive sense), Du Bois is not merely politicizing aesthetics but more importantly aestheticizing politics. As to the first, he sees a transformative role for art, broadly understood. He opens "Criteria" by saying "the thing [i.e., art] that we are talking about tonight is part of the great fight we are carrying on."[66] Du Bois most certainly sees himself as engaging in this fight. But why, one might ask, emphasize art rather than political action? This question mistakenly understates the fact that he sees art as a form of political action in a world of asymmetrical power relations that must stand alongside traditional modes of protest. Recounting his transition from relying exclusively on scientific rationality in addressing racial inequality, Du Bois explains: "The black world must fight for freedom. It must fight with the weapons of Truth, with the sword of the intrepid, uncompromising Spirit, with organization in *boycott, propaganda and mob frenzy*."[67]

In attributing the aestheticization of politics to Du Bois one should observe that he does not believe he is importing into the political and ethical domain something that ought to be kept out. Rather, he sees the aestheticization of politics as a method for African Americans to expand their self-description and the judgment of their white counterparts. He refers to the end result as a form of "wide judgment"—a "catholicity of temper" that is essential to properly regarding one's fellows.[68] For the role of the black artist generally, and the black rhetorician in letters particularly, is not merely to ask the question "What is a Negro anyhow?" but to provide a capacious answer to the question.[69] This is what Du Bois refers to as the "art of black folk" that "compels recognition." Compel here denotes force to be sure, but Du Bois has in mind not an imposition from the outside but inducement from the inside.[70]

Notice that these two claims—politicizing aesthetics and aestheticizing politics—serve as bookends for the essay. The first keeps in view the problem of racial injustice that orients Du Bois as a literary artist, whereas the second indicates that the content of his rhetoric must be aimed at expanding his white counterparts' ways of seeing and feeling. Cultivating wide judgment requires, as Du Bois attempts decades earlier in *Souls*, a dramatization of the struggles of black life under oppressive conditions—a jarring presentation of those who live behind the veil.

On Rhetoric and Judgment or Du Bois's Democratization of Propaganda

In my reading of "Criteria" and using it as a framework for orienting the reader to *Souls*, I have tied rhetoric and propaganda closely together. But an immediate worry emerges about propaganda's relationship to manipulation and thus its antidemocratic qualities. Let me address this before turning explicitly to *Souls* in the next chapter since it permits a clearer discussion of rhetoric to which I have thus far gestured.

Recall Du Bois's explicit aim to widen the judgment of the audience in "Criteria," and my earlier analysis of the words "listen" and "see" in *Souls*. The first of these helps us understand what he intends by the second. He does not intend for readers to alienate their judgment to his authority—that is, he does not aim for domination. Rather, he asks readers to put the capacity for judgment to work, including its ability to be expanded. Rhetoricians seek to stir the souls of those they engage so that they may arrive (and see themselves as participating in that arrival) at a truth hitherto unavailable.

It is not at all clear, one might think, how the rhetoric of *Souls* can hope to generate the deep transformation Du Bois imagines that affirms rather than stifles reflective agency. Or to put it in the form of a question: What does it mean for Du Bois's audience to see themselves as participating in the arrival of a truth hitherto unavailable? After all, Hill describes rhetoric as the imposition of power and Du Bois describes rhetoric as propaganda. In 1920, as indicated by the epigraph, he tells us that "the truth of art tampers."[71] All of this seems to point to manipulation. Obviously this would not involve us in affirming the reflective agency of the recipient, and it most certainly does not support an interpretation of Du Bois's use of rhetoric as democratic. This was the same problem that seemed to afflict Walker's reliance on prophecy in chapter 1 as a means to speak to the reader. Why not, one might ask, interpret propaganda more straightforwardly and subsequently read *Souls* as a book engaged in manipulation, even if for good ends?

As with Walker, Du Bois, and many in the tradition, one way of approaching this issue is to compare persuasion and manipulation. When we manipulate someone, we typically move them to a belief or action that is inconsistent with the reason for which they hold that belief or engage in that action. As a result, there is a disconnect between the belief they hold and the reason for holding that belief, making one feel that the belief in question, properly speaking, is not the person's own. To manipulate a person in this respect is to dominate them clandestinely—we come to substitute the manipulator's judgment for our own. Indeed, this was Plato's classic concern in the *Gorgias*.[72] "The rhetorician's mastery of language," says Peter Euben of Gorgias's view, "enables his student to master anyone, anytime, anyplace, and for any ends."[73] Manipulation thus violates what we might call an *identifiability condition*: manipulated people mistakenly recognize themselves in the beliefs they now hold that are false to their real interests.[74] This violation undermines one's reflective agency.

There is another view of rhetoric that does not necessarily fall prey to this conflation and which Aristotle defends in *On Rhetoric* and which Hill reiterates in his *Principles of Rhetoric*. Bryan Garsten and Danielle Allen have reclaimed the Aristotelian view of rhetoric for thinking about contemporary reflections on deliberative democracy.[75] Properly understood, rhetoric reflects the cooperative aspirations of democratic life, rather than the more tyrannical imposition of the rhetorician's views. This is because the rhetorician hopes that the audience—those to whom he or she writes and speaks—will assent to the particular views in question as being their own so that they comport their political and ethical lives in light of those views. Think back to Du Bois's claim that the rhetorician uses goodness not as an ethical sanction but as a method for gaining human sympathy and interest. I follow this distinction between rhetoric-as-manipulation and rhetoric-as-persuasion mainly because it is a division to which Du Bois was attentive given his education and what he lays out in "Criteria" and because it helps us better understand how *Souls* can aspire to contribute to the political and ethical development of America. The latter, as Du Bois argues in "Criteria," relates to cultivating the "wide judgment" he defines as the aim of the black rhetorician.

In contrast to manipulation, when we persuade someone to hold this or that belief or engage in this or that action, there is a sense of ownership on the part of the one who is on the receiving end of persuasion. This is why Du Bois specifically uses "listen" and "see" to describe how the audience should orient themselves to his words. The person can say at the end of having listened and read carefully, "I'm persuaded." And "I'm persuaded" is meant to also denote that one now understands as in, once more, "I see." This is crucial if what one intends is for the person or community to be able to affirm, *on their own*, the new belief they now hold. This is what we might refer to as the content of the wider judgment. As Hill explains of the role of persuasion: "Persuasion may go on long after the feelings have been reached; for it is necessary, not only that the feelings should take the right direction, but that they should take it with a will."[76]

On this point, Du Bois agrees. For although he rightly emphasizes the coercive force of the law in protecting African Americans, he also believes the law alone does not entail the kind of deep transformation at the level of character necessary for achieving racial equality.[77] As he says elsewhere, the cure to racial injustice, if one were ever to be found, is not possible by "simply telling people the truth"; it comes about by "inducing them to act on the truth."[78] To induce them to act on the truth is to have it reflectively emanate from their will.

The statement "I'm persuaded" refers to the process of internal transformation by the auditor that aligns his or her belief with the rhetorician. As mentioned earlier, this is why movement is so important; one is literally moving from one side to another. This alignment indicates the active involvement of the auditor and affirms a view of the persuader (in this case Du Bois) as a partner in bringing about the internal transformation. In contrast to Robert Stepto's claim that the "rhetorical posture" of *Souls* expresses a "strategy for greater authorial control," it appears to do the opposite.[79] This is the point Du Bois affirms in his assessment of *Souls* in 1904: "In thus giving up the usual impersonal and judicial attitude of the traditional author I have lost in authority but gained in vividness."[80]

The diminishment of his authorial voice makes sense in the context of inviting his readers to be co-participants in arriving at shared judgments regarding the plight of African Americans. The statement "I'm persuaded" thus expresses something that individuals who are persuaded have reflectively done for themselves, which connects the belief they now hold with reasons for holding that belief. Hence Du Bois says in the first sentence of "The Forethought," already discussed: "Herein lie buried many things which if read with patience *may* show the strange meaning of being black here in the dawning of the Twentieth Century."[81] We see a similar use of the modal verb "may" when he says that he will narrate in detail the stories of black life so "that men *may* listen to the striving in the souls of black folk." This use of "may" captures a point so central to classical rhetoric. As Aristotle explains of the rhetorician's lack of control, it is the one on the receiving end of persuasion that "determines the speech's end and object."[82] Listeners are, in essence, responding to a situation in light of reasons to which *they* take *themselves* to be committed, even as the rhetorician is a co-participant in helping them see those reasons. This is why it makes sense to say Du Bois seeks to affirm the reflective agency of his reader.

I offer two observations about Du Bois's interest in the reflective agency of his reader and how we should understand the democratic character of rhetoric. His method has a dual function that points to both his black and white audiences that I will amplify in the next chapter. Du Bois is terribly concerned to affirm the self-esteem of African Americans, even amid the horrors of life. This is part of the great fight that Du Bois finds it necessary to remind his audience of in 1926. The examples are numerous, but in *Souls* we might think of the story of Josie Dowell, Alexander Crummell, the fictional story of John Jones, and Du Bois's understanding of the sorrow songs. Given the tragic fate of the first three individuals, it seems odd to put it in terms of affirming self-esteem. And by self-esteem, I mean what Tommie Shelby refers to as "a secure conviction that one's fundamental purposes are worthwhile."[83] Or to align it more closely to

Du Bois: African Americans are a people from whom worthwhile purposes both individually and collectively are possible. Despite the impact of white supremacy, then, the first three chapters underscore the excellence that African Americans should aspire toward, while the last of the four explicates the spiritual excellence African Americans qua African Americans have already displayed and contributed to the polity in the form of the sorrow songs. I will have more to say about the first two of these chapters in a moment. But these chapters should be read as Du Bois's attempt to counteract the negative influence of misrecognition—that is, of "measuring one's soul by the tape of a world that looks on in amused contempt and pity" that frames *Souls*.[84] Just as he invites the judgment of his white readers to be co-participants in the arrival of a truth hitherto unavailable, he does the same for those who live behind the veil. The hope is that even amid the terror of white supremacy, black Americans might nonetheless see the performance value of their lives.

In proceeding this way, and in contrast to Robert Gooding-Williams's interpretation of Du Bois wherein "African American politics is a practice of rule,"[85] *Souls* aspires to render compatible two accounts of politics that are central to American political thought broadly. The first is a vision of politics that focuses on ruling in the form of *giving direction* or *pointing the way*. This was obviously part of Du Bois's well-criticized elitism, even if only an elitism of an intellectual and professional vanguard. The second is a form of politics that affirms the reflective agency of the citizenry. Du Bois says in chapter 3, "Of Mr. Booker T. Washington and Others," where he deals with the question of leadership, yoking the two views of politics together as part of one understanding of democracy: "Honest and earnest criticism from those whose interests are most nearly touched,—criticism of writers by readers, of government by those governed, of leaders by those led,—this is the soul of democracy and the safeguard of modern society."[86] Indeed, as the conclusion of the book suggests, the weary traveler—the figure of the leader—is sustained by the encouraging voice of the masses below. In *Souls*, Du Bois stands before the judgment of the African American community asking them, as he does of his white audience, to study his words with him, "seeking the grain of truth hidden there."[87]

What, then, of his white audience? It seems that we miss the point of involving the judgment of the reader, if we do not attend to the relational and binding character of what Du Bois is attempting. Recall that Du Bois says to his audience, study my words "with me." Arriving early on in "The Forethought" of *Souls*, this is an invitation that frames the book. But an invitation to what? What he has in mind is that speaker and listener, author and reader may arrive at *shared* judgments regarding the subject matter and the claim it makes on them. In suggesting that they (speaker and listener) will arrive at shared judgments regarding the plight of blacks and the deficiencies of the polity, Du Bois also believes they will have tied themselves together in a community based on shared emotional dispositions regarding the subject matter.

To refer to a "community based on shared emotional dispositions" in no way implies that Du Bois means to refer to non-cognitive states. Involving the judgment of the reader in an effort to arrive at an accurate picture of the plight of African Americans, as Du Bois does, means that the emotional states that follow have an irreducible cognitive component. That is, they are in themselves judgments of value regarding the social world and the persons that inhabit it. To invoke the contemporary language of Robert Solomon as a description of Du Bois's outlook: "Emotion is not merely a feeling, as, say, pain is a feeling. It is also an outlook, an attitude, a reaching out to the world. . . . Thus, the conceptual geography of emotion suggests that the realm of emotion is neither the mind nor the world but both together: the world as experienced."[88] As such, Du Bois's reliance on the emotional dimension of persons also functions as a cognitive-affective approach to achieve a proper appreciation of the lived experience of one's fellows.

This final moment permits us to draw together the themes here with those pursued in the previous chapters. The shared horizon of concern is possible because of the space of contestation the idea of the people makes possible, even as the space becomes the locus for persuading white Americans to embrace an expanded view of themselves and the political community. Notice, Du Bois's account at once presupposes the aspirational view of the people Thomas Jefferson defended in the previous chapter and does so by turning to aesthetics as a means to awaken his fellows to a new society on par with Whitman. But he adheres more consistently than Jefferson or Whitman to the idea of openness and the struggle over whom we ought to be as a polity that connects him to Wells on one side and Holiday on the other. This is why, to recall Du Bois's language, it is a great fight. Whereas Jefferson's view collapsed into a form of particularism that threatened to arrest the developmental quality of the polity—a path Delany followed—Du Bois's seeks to forge an American polity consistent with the principle of openness that democratic legitimacy entails. The relational and binding quality that *Souls* seeks to forge follows from making the reader a co-participant in the arrival of a truth hitherto unavailable.

For him, a properly realized community based on shared emotional dispositions would embody not only conceptions of what one's community is about but also how one should relate to those being disregarded and dominated. Or to put it once more in the language of "Criteria of Negro Art," a properly realized community would be shaped by sympathy and human interest.

Calling the People to a Higher Vision

ON *THE SOULS OF BLACK FOLK*

There is unity in the book, not simply the general unity of the larger topic, but a unity of purpose in the distinctively subjective note that runs in each essay. Through all the book runs a personal and intimate tone of self-revelation. In each essay I sought to speak from within—to depict a world as we see it who dwell therein. In thus giving up the usual impersonal and judicial attitude of the traditional author I have lost in authority but gained in vividness.

—W.E.B. DU BOIS, "THE SOULS OF BLACK FOLK"

W.E.B. DU BOIS'S RECOLLECTION of Sam Hose's lynching (referenced in chapter 5) as the breaking point in his intellectual development—his move away from strict reliance on social science and its concern with presentation of "facts"—is complicated and varied. The famous memory of Hose's knuckles on display down a road he was traveling tracks the unfolding of Du Bois's traumatic encounter with racial disregard that ends in pessimism about the United States. By the end of his life, Du Bois could not "take any more of this country's treatment." "Chin up," he wrote to a friend, "and fight on, but realize that American Negroes can't win."[1] Perhaps he was right, the jury is still out. But his path ended where Martin Delany's truly began. Ironically, Du Bois's struggle in the United States, even if it ended in disappointment, created the condition for a new generation to deploy their energies in the ongoing battle for racial justice.

There is little space here to tell that story. But at the beginning of the journey—the place where we will sit—is Du Bois's sense that mere presentation of facts regarding the lives of black people was not enough. Where black people were concerned, facts seemed inadequate to secure truth. In *The Souls of Black Folk* of 1903, he is clear: social scientists give too much attention to tallying the "bastards and . . . prostitutes" among black people and too little attention paid to the "vast despair" that darkens black life.[2] "The car-window sociologist," he writes later in the book, is precisely the calm, cool, and detached scientist that is unable to effectively capture the stirrings of souls and the pain exacted on them.[3] What would it mean to focus on that pain—to travel, even if imaginatively, through the souls of black folk? How might it move the audience to truth's home? What vision of America might emerge if we begin with the pain of black people?

These questions should help us understand one of Du Bois's brief self-appraisals of *Souls* that opens this chapter. There is a personal note that runs throughout the book.[4] *Souls* is a narrative from one who is "bone of the bone and flesh of the flesh of them that live within the Veil."[5] Du Bois's attachment to his subjects allows him to vividly capture the color line and its effects on black and white lives. He aimed for a new mode of presentation that could vivify his interventions. Even in 1903, several years after Hose's lynching, Du Bois was still interested in the facts of black life and white wrongs; he was still after the truth of it all. Similar to Ida B. Wells, he came to think fact-finding and vivid storytelling were part of the epistemology of truth's discovery and social uptake. As Sheila Lloyd rightly notes, in *Souls* the "language of social analysis and critique is supplemented by romantic vocabulary and imagery."[6]

It is unclear if Du Bois read Frederick Douglass's meditations on the importance of the photograph to a community's cultural life. Perhaps he did. But what is clear is that Douglass captures a sentiment—noble in his estimation—that is on display in Du Bois's work: "Only a few men wish to think while all wish to feel, for feeling is divine, and infinite."[7] Du Bois's use of "vividness" in the epigraph to characterize his compositional practice in writing *Souls* captures the evocative character of the text as well as the intensity of the emotions it seeks to elicit. His authority may well be diminished, but this is part of his invitation to discover the truths in the text. "Books," writes Walt Whitman in a line that could have been written by Du Bois, "are to be called for, and supplied, on the assumption that the process of reading is not a half-sleep; but, in the highest sense, an exercise . . . the reader is to do something. . . . must himself or herself construct indeed the . . . argument."[8] This is precisely the logic of rhetoric described in the previous chapter; it ties Du Bois to Wells, Whitman, and Douglass and all to the idea that coming to discover the truth is a co-partnership.

In invoking Douglass and Whitman, even if ever so briefly, I am proposing that Du Bois draws together two features that we have already encountered: a commitment to his readers' reflective agency and a belief that the vividness of the pictures he paints in words may move his audience to a position of ethical rectitude. Here is *Souls'* perfectionism—a romantic aspiration to transform the polity and call the people to a higher vision. It is no wonder Du Bois tells us in *Dusk of Dawn* as he reflects on the period in which he wrote *Souls*: "My attention from the first was focused on democracy and *democratic development* and upon the problem of the admission of my people into the freedom of democracy."[9]

In chapter 4, I argued that the idea of the people central to democracy opens up space for evocative appeals. In chapter 5, I maintained in my discussions of Whitman, Wells, the NAACP, and especially Billie Holiday that the aesthetic fills out such appeals. There, of course, our focus was on the horror of lynching as a means to transform the citizenry. In chapter 6, we considered at length the context of Du Bois's "Criteria" essay, and I illuminated both the substance of that text and its intimations in *Souls*. I offered an account of why it makes sense to think about *Souls* from the perspective of "Criteria" and, thus, as a project of positive propaganda. The persuasive goals of the Du Boisian rhetorician is of a piece with the propagandist's desire to realize truth and goodness. Du Bois turns out to be an artist of letters, or as William Ferris puts it, a "vivid word painter,"[10] serving as a co-partner in helping his audience arrive at a broader or truer picture of black life. *Souls* functions as a bridge to usher the people into a new image of themselves. We can now say that when Du Bois tells us in 1926 that the artist has used visions of goodness to secure sympathy and human interest, he was describing goals he pursued in 1903.

I turn explicitly in this context to *Souls* and offer an interpretation of three of its central chapters: chapter 1, "Of Our Spiritual Strivings"; chapter 4, "Of the Meaning of Progress"; and chapter 12, "Of Alexander Crummell." These three chapters provide us with a way of viewing the entire book. Attending to the first of these chapters brings into sharper relief the problem to which the rest of *Souls* is directed—the problem of frustrated and unrealized souls that Du Bois sees in the eyes of "the other black boys."[11] The gendered language that binds chapters 1 to 12 is mediated by the figure of Josie Dowell that emerges in chapter 4. Josie (following her common identification) is a poignant example of a figure whose aspirations succumb to the "progress" of white supremacy. Joseph Winters is correct when he says: "Josie's life and death constitute a central place in Du Bois's vision."[12] By treating Josie's fate as an iteration of the problem outlined in "Of Our Spiritual Strivings," the reader is positioned to see Du Bois's general concern as affecting black life as such. The discussion of Josie suggests that for him white supremacy endangers the freedom of both black men and women. This complicates even if it does not settle the constrained character of Du Bois's feminism.[13]

Unlike most discussions of *Souls*, I focus on the theme of the soul rather than the more commonly discussed ideas such as the "veil" or "double-consciousness" to sharpen both the site of the problem and the place for transformation.[14] The "veil" and "double-consciousness," although important, play subordinate roles in this analysis. We have already noted the importance of the soul in part 1, and it remained a central category in the latter part of the nineteenth century. Defenders of white supremacy denied that black people had souls, which often functioned as reasons for their ill treatment. From Bucker Payne's *The Negro: What Is His Ethnological Status?* (1867) to G.C.H. Hasskarl's *"The Missing Link?" or The Negro's Ethnological Status* (1898) to Charles Carroll's *The Negro a Beast; or, In the Image of God* (1900)—all these works turned on the denial to black people of souls. Du Bois's book emerges against this backdrop and responds to these denials.[15]

Instead of focusing exclusively on *Souls* as a counterresponse, I explore how the idea of the soul enables Du Bois's discussion of the emotional and ethical dimensions of the self that aspire for goods in this world. These goods are material, to be sure, but also socio-psychological—the ability to form plans of life, have confidence (i.e., self-esteem) in one's capacity to construct and pursue those life plans, and thus hope in realizing those plans with communal support. The ability to form plans of life and have confidence in them rests on a foundation of shared supportive goods, such as enjoying equal ethical and political regard in society, that are essential to our pursuits but not equivalent to them.[16] All of this is presumed to be necessary to the soul's enrichment. The soul, I contend, thus functions as a metaphor for what we might call the immanence of transcendence. The goods we seek emerge from this world, but our ability to secure them often transcends our agency and requires communal support.

Similar to other thinkers, Du Bois is concerned with how the soul is deformed or frustrated due to the workings of white supremacy. Recall

David Walker's 1829 concern with the enslaved woman and free enslaved man, or think of Maria Stewart as she agonizes in 1833 that servitude has sapped the ambition and courage of black people, or Hosea Easton's worry in 1837 that black lives are deformed due to racial prejudice, or finally Martin Delany's 1852 observation that the elevation of black life is arrested in the United States. Du Bois captures all these concerns in his thinking of the soul. To be a slave of the community in Frederick Douglass's sense of that idea is not only to have the material conditions of life perpetually endangered but more significantly to have a soul that is deformed or that ceases to strive. Centralizing the soul in this analysis allows us to track both the tragic resonances of the text and its perfectionist arc that Du Bois retrospectively describes under the heading of "democratic development."

Against this background, Du Bois's chapter on Crummell (chapter 12), mediated and enriched by his discussion of Josie, comes to serve a specific purpose. He is a proxy for black lives. The Crummell chapter functions as a window onto the vast reaches of black aspirations and the way the practical workings of white supremacy obstruct the realization of those aspirations. These two features conspire in an emotional dance that Du Bois hopes will generate transformation. His description of the soul intends to unite black and white audiences in order to generate sympathy and human interest—they each seek to "know the world" and "know [themselves]."[17] And yet, it is the fact of unrealized aspirations due to white supremacy— the asymmetry between black and white lives—that he hopes will induce shame.

The Immanence of Transcendence: Reading "Of Our Spiritual Strivings"

The publication of *The Souls of Black Folk* was a cultural event. As a reviewer in the *Nation* put it in 1903: the book is a "profoundly interesting and affecting book, remarkable as a piece of literature."[18] John Spencer Bassett, the *South Atlantic Quarterly* editor, nicely captured the thrust of the book: "It is a plea for soul opportunity."[19] In his sprawling but decadent philosophical idealism of black life and history, *The African Abroad* of 1913, Ferris says of *Souls*: "Du Bois is a literary artist who can clothe his thought in such forms of poetic beauty that we are captivated by the opulent splendor and richness of his diction, *while our souls are being stirred by his burning eloquence.*"[20] In keeping with Ferris's remark, William Braithwaite goes further in 1919, claiming that *Souls* "began a poetic tradition." Stretching "poetry" to include prose, Braithwaite continues: "It is only through the intense, passionate, spiritual idealism of such substance as makes 'The Souls of Black Folk' such a quivering rhapsody of wrongs endured and hopes to be fulfilled that the poets of the race with compelling artistry can lift the Negro into the only full and complete nationalism he knows—that of the American democracy."[21] This is the central reason why the idea of the soul looms large in the book.

How does Du Bois understand the soul? How does his account of the soul illuminate the problem of white supremacy? How do these questions center the lives of black people as the abiding concern of the text rather than allowing the text to function as a meditation on the interior life of Du Bois? With this last question, I resist the tendency to situate Du Bois in *Souls*, thereby focusing squarely on his textual presence.

ON THE IMPORTANCE OF THE SOUL

The use of "souls" in Ferris's passage and the invocation of "spiritual idealism" by Braithwaite denote the ethical and emotional nature of human beings that Du Bois is seeking to transform. In earlier thinkers, we observed the soul in conjunction with the spirit to capture what humans are and the energy that fuels their aspirations. These thinkers seemed less interested in talking about the soul as an intangible and immortal property. Du Bois stands in this tradition, although he fills out the discussion considerably. The soul is not a transcendent property that exists beyond the material self that we see in Plato, nor does it represent an interior dimension within us and through which God speaks as we see in St. Augustine.[22] As Jonathon Kahn rightly notes: Du Bois "constructs the souls of black folk entirely out of the desires, efforts, practices, and accomplishments of African American life as it is lived."[23] In this the soul has a communal character. Soul is the bearer of character, and character the bearer of the soul.

This is only part of Du Bois's picture. The soul is also that part of us that longs for and aspires toward ways of being and living in the world. The soul is always grasping for what stands beyond it and which is presumed to be the source of its fulfillment. To have soul is to feel the vibration of the longings and desires of a past—a communal past—coursing through you, even as your soul may burn with desires yet realized. This way of thinking of the soul is perfectionist in form. We might think of it in William Wordsworth's sense in which the soul, emerging out of and communing with nature, discovers its creative and unexpressed capacities.[24] This brings to mind Ralph Waldo Emerson's understanding of the soul when he speaks of nature as having higher goals in producing new individuals and communities. He refers to this as "*ascension*, or the passage of the soul into higher forms."[25] Closer to Du Bois, we might think of Anna Julia Cooper's test of democracy: "if it does not turn out better, noble, truer men and women,—if it does not add to the world's stock of valuable souls . . . I will have none of it."[26] This is not literary ornamentation—the word "soul" does substantive work. Wordsworth, Emerson, and Cooper are committed to perfectionism. Their perfectionism is not about plans of life receiving political endorsement, say, from the state. Rather, perfectionism refers to the development and improvement of character but always understood within a shared horizon, whether that be of nature broadly or one's social and political communities.[27]

For Du Bois, this desiring feature of the soul is unlikely to be radically unique. In this we find its dangers and possibilities. What is aspired for is often shaped by our communities and for just that reason the soul can also express the wounds of a community. Here, for example, we might think of Frederick Douglass's description of the Negro spirituals: "They told a tale of woe . . . they breathed the prayer and complaint of souls boiling over with the bitterest anguish. . . . The songs of the slave represent the sorrows of his heart."[28] Du Bois's description of the Negro spirituals—the sorrow songs—is close to Douglass's account. They are, for Du Bois, tales of despair laced with threads of faith in freedom.[29]

The soul may also express the deformed and destructive wishes of a community. This is what Du Bois has in mind in the famous chapter 2 of *Darkwater*. The chapter itself is a revised version of his 1910 essay "The Souls of White Folk" and his 1917 article "Of the Culture of White Folk."[30] Du Bois describes the souls of white people and their longing for sole possession of the earth as the source and plenitude of their identity. For him, the proprietary model of whiteness—a model that shapes so much of the contemporary analysis of racial capitalism—is housed within an ethical-religious framework.[31]

Whiteness is a religious worldview in the sense of providing those who inhabit it with idioms for constructing reality, ways of understanding their lives within it, and giving their lives purpose and meaning. "A nation's religion," Du Bois says, "is its life."[32] The insidious dimension of whiteness is that it depends, for its intelligibility, on the denial to others of the opportunity to fashion their own lives and communities.

This is the psychological wage of whiteness to which Du Bois famously refers in *Black Reconstruction*. His point is not merely that whiteness provides compensatory relief to white Americans for being exploited by economic processes. He also means to capture how whiteness shapes the appetitive and spiritual dimensions of character formation, and it can take on horrific form as we observed in our discussion of lynching. In both the general sense and the specific manifestation of lynching spectacles, the point is that one is cultured in whiteness. Here is how Du Bois describes the matter in *Darkwater*, as he distills his conversations with the "sweeter souls of the dominant world."

> My poor un-white thing! Weep not nor rage. I know, too well, that the curse of God lies heavy upon you. Why? That is not for me to say, but be brave! Do your work in your lowly sphere, praying the good Lord that into heaven above, where all is love, you may, one day, be born—white!

To this Du Bois responds:

> I do not laugh. I am quite straight-faced as I ask soberly:
>   "But what on earth is whiteness that one should so desire it?" Then always, somehow, some way, silently but clearly, I am given to understand that whiteness is the ownership of the earth forever and ever, *Amen!*[33]

As a religious worldview, whiteness cultivates in its occupants an orientation toward the world, and dominion over the objects in the world is the soul's expression. Hence Du Bois says: "All through the world this *gospel is preaching*. It has its literature, it has it *priests*, it has its secret propaganda and above all—it pays!" To say whiteness has its literature, priests, and negative propaganda (we can assume, he means) and pays is just to say whiteness has a culture of support.

Darkwater is a critical text for understanding Du Bois's idea of the soul and many other transformations in his thinking about democratic leadership, the social-psychology of whiteness, and the impact of whiteness on political economy. But for our purposes, it is the all-important first chapter of *Souls* on which we focus. In that chapter, "Of Our Spiritual Strivings," we see the representation of the soul yearning and being denied. This captures the perfectionism and tragedy at the heart of the book Du Bois deploys in his efforts to transform his white counterparts. Together, perfectionism and tragedy also help us see that under conditions of domination, the soul's integrity may understandably buckle and do so without any secondary lessons for life. In the face of our normal quests to be more than what we are, we may find that the cruelty and unfairness of life dash our plans, and often due to no fault of our own.[34] We may also realize that our failure is not the result of bad luck but a consequence of what Claudia Card calls the "unnatural lottery"—a path-dependent form of bad luck visited upon the oppressed while absolving others of their responsibility in its reproduction through norms and institutions.[35] Du Bois notices it, he understands it, but he asks his readers not to be paralyzed by it for the sake of ethical and political resistance. We need to move carefully through some of the chapter's initial paragraphs to see how and why the soul emerges as a significant category.

ON THE IMMANENCE OF TRANSCENDENCE

Consider the first two paragraphs in "Of Our Spiritual Strivings." In paragraph 1, Du Bois focuses our attention on the question, "How does it feel to be a problem?" He fleshes out "problem" in terms of exclusion from the polity and the inability to legitimately use the community's resources to flourish. This is the point he pursues in paragraph 2 where he recounts his experience of exclusion and of having recognition withheld. There, he discusses exchanging cards in school and he tells the reader: "The exchange was merry, till one girl, a tall new comer, refused my card,—refused it peremptorily, with a glance." This is the famous moment when Du Bois realizes he is different and shut out "from their world [his white counterparts'] by a vast veil."[36]

Three moments mark the full arc of paragraph 2. The first moment, the one just discussed, is about Du Bois. The second is about those he refers to as the "other black boys" and what marks him off from them. The third moment is a reunion of the two but one that continues to foreground the lives of the other black boys.

Of the second moment, Du Bois writes: "But they [his white counterparts] should not keep these prizes, I said; some, all, I would wrest from them. Just how I would do it I could never decide: by reading law, by healing the sick, by telling the wonderful tales that swam in my head,—some way." What is important about this passage is Du Bois's explicit claim that he would not permit white Americans to keep all of the opportunities.[37] His insistence on keeping some for himself is a refusal to allow the veil to sever, at a perceptual level, his lived reality from his imagined longings. His response stands in stark contrast to that of the other black boys. Here is how Du Bois describes them: "With other black boys the strife was not so fiercely sunny: their youth shrunk into *tasteless sycophancy*, or into *silent hatred* of the pale world about them and mocking distrust of everything white, or wasted itself in a bitter cry, *'why did God make me an outcast and stranger in mine own house?'*"[38]

Du Bois is characterizing both the other black boys and his relationship to them. Oppression constrains all black people in the nineteenth and early twentieth centuries and thus they all live under a shared condition of domination. "A half-awakened common consciousness," he writes in chapter 4, develops from "common joy and grief." But black people's relationship to that condition is not the same: "All this caused us to think some thoughts together; but these, when ripe for speech, were spoken in various languages."[39] This marks internal difference, even amid the experience of shared disregard. This is why Du Bois says the strife between the black boys and white America was not aggressively enjoyed.

This conflict, however, gives rise to settled orientations that Du Bois sees as troubling. *Sycophancy* refers to a kind of servile orientation to secure a good or to gain favor. It captures the subordinate status of the one seeking favor—a form of servility marked by insincerity. Unlike the attribution of sycophancy to Booker T. Washington in chapter 3 of *Souls*, in this context there is no suggestion that this is desired. Du Bois is clear that sycophancy is rightly perceived as tasteless—a failure to show self-respect, and thus a failure to elicit respect from others. *Silent hatred* refers to a form of pent-up anger which, importantly, is not directed at specific white individuals that may be the cause of one's harm. Rather, hatred is directed at all white people; it captures an abiding orientation toward one's white counterparts. The *plea to God* regarding one's status as an outcast goes deeper than the first two since it wonders about the spiritual deservedness of one's status. Here, one's orientation toward oneself is marked by existential doubt.

At the center of *Souls* is Du Bois's concern with black people's psychological health and ethical-political status. The orientations of sycophancy, hatred, and self-doubt of one's worth seem not to function as motivation for resistance against the forces of domination. Du Bois is not here criticizing. Rather, he is pointing the reader to the problem—the problem with white people that creates problems for black people. He thus describes how the workings of white supremacy structure the objects of one's soul and the horizon of the soul's imaginings. As he says later in the chapter: "The facing of so vast a prejudice could not but bring the inevitable self-questioning, self-disparagement, and lowering of ideals which ever accompany repression and breed in an atmosphere of contempt and hatred."[40] We might say that he is showing us that the soul's integrity is not always improved by suffering but may buckle under domination's weight. We may be left in ruins.

Du Bois's thinking connects with our earlier discussion of hope, but here it is localized in one's normal relationship to life. This is not the grand framing of how black people qua black people should orient themselves to the nation's transformative possibilities in the absence of available evidence—the debate among Delany, Douglass, and Cooper. Rather, Du Bois's interest is the following: Given the workings of racial domination, how do black people get on with the business of forming plans of life? If the soul is the seat of aspiration, it is also the place of hope—a source of motivation.

It is this mundane but no less significant way of thinking about hope that concerns Du Bois. As Katie Stockdale rightly notes, "oppression can threaten and damage hope," it can diminish "the likelihood that a person's hopes will be realized" and it harms our "capacities for hope: the very ability to cultivate or sustain hopes for one's own life."[41] What Stockdale observes is precisely what Du Bois implies in his characterization of the other black boys. As the soul comes under assault, and insincerity, hatred, and self-doubt settle in as abiding states, aspirations are either deformed or go unarticulated and unpursued. Things are not fiercely sunny for the other black boys; their efforts are marked by the recognition of being diminished, due to no failure of their own will. The critical question, for Du Bois, is how to sustain hope in the face of oppression.

Du Bois himself was not immune to the darkening of the soul and evisceration of hope. In chapter 11, "Of the Passing of the First Born," he offers an elegiac meditation on his son's death, Burghardt Gomer Du Bois. Chapter 11, along with chapters 12 ("Of Alexander Crummell") and 13 ("Of the Coming of John"), is part of one sustained reflection on the unnatural lottery and its effect on black lives. To this we should add chapter 4 ("Of the Meaning of Progress) and the figure of Josie.

Burghardt was born on October 2, 1897, and died of diphtheria several months shy of his second birthday. The death was not wholly "natural"; white doctors would not treat his son and black doctors were scarce. In the chapter, Du Bois sees in Burghardt the embodiment of his own hope: "I too mused above his little white bed; saw the strength of my own arm stretched onward through the ages through the new strength of his; saw the dream of my black fathers stagger a step onward in the wild phantasm of the world."[42]

What is striking about the chapter is how he describes the meaning of Burghardt's death—the freedom he seemingly finds. If we pay careful attention, we can detect that Burghardt escaped (in one sense) the fate of the black boys:

All that day and all that night there sat an awful gladness in my heart,— nay, blame me not if I see the world thus darkly through the Veil,—and my soul whispers ever to me, saying, "Not dead, not dead, but escaped; not bond, but free." No bitter meanness now shall sicken his baby heart till it die a living death, no taunt shall madden his happy boyhood. Fool that I was to think or wish that this little soul should grow choked and deformed within the Veil! I might have known that yonder deep unworldly look that ever and anon floated past his eyes was peering far beyond this narrow Now. . . . Well sped, my boy, before the world had dubbed your ambition insolence, had held your ideals unattainable, and taught you to cringe and bow.[43]

This is a poignant passage. Du Bois comes to find gladness, even if laced with profound sadness, in his son's death. The reason is that Burghardt escaped the deadening effects of white supremacy. This perverse characterization in which death equals freedom, and life amounts to a living death in America, haunts the entire text. Du Bois tries desperately to hold this thinking at bay.

As that chapter concludes, Du Bois ultimately thinks better of his characterization, even as it is laced with a tragic recognition. The upheaval of his emotions gives way to settled ones. The meaning he attaches to Burghardt's death cuts too deep; it leaves little room for much else by way of living. It is a closed tragedy, with none of the lessons for others to deploy in their own lives. It is a truth, but it cannot be the only truth, or so Du Bois insists. His loss of innocence and refusal to allow racism to constrain his soul invoked in chapter 1 are now literally recast in chapter 11 as the narrative death of an innocent. Like that initial discussion, Du Bois's elegy refuses to accept death as freedom—refuses to allow white supremacy to have the last word. He models an orientation for his black reader—a posture toward the viciousness of American life. Should not the reader do the same? Should they not, after all, insist on another truth—namely, that white supremacy produces losses of such a catastrophic nature, such as taking comfort in the death of one's child because it means they escaped racism, that no one should have to endure?[44] As with the other black boys, white supremacy has taken something from him. But Du Bois refuses to allow his soul to die. Loss is real, he says to his readers, and grief hurts. Both mark out the cruelty of American life; but they must not consume. He refuses to surrender, but nor does he suggest that a better future is assured: "Idle words; he *might have* borne his burden more bravely than we,—aye, and found it lighter too, some day."[45] As Joseph Winters notes, "possibility and loss" always mingle in Du Bois's thinking when we recognize that we do not exercise sovereign authority over those with whom we engage.[46] It is the particular character of possibility and loss—the liminal condition it creates for black people—that gives rise to black hope: "a hope not hopeless, but unhopeful."[47]

As his thinking in chapters 1 and 11 suggests, Du Bois takes himself to be in and of the black community, but he carves out some distance between himself and the lives of black people. This is not primarily because of Du Bois's well-acknowledged refined sensibilities. Something else is at work—a desire to use the reality of black life as a means to train our insights.

Throughout *Souls*, Du Bois's authorial position emanates from what Robert Stepto rightly calls a "more completely realized development of a proudly self-conscious (as opposed to 'double-conscienced') racial voice."[48] The original article title of chapter 1 that appeared in the 1897 issue of *The Atlantic* was "Strivings of the Negro People" before he moved to the more subjective and intimate title, "Of Our Spiritual Strivings." Notwithstanding this self-identity (or perhaps because of it), Du Bois distinguishes between himself and his refusal to give up and the other black boys because he means for the reader to focus on lives that go unrealized.

By shifting our attention to the status of the other black boys in *Souls*—their responses to domination and exclusion—and making them the central concern for Du Bois, we can resist Shamoon Zamir's argument that the first two paragraphs in *Souls* are "strongly anchored in autobiography, with Du Bois gradually and with qualification moving out toward claiming some sort of representative status for his own experience."[49] Instead, we can read Du Bois as asking his readers to bear witness to the deformed or exhausted souls among his people that characterized his thinking of the 1890s. His point in focusing on the other black boys is to say to his audience, take heed. There are lessons, we should read Du Bois as saying, to be learned from my people's deformed or frustrated lives. What precisely they are depends on his two audiences—his black and white readers. But tragedy must educate.

In emphasizing the soul and the danger posed to it by white supremacy, I do not mean to downplay the material consequences of domination and exclusion—you are unable to vote, you live at the whim of another and remain perpetually vulnerable, your economic pursuits are frustrated, and you are unable to move freely from place to place without fear. Throughout the text, for example, in chapters 1 and 3, Du Bois underscores the political importance of the right and ability to vote freely. And in chapter 7, "Of the Black Belt," Du Bois focuses on how material opportunities are denied to African Americans because they are wholly under white people's control. Here, debt peonage and sharecropping loom large as does the inescapability of debt: "A young black fellow. . . . He is twenty-two, and just married. Until last year he had good luck renting; then cotton fell, and the sheriff seized and sold all he had. So he moved here, where the rent is higher, the land poorer, and the owner inflexible. . . . Poor lad!—a slave at twenty-two."[50] From the Jim Crow car to debt peonage and share-cropping, the chapter narrates a story of inescapable debt, tied to the devaluation of black life that robs one of freedom.

As with the franchise and freedom of economic opportunities, the importance of the soul is always in close proximity. In his summary reflection in the conclusion of chapter 1, Du Bois writes: "The power of the ballot we need in sheer self-defence, else what shall save us from a second slavery? Freedom, too, the long-sought, we still seek,—the free-dom of life and limb, the freedom to work and think, the freedom to love and aspire."[51] These words—"freedom to love and aspire"—do not appear in the original 1897 essay. With their addition, we can see that similar to thinkers we have already considered, the foundational danger for Du Bois is of a soul whose striving is deformed or ceases to aspire altogether.[52]

This idea of the soul gives Du Bois's discussion of the veil first intro-duced in paragraph 2 of the chapter and double-consciousness in para-graphs 3 and 4 its rich and unsettling character. Here is the classic passage to which readers often refer:

> After the Egyptian and Indian, the Greek and Roman, the Teuton and the Mongolian, the Negro is a sort of seventh son, born with a veil, and gifted with second-sight in this American world,—a world which yields him no true self-consciousness, but only lets him see himself through the revelation of the other world. It is a peculiar sensation, this double-consciousness, this sense of always looking at one's self through the eyes of others, of measuring one's *soul* by the tape of a world that looks on in amused contempt and pity.[53]

The passage contains a set of interrelated claims. The first relates to the epistemic insight that attends black vision. Black people are perceptually enhanced because they are able to discern aspects of the world based on their subordinate status. They see, as it were, from below and this provides insight into the kinds of practices required to sustain domination and the position of those engaged in denying justice.[54] Those differently raced and in dominant positions often overlook their complicity in injustice and thus reason from a place of ignorance.

The second claim relates to the intersubjective status of identity formation. Recognition is central to who we are and black people may often forge their identities through the distorted lens of racial disregard.[55] This is not merely an issue of nonrecognition, what the young girl performed when she refused Du Bois's card; this is a matter of misrecognition. Both in his time, say in the 1890 works of William James, Anna Julia Cooper, and George Herbert Mead, and in our time with Charles Taylor, the idea is that misrecognition "can inflict a grievous wound, saddling its victims with a crippling self-hatred."[56] One of the central features of double-consciousness is the infliction of what Tommie Shelby calls an "expressive harm, a form of stigmatizing, insulting, or demeaning [of] others"[57] that comes to diminish one's self-esteem. This is why it becomes challenging to muster hope. Du Bois's language of looking at oneself through others' eyes points to the importance of recognition. In his view, and not unlike earlier thinkers and contemporary scholars, misrecognition by one's fellows touches the soul, darkens its light, and threatens to prevent it from illuminating one's path forward.

Understanding the themes of paragraphs 3 and 4, I think, retrospectively sharpens the third, and final, moment of paragraph 2. At the end of that paragraph, Du Bois returns to the shared experience of exclusion. But amid that common condition, the reader can now hold in view the distinction between Du Bois and the other black boys. This informs and structures how we should read the last sentence of paragraph 2 wherein he invokes William Wordsworth's 1807 romantic era poem, "Ode. Intimations of Immortality from Recollections of Early Childhood" (or "Intimations Ode").

When Du Bois says that the "the shades of the prison-house closed round about us all," he implicitly invokes Wordsworth's poem. But what is the point of the poem? Among its many themes, Wordsworth is principally interested in the immortality of the soul and he sees the soul as a cipher for divinity.[58] "Intimations Ode" is part of a longer historical shift that tightly binds God and the soul to the unfolding and revelation of nature's possibilities and the idea of human beings as an extension of nature. The soul exists in this world as it bears the trace of another—spiritual—world that came before.[59] This was part of a "general tendency" in romanticism according to M. H. Abrams's classic study, "to naturalize the supernatural and humanize the divine."[60]

Despite the shift to naturalism (something that Du Bois shares with the romantics), Wordsworth's use of the prison house represents a lament regarding the soul's emergence from youth into adulthood. He has in mind childhood recollections of the divine light that precedes birth and which, once born, slowly fades over time.[61] Understanding the soul and childhood in this way was not unique to Wordsworth; we see it in more and lesser degrees in William Blake, Samuel Coleridge, and Ralph Waldo Emerson. To take the most proximate example, we see Emerson in his 1842 essay "The Transcendentalist" lamenting that the individual loses touch with a prior experience of the divine because of the intrusion of life and life's movement.[62] Grappling as they did with religion's fate under modern conditions, romantics like Wordsworth and Emerson were interested in retaining the immanence of divinity in this all-too-natural world. For it was with the trace of God in us that we might still recognize the light and beauty of this world.

Du Bois's use of the prison house metaphor has an analogical relationship to Wordsworth's poem on an initial read. Du Bois imitates Wordsworth's by recalling his childhood and the way racism steals his innocence. This is the interpretation we see in different ways from Gooding-Williams and Zamir.[63] Gooding-Williams is quite explicit in his reading: Du Bois revises "Wordsworth's descendentalism by imagining himself as descended from a sublime and glorious origin into the jail cell of American racism."[64] Du Bois thus figures not merely as the author of *The Souls of Black Folk* but also and importantly its subject matter.

In invoking Gooding-Williams's and Zamir's analyses, we might consider the following. In reading Du Bois's invocation of Wordsworth as a means for revealing something about himself, are we still able to keep in view the distinction between Du Bois and the other black boys? The answer is likely no, and the reason is that we will mistakenly take Du Bois's story about his loss of innocence as also the exemplary story about the lives of other black boys. Recall Zamir's argument that Du Bois claims a representative status for his own experiences. This reading is encouraged by Du Bois, as he seeks to authorize his experiences as a black person and thus legitimize his appeal to white and black Americans. Who denies that Du Bois was looking to establish himself as black America's voice? But this angle of interpretation, if insisted upon too intensely, misses something crucial that Du Bois is also after. It is because of his life before the veil descends, in contrast to the other black boys, that makes him sufficiently resilient in the face of white supremacy in ways that the other black boys appear not to be. It is the lives of the other black boys to which the book attempts a response.

I suggest, then, that we deemphasize Du Bois as the subject of *Souls*. I propose that we give less weight to the kind of interpretation we find in Zamir and Gooding-Williams in which Du Bois becomes the issue of the book. I am asking that we take the title—*The Souls of Black Folk*—as our main focus. If we do so, I think we can do better justice to Du Bois's expressed interest in the lives behind the veil.

This permits another insight, one that keeps white supremacy clearly in view and its influence on black people's self-description and life chances. For Du Bois, it is not a prior experience with the divine or some loss of innocence that the other black boys lament, that leaves them wondering why they are outcasts in their own house. Rather, it is the human longing—the black boys' desire to grow and dream unencumbered. The prison house not only closes around the souls of black folk, but without proper fortification it seemingly darkens its inner light. This means that in *Souls*, Du Bois is interested in getting the nation to show care and concern for black people and to establish the conditions that must obtain for them to strive with the possibility of flourishing.

This reading situates Du Bois's thinking within a broader horizon of concern we have thus far considered. What is required is that black people not accept the image of themselves they see when they look through their white counterparts' eyes. This shaped the call for racial solidarity of the 1830s, 1840s, and 1850s, and informed the Harlem Renaissance's counter-response to the misrecognition and misdescription of black people that we examined in the last chapter. Du Bois captures his worry about accepting the content of misrecognition in a particularly poignant manner in paragraph 5:

> Through history, the powers of single black men flash here and there like falling stars, and die sometimes before the world has rightly gauged their brightness. Here in America, in the few days since Emancipation, the black man's turning hither and thither in hesitant and doubtful striving has often made his very strength to lose effectiveness, to seem like absence of power, like weakness.[65]

All this suggest that Du Bois intends for the reader to focus not on his response but on the reactions by other black people that reveal their struggles and frustrations in an age seemingly marked by freedom. As was the case in earlier figures, he is also keen to point out that the soul only *seems* to be weak and without power, indicating his goal to remind black people of their innerspring of energy.[66] Alexander Crummell serves as the reminder.

Of Josie Dowell

Before turning to Crummell, we need to make explicit the reach of Du Bois's concerns. As stipulated in chapter 1 of *Souls*, it is the other black boys to which he directs his attention. The language of "boys" and the frequent references to "black men" and their powers and dreams in contrast to the infrequent references to black women is a source of concern. Throughout *Souls*, to appropriate Joy James's understanding, Du Bois "holds on to a masculinist framework that presents the male as normative."[67] The black "male,"[68] as it were, becomes the subject of his concerns, the presupposition of his thinking, and the transformative site on which to build a better future. But were we to stay here (James hardly does, although many do), Du Bois would find himself challenging the ways the lives of black men are rendered invisible, while inadvertently (perhaps) producing his own blind spot as it relates to the status of black women. We will be left with the claim, as Hazel Carby classically put it, that "gendered structures of thought and feeling permeate . . . *The Souls of Black Folk*," and the specific result is that black women are not imagined as "viable political, social, or intellectual" futures in the text and for African Americans.[69] The figure of Josie and the intellectual context of Du Bois's reflections trouble the account above. In doing so, Du Bois pulls Josie in rather than excludes her from the orbit of concerns that frame chapter 1 of *Souls*.

There are at least three different kinds of issues we might find ourselves worrying about with Du Bois on the question of gender equality. It is worth distinguishing them because they bear directly on the broader commitment to equal regard for persons as a feature of democratic life. We also want to be clear about the aptness of our worry. Patriarchy, on the one hand, and insensitivity to the gendered character of social life and the unequal burdens involved, on the other, are not the same thing. The latter need not entail the former, although the former most certainly includes the latter. So distinguishing between different kinds of problems will help sharpen the analysis, the criticism, and perhaps mode of intervention. Ultimately, one has to decide the terms on which Du Bois will be taken (if you take him at all).

There is the straightforward position of patriarchy, in which men and women are hierarchically arranged and in which "the male" is normative. This account involves practices of domination and exclusion based on gender and it also subscribes to clear gendered roles and duties. Given Du Bois's activism and his elevation of women's rights and their heroism, it can scarcely be thought that he was committed to this first position.

We can distinguish the account above from a second position that eschews patriarchy, that renders the embodiment of "male" and "female" lives as equal and so brings into view the distinctive harms that attend being a woman, but that nonetheless still subscribe to clear gendered roles and duties. Of this second kind that sits at the opposite end of the first, you can find in the nineteenth and early twentieth centuries several African American women activists and intellectuals, such as Anna Julia Cooper, Fannie Barrier Williams, and Mary Church Terrell, pushing for social and civic equality but having little concern with speaking about the distinctive work of black women versus black men. For example, in her first presidential address to the National Association of Colored Women in 1897, Terrell is clear: "Special stress has been laid upon the fact that our association is composed of women, not because we wish to deny rights and privileges to our brothers . . . , but because the work which we hope to accomplish can be done better, by the mothers, wives, daughters, and sisters of our race than by the fathers, husbands, brothers, and sons."[70] What should be observed about this category, and here I partly agree with Farah Jasmine Griffin, is that as a tool of critical analysis gender was not fully worked out in the nineteenth and early twentieth centuries.[71] This permitted the language of "men's work" or "women's work," even as that language was housed within criticisms of patriarchy, sexism, and white supremacy.

There is a third—middling—approach. This position eschews patriarchy but, as James says, sees the "male" as normative. This view often reasons from the standpoint of "men" and their embodiment (real or imagined) and carries a set of characterological entailments for civic participation, say, "manly" assertiveness. It leads one to ask, as Shatema Threadcraft has recently done of Du Bois: "Must women behave like men to participate in the struggle for racial equality, and finally, as citizens?"[72] Like the first, this account also involves clear gendered roles and duties. Inequality sneaks in through the backdoor, as it were, but however it gets in, it is there all the same.

As it relates to Du Bois, the internal workings of the third category are not as straightforward as they appear and reveal deeper issues that defined the late nineteenth and early twentieth centuries. As we have already observed in our previous discussion of David Walker and Maria Stewart, tying manliness to citizenship need not undercut the claim that women should be free and equal in the pursuit of their aspirations. The theme of manliness in the writings of African Americans was a counterresponse to the ways civic standing, whiteness, and gender were tied together in

American discourse. As Gail Bederman puts it: "African Americans all understood that the only way to obtain civic power was through gender— by proving that they, too, were men."[73]

In his writings, Du Bois often ties manliness to civic assertiveness. When he criticizes Washington in chapter 3 for giving up on civic rights, he says: "on the contrary, Negroes must insist continually, in season and out of season, that voting is necessary to modern manhood, that color discrimination is barbarism."[74] It is not only civic standing that is endangered but more broadly the ethical status of black people. Du Bois's manner of critique leaves the impression that Washington's presumptive failures to embody manhood mean that he has traded it in for something like feminine submission. As Carby writes of the criticism: "Not only is the reader left in little doubt that Washington is not a man by Du Bois's measure of black masculinity, but his compromise with the dominant philosophy of his age is to be understood as a form of prostitution."[75]

We move too quickly if we conclude on this point. What is tightly bound up in Du Bois's critique of Washington is the linking of the franchise to manhood, and both to civilizational development (as connoted by his contrasting reference to barbarism). The idea of civilizational development (observed by Carby but not used in her analysis of Du Bois) conditions how we ought to understand manliness.[76] For Du Bois, manliness is denotative of a set of virtues for one to live up to rather than being something that inheres in those identified as "male." This fits with the tropes and symbols of evolution that generally defined the period, for good or ill. As Bederman writes: "Ideologies of 'manliness,' like ideologies of race, were imbued with 'civilization's' millennial evolutionism."[77] This is why Wells deployed civilizational discourse as part of her political-ethical challenge to lynching practices. She knew its importance to the culture of American life. For Du Bois's part, he is not interested in effeminizing Washington, as Carby suggests. The proper contrast is not between masculinity and femininity but between civilized manhood and uncivilized barbarism and immaturity. As Du Bois thought Washington did, giving in to color discrimination and allowing it to obstruct black Americans' quest for the franchise is tantamount to embracing barbarism.

There are important implications here for how we understand his discussion of Josie, who figures centrally in the chapter that follows Du Bois's criticism of Washington. Du Bois's argument implies that civilizational development is not fixed but something still susceptible to development. He ties manhood to the franchise in 1903 and yet only six years later in 1909 he says that "women are among the greatest leaders of social reform. . . . Of course there are fools a plenty to tell them they don't need the ballot and to feed them the ancient taffy about homes and babies. . . . But this is the second forward coming of the women and beneath it is a ground swell that none can long resist."[78] Notice that this too is put in terms of a distinction between older (here now called "ancient" ideas) and presumably civilized and enlightened ideas. The ancient taffy about homes and babies is not a critique of domesticity, but it refuses to use the domesticity script as the exclusive framework to define the good life for women. By 1920, Du Bois laments as he reflects on the condition of black women: "They existed not for themselves, but for men; they were named after the men to whom they were related and not after the fashion of their own souls."[79] Already in *Souls* and in his discussion of Josie, we can detect elements of this later view.

Although *Souls* seemingly ties manliness to civic standing, especially in chapter 3, Josie emerges in chapter 4 as a person over whom the reader is meant to lament. Josie is a black woman whose soul's aspiration is destroyed by the ironies of American progress. In thinking about Josie, we should consider two questions. How does she figure in Du Bois's narrative? What is the status of her plight in relation to the other black boys?

In chapter 4, Du Bois recounts the summers of 1886 and 1887 where he taught school in a small town in Alexandria, Tennessee, and his return after ten years. The chapter textually marks this division of time. During the two summers, Du Bois was a student at Fisk University, and Josie and others would become his students in that small town. Josie is the first named figure in the chapter, appearing in paragraph 4. She effectively functions as his introduction to the people of the town. She is also the first figure named in the second part of the chapter when he discusses his return. In the first part Josie is full of life and at the beginning of the second part she is dead. Aside from Josie, there are only three other characters in *Souls* whose life's story structures chapters: Burghardt, John, and Crummell.

In the first portion of the chapter, Du Bois partly discusses Josie's dreams as bound to the household—tied to her concern for her family. In describing the Dowell family, he says:

Then there was Josie herself. She seemed to be the centre of the family: always busy at service, or at home, or berry-picking; a little nervous and inclined to scold, like her mother; yet faithful, too, like her father. She had about her a certain fineness, the shadow of an unconscious moral heroism that would willingly give all of life to make life broader, deeper, and fuller for her and hers.

But Josie's aspirations also extend beyond the home, denoting Du Bois's capacious vision of the future of black women. Here, Du Bois links Josie's way of longing and seeing her place in the world with two others, notably younger men. He draws a contrast between those of an earlier time and Josie and others:

> The mass of those to whom slavery was a dim recollection of childhood found the world a puzzling thing: it asked little of them, and they answered with little, and yet it ridiculed their offerings. Such a paradox they could not understand, and therefore sank into listless indifference, or shiftlessness, and or reckless bravado. There were, however, some—such as Josie, Jim, and Ben—to whom War, Hell, and Slavery were but childhood tales, whose young appetites had been whetted to an edge by school and story and half-awakened thought.

When Du Bois ties Josie to the others it is not to foreground a distinctively "male" characteristic that she has somehow come to possess. Josie stands on a horizontal plane with Jim and Ben, just as her story's importance is on equal footing with the stories of Burghardt, John, and Crummell. In the quoted passage, Du Bois defines a generational divide, one marked by women like Josie who see the future as a space of open opportunity. For him, Josie rightly sees, even if dimly (half-awakened, as he says), in the power of education the ability to remake her future and that of her family. In this, her place at home and her vision of a future beyond are bound together in one orientation: "Best of all I loved to go to Josie's, and sit on the porch, eating peaches, while the mother bustled and talked: how Josie had bought the sewing-machine; how Josie worked at service in winter . . . how Josie longed to go away to school."[80]

Josie emerges as a person who seeks soul-opportunity. Du Bois fleshes this out in terms of her desire to learn and do so partly by going away. We can easily infer from what Du Bois says about Josie that she is a woman with dreams, and those dreams are both in and beyond her presumed role as a woman. She fashions herself, Du Bois thinks rightfully so, after a vision she gives herself, rather than after a script provided to her by others. Strikingly, she is more like Du Bois of chapter 1 than the other black boys, at least in this first part of the chapter.

The second part opens with Du Bois's return after ten years. His reintroduction to the town is with reference to Josie. "Josie was dead, and the gray-haired mother said simply, 'We've had a heap of trouble since you've been away.'"[81] It isn't clear how Josie died; we do sense that physical exhaustion due to excessive laboring was part of it. What is clear is that

her moral heroism kept her devoted to her family until she could no longer survive. Josie's brother was incarcerated and others labored under the
thumb of their white counterparts, caught in the system of debt Du Bois
describes in vivid detail in chapter 7. Of the town's schoolhouse—the place
where Du Bois once taught the town's future—he writes: "My log schoolhouse was gone. In its place stood Progress; and Progress, I understand,
is necessarily ugly."[82]

The second part aims to underscore the underbelly of progress in both
general and particular senses. Of the first, time progresses, but often at
the expense of or in complete denial of the marginalized. Here, as Winters
explains, Du Bois's general commitment to progressive and evolutionary
narratives is laced with recognition of loss. Du Bois "describes images of
ruins and broken parts, intimating that loss is inscribed in the topography
and architecture of this Tennessee community."[83] He means for his readers to bear witness to the ruins.

But that is not all. As Du Bois comes to understand Josie's fate, he
writes: "She grew thin and silent, yet worked the more." A few sentences
later: "Josie shivered and worked on, with the vision of school-days all fled,
with a face wan and tired."[84] Not only the landscape but the very body wears
and reflects the brokenness visited upon the people of the town. Josie's fate
is not the result of a lack of skill and commitment but owed to forces beyond
her control. She is an introduction to the town's aspirations, and she is also
a reintroduction to the denial of those aspirations. Du Bois concludes the
chapter: "How shall man measure Progress there where the dark-faced
Josie lies?"[85] The reader is asked to measure progress based on the fate of
a black woman.

This centering of Josie brings her into the orbit of concerns laid out
in chapter 1 of *Souls* but with an important difference. The other black
boys were partly captured by the insidious logic of double-consciousness,
leading to insincerity, hatred, and self-doubt. In the discussion of Josie,
it is not that white supremacy deforms her self-understanding, as much
as it impacts her wider environment. She is hemmed in by a culture that
disregards black people, leading Du Bois to ironically title the chapter,
"Of the Meaning of Progress." The point is for Josie and her community's
tragedy to cut against the triumphalism so often associated with progress
discourse in American life. This permits us to cast Du Bois's understanding of Josie in its proper light. It is not, as Carby suggests, that Du Bois
deems Josie an unviable expression of the future of black life; it is that
the standards of the wider society devalue people like Josie such that her
vision becomes an unachievable expression of the future.[86]

How can we hope that Josie's story, like many other stories in *Souls*, will move the reader? Du Bois's main suggestion comes in his chapter on Alexander Crummell. In turning from Josie to Crummell, we should keep in mind once again the words from the opening of *Souls*. There he tells us he will narrate stories so that "*men may listen to the strivings in the souls of black folk*."[87] We now move to the final phase of the argument, bringing this chapter and part 2 to a close.

Of Alexander Crummell

Thus far I have specified two different kinds of problems to which *Souls* responds. The first includes how white supremacy deforms the soul because it influences the self-understanding of black people. The themes of insincerity, hatred, and self-doubt that define the other black boys' settled states connote white supremacy's movement into the inner citadel of the self. The second problem, captured by Josie, is less about white supremacy's movement into the interior of the self and more about how it shapes the external environment frustrating aspirations. The first has to do with black people's relationship to themselves amid white supremacy, the second is about white people's responsibility for what they have wrought. These two features as well as Du Bois's ethical-political response come together in "Of Alexander Crummell." Here, we return to Du Bois's rhetorical framework as he attempts to enlist the judgment of his readers. The story of Crummell's life addresses the psychological health of his black readers and seeks to engender the emotional states of sympathy and shame in his white readers.

PERFORMANCE VALUE: THE "TALE OF A BLACK BOY"

Chapter 12, "Of Alexander Crummell," opens with a stunning line that recalls Du Bois's thinking from chapter 1: "This is the *history of a human heart*,—the tale of a *black boy* who many long years ago began to struggle with life that he might *know the world and know himself*."[88] Let us focus on the representative status of Crummell suggested by this line. In the chapter, the reader is taken on a journey through Crummell's life and the various obstacles to his quest to live a good life. In each stage, Du Bois notes the temptations of hate, despair, and doubt that threaten to become settled dispositions. In each instance, Crummell successfully resisted. Still, Du Bois laments that the world does not know of him: "In another age he might have sat among the elders of the land in purple-bordered toga; in another country mothers might have sung him to the cradles."[89] By the end of the story, it appears that Crummell has failed.

What is the point of the story? Despite the appearance of failure, Du Bois means for his black audience to see the performance value of Crummell's life as reason for their own motivation. Ronald Dworkin eloquently captures the meaning of performance value: "We value human lives lived not for the completed narrative . . . but because they too embody a performance: a rising to the challenge of having a life to lead. The final value of our lives is adverbial, not adjectival."[90] This is captured in English parlance as when we say of a person, they played or lived *well*.

The idea of performance value is precisely what Du Bois has in mind when discussing Crummell: "He did his work,—he did it *nobly* and *well*; and yet I sorrow that here he worked alone, with so little human sympathy."[91] Du Bois is less interested in what Crummell has left behind as a result of his work (although that does matter) and more concerned with how we should value the performance of his life amid adversity. It is so important to Du Bois that he wonders how the final claimant—Jesus—will judge Crummell. The adverbial framing reappears: "I wonder where he is to-day? I wonder if in that dim world beyond, as he came gliding in, there rose on some wan throne a King,—a dark and pierced Jew, who knows the writhings of the earthly damned, saying, as he laid those heart-wrung talents down, 'Well done!'"[92]

These words—nobly, well, and well done—are meant to capture the exemplary quality of Crummell's life. But its exemplarity inheres not in the fact that it is a unique life or stands outside the veil but because it models a way of resisting-by-living amid disregard. Importantly, when Du Bois narrates in chapter 3 the various paths that black people have taken in response to resistance, he writes of the third important approach: "finally, a determined effort at self-realization and self-development despite environing opinion."[93] Crummell embodies this approach.

Du Bois thus intends for the story of Crummell's life to do ethical work. This, of course, is generally what African American thinkers intend when they work in the narrative or storytelling mode. The aim is always about moving the reader to a new position. In this specific case, Du Bois sets up a relationship of equality between Crummell (and the workings of his blackness in the world) and black people. Here, he stages a moment of implied recognition but now reconfigured through the framework of the exemplar. As Lawrie Balfour says of the meaning of exemplarity: "Without offering general rules for political emulation, exemplarity engages the reader, eliciting judgment and providing an example of judging."[94] I add to this: providing an example of judging oneself in the face of disregard. Or to put it differently, the example potentially reflects back to us that which is latent within us, functioning as a means of self-assessment.

We should begin to see that this targets the problem of recognition central to chapter 1. It is not that Du Bois rejects recognition as the foundation of self-esteem. We cannot escape the imposition and necessity of the social world to our self-understanding and self-realization. But an important set of questions emerge as Du Bois thinks about white supremacy and its effects on the souls of black people. How should others factor into black people's cultivation of self-worth? What contribution do others make to the character of black lives—to the meaning of their lives, their sense of worth, and the feeling of significance of the projects they pursue?

These questions place Du Bois very much in line with earlier thinkers. Similar to them, he believes it is possible to cultivate a sense of self-esteem that is not tethered to the source of one's oppression. I am here using "self-esteem" (my word, not Du Bois's) in a technical sense. As Tommie Shelby puts it: "*Self-esteem* has two aspects: (1) a secure conviction that one's fundamental purposes are worthwhile and (2) confidence in one's ability to realize these purposes."[95] These two aspects map onto the two problems with which we have been concerned. The first is about one's relationship to oneself. The second is about the relationship to the wider environment that supports or frustrates one's aspirations. For the moment, I only want to focus on the first of these.

One's relationship to oneself sits within a framework of social endorsement; how we see ourselves and the things we desire derives partly from what is reflected back to us when we look at the world. Du Bois's aim is to rethink the parties involved in the recognitive relationship. This is why Crummell figures importantly. He was a witness to the horror of black life. In the face of that, he was tempted by hate—a form of hate standing "between him and the world." He "loved . . . neither the world nor the world's rough ways." But he resisted in the name of a higher "vision of life." He was rejected by the house of God in which he was trained, but amid that disappointment he held despair at bay. Here, once more, he was guided by "his plan of life." He finally struggled through doubt in himself and in his people. And yet: "He never faltered, he seldom complained; he simply worked, inspiring the young, rebuking the old, helping the weak, guiding the strong."[96]

What is significant is the analogical connection between sycophancy, hate, and self-doubt from chapter 1 and hate, despair, and doubt in chapter 11. This is not precisely a one-to-one correspondence. Sycophancy has no corresponding disposition in Crummell and is replaced with despair. Both sets of dispositions, however, are stimulated by white supremacy. Crummell refuses to allow these to become settled states of his character. He refuses to believe what white people think and say about him. In leaning on this powerful story, Du Bois seeks to persuade his black counterparts that the value accorded white people need not serve as the mediator between their self-understanding and their ability to craft worthy visions of their lives.[97] Notice what Du Bois is trying to do. He seeks to build up the self-esteem of black people by using Crummell as a model for how one should value the performance of one's life, though your white counterparts reject you all the same.

This way of proceeding is so influential in the tradition of African American political thought and practice. Recall that in the nineteenth century, black people turned inward to cultivate a community of regard. Through churches, periodicals, and the colored convention movements, the community of regard reflected back to black people what was possible. After the period in which *Souls* was written, the Harlem Renaissance used black art as a means to cultivate a healthy image of black people in their own eyes. Although this book will not say much about the Black Power movement, even a cursory look at that movement and excavation of the term itself reveal a similar logic. What all share is an attempt to nurture the self-esteem of African Americans—to fortify their souls in the face of the onslaught of white supremacy and to stabilize in their own minds the sense of worth in themselves and the projects they pursue.

"THE HISTORY OF A HUMAN HEART": CULTIVATING SYMPATHY AND ELICITING SHAME

Performance value, although important, will never finally be enough. It may fortify the soul and stimulate hope, but in the long run, we each desire to have some of the goods of life we seek realized. Finally, self-esteem depends, as Shelby rightly notes, on efficacy. This is a problem Du Bois understands. He intends for his white audience to wonder why, amid Crummell's skill and character, all one is able to take note of is his unrealized striving. The narrative weight and rhetorical appeal of *Souls* press this question most forcefully. To rethink the parties of recognition is not to say one can or should forgo the support of one's white counterparts. This is because the full expression of one's freedom requires a culture of support that shapes the socio-institutional ecology in which one stands. Recall the story of Josie.

At precisely this moment, we should also detect Du Bois's response to the role white Americans play in the horror of black life. The path to improving the American polity, he proposes, must journey through the striving and tragedy of black souls—the history of human hearts. He ties the health of American democracy to this journey and one's willingness to undertake it. In this, Du Bois's approach is of a piece with the one laid out by Wells in the 1890s and that he replicates here and in his work as editor of *The Crisis*.

Du Bois not only retrieves the past, he underscores remembrance as a central practice in dealing with the workings of white supremacy. Similar to the form of the entirety of *Souls*, Du Bois structures his readings of Josie and Crummell with the goal of having his white reader travel through the suppressed or denied memories of the nation to which they belong. But rather than allow America's collective memory to serve as a reaffirmation of its presumed greatness and thus silence the claim of justice, Du Bois calls forth America's ghosts—the past—to discipline and direct the present. Josie and Crummell are two of America's representative ghosts. When ghosts are present, we are always dealing with matters of unfinished business.

All this helps explain why *Souls* is retrospective in form; it looks back on how racism has ravaged the lives of black people and squandered the possibilities of American democracy. This returns us, even if briefly, to chapter 1:

> Merely a concrete test of the underlying principles of the great republic is the Negro Problem, and the spiritual striving of the freed-men's sons is the travail of souls whose burden is almost beyond the measure of their strength, but who bear it in the name of an historic race, in the name of this the land of their fathers' fathers, and in the name of human opportunity.
>
> And now what I have briefly sketched in large outline let me on coming pages tell again in many ways, with loving emphasis and deeper detail, that men may listen to the striving in the souls of black folk.[98]

In taking his audience on a journey through lives already lived, white Americans, Du Bois contends, must come to see their authorship in the tragedies of black life.

But why? What is he after? For Du Bois, the goal is not exclusively about reckoning with the past but doing so with clear ethical-political goals in mind. In good rhetorical fashion, his aim is to move the reader. He seeks to elicit sympathy from white Americans because, like African

Americans, they too long to have their soul's desires fulfilled. This is a moment of ethical symmetry.

Yet—and this is the critical point—Du Bois intends for that emotion to bear the stain of white Americans' prior desire to frustrate the flourishing of black lives. White Americans must begin, as African Americans have often had to begin, with the betrayals of American life. He is not exclusively interested in *what* white Americans have done but in *who* they are in what they have done. He is not interested in eliciting guilt. Du Bois is after shame—the feeling that we have failed to live up to the vision of ourselves to which we are committed or to which we should be committed. This forms the ground of Du Bois's perfectionism or developmental view of democracy. The goal to reshape the polity—to enable the people to imagine themselves anew—must anchor itself within the tragedy of black lives.

Why should one believe that it is the cultivation of sympathy to which the rhetoric of *Souls* is directed? The simple answer is that throughout *Souls* Du Bois often argues for the importance of sympathy. He understands that arousing one's emotions is a central activity of the rhetorician. In chapter 6, "Of the Training of Black Men," he writes: "It was not money these seething millions want, but love and sympathy, the pulse of hearts beating with red blood."[99] In chapter 9, "Of the Sons of Master and Man," remarking on the ironic form of affection that emerged from the institution of slavery in comparison to what followed in its wake, he explains: "This is a vast change from the situation in the past, when, through the close contact of master and house-servant in the patriarchal big house, one found the best of both races in close contact and sympathy."[100] Finally, we recall the line already quoted from the chapter on Crummell but now in its full context:

> He did his work,—he did it nobly and well; and yet I sorrow that here he worked alone, with so little human sympathy. His name today, in this broad land, means little, and comes to fifty million ears laden with no incense of memory or emulation. And herein lies the tragedy of the age: not that men are poor,—all men know something of poverty; not that men are wicked,—who is good? Not that men are ignorant,—what is Truth? Nay, but that men know so little of men.[101]

Whenever Du Bois employs the language of sympathy, it conveys a sentiment that brings the life of another into view. So little human sympathy, referenced in the passage, is tied to knowing so little of men. To be sympathetic means that one understands a person from their point of view (knowledge of the person) in a way that generates concern for them.

Because sympathy involves understanding from the position of those with whom one sympathizes, the capacity for sympathy is constitutively connected to our ability to *re-present*—that is, imagine—in one's mind what will often not be directly seen. The idea of imagining is really a metaphorical way of traveling with the person or community seeking sympathy. One expression of sympathy's success is not merely that individuals are persuaded but that they are *moved* by your predicament.

In narrating Crummell's life and using him as a proxy, Du Bois intends to undermine the dividing force of the veil so that the reader can come to appreciate and sympathize for those who stand behind it.[102] The veil not only divides the ethical-political status of blacks and whites (the "world within and without the Veil")[103] but also signals an emotional geography that follows from this division (which leads to so little human sympathy). The veil represents (among other things) the division between the "outer" or experiential condition of blacks in America and the "inner" disposition that experience should properly influence among white Americans. Notice further that this division between "outer" and "inner" is precisely what, from the perspective of "Criteria of Negro Art," Du Bois believes the rhetorician must overcome in an effort to expand the judgment of the reader.

Overcoming the divide between "outer" and "inner" relates directly to Du Bois's ironic use of sympathy between master and house-slave, which he takes up in chapter 9. It is important to observe that this analysis comes in the sociological portion of the book—chapters 7–10—where he remarks, "We seldom study the condition of the Negro To-day honestly and carefully."[104] The ironic use of sympathy shows what happens when the divide is not appropriately bridged. As Du Bois explains,

> This is a vast change from the situation in the past, when, through the close contact of master and house-servant in the patriarchal big house, one found the best of both races in close contact and sympathy, while at the same time the squalor and dull round of toil among the field-hands was removed from the sight and hearing of the family. One can easily see how a person who saw slavery thus from his father's parlors, and sees freedom on the streets of a great city, fails to grasp or comprehend the world of the new picture.[105]

In this context, Du Bois emphasizes a form of sympathy born of contact, but its meaning is distorted because the truth of black life is "removed from the sight and hearing of the family." Removing the problems from sight and hearing signals the superficiality of contact. He commends proximity, but it needs to be genuine. He thus juxtaposes close contact as determined by the norms of the "big house," and the close contact that puts in view the daily "squalor" and "toil" of black life as imposed by the norms of the veil. The former gives to white Americans a distorted view of what freedom means and leaves blacks in a position where they suffer as a result.

In focusing on the details of Crummell's life and the character it represents, Du Bois means to counteract this distortion and its effects. Here we return to the opening line from the chapter: "This is the history of a human heart,—the tale of a black boy who many long years ago began to struggle with life that he might know the world and know himself." Crummell's life allows Du Bois to stage the experiential separation between whites and blacks (revealing the substantive difference between freedom and domination), even as he alerts the reader to a deeper connection between the races. The division between the races becomes palpable as he recounts the tragic details of Crummell's life that result from disregard and domination. This condition accentuates the absence of freedom and equal regard and requires a response. The motivating force for addressing this situation, Du Bois hopes, comes about because of a fundamental human quest for self-realization that black and white Americans share. In describing the chapter as a history of "a human heart," Du Bois humanizes for the reader the subject of the narrative so that the white reader may be "touched."[106] The result of being "touched" by the narrative, or so Du Bois intends, is that the reader will come to feel appropriately and therefore understand the nature of Crummell's plight and that of those like him.

Following Du Bois on this journey reconceptualizes freedom for the reader. The meaning of freedom no longer consists in using the norms of the "big house," for that merely obscures the horrors of black life and leads to a disingenuous sense of close contact. Rather, freedom consists in removing the obstacles to self-realization. Freedom is now conceptually tied to making Crummell's goals and the goals of those like him genuine possibilities in the United States.

This is not a narrow sentimentalism. Du Bois's attempt at humanization aspires to bring about a perceptual shift. In standing inside the veil bearing witness to Crummell's life, the life of this "black boy" potentially moves from outside the affective orbit of the white reader to its inner domain. The white reader is at once, or so Du Bois hopes, moved by the *shared* quest for self-development and chastened by its specific frustration in the lives of those darker individuals with whom they share the polity:

You will not wonder at his weird pilgrimage,—you who in the swift whirl of living, amid its cold paradox and marvelous vision, have

fronted life and asked its riddle face to face. And if you find that riddle hard to read, remember that yonder black boy finds it just a little
harder; if it is difficult for you to find and face your duty, it is a shade
more difficult for him; if your heart sickens in the blood and dust of
battle, remember that to him the dust is thicker and the battle fiercer.
No wonder the wanders fall! ... The Valley of the Shadow of Death
gives few of its pilgrims back to the world.[107]

The specific and unjustified suffering of the "black boy" becomes the
object of reflection about which one should properly feel sympathy. Du
Bois pursues a similar path in his chapter on Josie. As with that chapter,
the reader comes face-to-face with the destructive influence of racism, but
it serves to underscore the fundamental gap at the core of the polity that
stifles affirmative gestures by fellow human beings. The problem, we can
imagine him saying to his white reader, is not with some presumed deficiencies of Crummell or Josie; the problem is with you.

The success of Du Bois's narrative depends not on a view of impartial judgment but on the partiality of the reader. As we discussed in the
previous chapter, when he seeks to persuade his readers he meets them
where they stand; he addresses their existing bundle of commitments, values, and norms with the hope of expanding their content. As he explains
in chapter 9, where sympathy is invoked by name: "Such an essentially
honest-hearted and generous people cannot cite the caste-leveling precepts
of Christianity, or believe in equality of opportunity for all men, without
coming to feel more and more with each generation that the present drawing of the color-line is a flat contradiction to their beliefs."[108]

We must take great care in reading this line. Du Bois is clear that *Souls*
is about democratic development. We have seen this before in Walker,
Douglass, and Wells. Similar to them, Du Bois is well aware that the content of those beliefs as currently structured does not, in fact, have African
Americans in view as proper subjects of their application. After all, Du Bois
recounts Crummell's attempt to go to school in New Hampshire, "but the
godly farmers hitched ninety yoke of oxen to the abolition school house
and dragged it into the middle of the swamp."[109] This is precisely why
the perceptual shift above is necessary. Thus, when Du Bois appeals to
conventional wisdom (e.g., the precepts of Christianity or equality of
opportunity), he does so in an effort to extend its content and move the
reader to a position that they might not have otherwise adopted. It is this
new, expanded view that Du Bois subsequently uses as a way to defend the
proposition of contradiction or inconsistency. So in saying that he seeks

to get his readers to see and feel that the suffering of African Americans is out of step with what America claims to be about, one must keep in mind that the content of this description of America is not a reality but an aspiration toward which Du Bois is trying to move the nation.

In showing the inconsistency between the expanded principles—principles of equality or the dignity of persons that are now structured in light of African Americans—and the failure to apply them equally, Du Bois seeks to generate in the reader a sense of shame for having contributed to their suffering. If sympathy looks outward to others, shame looks inward to the self that has either contributed to the suffering of those on the outside or played witness to that suffering.[110] As Bernard Williams rightly notes, "Shame looks to what I am."[111] Shame entails falling below a standard I otherwise embrace or should embrace, but this falling below can only come into view because of the negative results that follow and which sympathy puts on display.

Although Du Bois does not use the language of shame, there is little doubt this is what he intends. As he says in the "The Afterthought" of *Souls*, "Let the ears of a guilty people tingle with truth."[112] There are two terms here—"guilty" and "truth"—that require elucidation. To be guilty, as Du Bois employs it, is to be justly chargeable with harming another (in this instance African Americans). One might think, however, that there is imprecision in this sentence, especially given that he hopes that *Souls* will touch or move the reader. The imprecision emerges because we can readily think of cases in which people are found guilty of an offense for which they do not take responsibility. But the fact that Du Bois wants the guilt to resonate with the offenders (to tingle their ears) means that he takes himself to be laying out their failure to live up to a standard with which they identify. Properly speaking, this is shame because it points as Williams suggests to what I am and have failed to embody.

The sympathetic identification with African Americans that contributes to an expansion of the ethical-political horizon is now employed by Du Bois to shame the reader. That sympathy is paired with shame is important, especially given that thinkers typically deploy shame in isolation from other emotions.[113] The problem in doing this is that it will invariably be the case that the reaction to shame will be one of evading the situation that requires attention—one will recoil from rather than engage with shame and the source from which it springs. This is precisely why the structure of *Souls* moves from attempting to cultivate sympathetic identification in several of the early chapters to eliciting shame in the reader by the end of the book. It is the work of sympathy—creating a shared normative and affective horizon—that increases the chances that a sense of shame will emerge. (Of course, there are no guarantees where democratic transformation, with its reliance on affect, is concerned.) In doing so, Du Bois intends for his readers to feel diminished by the end of the book—a sense that something about who they are as displayed in their treatment of blacks is wrong. The psychological and characterological effect of this is to lower "the agent's self respect and diminish him in his own eyes" to begin the work of repair.[114]

This helps explains Du Bois's reference to truth. For the truth that will tingle the ears of white Americans is a truth about normative dissonance that is on display in their mistreatment of African Americans. To let the ears of guilty people tingle with truth, then, is meant to arouse in them a sensation of aversion to a picture of themselves and the society to which they belong that results in harming blacks. This is the realization that shame makes possible for the reader. Du Bois's aim here is not, properly speaking, for readers to feel bad because they have been shamed but to feel bad because they have failed to realize the good.

Failing to realize the good crystallizes an important undercurrent to Du Bois's evocations of sympathy and shame. First, sympathizing with the plight of African Americans in their frustrated attempts to achieve self-realization (a) reveals to the persuaded reader something that they find central to the flourishing of life and (b) potentially awakens in them a sense of disappointment over the failure of the polity and all who belong to it (including themselves) for not providing the space in which that flourishing can be actualized. Second, precisely because the reader sees self-realization as central to the flourishing of life, but nonetheless frustrated in African Americans because of racism, the reader is forced to ask and confront the following questions: Who am I? What kind of community do I belong to that obstructs the living of life? These are the questions that must be generated within and by citizens if they are going to genuinely transform society. But they are questions that allow readers to probe the justice and injustice of their community.

As these questions suggest, if shame diminishes the standing of persons in their own eyes, it is equally meant to be generative of a new way of living by alerting the reader to the demand of a democratically just society. Shame honors the judgment of the reader by encouraging a self-critical stance toward one's treatment of African Americans that reflexively reveals the ethical deficit within oneself and one's community. As Williams explains, "shame may be expressed in attempts to reconstruct or improve oneself."[115] Like the deployment of horror in chapter 5, shame thus provides an opportunity for self-development because it entails a view of one's ethical-political identity in relation to which transformation is made possible and rendered intelligible. This is precisely why the hope of *Souls* is that it will not fall "*still-born into the world-wilderness*" but rather may "*spring . . . from out its leaves vigor of thought and thoughtful deed to reap the harvest wonderful. . . . Thus in Thy good time may infinite reason turn the tangle straight, and these crooked marks on a fragile leaf be not indeed.*"[116]

———◆———

The discussion of the soul in "Of Our Spiritual Strivings," of Josie and Crummell, and the role of sympathy and shame recalls the importance of rhetoric. This understanding of the soul fits within a tradition that sees the rhetorician as central to self and communal development. Recall the words of Ferris: "our souls are being stirred by [Du Bois's] burning eloquence." In Plato's *Phaedrus*, Socrates tells us that the art of rhetoric represents "a way of directing the soul by means of speech."[117] In so directing, Cicero says, the aim of rhetoric "is to rouse the people when languishing and to restrain them when impetuous." "Who," he asks, "can exhort people to virtue more passionately than the orator, and who can call them back from vice more vigorously?"[118] The desire to direct the soul (in Plato's sense), call the soul back from vice (in Cicero's way of thinking), or stir the soul (as Ferris's describes) underwrites the structure of Du Bois's appeal.

We can now say this way of thinking includes many of the figures already encountered, relying as they did on the aspirational view of the people and seeking with faith to direct the people to higher visions of themselves. The aspirational view of the people is grounded in a perfectionist understanding of self and society. And they believe that an affective-aesthetic framework helps to realize development. It is worth restating that for aspirational politics to have any chance of working in this context, these thinkers insist, the history of racial disregard must function to inform the content of one's aspirations. This is simply because, as Du Bois, Wells, Douglass, Easton, and others suggest, the cultural life of the United States is so closely bound to white supremacy that we must remain on alert for when racial disregard threatens to bleed into the present. This suggests that the ongoing social learning of the citizenry must bear the trace of its tragic past in order to remain responsive to the demands of freedom and equal regard in the present.

This is not, however, the only or even primary way Americans understand the meaning of the aspirational people and its relationship to the past. Both historically and philosophically, we have often treated white supremacy as a denial of the true or real creed in "the hearts of ordinary Americans" rather than seeing it as a competing feature of America's cultural life. "The American dilemma," writes Gunnar Myrdal in his extraordinary text of 1944, "is the ever-raging conflict between on the one hand, the valuations preserved on the general plane which we call the 'American creed' . . . and, on the other hand, . . . group prejudice against particular persons or types of people."[119] Here, the people as aspiration functions in the recovery mode—that is, through the people we recover what they really are and have been that is betrayed by white supremacy. Myrdal's approach, although quite unintended, involves a troubling characterization of how to assess the nation's response to racial inequality. He captures a style of evasion that is so central to American life. The Myrdalian approach measures ethical and political progress by society's proximity to the American Creed and society's cultural distance (often through repression or disavowal) from the trauma of racial disregard. The creedal approach to racial inequality ironically nurtures a politics of forgetting. White supremacy is anomalous to the American polity and not a feature of the nation's identity with which we must constantly reckon. This does not enrich aspirational politics in its quest to reconstitute the cultural life of society; it deforms its meaning.

The conclusion turns to this ill-formed aspirational politics (and its post–World War II varieties) and to a signature source of resistance. This is necessary to dramatize how the brand of aspirational politics developed over the last chapters does not fall prey to its deformed variety. Our final reflection will make central what has hitherto been suggested—namely, remembrance of the past as a feature of democratic life. This is a species of what we might call critical responsiveness and no thinker fills this out better than James Baldwin. In many ways, he is not novel in this regard. Du Bois, you could say, was after this. But then again, I am not interested in novelty but a form of repetition and emphasis. It is to Baldwin, postwar liberalism, and the horizon of the civil rights movement that we now turn.

James Baldwin's Gift

BOOK CONCLUSIONS CAN BE ARBITRARY, especially when the drama of their subject matter is still unfolding. In the twenty-first century, the resurgence in white supremacy compounded by rising economic inequality, climate catastrophe, and the erosion of democratic habits grip the nation.[1] Still, we have reached a point in the journey where we should settle down and wait for others—if they come along—to pick up where this book must now end. So where have we been and what final insights might we offer to those who look toward a future not yet, a people, for good or ill, still in the process of becoming?

Throughout our journey, I have tried to reflect on how a group of African American thinkers and artists understood their efforts to transform the United States amid racial disregard. I have wondered about the specific vision of democracy that underwrote their appeals to the nation and the descriptions of self and society they presupposed. These two broad issues have allowed me to trace how the categories of aspirational people, aesthetics, affect, faith, and character functioned as central tools in their understanding of democratic life and its development. I have argued throughout that these thinkers see democracy as a way of relating to one's fellows that acknowledges their freedom and equal ethical and political standing and shows care and concern in that acknowledgment. This requires a way of perceiving the world; it requires a soul rightly attuned to the claims of others. The preoccupation with the soul or character helps us understand the aesthetic and affective registers on which many of these thinkers worked. Their shared approach is perfectionist in form. But this is not because they hold some strong view of the good life they imagine the state will coercively implement but because they see democracy as a cooperative enterprise of soul-craft politics. We should not recoil from this; we should embrace it because although the institutional and legal structures of democracy are of the utmost importance, they require for their healthy functioning a citizenry rightly oriented. They need citizens capable of asking themselves, who are we in the lives we lead and the actions we undertake concerning each other? A nation unable to ask those questions is already dead or approaching its end.

Although the primary subject matter has been that of white supremacy and racial disregard, I hope the reader can now see that the resources of these thinkers extend well beyond the problems at hand. They represent an archive of democratic thinking and an inheritance from which we ought to draw.

———

Given the history of American moral and political thinking, with our tendency toward triumphalist or exceptionalist national narratives, aspirational politics is always in danger of being deformed—of disavowing the darkest features of the society to which it otherwise claims to respond. Perhaps it is a defect of our beginnings, but in the United States, we often deny our deficiencies. Either they are placed on the shoulders of minorities that are claimed not to reflect "who we truly are" or they are thought to follow from those (usually, and tragically, the victims of the nation's deficiencies) who fail to make the most of the opportunities afforded them. We make these moves—I suppose we think we must—because we consistently begin with an exalted sense of the nation. Although this way of thinking seems out of fashion among academics, I am inclined to say that the idea of exceptionalism still holds sway within the discursive and symbolic fields of American life. So something must be said about how we should guard against this tendency. How should we stand to our past so that we might live our future in the fullness of civic affection that democracy requires?

In these final moments, I turn to the dominant model of racial liberalism that defined the second half of the twentieth century and its deformed aspirational politics. We see it popularized in powerful form by Swedish sociologist Gunnar Myrdal's 1944 work, *An American Dilemma: The Negro Problem and Modern Democracy*.[2] In that work, he deploys liberalism's commitment to freedom, equal regard, and social justice to address racial inequality.[3] From the 1940s to the 1960s, racial liberalism shaped social, legal, economic, and political engineering. Myrdal is a representative example of a way of thinking about the United States' history of racial discrimination and its quest to realize a just society. In *An American*

Dilemma, we find a "once-born" liberalism, with little place for sin and tragedy.[4] To read him as I do is to get at his aspirational politics and the underlying *attitude* informing his vision, by which I mean a point of view from which to consider matters. Myrdal's is an attitude of *evasion*. It remains with us today.

Against the backdrop of Myrdal, I focus on one of the most critical responses of the period—the thinking of James Baldwin. His writings captured the public imagination and shamed the political establishment as the black freedom struggle was coming clearly into view in the early 1960s. He gives us both prophetic fire and ministerial guidance. In response to his November 1962 *New Yorker* essay "Letter from a Region in My Mind," which subsequently was included in *The Fire Next Time* of 1963, *Variety* said the essay was "a savagely bitter upbraiding of white 'hypocrisy' about civil liberties." Baldwin "thoroughly frightened much of the white community which has been complacently devoted to token gestures."[5]

We turn to Baldwin because in him, we find an attenuated aspirational politics, born as it was from seeing both the promises and the betrayals of the United States. I am not after an undiscovered Baldwin. Well-trodden paths are often worth revisiting.[6] Rather, I place him in the flow of ideas we have encountered. He channels past reflections that culminate in a vision of faith darkened by the struggle for racial regard and maintains a commitment to the United States. His writings are not primarily programmatic; instead, Baldwin offers a way of seeing the texture of our historical topography so as to inform the programs of action we undertake. His is an attitude of *critical responsiveness*.[7]

Baldwin's attenuated vision is productive; it demands that we remain alive to how the past bleeds into the present. Critical responsiveness is a central value of a democratic society, but especially one marked by deep practices of inequality and domination. It carries that perceptual sensitivity that has developed across the pages of this book. In Baldwin's hands, critical responsiveness helps us think less about progress as a movement away from the past and more in terms of the skills with which we remain actively alert to and mindful of history's reappearance. In commending critical responsiveness as an ethical and political virtue, Baldwin resists what Saidiya Hartman refers to as the "antinomies of redemption . . . and irreparability."[8]

Compared to Myrdal and those standing in his shadow, Baldwin represents a different attitude. In his writings, we discover his confrontation with the *irrevocable deeds* of white supremacy and yet the necessity of responding to it all the same because, alas, we are responsible for the communities we inhabit. To call it irrevocable is to focus on the soul-scarring character of white supremacy, for which, as he says, neither he "nor time nor history will ever forgive."[9] And yet, I want to insist that the scarred soul of the nation ironically shapes Baldwin's perfectionism—his view of identity, history, and the ethical themes of responsibility, forgiveness, redemption, and atonement. Through him, we discover a nation traumatized by self-inflicted wounds, and he hopes that we remember just enough to act responsibly but not so much that we give up. This is Baldwin's vision of faith without redemption: both his inheritance and his gift.

Racial Liberalism and the Once-Born Soul

Gunnar Myrdal's *An American Dilemma* represents a major statement on race and inequality in the United States. Doubting the ability of Americans to offer an objective analysis of race in America, the Carnegie Corporation commissioned the study in 1938 and selected the Swedish economist Myrdal. He in turn enlisted some of the most gifted scholars of race in the fields of history, sociology, economics, and political science. In the study, Myrdal links racial inequality to economic exploitation and asymmetrical power relationships. At the very outset, he remarks "that practically all the economic, social, and political power is held by whites." Shortly thereafter, he explains that the study views the "American civilization" from the "most disadvantaged population group." And in the longest section of the two volumes, "Part IV: Economics," we discover: "The Negro population has much less than one-tenth of the total consumer income in the United States."[10] These lines point toward Myrdal's interest in political economy and his structural analysis in thinking about race in the United States.

Despite this apparent interest and analysis, Myrdal embraces a specific kind of moralism latent in American culture. He opens and closes the massive study (parts 1 and 11, respectively) by framing the problem of racial inequality in terms of the crisis of moral commitments among whites and their betrayal of what he calls the American Creed. This remains the most enduring part of the study. The text's moral vision aligns itself with the political bent of postwar analysis on race that emphasized the psychological states of individual whites and prioritized education and nondiscriminatory policies to bring the nation in line with its deeply held beliefs. The politics of the day and for several decades thereafter also drew support from the study.[11]

The framing matters. The decision to structure the book in the way he did shapes how we ought to understand the underlying ideological commitments of the American polity, the history of racial disregard, and the status of white persons in addressing the problem. The book aspires to tell an *origin* story about who Americans are. In this case, origin functions less like a *beginning* to which we return and often to chart a future that may be discontinuous with the past we left. Beginnings, as Edward Said and Eddie Glaude suggest in different ways, permit us to begin again. Origin is often determinative; it has a "divine, mythical and privileged" character that "dominates what derives from it."[12] This is why it is vital to Myrdal to sketch in the first chapter the "*origin* of the American Creed."[13] Behind racial inequality in the United States, he wants us to believe, we discover a true community that beckons us—a vision of American identity in its pure form. According to this archaeological approach,[14] we must uncover who Americans are to orient them toward the future.

The pure form of American identity and Myrdal's religious belief that American democracy is fated to win the battle against white supremacy bring to mind William James's classic account of the once-born soul. Admittedly, Myrdal only invokes James once in *American Dilemma*, and even there he is not referencing James's 1902 work. So why reach for James's text? I want to suggest that the heuristic of the once-born soul best captures Myrdal's brand of liberalism. Heuristics are mental shortcuts that economize our thinking and when they are about the world, they declutter the landscape. They can often be too neat. In this case, that is the point. For Myrdal, the American Creed functions in this way, and behind that Creed is the once-born soul.

In his *Varieties of Religious Experience*, James distinguishes between two ideal types: once-born and twice-born souls. He acknowledges that most of us are of a mixed variety, but what is of significance is that these different types of souls embody attitudinal orientations toward life. The first-born has a healthy-minded attitude and often "looks on all things and sees that they are good." In the "systematic variety" of healthy-mindedness, it "selects some one aspect of [the world] as [its] essence for the time being, and disregards the other aspects."[15] In order to resist humanity's constant struggle and violation of its own highest image, the once-born consistently retreats to an affirmative feature of human life and claims that feature as humanity's essence. In contrast, James says, the twice-born soul notes both the light and persistence of the dark features of human nature. "The doctrine of the twice-born," he explains, "hold[s] as it does more of the element of evil in solution—is the wider and completer" view. James's point is not that the once-born soul cannot acknowledge evils, but they factor as anomalies of human life and thus the once-born is prevented from accept-ing evil as a real feature of human nature.[16] As he says of the once-born: "the world is a sort of rectilinear or one storied affair, whose accounts are kept in one denomination, whose parts have just the values which naturally they appear to have." The once-born lives on the "plus side" of life.[17]

The textual echo of the once-born lives in *An American Dilemma*, but to notice it we must track Myrdal's description of the problem. In the introduction, he captures the heart of the issue:

> The American Negro problem is a problem in the heart of the Ameri-can. It is there that the interracial tension has its focus. It is there that the decisive struggle goes on. This is the central viewpoint of this treatise. Though our study includes economic, social, and politi-cal race relations, at bottom our problem is a moral dilemma of the American—the conflict between his moral valuations on various levels of consciousness and generality.[18]

White Americans are pulled in two directions. On the one hand, they believe in freedom and equality, which defines the American Creed. Yet, on the other, there are a variety of prejudices against African Americans that betray the Creed. For Myrdal, each white American carries within their breast this tension, and it dogs their psyche and wreaks havoc on the external commu-nity in which black people live. Although Myrdal notes that there "are no homogeneous attitudes . . . but a mesh of struggling inclinations, interests, and ideals," he maintains that the American Creed is the "morally higher" valuation that orients the polity and is underwritten by much of American life.[19] But he is keen to note that the issue is not a "Negro problem" but a "white man's problem" as many African American thinkers before and after him argued.[20]

The tension between America's professed commitments and its treat-ment of African Americans should now be familiar. David Walker's question: Do you not understand the words of your Declaration of Inde-pendence, has this tension in mind. Ida B. Wells's internationalizing of lynching dramatized how far the United States was from its professed principles. W.E.B. Du Bois's sense that the fate of black people in the United States was "a concrete test of the underlying principles of the great republic" resembles Myrdal's later approach.[21]

These figures share with Myrdal a reliance on America's dominant political and ethical language. But the use of similar terms and tropes— the rhetorical context—obscures the subtle differences in use that we must now recover. They resist what Sacvan Bercovitch calls the "rituals of consensus."[22]

Here again, framing matters and helps us recall earlier claims. For African American thinkers, the treatment of black people and the nation's principles functioned as co-equal, even if contingently related features of the American republic.[23] They did not believe that ideas of equality and freedom necessarily entailed practices of domination. But they also acknowledged that racial disregard functioned alongside notions of freedom and equality because those ideals were ideationally tied to whiteness. When Wells referred to the unwritten laws that police black and white lives and Du Bois discussed the wages of whiteness they were tracking this darker tradition of American life. This darker tradition makes the nation, as Frederick Douglass knew, false to a racially just future. Their sensitivity to the competing visions of American life generated a set of appeals less about the psychological state of discrete white persons and more about the social-ecology of American cultural life in which persons and institutions were entangled in and habituated to practices of disregard. White supremacy is neither exhaustive of nor antithetical to American identity; it is a dynamic cultural formation that requires, as they argued, a countercultural (albeit internal) reimagining of American life. They aimed for a transvaluation of freedom's scope and equality's conditions that did not recover America but discovered it anew. Their idea that human beings and society are susceptible to improvement coupled with their open-ended view of the people as central to the legitimating logic of democracy shaped their faith in ethical and political possibilities.

Myrdal proceeds differently. He treats the history of racial domination as an aberration within American life and thus sets about the task of recovering and educating the citizenry about their true commitments. When we compare, we see the difference. One looks to a past thought to exist (origin story), while the other looks to a future without precedent (a new beginning). But for African Americans, the ethical and political goals take shape precisely because of the centrality of the past to one's point of view. This Socratic-like concern with turning the soul toward the truth became one of the central focuses of Du Bois's *The Souls of Black Folk* and the defining feature of Baldwin's corpus. Myrdal partitions the past between those features that "truly" convey American ideals and those that reflect anomalies within the national identity. This is why he says "in principle the Negro problem was settled long ago." For him, the scope of freedom was clear and the conditions of equality were properly understood, but the application was limited.[24] Similar terms swirl about Myrdal and African American thinkers, but they disagree about what they mean and where they locate themselves in America's cultural life.

Myrdal's thinking is of a piece even as it pushes against a general crisis in both Europe and the United States—a predicament in which the very meaning of human progress was at stake.[25] With two world wars, the development of spiritual malaise, and the persistence of racial inequality, it was no longer clear (perhaps it never was) that humans were moving in a positive direction. In his 1938–39 Gifford Lectures, for example, theologian Reinhold Niebuhr argues that modernity denies the "idea that man is sinful in the very centre of his personality, that is in his will."[26] In *Dusk of Dawn* (1940), Du Bois struggles to generate an affirmative picture of his white counterparts: "All my life I have had continually to haul my soul back and say, 'All white folk are not scoundrels nor murderers. They are, even as I am, painfully human.'"[27] In the same year, German sociologist Karl Mannheim goes further, capturing what he takes to be the spirit of the age: "For many of us the problem of human nature and the possibility of changing it has only been raised through the events of the last few years. Two prejudices seem to have collapsed simultaneously: first, the belief in a permanent 'national character,' secondly, the belief in the 'gradual progress of Reason in history.'"[28]

Myrdal rejects both of Mannheim's views and he does so because the stakes are high. This comes out if we look very briefly at his and Alva Myrdal's *Kontakt med Amerika* (*Contact with America*) of 1941. Amid the war, the Myrdals grappled with the danger posed by the Third Reich and Sweden's political position of neutrality. They wrote *Kontakt* hoping to make the Swedes positively disposed toward the United States. As Maribel Morey puts it: the Myrdals "wanted to make clear to Swedes that there was an inherent difference between modern-day Germans and Americans, that the United States was worthy of Swedes' allegiance during the war."[29] They were not blind to human failings, but the political urgency of the moment precluded Niebuhr's pessimistic view of human nature, the ambivalence of Du Bois, and the resignation of Mannheim. Myrdal proceeds on the basis of a morally coherent national character in the form of the American Creed and envisions its unfolding—an unfolding of democracy itself—as defeating racial inequality.

There is a richness to this view and there are dangers as well. The Myrdals acknowledged that racial discrimination was the most significant test of the West, in both Germany and the United States. But unlike in Germany, the Myrdals argued that "no people on earth are (or ever were) so passionately interested in finding and crying out their own deficiencies as Americans."[30] The irony should not be lost on us today. When we compare the two countries, Germany stands out as a nation of remembrance. Germans seemingly agonize over their past. Rather than erecting monuments to a Lost Cause as we have done in the United States that reflect our ethical deficiencies, they display the iconography of their shame to which they voluntarily bear witness. But in 1941, the Myrdals suggested that there is something special about Americans. Here, the once-born soul shows itself. If Americans are unique in alerting themselves and the world to their deficiencies, it is mainly because those faults do not reflect who Americans are. As a social scientist and not a metaphysician, Myrdal attempts to chasten his faith in democracy. As he says in *American Dilemma*, "history is not the result of a predetermined Fate." Nevertheless, he remains confident that the "trends" reveal the "gamut of possibilities for the future."[31] In looking at those trends, as Walter Jackson explains, Myrdal "squeezed the most optimistic interpretation possible out of the data he examined."[32] He asked his readers to live on the plus side of life as the once-born often does.

Innocence as Crime

Myrdal's text is not merely descriptive; it articulates a normative aspiration. His elevated notion of our national identity whispers to our soul like ministering angels and comforts the heart. So it is unsurprising that *An American Dilemma* became a text not only for the academic but for the layperson as well, as abridged versions were produced for the policymaker and student alike. President Harry Truman's Committee on Civil Rights, for example, and its 1947 report *To Secure These Rights* were heavily influenced by Myrdal's text and became an important blueprint for thinking about federal action on civil rights. And there is a contextual sensitivity at work in the text that anchors the reader. *An American Dilemma* is filled with examples, both interpersonal and structural, of white supremacy and black domination. But they inhabit the text in a particular way and shape how the nation should think about its identity amid racial disregard.

Ultimately, narrating the American Dilemma works by fragmenting not what we remember but *how* we remember it. As a result, the past flows away from us into the gutter of our horrible deeds, giving us the impression that they form no part of our shared identity—that they do not touch the nation's soul.[33] The details of the past are called forth and seemingly shape the present. But Myrdal sequesters them, allowing Americans to say in the 1940s, as they so often say today: "That is not who we are."

Of course, Myrdal was very much concerned by what he considered a debilitating pessimism in social scientific analysis.[34] He wanted to destroy neither hope in a better future nor faith in one's ability to realize it. There is much to admire in his effort to see the social scientist as part analyst and part advocate. In the end, we must get on with politics—in both its recognizable institutional form and its all-important cultural expression. Through politics we craft and attend to our shared lives and in doing so we also communicate the worth of citizens.

But he moves too far in the opposite direction, encouraging his readers to take comfort that the vision of life on display was not theirs. He sanctions the thought that the prejudices that constrained black life were not also of America's will. Ever on the quest for an unsullied ethical identity, Myrdal ironically deforms our way of seeing the full picture of our humanity. In that deformation, he leaves us less than human—less responsive to our shared, even if tragic inheritance and less attuned, as a result, to the sources of injustice.

I admit that less than human may seem an exaggeration and a terrible indictment. But if part of being human in a democratic society demands that we are responsive to our fellows, then the issue is not merely about what we must (as a society) be responsive to but why. Myrdal is clear about what the United States must address, but he isn't at all clear about why in the 1940s the United States found itself in need of a response in the first place. Just what is it about this country that has given life to racial inequality?

At precisely this moment, we can hear James Baldwin's worry two decades later in his 1964 essay "The White Problem." The backdrop of this striking essay is a weighty context and it is worth recounting some of the notable events:

the crisis of integration most visibly on display at the University of
    Mississippi and the ensuing white mob violence in 1962;
the Birmingham children's crusade march in May 1963;
the Birmingham riot in May 1963;
the assassination of civil rights activist Medgar Evers in June 1963;
the March on Washington in August 1963;
the horrific 16th Street Baptist Church bombing by Ku Klux Klan
    members that killed four little girls in September 1963;
the assassination of President John F. Kennedy in November 1963.

The political climate was intense, but behind it all were past debts coming due and a nation in denial. "What is most terrible," Baldwin writes, "is that American white men are not prepared to believe my version of the story. . . . In order to avoid believing that, they have set up in themselves a fantastic system of evasions, denials, and justifications, [a system that] is about to destroy their grasp of reality, which is another way of saying their moral sense."[35]

This is the claim of innocence that Baldwin makes central to his writings. As Lawrie Balfour and George Shulman have argued separately, his use of the word "innocence" functions as a tool of political and epistemic analysis.[36] Innocence denotes attitude and point of view, which, as Baldwin argues, infuses the cultural field of the United States and shapes the outlook of white Americans. Innocence involves closing one's eyes to others in their historical particularity to affirm an alternative and false reality. What precisely is that false reality? He names it in that same essay of 1964:

> The people who settled the country had a fatal flaw. They could recognize a man when they saw one. They knew he wasn't . . . anything else but a man; but since they were Christian, and since they had already decided that they came here to establish a free country, the only way to justify the role this chattel was playing in one's life was to say that he was not a man. For if he wasn't, then no crime had been committed. That lie is the basis of our present trouble.[37]

We will return to the language of "fatal flaw," but we should pay attention to something else for the moment. Like Myrdal, we see the attribution of the problem to white people but take note of Baldwin's description. Here, he detects the attitude of evasion.

To confront black pain and death involves acknowledging something about one's community. This is because for Baldwin white and black Americans are not merely caught in a master-slave relationship; it is, "literally and morally, a *blood* relationship."[38] He is referring to the historical horror of the rape (literally) of black women by white men and the idea of kinship that carries (morally) with it ideas of responsibility and accountability. In his view, acknowledgment shatters illusions, something that Baldwin argues is a difficult even if necessary thing for a society to do. Here is the difficulty: "The danger," he tells his nephew in *The Fire Next Time*, "in the minds of most white Americans, is the loss of their identity. Try to imagine how you would feel if you woke up one morning to find the sun shining and all the stars aflame. Any upheaval in the universe is terrifying because it so profoundly attacks one's sense of reality."[39] He models sympathetic identification to help his nephew (a stand-in for black people) understand those he must deal with.

Behind this remark is Baldwin's ongoing confrontation with identity as a form of estrangement and deformation. If he tries to enable black people to see their white counterparts, he also seeks to describe to white Americans the illusions that grip them and the costs. So his preoccupation with identity is also a call for his fellows to be suspicious of how they think of themselves. *Estrangement* is about how the meaning of American identity evades the reality of historical inheritance. When Baldwin uses reality in an affirmative sense and in relation to the past, he means its fullness. Estrangement from the fullness of one's past has striking consequences. When white Americans narrate the meaning of the Civil War, Reconstruction, the civil rights movement, or the election of the first African American president, these stories function as instances of the nation's latent commitments manifest—the power of America's origin story righting the course of events.[40] These moments in American history are not interpreted, as Baldwin would encourage us to do, as deep criticisms of and tensions within the complicated identity of the nation. For that reason, the nation does not interpret them as departures from the Founders' commitments. They do not, in other words, show us a scarred nation attempting to be born again.

Deformation of our ethical capacities (the "moral sense" as Baldwin refers to them) results from estrangement. He argues that the intensity of one's attachment to the innocence of American life matches the ease with which one abdicates responsibility for the communities to which one belongs. "People who imagine," he writes a year later in "The White Man's Guilt," "[that] history flatters them (as it does, indeed, since they wrote it) are impaled on their history like a butterfly on a pin and become incapable of seeing or changing themselves, or the world."[41] Our ethical capacities matter not merely because they make us attuned to the world but also because we find our ability to remake the world in that very attunement.

There is a striking implication Baldwin asks his readers to consider that recasts the political goals of the United States: *As a form of estrangement, American identity evades democratic freedom.* His picture of freedom should now be familiar. From the 1830s through the 1940s (covering roughly the scope of this book), African Americans pushed against domination, but they also tried to get the nation to embrace a non-sovereign understanding of freedom. Freedom requires cultural and institutional support and thus requires one to be seen or taken in a certain way to complete freedom's meaning—that is, the ability to pursue one's plans of life without fear or threat of being subjected to the use of arbitrary power. We are inescapably dependent on each other. But dependency involves vulnerability, potentially revealing the inadequacies or limitations of the identities or understandings on which we rely. Being free will often require us to embrace that figurative and frightening idea of death about which Walt Whitman and Baldwin believe is central to a democratic society. However necessary, freedom turns out to be a hard thing to bear for those that claim innocence. This is why Baldwin says at the very outset of his 1961 work, *Nobody Knows My Name*, a work that is ostensibly about him grappling with his own identity: "Nothing is more desirable than to be released from an affliction, but nothing is more frightening than to be divested of a crutch."[42]

Here is the rub, and however obvious it may seem we must never tire of saying it and encouraging each other to accept its truth: *The things to which one must attend do not disappear because we close our eyes, and the inherited costs display themselves in the form of reinscribed harms that demand a response.* This point of view gives us a different take on our narration of American history. Reconstruction or the civil rights movement or even Black Power was not merely a site of transformative possibilities but the manifestation of repressed trauma haunting the present. As Avery Gordon puts it: "Haunting . . . always registers the harm inflicted or the loss sustained by a social violence done in the past or the present. But haunting . . . is distinctive for producing something-to-be-done."[43] Civic kinship does not dissolve because we refuse to acknowledge the claim it makes on us. Reflecting on his meeting with Attorney General Robert Kennedy in 1963—a meeting in the wake of the Children's Crusade and Birmingham upheaval—Baldwin famously says to sociologist Kenneth Clark: "There are 20 million Negro people in this country, and you [referring to the attorney general] can't put them all in jail."[44] That is to say, you cannot put them all in jail for demanding, however they do so, ethical and political rights that were always theirs. The things we must attend to remain, but now with compounded harm. What do citizens of such a nation become? What price do we pay for disavowal? Baldwin's answer: "they have become in themselves moral monsters."[45]

When Baldwin uses the language of moral monsters, and here we must proceed with care, we should think of Wells. Both sought to alert their audiences and readers to the cost of rejecting in others what one claims to honor in oneself: "Our dehumanization of the Negro . . . is indivisible from our dehumanization of ourselves: the loss of our identity is the price we pay for our annulment of his."[46] Baldwin has no interest in dehumanizing

JAMES BALDWIN'S GIFT [279]

those he calls moral monsters. Similar to Wells's use of "barbaric," he does not deploy the term as determinative of who and what white Americans are fated to be. This is why, as he says, it is a terrible indictment because he thinks (and we ought not to think otherwise) his listeners can recognize the offense his claim represents—the offense to their character and way of being in the world. He demands that citizens be discursively agile—that they see the figurative use of the language as getting as close as possible to a terrible transformation of the self. What makes it a terrible indictment in another sense is the implication: many white Americans have shut off in themselves that part of them that responds to the pain of others, in particular civic others. To be a moral monster is to betray, we might say, the demand of thick relationships that define our shared political lives. This is the price of innocence and what makes it a crime.

Responsibility and History

Nothing short of rebirth is required—a reawakening by embracing the nation's trauma *as also* what the nation is. Baldwin's plea is that Americans assume a different attitude, critically embrace their past, and allow both to structure a collective vision of responsibility. But just as Myrdal's view involved a picture of innocence against which Baldwin rails, I want to suggest it also involved a narrow conception of responsibility inadequate to the fullness of history. Baldwin offers us more.

Let us linger a bit longer in the 1960s—the maelstrom of American possibility and trauma. Before an audience in 1963, Baldwin, Nathan Glazer, Sidney Hook, and Myrdal gathered for *Commentary*'s symposium, "Liberalism and the Negro." Moderated by the editor of *Commentary*, Norman Podhoretz, Baldwin found himself (with Myrdal as the European observer) in the presence of three generations of white liberal New York intellectuals.[47] The symposium was subsequently published in 1964, marking the twentieth anniversary of Myrdal's study. The symposium took stock of America's progress, African Americans' ethical and political status, and the nation's most significant dilemma.

One immediately notices that Baldwin stands apart from America's liberal defenders. The focal point of tension is not between Baldwin and Myrdal as one might have anticipated (at least not explicitly), and not even between Baldwin and Glazer that most scholars discuss. Glazer's attempt to assimilate racial inequality to the issue of ethnic integration ignored that the postwar landscape absorbed the variety of Euro-American ethnicities into whiteness, leaving in its place the white-black paradigm.[48]

Still, that is not the most significant conflict. Instead, the heart of the disagreement is between Baldwin and Hook.

Behind Hook's critical engagement with Baldwin is a broader claim about the role of history in thinking about ethical and political life. Hook tells the audience that the ethical principles of American life (i.e., the principles of the Declaration of Independence) must guide the citizenry. He concedes there is much to do to improve the life and standing of African Americans, but he insists there is little doubt that the nation has made and will continue to make progress. As Hook claims Baldwin does, to argue otherwise is to "paralyze our ethical impulses."[49]

Throughout the exchange, Hook is more Myrdalian than Myrdal. I do not know if he read the text, but Hook inhabits the logic of *An American Dilemma*, perhaps without even knowing. The haunting presence of totalitarianism—the ghosts of world wars—occupies his attention. He leans into an ideological defense of liberal democracy that is indistinguishable from his appreciation of the United States as an ethical republic. To him, Baldwin looked more like the social protest novelist Richard Wright, and Hook had already criticized him (and others) in 1949 for pushing negative ideas about the United States.[50] This ideological context and Hook's politics of vindication shaped his attitude toward the past in thinking about racial justice and his account of responsibility:

> Those people in the South today who turn their eyes away from the Negro problem are responsible for the situation to the extent that they can relieve it. But they are not responsible for the initial acts which developed the situation in which they find themselves. . . . They can be charged with responsibility for not playing a greater role, for not taking a more active part in the political process. But there's a tremendous difference between responsibility for a problem which we run away from and collective guilt for the crimes of racists.[51]

We should observe two issues. First, Hook conceives of the "Negro problem" as a problem for black people that is in need of being fixed by those with whom they share society. This gives a specific character to the issue at hand: the problem inheres in the situation of African Americans (it is the "Negro problem") and thus Hook takes the background conditions for granted. We do not, in other words, treat the problem as a feature of the historical development of the socio-institutional ecology of American life and as something for which we must take responsibility.[52] This leads to the second observation. In Hook's thinking, we can discern the outline of what Iris Marion Young refers to as a liability model of responsibility. On this view, we must be able to assign culpability to agents causally tied to consequences for which responsibility is sought.[53] This leads him to suggest in the passage above: They were racists then, we are not now, and our responsibility extends no further than the actions we in the present have committed. History remains, but its role is diminished, lest we endanger human agency and social transformation.

The worry about ethical and political paralysis and the desire to get Americans to act in the name of racial justice may sound familiar. Hook sounds like Douglass, Anna Julia Cooper, or even Du Bois from an earlier time insofar as they all concerned themselves with seeing humans as agents of change. But there is a difference that reveals the historical blindness of the American Creed and refuses the easy equivalence between those thinkers and Hook.

I do not want to go too far with this claim; we have read and seen too much. In the nineteenth and twentieth centuries, African American thinkers shared the democratic desires of Myrdal and Hook. They believed, even in different degrees, that resisting domination, realizing equal regard, and affirming the virtue of self and societal creation in the name of social justice were central values of a democratic order. Accordingly, they focused on exercising the franchise and enjoying the fruits of equal opportunity while simultaneously attempting to transform the wider culture to receive them in society.

However, their attitude toward America's brutal racial history framed their commitments to democracy differently. If the American Creed was a once-born faith because it had little space for lasting anguish and little patience for the specters of the past, then black perfectionism wedded to a vision of American society not yet proposed a different path. African American thinkers argued that the way to a new America must run through the trauma of black life—a twice-born faith in James's sense that did not remit the nation's failures but held promises and betrayals clearly in view.

Hook's way of thinking reflects one of the most important entailments of American innocence—the idea that the citizenry stands exclusively within its present horizon of experience. The result is a clean American story, connecting Hook in the 1960s to Myrdal in the 1940s. But, of course, other beliefs were circulating that stood in marked contrast—the idea that the present may bear the trace of a past from which the nation cannot finally escape. Baldwin famously alerts his readers to this in *The Fire Next Time*, which I briefly referred to in the introduction. This line can find no home in Hook's 1963 remarks: "This is the crime of which I accuse my country and my countrymen, and for which neither I nor time nor history will ever forgive them, that they have destroyed and are destroying hundreds of thousands of [black] lives."[54] Destruction not only happened, but it continues anew.

To speak as he does indicates that Baldwin is not merely interested in us recalling past events. "It is not a question of memory," he explains in 1955. "Oedipus did not remember the thongs that bound his feet; nevertheless, the marks they left testified to that doom toward which his feet were leading him."[55] He thinks merely recalling the past is often about distance: "what we call history is perhaps a way of avoiding responsibility."[56] To stand in an intimate relationship with the past requires us to acknowledge how it shapes the ground of our identity and the practical judgments that work themselves into the world through our words and deeds. "The man does not remember the hand that struck him," Baldwin insists, "the darkness that frightened him as a child; nevertheless the hand and the darkness remain with him, indivisible from himself forever, part of the passion that drives him wherever he thinks to take flight."[57]

The foundational role Baldwin accords the past is likely to make us nervous. There is an Old Testament sensibility in his writings in how failures in history come to weigh on the present. And worries over guilt or blame swirl about us when asked to see ourselves as responsible for the past. In our contemporary moment, I am reminded of Republican senator Mitch McConnell's response to reparations for slavery: "I don't think reparations for something that happened 150 years ago for whom none of us currently living are responsible is a good idea."[58]

For a society preoccupied with innocence and that thinks of responsibility always through a liability model, Baldwin will appear to be asking us to take the fall for something we did not do and over which we had no control. We heard it in Hook, and in Baldwin's famous exchange with the cultural anthropologist Margaret Mead in 1970 we can hear it again. Baldwin asks her to think about our connection to each other across time and how our past may bind us. To that suggestion, she responds: "I think if one takes that position it's absolutely hopeless. I will not accept any guilt for what anybody else did. I will accept guilt for what I did myself." The reason, she continues: "If we can't control it, we're not guilty."[59]

Despite Baldwin's claims, he is not interested in blame or guilt. "I'm not interested in anybody's guilt," he writes in 1964, "I know you didn't do it, and I didn't do it either."[60] To Mead's concern he says, "But I'm not trying to make us guilty."[61] Similar to Hook and Mead, Baldwin is after responsibility, but not of the liability kind. "But I am responsible for it," he continues, "because I am a man and citizen of this country and you are responsible for it, too."[62] The "it" here is the racial nightmare of American life that functions as a shared inheritance.

At just this moment, Baldwin's insight shines through, but it requires us to keep the connection between dependency and democratic freedom in view. Suppose, as I have argued throughout, freedom denotes dependency, the necessity of a socio-institutional ecology (i.e., the demos in its collective capacity) that creates ethical and political conditions for completing one's freedom. In that case, the lack of a healthy ecosystem that produces and reproduces injustices will prevent freedom's realization. For Baldwin, we should not think of this as merely a structural-institutional problem because reproduction also lives through us—in our habits and sensibilities. When these institutions are at work, they create an environment of identity formation that also bears our stamp. They reflect and reproduce who we are. The reproduction of racial injustices across time requires a corresponding capacious idea of responsibility to match. What Baldwin is after in his writings we find nicely stated by Iris Marion Young: "shared responsibility is a responsibility I personally bear, but I do not bear it alone. I bear it in the awareness that others bear it with me; acknowledgement of my responsibility is also acknowledgement of the inchoate collective of which I am a part, which together produces injustices."[63] Our racial history thus requires that we view responsibility as also something we can share, even when we cannot causally see such acts of injustices flowing from our will.

So Baldwin thinks we awaken *our* responsibility by holding the nightmare in view. Hook suggests otherwise. Hook thinks the American Creed can only survive by releasing it from its burdens.[64]

I will come back specifically to Baldwin's account of responsibility. Given how he thinks about history, it does not seem possible that even a shared idea of responsibility can ultimately redeem the nation. This seems to cut against the meaning of aspirational politics—the idea of a people not yet. But let us stay with this theme of responsibility and the American Creed because it reflects a broader and confused view internal to the postwar and civil rights movement landscape for many white liberals. It allows us to see the dangers of the liability model. If the American Creed must be unburdened, as Hook suggests, then what, if anything, constitutes the persistent challenges that African Americans faced?

In his 1965 report, *The Negro Family: The Case for National Action* (otherwise referred to as *The Moynihan Report*), Assistant Secretary of Labor Daniel Patrick Moynihan provides an answer in the concluding pages. "The present tangle of [Negro] pathology is capable of perpetuating itself without assistance from the white world."[65] *The Moynihan Report* is a wonderful example of the dominant model of racial liberalism, invoking as it did Myrdal in its opening pages: "What Gunnar Myrdal said in *An American Dilemma* remains true today: 'America is free to choose whether the Negro shall remain her liability or become her opportunity.'"[66] This formulation from the introduction stands oddly in relation to the line that appears in the report's conclusion. Despite liberals seeing black people as suffering under the pressure of racial disregard (that America can choose to address), the tragedy of black life seemingly stands independent of those pressures (a cultural pathology that reproduces itself through the actions of black people). While the first aimed to secure sympathy among the broader public, it was troubled and often undercut by the second claim.

The second claim appears durable across time.[67] In the 1960s and 1970s, politicians tied the cultural "weaknesses" of black people to their penchant for "rioting" (more accurately called civil protest) and violence. In the late 1970s and 1980s, those same cultural "deficiencies" were used to explain and overstate African Americans' dependency on the state. Gone was the biological racism of an earlier time and culture was installed in its place, but now racially differentiated. What race refers to has changed, but the shift seemingly carries a persistent antagonism. There is, in other words, an affirmation of black people as a collectivity that require assistance and yet they stand apart from the wider society. Black people become either a patient in need of aid or a community one must discipline.

Here is the implication. How history presses on and shapes us falls from view. Rather than rely on the historical connection between self and society suggested by black life and the troubling context of choice, liberal thinkers have focused on the responsibility of black people to rightly choose regardless of context. And for many, the failure of black people to rightly choose bespeaks their unique pathology. In short, or so the argument goes, the problem is with them, and not with white people, and most certainly not with the ethical life of the United States.[68]

From Baldwin's perspective, we must see that the workings of the past in the present cannot be properly shouldered by the model of responsibility commonly at work. The liability model misses how racial inequalities are often based on a logic of societal disregard that in itself structures the life chances of black people, while disavowing society's involvement.[69] The point is not that the liability model is wrong, but it most certainly is inadequate to meet the normative demand of democracy given our specific racial history. And with that inadequacy comes another—namely, a failure to convey the equal ethical and political standing of a group of people who are otherwise claimed as fellow citizens. Only a shared vision of responsibility can meet the challenge. But this requires that we are honest about our history and ourselves.

———◆———

History, especially America's racial past, can be terrible; its trauma, held too tightly or focused upon too minutely, threatens to dash our hopes and undo our efforts. Whether in Douglass's engagement with Martin Delany in the nineteenth century or Du Bois's meditation in *The Souls of Black Folk* at the turn of the twentieth, the issue was partly about how society should stand to the past. Baldwin is asking his readers to see the past as the scaffolding of their identity. The "great force of history comes from the fact that we carry it within us, are unconsciously controlled by it in many ways, and history is literally present in all that we do."[70]

But for all of them, this may be productive. They are not the figures of which Nietzsche warned whose historical sense ran too deep, rooting them in place and rendering them unable to move. This was Hook's or Myrdal's fear, you might say. In contrast, Baldwin offers a different point of view. In "great pain and terror," he writes, "one enters into battle with that historical creation, Oneself, and attempts to re-create oneself according to a principle more humane and more liberating: one begins the attempt to achieve a level of personal maturity and freedom which robs history of its tyrannical power, and also changes history."[71] Baldwin insists that what we lose in comfort as we battle with the past we may gain in ethical and political maturity.

Baldwin regularly uses the word "mature" or allusions to it. "Nothing can save us," he writes in 1964, "if we cannot achieve that long-, long-, long-delayed maturity." A year later he tells the nation what results from this delayed maturity: "The fact that [white Americans] have not yet been able to do this—to face their history, to change their lives—hideously menaces this country."[72] His use of "maturity" is also his way of signaling what the civil rights and Black Power movements were attempting to stimulate in the nation: growth. However, the desire to retain our innocence comes at a grave cost. When the story of social movements, for example, cannot be folded into the origin story made manifest, they necessarily become harbingers of destruction. This obscures that both emerge from the same crisis of racial disregard and that the latter (Black Power) represents a transformation of the former (civil rights movement) due to the nation's disavowal.

Baldwin's insistence on Americans becoming mature echoes the writings of earlier black thinkers from the nineteenth century, even as he exemplifies an important thread that continues into the civil rights generation of the twentieth century. It is present in Ralph Ellison, Martin Luther King Jr., and Toni Morrison. All agree with Baldwin's quest to cultivate a historical sense. "Perhaps more than any other people," Ellison explains in 1964,

> Americans have been locked in a deadly struggle with . . . history. We've fled the past and trained ourselves to suppress, if not forget, troublesome details of the national memory, and a great part of our optimism, like our progress, has been bought at the cost of ignoring the process through which we've arrived at any given moment in our national existence.[73]

None of these thinkers abandon aspirational politics, but they filter it through the history of America's racial horror and thereby seek to discipline its expression.

From Walker to Baldwin, African American perfectionists asked their audience to see something as profoundly wrong with who white Americans take themselves to be in their relationship to and treatment of black people. The previous chapters narrated a way of thinking about democracy that did not turn us away from the horror of American life but toward it as a condition for growth. Myrdal, Hook, and Moynihan share with this tradition its goal to think about racial disregard as an ethical-political problem. But they framed the response in archaeological terms, as a method of recovering who we are in our essential and untraumatized nature. As a result, they found themselves engaged in handwringing—something that has become customary for the nation—about how fixation with the past paralyzes the nation. They therefore were uninterested in asking the questions that Baldwin thought we must ask: How should we stand in relation to the irrevocable deeds of white supremacy? What is the fate of responsibility in a democratic society given the brutal racial history of the United States? What is left of aspirational politics if the past always haunts the present?

The Sensibility of the Twice-Born: Faith without Redemption

I have sketched a point of view that Baldwin asks us to assume. It involves us rejecting the idea of our racial innocence in order to accept the fullness of our past. That is, to be critically responsive to it. But, in doing so, we are also positioned to embrace a form of freedom adequate to meet the demand of our shared democratic life. With this comes a corresponding robustness to our view of responsibility, what I have called a shared idea of responsibility.

There is one lingering issue to address that has to do with the weightiness of our history. It comes in the form of the very notion of an irrevocable deed I mentioned in the introduction. For if deeds are irrevocable, and their consequences seem to extend into the present, it is not clear why one would ever attempt to respond. One might worry that how Baldwin asks us to think about the past threatens to endanger the very notion of aspirational politics. His claim in *The Fire Next Time* that the country's crimes against black people are something for which he nor time nor history can ever forgive or his insistence in "The White Problem" that the act of enslavement was the country's "fatal flaw" seems to deny transformation. The reason we are likely to think this is because of how we have historically envisioned politics. For if aspirational politics holds out the possibility of change and progress where racial justice is concerned, it must be because the nation can redeem itself. Perfectionism, one might think, must imply salvation.

I ask you to think about the matter differently. To take Baldwin seriously—indeed, the arc of this book—requires us to disentangle transformation and progress from redemption. This is not a tactic and it isn't a program; it is an attitude or mood that nurtures democracy and tries to sustain the citizenry for an incomplete and incompletable journey.

"I don't think," Baldwin says to Hook in that roundtable discussion, "we can discuss this [the ethical character of the nation] properly unless we begin at the beginning."[74] When he asks us to return to the beginning and the weightiness of our past, he asks us to think of the nation as Josiah Royce once thought of an individual that wrecked their moral universe. Here is how Royce put it in that extraordinary text of 1913, *The Problem of Christianity*:

> In his own deed he has been false to whatever light he then and there had and to whatever ideal he then viewed as his highest good. Hereupon no new deed, however good or however faithful, and however much of worthy consequences it introduces into the future life of the traitor or of his world, can annul the fact that the one traitorous deed was actually done.[75]

For Baldwin, the deeds are the enslavement of black people and the corresponding hierarchy of value we call white supremacy. He cannot absolve white Americans of a deformation they initiated in the nation's name, and this point holds even as he encourages his nephew to "accept them with love."[76] At this moment, Baldwin asks his black audiences to love white people, but he also thinks this goes a long way in unburdening black people with responsibility for *saving* their white counterparts. Love is powerful, but the work of civic love always requires partners: "If we—and now I mean the relatively conscious whites and the relatively conscious blacks, who must, like *lovers*, insist on, or create, the consciousness of the others—do not falter in our duty now, we may be able, handful that we are, to end the racial nightmare."[77] The love from black people may point the way to accepting one's past and is therefore important in that regard, but until "they understand [their history], they cannot be released from it."[78] Time and history cannot serve in that role either. Although they are useful in marking the temporal distance from one's beginnings, they cannot dissolve the inherited consequences of those actions.

To be released from the past or forgiven for it (these things mean the same for Baldwin) is not the same as absolving one of the horrors that the past represents in time. In his conversation with Mead, he refers to this as "the dynamic that exists in time."[79] Those deeds are irrevocable and seeded the ethical and political life we now live and share. To this thought, Mead recoils: "Then we've nowhere to go."[80] It now appears that Baldwin has seemingly traded one origin story for another, that in abandoning the optimism of the American Creed he has embraced pessimism. No, he says, because "we have atonement."[81]

To atone is to engage in reparative work; it orients the soul as one undertakes the work of correction, of improvement, of development. An atoning community looks backward to the beginning that has given life to the harms, is perceptually attuned to how the harms ripple through time, and engages in ameliorative actions so that those in the future may live more humanely in the light of their past.

In this way, atonement gives a specific meaning to our present actions in redressing racial inequalities and injustices that contrast with the language of redemption. Redemption would aim to restore that which was broken and deliver us from the harms that follow as a result. To be, for example, redeemed through Christ is to be delivered from one's sins. Christ on the cross is a powerful and rich image; it represents the emptying of the self in the form of sacrifice for humanity thus releasing us from our sins. Baldwin, however, does not invoke Christ in this role to address the tragedy of America's racial history. Moreover, it is unclear what redemption could mean, as he puts it, given the many thousands gone. "Endlessly varied," says Royce, "are the problems—the tragedies, the lost causes, the heartbreaks, the chaos, which the deeds of traitors produce. . . . But all this constitutes the heart of the sorrow."[82] There is no narrative of escape, no redeemer, and no metaphysical certainty guaranteed to us by our origin story. And with this, Baldwin dispenses with the idea of redemption.

We should do the same. While it is true, as I have argued, that the normative vision of democracy released dynamic energy and potential, it is also true that in doing so, American democracy relies on a vision of futurity that grounds the legitimacy of democracy. This has served as the reservoir from which others have drawn in their struggle for justice and in their success in securing a bit of it. But our belief in national absolution is destructive. It sends us off questing after a pure past of ethical upright-ness. It leads us to attach too much value to victories of racial progress and to read our historical successes as redemption. It encourages us to believe it is permissible to monetize and materialize the reparative work of atone-ment. In Jesse McCarthy's words, it obscures that "reparations should be about bending the social good once again toward freedom and the good life."[83] It blinds us to the fact that responding to our racial history, similar to living our democracy, depends on what Baldwin says are choices we have "got to make for ever and ever and ever, every day."[84]

To be sure, white supremacy is, for him, America's sin. The source of this sin is naturalistic, not metaphysical, and is rooted in this-worldly choices. Still, sin talk has symbolic power. Sin illuminates a form of wrongdoing that cuts deep—that not only touches the soul but has a hand in the soul's formation. If our history of racial disregard lives in us, Bald-win insists, then it follows that even our affirmative confrontation with it only makes sense because we embrace the past. Or to put it differently, our affirmative gestures of redress—that is, the legal, political, and cultural expressions—are only intelligible because they bear the trace of a stain we have inherited. We can atone for our racial crimes, but even through our reparative work we are reminded of the fatal betrayal, the fatal flaw.

On the first read, this will most certainly feel like a terrible conclu-sion and an offense to freedom. In a few lines it may appear that I have betrayed the perfectionism I have sought to defend across these pages. But I want you to understand where this perfectionism begins and where it leads. How does one think about the development of self and society if not by tracking how both grapple with the darkest features within. The perfectionist ethos—the ascension of the soul into higher forms—in Bald-win's hands is not about overcoming and thus escaping our trauma but often living in the light of a trauma that constantly threatens to intrude on our lives. In some ways this was already at work in many of the thinkers we considered, and as a result they sought to fortify our soul and properly attune our senses, but it is a constant theme in Baldwin.

To assume this point of view involves a radical transformation. It envisions a society struggling to remain alive to the danger of its racial past in the present, to be perceptually on alert to how it might display itself in time. This is why Baldwin describes our confrontation with our past as a battle; we do not find success in defeating the past but in preventing it from becoming tyrannical. Being alive to our beginnings *may* permit us to begin again. We don't overcome our national trauma and we do not secure salvation from our inheritance. In struggling with and against both, we potentially communicate new senses of worth to each other through words and deeds. This is community work—the hard work of democracy— and it can also be the darkened light of *our* faith forged through the tragedy of *our* history.

NOTES

Introduction

1. W.E.B. Du Bois, *Darkwater: Voices from within the Veil* (1920; New York: Oxford University Press, 2007), 68.

2. Ta-Nehisi Coates, "Trayvon Martin and the Irony of American Justice," *The Atlantic*, July 15, 2013, https://www.theatlantic.com/national/archive/2013/07 /trayvon-martin-and-the-irony-of-american-justice/277782/. This argument is expanded and deepened in Coates, *Between the World and Me* (New York: Spiegel and Grau, 2015); Coates, *We Were Eight Years in Power: An American Tragedy* (New York: One World, 2017). For my specific worries about Coates, see Melvin L. Rogers, "Between Pain and Despair: What Ta-Nehisi Coates Is Missing," *Dissent Magazine*, July 31, 2015, https://www.dissentmagazine.org/online_articles/between-world-me -ta-nehisi-coates-review-despair-hope; Rogers, "Keeping the Faith," *Boston Review*, November 1, 2017, http://bostonreview.net/race/melvin-rogers-keeping-faith.

3. Calvin L. Warren, "Black Nihilism and the Politics of Hope," *CR: The New Centennial Review* 15, no. 1 (2015): 217. For his extended argument, see Warren, *Ontological Terror: Blackness, Nihilism, and Emancipation* (Durham: Duke University Press, 2018).

4. Jared Sexton, *Amalgamation Schemes: Anti-Blackness and the Critique of Multiracialism* (Minneapolis: University of Minnesota Press, 2008); Sexton, "The Social Life of Social Death: On Afro-Pessimism," *Social Text* 28, no. 2 (2011): 31–56; Sexton, "Afro-pessimism: The Unclear Word," in *Rhizomes Cultural Studies in Emerging Knowledge* 29, http://www.rhizomes.net/issue29/sexton.html; cf. Frank Wilderson, "Gramsci's Black Marx: Whither the Slave in Civil Society?" *Social Identities* 9, no. 2 (2003): 225–40; Wilderson, *Red, White, and Black: Cinema and the Structure of U.S. Antagonisms* (Durham: Duke University Press, 2010); Wilderson, *Afropessimism* (New York: Norton, 2020). The reader can find a different articulation of the permanence of racism that does not extinguish political engagement in Derrick Bell, *Faces at the Bottom of the Well: The Permanence of Racism* (New York: Basic Books, 1992).

5. Michel Rolph Trouillot, "The Otherwise Modern: Caribbean Lessons from the Savage Slot," in *Critically Modern: Alternatives, Alterities, Anthropologies*, ed. Bruce M. Knauft (Bloomington: Indiana University Press, 2002), 222; cf. 224.

6. Barnor Hesse and Juliet Hooker, "Introduction: On Black Political Thought inside Global Black Protest," *South Atlantic Quarterly* 116, no. 3 (July 2017): 449.

7. See generally Philip A. Klinkner and Rogers Smith, *Unsteady March: The Rise and Decline of Racial Equality in America* (Chicago: University of Chicago Press, 2002).

8. Michelle Alexander, *The New Jim Crow: Mass Incarceration in the Age of Colorblindness* (New York: New Press, 2012); F. Michael Higginbotham, *Ghosts of Jim Crow: Ending Racism in Post-Racial America* (New York: New York University Press, 2013); Eddie S. Glaude Jr., *Democracy in Black: How Race Still Enslaves the American*

Soul (New York: Crown Press, 2016); Richard Rothstein, *The Color of Law: The Forgotten History of How Our Government Segregated America* (New York: Liveright, 2017); Elizabeth Hinton, *From the War on Poverty to the War on Crime: The Making of Mass Incarceration in America* (Cambridge, MA: Harvard University Press, 2017).

9. Hayden White, *Metahistory: The Historical Imagination in 19th-Century Europe*, Fortieth-Anniversary Edition (1973; Baltimore: Johns Hopkins University Press, 2014), chap. 1; White, *The Content of Form: Narrative Discourse and Historical Representation* (Baltimore: Johns Hopkins University Press, 1990); cf. David Scott, *Conscripts of Modernity: The Tragedy of Colonial Enlightenment* (Durham: Duke University Press, 2004), 7, 32.

10. Wilderson, *Afropessimism*, 102; cf. Warren, *Ontological Terror*, 16–20.

11. Scott, *Conscripts*, 7.

12. I use the language of "closed tragedy" to distinguish what I am suggesting from Scott's more generative account of tragedy. Ibid., chap. 5.

13. The classic statement of the American Creed is found in Gunnar Myrdal, *An American Dilemma: The Negro Problem and Modern Democracy*, with introduction by Sissela Bok, 2 vols. (1944; New Brunswick, NJ: Transaction, 2009).

14. For the classic statement of institutional racism, see Kwame Ture and Charles Hamilton, *Black Power: The Politics of Liberation* (New York: Vintage, 1967), chap. 1, especially 4–5.

15. Frederick Douglass, "What to the Slave Is the Fourth of July" (1852), in *The Frederick Douglass Papers: Series One, Speeches, Debates, and Interviews*, ed. John W. Blassingame, vol. 2 (New Haven: Yale University Press, 1982), 366.

16. For an extended reflection on this contested and generative relationship, see Melvin L. Rogers and Jack Turner, "Political Theorizing in Black: An Introduction," in *African American Political Thought: A Collected History*, ed. Melvin L. Rogers and Jack Turner (Chicago: University of Chicago Press, 2021), 1–29.

17. Rogers Smith, "The 'Liberal Tradition' and American Racism," in *The Oxford Handbook of Racial and Ethnic Politics in the United States*, ed. David L. Leal, Taeku Lee, and Mark Sawyer (New York: Oxford University Press, 2018), http://doi.org/10.1093/oxfordhb/9780199566613.013.13; cf. Smith, "Understanding the Symbiosis of American Rights and American Racism," in *The American Liberal Tradition Reconsidered: The Contested Legacy of Louis Hartz* (Lawrence: University Press of Kansas, 2010), 55–89. For a similar move, see Charles W. Mills, *Black Rights/White Wrongs: The Critique of Racial Liberalism* (New York: Oxford University Press, 2017).

18. The freedom literature is extensive, but on freedom as an aversion to domination in its contemporary form, I have in mind Iris Marion Young, *Justice and the Politics of Difference* (Princeton: Princeton University Press, 1990), especially chap. 2; Philip Pettit, *Republicanism: A Theory of Freedom and Government* (New York: Oxford University Press, 1997); Pettit, *On the People's Terms: A Republican Theory and Model of Democracy* (New York: Cambridge University Press, 2012); Danielle S. Allen, *Talking to Strangers: Anxieties of Citizenship since Brown v. Board of Education* (Chicago: University of Chicago Press, 2004); Ian Shapiro, *Politics against Domination* (Cambridge, MA: Harvard University Press, 2016).

19. I refer the reader to Alexis de Tocqueville's classic statement on "equality of condition" in *Democracy in America*. There Tocqueville means to capture the

emerging leveling conditions in society and the corresponding norm it reflects. "The noble has gone down in the social scale, and the commoner gone up; as the one falls, the other rises. Each half century brings them closer, and soon they will touch." Alexis de Tocqueville, *Democracy in America*, trans. George Lawrence, ed. J. P. Mayer (1835 and 1840; New York: Perennial Library, 1988), 11. Other elaborated accounts of social regard include Elizabeth Anderson, "What Is the Point of Equality?" *Ethics* 109, no. 2 (1999): 287–337, especially 313–14; Carina Fourie, "What Is Social Equality? An Analysis of Status Equality as a Strongly Egalitarian Ideal," *Res Publica* 18, no. 2 (2012): 107–26; Danielle Allen, *Our Declaration: A Reading of the Declaration of Independence in Defense of Equality* (New York: Norton, 2014), chap. 14; Allen, "A New Theory of Justice: Difference without Domination," in *Difference without Domination: Pursuing Justice in Diverse Democracies*, ed. Danielle Allen and Rohini Somanathan (Chicago: University of Chicago Press, 2020), 37–42; Roberto Frega, *Pragmatism and the Wide View of Democracy* (New York: Palgrave Macmillan, 2019), 78–81.

20. The classic versions of the anomalous view of white supremacy: Myrdal, *American Dilemma*; Louis Hartz, *The Liberal Tradition in America* (New York: Harcourt, Brace, and Company, 1955). For an analysis of the anomaly thesis, see Charles Mills, *Black Visible: Essays on Philosophy and Race* (Ithaca: Cornell University Press, 1995), chap. 6; Smith, "The 'Liberal Tradition' and American Racism."

21. Michael C. Dawson, *Black Visions: The Roots of Contemporary African-American Political Ideologies* (Chicago: University of Chicago Press, 2001).

22. For historical and textual reasons, I refer to democracy in part 1 as republicanism.

23. Alasdair MacIntyre, *After Virtue*, 3rd ed. (1981; Notre Dame, IN: University of Notre Dame Press, 2007), xi, especially chap. 15; cf. Sheldon Wolin, "Political Theory as a Vocation," in *Fugitive Democracy and Other Essays*, ed. Nicholas Xeno (Princeton: Princeton University Press, 2016), 27. I am not here claiming that I agree with all that MacIntyre argues. For critical assessments, see Susan Moller Okin, *Justice, Gender, and the Family* (New York: Basic Books, 1989), 60–61; Jeffrey Stout, *Democracy and Tradition* (Princeton: Princeton University Press, 2004), 134–35.

24. Scott, *Conscripts*, 4.

25. Alasdair MacIntyre, "Epistemological Crises, Dramatic Narrative and the Philosophy of Science," *Monist* 60, no. 4 (1977): 461.

26. Robert Gooding-Williams, *In the Shadow of Du Bois: Afro-Modern Political Thought in America* (Cambridge, MA: Harvard University Press, 2009), 2–4; cf. Rogers and Turner, "Political Theorizing in Black: An Introduction," 1–29, especially 4–17; Frank Kirkland, "Modernity and Intellectual Life in Black," in *African-American Perspectives and Philosophical Traditions*, ed. John P. Pittman (New York: Routledge, 1997), 136–65; Michael Hanchard, "Afro-Modernity: Temporality, Politics, and the African Diaspora," *Public Culture* 11, no. 1 (1999): 245–68; Hanchard, "Contours of Black Political Thought: An Introduction and Perspective," *Political Theory* 38, no. 4 (2010): 510–36; Lawrie Balfour, "*Darkwater*'s Democratic Vision," *Political Theory* 38, no. 4 (2010): 537–63.

27. In saying this, I do not deny that many of these thinkers take up the global struggle of race. This book, however, focuses on their specific concerns regarding

black people in the United States. Readers should consult works that draw resources from black political thought more broadly or black internationalism. These works are defined by (a) an emphasis on the ways African Americans often think about race in global or international terms to guard against the reinscription of the ideology of American imperialism, and/or (b) are informed by and draw political philosophical and practical resources from non-white thinkers beyond the United States, and/or (c) meditate on concepts that traditionally are the province of political theory through the lens of the global racial struggle and thus readily draw connections between figures in and beyond the United States.

The following representative list includes those that fall in one or more of the argumentative categories above: Cedric Robinson, *Black Marxism: The Making of the Black Radical Tradition* (1983; Chapel Hill: University of North Carolina Press, 2000); Carol Anderson, *Eyes off the Prize: The United Nations and the African American Struggle for Human Rights, 1944–1965* (New York: Cambridge University Press, 2003); Anthony Bogues, *Black Heretics, Black Prophets: Radical Political Intellectuals* (New York: Routledge, 2003); Nikhil Pal Singh, *Black Is a Country: Race and the Unfinished Struggle for Democracy* (Cambridge, MA: Harvard University Press, 2004); Ifeoma Kiddoe Nwankwo, *Black Cosmopolitanism: Racial Consciousness and Transnational Identity in the Nineteenth-Century Americas* (Philadelphia: University of Pennsylvania Press, 2005); Brent Hayes Edwards, *The Practice of Diaspora: Literature, Translation, and the Rise of Black Internationalism* (Cambridge, MA: Harvard University Press, 2003); Manning Marable and Vanessa Agard-Jones, eds., *Transnational Blackness: Navigating the Global Color Line* (New York: Palgrave Macmillan, 2008); Maurice Jackson and Jacqueline Bacon, *African Americans and the Haitian Revolution* (New York: Routledge, 2010); Minkah Makalani, *In the Cause of Freedom: Radical Black Internationalism from Harlem to London, 1917–1939* (Chapel Hill: University of North Carolina Press, 2011); Neil Roberts, *Freedom as Marronage* (Chicago: University of Chicago Press, 2015); Juliet Hooker, *Theorizing Race in the Americas: Douglass, Sarmiento, Du Bois and Vasconcelos* (New York: Oxford University Press, 2017).

28. Cf. "Democracies seek to sustain themselves and endorse the basic values of their citizens. But unless the citizenry is perfectly just, they act toward a future horizon in order to make their democracy good or better than it is at present." John R. Wallach, *Democracy and Goodness: A Historicist Political Theory* (New York: Cambridge University Press, 2018), 21. I am also broadly appropriating the idea of normative discursive practices, with its ideas of commitment and entitlement. See Robert Brandom, *Making It Explicit* (Cambridge, MA: Harvard University Press, 1994). See also Stout, *Democracy and Tradition*, part 2.

29. Here, the term "space of reasons" is taken from Wilfrid Sellars, *Empiricism and the Philosophy of Mind* (Cambridge, MA: Harvard University Press, 1997) and I mean it to denote the justificatory status of our norms.

30. I have in mind Cornel West's description of romanticism, but given the confusion that attends this term and the way it is easily assimilable to a metahistorical narrative of progressive unfolding of history, I have decided not to use it. On romanticism, see West, *The American Evasion of Philosophy: A Genealogy of Pragmatism* (Madison: University of Wisconsin Press, 1989), 214; cf. Richard Rorty, "Pragmatism and Romanticism," in *Philosophy as Cultural Politics: Philosophical Papers*, vol. 4

(New York: Cambridge University Press, 2007), chap. 7. For the specific language of perfectionism, see Stanley Cavell, *Conditions Handsome and Unhandsome: The Constitution of Emersonian Perfectionism* (Chicago: University of Chicago Press, 1990); Stout, *Democracy and Tradition*, chap. 1; Colin Koopman, *Pragmatism as Transition: Historicity and Hope in James, Dewey, and Rorty* (New York: Columbia University Press, 2009), 144–48.

31. Cf. Quentin Skinner, "Meaning and Understanding in the History of Ideas" (1969), in *Meaning and Context: Quentin Skinner and His Critics* (Princeton: Princeton University Press, 1989). See also R. G. Collingwood, *Autobiography* (New York: Clarendon Press, 1939), chaps. 5, 7, 10; Scott, *Conscripts*, chap. 1, especially 51–55.

32. Alexander Crummell, "The Need for New Ideas and New Aims" (1885), in *Africa and America: Addresses and Discourses* (Springfield, MA: Willey and Co., 1891), 19.

33. Ibid., 18.

34. Ibid., iii–iv.

35. W.E.B. Du Bois, *The Souls of Black Folk* (1903; New York: Oxford University Press, 2007), 16; cf. this to a similar invocation in his posthumously published *The Autobiography of W.E.B. Du Bois* (1968; New York: Oxford University Press, 2007), 275. For a very good reflection on this formulation in *Souls*, see Lawrie Balfour, *Democracy's Reconstruction: Thinking Politically with W.E.B. Du Bois* (New York: Oxford University Press, 2011), chap. 1. Primarily pursuing the literary arc of this tradition, Gregory Laski turns this theme into the guiding light of his reflections. See Laski, *Untimely Democracy: The Politics of Progress after Slavery* (New York: Oxford University Press, 2018).

36. Frederick Douglass, "Freedom Has Brought Duties" (1883), in *The Frederick Douglass Papers: Series One, Speeches, Debates, and Interviews*, ed. John W. Blassingame and John R. McKivigan, vol. 5 (New Haven: Yale University Press, 1992), 56.

37. Frederick Douglass, "We Must Not Abandon the Observation of Decoration Day" (1882), in *The Frederick Douglass Papers: Series One, Speeches, Debates, and Interviews*, ed. John W. Blassingame and John R. McKivigan, vol. 5 (New Haven: Yale University Press, 1992), 46–47.

38. For three helpful accounts on memory and the past, see Sheldon Wolin, "Injustice and Collective Memory," in *The Presence of the Past: Essays on the State and the Constitution* (Baltimore: Johns Hopkins University Press, 1989), 34; Eddie S. Glaude Jr., *In a Shade of Blue: Pragmatism and the Politics of Black America* (Chicago: University of Chicago Press, 2007), chap. 3; Juliet Hooker, *Race and the Politics of Solidarity* (New York: Oxford University Press, 2009), 105–15.

39. Bernard Yack, "The Myth of the Civic Nation," *Critical Review* 10, no. 2 (1996): 193–211; Antonio Negri, *Insurgencies: Constituent Power and the Modern State*, trans. Maurizia Boscagli (Minneapolis: University of Minnesota Press, 1999); Rogers Smith, *Stories of Peoplehood* (New York: Cambridge University Press, 2003); Margret Canovan, *The People* (Cambridge: Polity, 2005); Andreas Kalyvas, "Popular Sovereignty, Democracy, and the Constituent Power," *Constellations* 12, no. 2 (2005): 223–44; Sofia Nasstrom, "The Legitimacy of the People," *Political Theory* 35, no. 5 (2007): 624–58; Jason Frank, *Constituent Moments: Enacting the People in Postrevolutionary America* (Durham: Duke University Press, 2010); Bonnie Honig, *Emergency Politics:*

Paradox, Law, Democracy (Princeton: Princeton University Press, 2009); Paulina Ochoa Espejo, *The Time of Popular Sovereignty: Process and the Democratic State* (University Park: Pennsylvania State University Press, 2011); Kevin Olson, *Imagined Sovereignties: The Power of the People and Other Myths of the Modern Age* (New York: Cambridge University Press, 2016); Jonathan White and Lea Ypi, "The Politics of Peoplehood," *Political Theory* 45, no. 4 (2017): 439–65; Angelica Maria Bernal, *Beyond Origins: Rethinking Founding in a Time of Constitutional Democracy* (New York: Oxford University Press, 2017).

40. Here I draw on two kinds of works: first, those broadly interested in understanding the relationship between democracy and rhetoric; second, those broadly interested in the history of rhetoric as a feature of political life. For the first, see John O'Neil, "The Rhetoric of Deliberation: Some Problems in Kantian Theories of Deliberative Democracy," *Res Publica* 8, no. 3 (2002): 249–68; Allen, *Talking to Strangers*; Benedetto Fontana, Cary J. Nederman, and Gary Remer, eds., *Talking Democracy: Historical Perspectives on Rhetoric and Democracy* (University Park: Pennsylvania State University Press, 2004); Bryan Garsten, *Saving Persuasion: A Defense of Rhetoric and Judgment* (Cambridge, MA: Harvard University Press, 2006); Bernard Yack, "Rhetoric and Public Reasoning: An Aristotelian Understanding of Political Deliberation," *Political Theory* 34, no. 4 (2006): 417–38. For the second, see Quentin Skinner, *Reason and Rhetoric in the Philosophy of Hobbes* (New York: Cambridge University Press, 1996), part 1; Wendy Olmsted, *Rhetoric: An Historical Introduction* (Malden, MA: Blackwell, 2006).

41. On this point, see George Shulman, *American Prophecy: Race and Redemption in American Political Culture* (Minneapolis: University of Minnesota Press, 2008).

42. I am, in this regard, sympathetic to Erica Edwards's intervention regarding the internal workings that both empower and disempower charisma's allure in African American thinking. See Edwards, *Charisma and the Fictions of Black Leadership* (Minneapolis: University of Minnesota Press, 2012).

43. On the cognitivist account of the emotions, see Noel Carroll, *The Philosophy of Horror or Paradoxes of the Heart* (New York: Routledge, 1990), 26; Robert Solomon, *A Passion for Justice: Emotions and the Origins of the Social Contract* (Lanham, MD: Rowman and Littlefield, 1995); Martha Nussbaum, *Upheavals of Thought: The Intelligence of Emotions* (New York: Cambridge University Press, 2001); Sharon Krause, *Civil Passions: Moral Sentiment and Democratic Deliberation* (Princeton: Princeton University Press, 2008).

44. James Baldwin, *The Fire Next Time* (1963), in *Baldwin: Collected Essays*, ed. Toni Morrison (New York: Library of America, 1998), 294 (hereafter *CE*).

45. Martin Luther King Jr., *The Strength to Love* (1963; Minneapolis: Fortress Press, 2010), 29.

46. Martin Luther King Jr., "Nonviolence: The Only Road to Freedom" (1966), in *A Testament of Hope: The Essential Writings and Speeches of Martin Luther King, Jr.*, ed. James M. Washington (New York: HarperOne, 1986), 58.

47. On the version of ethos that specifically has race in mind, see Cornel West, *Prophesy Deliverance!: An Afro-American Revolutionary Christianity* (Philadelphia: Westminster Press, 1982); Young, *Justice and the Politics of Difference*; Allen, *Talking*

to Strangers; Glaude, *In a Shade of Blue*; Imani Perry, *More Beautiful and More Terrible: The Embrace and Transcendence of Racial Inequality in the United States* (New York: New York University Press, 2011); Christopher J. Lebron, *The Color of Our Shame: Race and Justice in Our Time* (New York: Oxford University Press, 2013).

For the broader political theoretical treatment of ethos where race does not figure prominently, see Stephen K. White, *The Ethos of a Late-Modern Citizen* (Cambridge, MA: Harvard University Press, 2009); White, *Sustaining Affirmation: The Strengths of Weak Ontology in Political Theory* (Princeton: Princeton University Press, 2000); White, *A Democratic Bearing: Admirable Citizens, Uneven Injustice, and Critical Theory* (New York: Cambridge University Press, 2017). The more general turn to ethos can be found in the following works: William Connolly, *The Ethos of Pluralization* (Minneapolis: University of Minnesota Press, 1995); Jane Bennett, "How Is It, Then, That We Still Remain Barbarians? Foucault, Schiller and the Aestheticization of Ethics," *Political Theory* 24 (1996): 653–72; Romand Coles, *Rethinking Generosity: Critical Theory and the Politics of Caritas* (Ithaca: Cornell University Press, 1997); Bonnie Honig, "The Politics of Ethos: Stephen White, *The Ethos of a Late-Modern Citizen*," *European Journal of Political Theory* 10, no. 3 (2011): 422–29; Sophia Hatzisavvidou, *Appearances of Ethos in Political Thought: The Dimension of Practical Reason* (New York: Rowman and Littlefield, 2016); Webb Keane, *Ethical Life: Its Natural and Social Histories* (Princeton: Princeton University Press, 2016).

48. White, *Ethos of a Late-Modern Citizen*, 1.

49. Allen, *Talking to Strangers*, chap. 1.

50. Resistance functions as the organizing theme in Alex Zamalin, *Struggle on Their Minds: The Political Thought of African American Resistance* (New York: Columbia University Press, 2017).

51. White, *Sustaining Affirmation*, 10.

52. This is clearly on display in *The Paradox of Constitutionalism: Constituent Power and Constitutional Form*, ed. Martin Loughlin and Neil Walker (Cambridge: Cambridge University Press, 2008).

53. Evelyn Brooks Higginbotham, *Righteous Discontent: The Women's Movement in the Black Baptist Church, 1880–1920* (Cambridge, MA: Harvard University Press, 1993); Kevin Gaines, *Uplifting the Race: Black Leadership, Politics, and Culture in the Twentieth Century* (Chapel Hill: University of North Carolina Press, 1996). We see similar worries in Cathy Cohen, "Deviance as Resistance: A New Research Agenda for the Study of Black Politics," *Du Bois Review* 1, no. 1 (2004): 27–45; Saidiya Hartman, *Wayward Lives, Beautiful Experiments: Intimate Histories of Riotous Black Girls, Troublesome Women, and Queer Radicals* (New York: Norton, 2019).

54. Gaines, *Uplifting the Race*, 3.

55. Adolph Reed, *Stirrings in the Jug: Black Politics in the Post-Segregation Era* (Minneapolis: University of Minnesota Press, 1999); cf. Ange-Marie Hancock, *The Politics of Disgust: The Public Identity of the Welfare Queen* (New York: New York University Press, 2004).

56. John Dewey, *Human Nature and Conduct* (1922), in *The Middle Works: 1899–1924*, ed. Jo Ann Boydston, vol. 14 (Carbondale: Southern Illinois University Press, 1983), 32.

57. Cf. Lebron, *Color of Our Shame*, 2, 55–56; cf. Roberto Frega, "Bringing Character Back In: From Republican Virtues to Democratic Habits," *Ethics and Politics* 21, no. 2 (2019): 197–202.

58. James Baldwin, *Notes of a Native Son* (1955), *CE*, 7.

59. James Baldwin, "Words of a Native Son" (1964), *CE*, 708.

60. Lebron and I disagree somewhat on the use of the term "white supremacy"; he believes it is not a fine enough concept to be helpful (*Color of Our Shame*, 19). Nonetheless, he speaks in a way consistent with my claim: "I want to suggest that the fundamental move necessary to undermine racial inequality in the deepest sense is to understand it as the *problem of social value*—the fact that blacks do not occupy an equal place in the scheme of normative attention and concern upon which our society depends in the first place to justify the distribution of benefits and burdens" (46, original emphasis). Glaude speaks plainly and accurately when he says white supremacy marks a value gap, "the belief that white people are valued more than nonwhite people" (*Democracy in Black*, 30).

61. Ida B. Wells, "Lynch Law in America" (1900), in *The Light of Truth: Writings of An Anti-Lynching Crusader*, ed. Mia Bay (New York: Penguin, 2014), 394.

62. James Baldwin, *Nobody Knows My Name* (1961), *CE*, 406; cf. "The goal of the student movement is nothing less than the liberation of the entire country from its most crippling attitudes and habits" (182).

63. Martin Luther King Jr., *Where Do We Go from Here: Chaos or Community?* (Boston: Beacon Press, 1967), 8.

64. Allen, *Talking to Strangers*; Sharon Krause, *Freedom beyond Sovereignty: Reconstructing Liberal Individualism* (Chicago: University of Chicago Press, 2015); Roberts, *Freedom as Marronage*.

65. Martin Robison Delany, *The Condition, Elevation, Emigration, and Destiny of the Colored People of the United States* (1852; New York: Arno Press, 1968), 37.

66. Faith is not the target of Stephen Holmes's worry, but his now classic defense of gag rules and self-binding is part of his effort to reduce risk in political society that something like faith would reintroduce. See Holmes, *Passion and Constraint: On the Theory of Liberal Democracy* (Chicago: University of Chicago Press, 1995), chap. 5.

67. Robert Merrihew Adams, *Finite and Infinite Goods: A Framework for Ethics* (New York: Oxford University Press, 1999), 373.

68. Paul Tillich, *Dynamics of Faith* (1959; New York: Harper One, 2009), 1, especially chap. 1; cf. James Cone, *A Black Theology of Liberation* (New York: Orbis, 1970), 18–19.

69. Paul Tillich, *Systematic Theology: Three Volumes in One* (Chicago: University of Chicago Press, 1967), 14.

70. James Cone, *The Cross and the Lynching Tree* (New York: Orbis Books, 2013), 160.

71. Percy Bysshe Shelley, "A Defence of Poetry" (1840), in *Shelley's Poetry and Prose* (New York: W. W. Norton, 2002), 517.

72. Frederick Douglass, "Pictures and Progress" (1864–65), in *The Portable Frederick Douglass*, ed. John Stauffer and Henry Louis Gates Jr. (New York: Penguin, 2016), 351.

73. Cf. Paul Tillich, *The Courage to Be* (1952; New Haven: Yale University Press, 1980); Cone, *The Cross and the Lynching Tree*, 160.

74. For a powerful elucidation of this theme of the imagination in American letters as turning to rather than away from reality, see Toni Morrison, *Playing in the Dark: Whiteness and the Literary Imagination* (New York: Vintage, 1992), 35–37.

75. For the accounts of culture on which I rely, see Jeffrey Alexander and Philip Smith, "The Strong Program in Cultural Theory: Elements of a Structural Hermeneutics," *Handbook of Sociological Theory*, ed. Jonathan Turner (New York: Kluwer, 2001), 135–50; Stuart Hall, *Cultural Studies 1983: A Theoretical History*, ed. Jennifer Daryl Slack and Lawrence Grossberg (1983; Durham: Duke University Press, 2016), lectures 6–7; Ulf Hannerz, *Cultural Complexity: Studies in the Social Organization of Meaning* (New York: Columbia University Press, 1992); Young, *Justice and the Politics of Difference*, chap. 2; Perry, *More Beautiful and More Terrible*, introduction.

76. Perry, *More Beautiful and More Terrible*, 5.

77. Mathew Arnold, *Culture and Anarchy*, in *Culture and Anarchy and Other Writings*, ed. Stefan Collini (1869; New York: Cambridge University Press, 1993), 79.

78. Frederick Douglass, "An Address to the Colored People of the United States" (1848), in *Frederick Douglass: Selected Speeches and Writings*, ed. Eric Foner (Chicago: Lawrence Hill Books, 1999), 119; Hosea Easton, *A Treatise on the Intellectual Character, and Civil and Political Condition of the Colored People of the United States; and the Prejudice Exercised towards Them*, in *To Heal the Scourge of Prejudice: The Life and Writings of Hosea Easton*, ed. George R. Price and James Brewer Stewart (1837; Amherst: University of Massachusetts Press, 1999), 90; Frances Ellen Watkins Harper, "The Colored Political in America" (1857), in *A Brighter Coming Day: A Frances Ellen Watkins Harper Reader*, ed. Frances Smith Foster (New York: Feminist Press, 1990), 99.

Part I. Situating Oneself in the Political World

1. For a discussion of social death, see Orlando Patterson, *Slavery and Social Death: A Comparative Study* (Cambridge, MA: Harvard University Press, 1982). On the agency and claim-making power of slaves, albeit in different historical and philosophical registers, see Eugene D. Genovese, *Roll, Jordan, Roll: The World the Slaves Made* (New York: Vintage Books, 1976); Laurent Dubois, *A Colony of Citizens: Revolution and Slave Emancipation in the French Caribbean, 1787–1804* (Chapel Hill: University of North Carolina Press, 2004); Vincent Brown, "Social Death and Political Life in the Study of Slavery," *American Historical Review* 114, no. 5 (2009): 1231–49; Neil Roberts, *Freedom as Marronage* (Chicago: University of Chicago Press, 2015).

2. I interpret the Socratic injunction to involve an examination of social and political life as well. The reader may well wonder about doing just this given that the utterance itself seems to function as an individual ethic of sorts. But to read the Socratic injunction thusly is to understate what Socrates is doing in his famous defense speech, as conveyed by Plato. Socrates intends to communicate to his fellow Athenians what it means to live as a reflective community—a community that does not blindly defer to others ("How you, men of Athens, have been affected by my accusers, I do not know" [*Apology* 17a]) but who subjects to reflection what is being

presented to them ("Leave aside the manner of my speech . . . and instead consider this very thing and apply your minds to this: whether the things I say are just or not. For this is the virtue of a judge [referring to the Athenians], while that of an orator is to speak the truth [referring to himself]" [18a]).

3. Dorinda Outram, *The Enlightenment* (Cambridge: Cambridge University Press, 1995), 3. The locus classicus of this view is Immanuel Kant's essay "An Answer to the Question: What Is Enlightenment?" There he writes, "Enlightenment is mankind's exit from its self-incurred immaturity. Immaturity is the inability to use one's own understanding without the guidance of another. Self-incurred is this inability if its cause lies not in the lack of understanding but rather in the lack of the resolution and the courage to use it without the guidance of another. Sapere aude! Have the courage to use your own understanding! Is thus the motto of enlightenment." Kant, "What Is Enlightenment?" (1784), in *What Is Enlightenment? Eighteenth-Century Answers and Twentieth-Century Questions*, ed. James Schmidt (Berkeley: University of California Press, 1996), 58.

4. John Dewey, *A Common Faith* (1934), in *The Later Works, 1925–1953*, vol. 9, ed. Jo Ann Boydston (Carbondale: Southern Illinois University Press, 1986), 33.

5. David Brion Davis, *Inhuman Bondage: The Rise and Fall of Slavery in the New World* (New York: Oxford University Press, 2006), 31–32; Davis, *The Problem of Slavery in the Age of Emancipation* (New York: Alfred Knopf, 2014), 17; cf. Winthrop Jordan, *White over Black: American Attitudes toward the Negro, 1550–1812*, 2nd ed. (1968; Chapel Hill: University of North Carolina Press, 2012); George M. Fredrickson, *The Black Image in the White Mind: The Debate on Afro-American Character and Destiny, 1817–1914* (Middletown, CT: Wesleyan University Press, 1971); Mia Bay, *The White Image in the Black Mind: African-American Ideas about White People, 1830–1925* (New York: Oxford University Press, 2000); Bruce Dain, *A Hideous Monster of the Mind: American Race Theory in the Early Republic* (Cambridge, MA: Harvard University Press, 2003).

6. *Encyclopedia Britannica* (Philadelphia: Thomas Dobson, 1798), 2:794. For a more extensive reflection on the logic of modern racism, see Cornel West, *Prophesy Deliverance! An Afro-American Revolutionary Christianity* (Philadelphia: Westminster Press, 1982), chap. 2.

7. James Theodore Holly, *A Vindication of the Capacity of the Negro Race for Self-Government, and Civilized Progress as Demonstrated by Historical Events of the Haytian Revolution* (New Haven, CT: William H. Stanley Printer, 1857), 7.

8. Brown, "Social Death and Political Life," 1246. The most potent and compelling articulation of this position is found in Dubois, *Colony of Citizens*; cf. Susan Buck-Morss, *Hegel, Haiti, and Universal History* (Pittsburgh: University of Pittsburgh Press, 2009); Nick Nesbitt, *Universal Emancipation: The Haitian Revolution and the Radical Enlightenment* (Charlottesville: University of Virginia Press, 2008).

9. Robert Gooding-Williams, *In the Shadow of Du Bois: Afro-Modern Political Thought in America* (Cambridge, MA: Harvard University Press, 2009), 2–3; Melvin L. Rogers and Jack Turner, "Political Theorizing in Black: An Introduction," in *African American Political Thought: A Collected History*, ed. Melvin L. Rogers and Jack Turner (Chicago: University of Chicago Press, 2021), 1–29.

10. Compare my claim here to the brilliant insights of Adom Getachew, "Universalism after the Post-Colonial Turn: Interpreting the Haitian Revolution," *Political Theory* 44, no. 6 (2016): 821–44.

11. I primarily have in mind Philip Pettit, *Republicanism: A Theory of Freedom and Government* (New York: Oxford University Press, 1997); Pettit, *On the People's Terms: A Republican Theory and Model of Democracy* (New York: Cambridge University Press, 2012); Pettit, *Just Freedom: A Moral Compass for a Complex World* (New York: Norton Press, 2014).

12. Here I borrow from Rogers Smith, "Beyond Tocqueville, Myrdal, and Hartz: The Multiple Traditions in America," *American Political Science Review* 87, no. 3 (1993): 549–566. I tend, however, to see Tocqueville as sensitive to this and so I think Smith's argument needs to be qualified. On this, see Margaret Kohn, "The Other America: Tocqueville and Beaumont on Race and Slavery," *Polity* 35, no. 2 (2002): 169–193.

13. Ralph Ellison, "Going to the Territory" (1986), in *The Collected Essays of Ralph Ellison*, ed. John F. Callahan (New York: Modern Library, 2003), 505.

14. Axel Honneth, *Freedom's Right: The Social Foundations of Democratic Life* (New York: Columbia University Press, 2014), 17.

15. There are exceptions, of course. Several texts center Afro-modern thought as a way to gain traction on the otherwise unimagined possibilities of modernity. Here is a sample: West, *Prophesy Deliverance*; Cedric J. Robinson, *Black Marxism: The Making of the Black Radical Tradition* (London: Zed Press, 1983); Patricia Hill Collins, *Black Feminist Thought: Knowledge, Consciousness, and the Politics of Empowerment* (New York: Routledge, 1991); Michael C. Dawson, *Black Visions: The Roots of Contemporary African-American Political Ideologies* (Chicago: University of Chicago Press, 2001); Gooding-Williams, *Shadow of Du Bois*; Roberts, *Freedom as Marronage*.

Chapter 1. My Judgment Makes Me Political: David Walker's Transformative Appeal

1. Frederick Douglass, "Our Destiny Is Largely in Our Own Hands" (1883), in *The Frederick Douglass Papers: Series One, Speeches, Debates, and Interviews*, ed. John W. Blassingame and John R. McKivigan, vol. 5 (New Haven: Yale University Press, 1992), 68–69.

2. Henry Highland Garnet, "A Brief Sketch of the Life and Character of David Walker," in *Walker's Appeal, with a Brief Sketch of His Life* (New York: J. H. Tobitt, 1848), v–viii; Maria Stewart, "Religion and the Pure Principles of Morality" (1831), in *Maria W. Stewart, America's First Black Woman Political Writer: Essays and Speeches*, ed. Marilyn Richardson (Bloomington: Indiana University Press, 1987), 30; W.E.B. Du Bois, *Dusk of Dawn: An Essay toward an Autobiography of a Race Concept* (1940; New York: Oxford University Press, 2007), 97.

3. Although the essay is dated, Cedric J. Robinson's reflection on David Walker continues to provide a substantive outline of the trajectory of appropriation of Walker in historical scholarship. See Robinson, "David Walker and the Precepts of Black Studies" (1997), in *Cedric Robinson: On Racial Capitalism, Black Internationalism, and Cultures of Resistance*, ed. H.L.T. Quan (London: Pluto Press, 2019), 340–53.

4. Here I have in mind Tommie Shelby's remark that the *Appeal* is closer to a "sermon than to a learned disputation." Shelby, "White Supremacy and Black Solidarity: David Walker's *Appeal*," in *A New Literary History of America*, ed. Greil Marcus and Werner Sollors (Cambridge, MA: Harvard University Press, 2009), 196–201.

5. David Walker, *Appeal to the Colored Citizens of the World*, ed. Peter P. Hinks (1829; University Park: Pennsylvania State University Press, 2000). The reader should note two things about my use of the title. First, I have Americanized the term "coloured" to "colored." Second, this edition of the *Appeal* incorporates the changes Walker made between 1829 and 1830 when he issued three different editions.

6. For extended reflections on this, see Leonard P. Curry, *The Free Black in Urban America, 1800–1850: The Shadow of the Dream* (Chicago: University of Chicago Press, 1981), chap. 1; Alexander Keyssar, *The Right to Vote: The Contested History of Democracy in the United States*, rev. ed. (New York: Basic Books, 2000), 320.

7. Samuel Johnson, *A Dictionary of the English Language*, vol. 1 (London, 1755), 119; Peter Risenberg, *Citizenship in the Western Tradition: Plato to Rousseau* (Chapel Hill: University of North Carolina Press, 1992).

8. Aristotle provides the classic expression of thinking about citizenship in light of constitutional norms as deciding who is "entitled to participate in an office involving deliberation or decision"; see Aristotle, *Politics*, ed. Carnes Lord (Chicago: University of Chicago Press, 1984), bk. 3, chaps. 1, 3; bk. 4, chap. 1.

9. I share Stephen Marshall's puzzlement by Walker's use of the word "citizen," but I part ways in rejecting the claim that this is merely a utopian assertion. See Marshall, *The City on the Hill from Below: The Crisis of Prophetic Black Politics* (Philadelphia: Temple University Press, 2011), 28.

10. There is a strong affinity between the political power I associate with the practice of appealing in the nineteenth century and Elizabeth Wingrove's reflection on letter writing in eighteenth-century France. See Wingrove, "Sovereign Address," *Political Theory* 40, no. 2 (2012): 138.

11. Mary Sarah Bilder, "The Origins of the Appeal in America," *Hastings Law Journal* 48, no. 5 (1997): 922.

12. Will Kymlicka and Wayne Norman, "Return of the Citizen: A Survey of Recent Work on Citizenship Theory," *Ethics* 104, no. 2 (1994): 353. For this emphasis on citizenship as legal status in the American case, see Rogers M. Smith, *Civic Ideals: Conflicting Visions of Citizenship in U.S. History* (New Haven: Yale University Press, 1997).

13. Smith, *Civic Ideals*, 1.

14. T. H. Marshall, "Citizenship and Social Class," in *Citizenship and Social Class*, ed. Tom Bottomore (1949; London: Pluto Press, 1992), 3–51.

15. The capacity and practice of judging was central to the opportunity the Declaration of Independence opened for the colonists. On this point, see Danielle Allen, *Our Declaration: A Reading of the Declaration of Independence in Defense of Equality* (New York: Norton, 2014). This also finds support in the emerging African American institutions of the 1820s in which, as Stephen Kantrowitz explains, "African American activists created networks and institutions to bind their scattered communities together, investing themselves in projects as various as newspapers, Protestant

denominations, and Masonic lodges." Kantrowitz, *More than Freedom: Fighting for Black Citizenship in a White Republic, 1829–1889* (New York: Penguin Press, 2012), 5; cf. James Oliver Horton and Lois E. Horton, *In Hope of Liberty: Culture, Community, and Protest among Northern Free Blacks, 1700–1860* (New York: Oxford University Press, 1997), chap. 6; Manisha Sinha, *The Slave's Cause: A History of Abolition* (New Haven: Yale University Press, 2016), part 2.

16. The account of black nationalism and the place of Walker therein that I have in mind is Sterling Stuckey, introduction to *The Ideological Origins of Black Nationalism*, ed. Sterling Stuckey (Boston: Beacon Press, 1972), 1–25; cf. Stuckey, *Slave Culture: Nationalist Theory and the Foundations of Black America* (New York: Oxford University Press, 1987), 120. In this regard, I am thinking especially of the following defining traits of black nationalism Stuckey lays out: "[1] A consciousness of a shared experience of oppression at the hands of white people, [2] an awareness and approval of the persistence of group traits and preferences in spite of a violently anti-African larger society, [3] a recognition of bonds and obligations between Africans everywhere, [4] an irreducible conviction that Africans in America must take responsibility for liberating themselves" (introduction, 6). To this is added a fifth claim: "[5] a conception of the white man as the devil" (13). Others do not advance this view precisely because they share, as do I, a sense that Walker envisioned interracial cooperation; see Herbert Aptheker, "Its Setting and Its Meaning," in *One Continual Cry: David Walker's Appeal to the Colored Citizens of the World*, ed. Herbert Aptheker (New York: Humanities Press, 1965), 1–61; Peter Hinks, *To Awaken My Afflicted Brethren: David Walker and the Problem of Antebellum Slave Resistance* (University Park: Pennsylvania State University Press, 1997), 250.

17. Wilson Jeremiah Moses, *Black Messiahs and Uncle Toms: Social and Literary Manipulations of a Religious Myth*, rev. ed. (University Park: Pennsylvania State University Press, 1993), 38–46. The exception here is Eddie Glaude, *Exodus! Religion, Race, and Nation in Early Nineteenth-Century Black America* (Chicago: University of Chicago Press, 2000), 34–43. Another, secular version of the elitism critique is found in Gene Andrew Jarrett, *Representing the Race: A New Political History of African American Literature* (New York: New York University Press, 2011), 43–46.

18. E.g., Wilson Jeremiah Moses, *The Golden Age of Black Nationalism, 1850–1925* (New York: Oxford University Press, 1988); Kevin Gaines, *Uplifting the Race: Black Leadership, Politics, and Culture in the Twentieth Century* (Chapel Hill: University of North Carolina Press, 1996); Adolph Reed, *Stirrings in the Jug: Black Politics in the Post-Segregation Era* (Minneapolis: University of Minnesota Press, 1999); Romand Coles, "'To Make This Tradition Articulate': Practiced Receptivity Matters, or Heading West of West with Cornel West and Ella Baker," in Stanley Hauerwas and Romand Coles, *Christianity, Democracy, and the Radical Ordinary: Conversations between a Radical Democrat and a Christian* (Eugene, OR: Cascade Books, 2008), 45–86; Robert Gooding-Williams, *In the Shadow of Du Bois: Afro-Modern Political Thought in America* (Cambridge, MA: Harvard University Press, 2009). An exception to this is Erica R. Edwards, *Charisma and the Fiction of Black Leadership* (Minneapolis: University of Minnesota Press, 2012).

19. Sheldon Wolin, *Tocqueville between Two Worlds: The Making of a Political and Theoretical Life* (Princeton: Princeton University Press, 2001), 63.

20. Cf. John H. Schaar, *Legitimacy in the Modern State* (New Brunswick, NJ: Transaction, 1981), chap. 1; George Shulman, "Thinking Authority Democratically: Prophetic Practices, White Supremacy, and Democratic Politics," *Political Theory* 36, no. 5 (2008): 708–34; cf. Shulman, *American Prophecy: Race and Redemption in American Political Culture* (Minneapolis: University of Minnesota Press, 2008); Jason Frank, *Constituent Moments: Enacting the People in Postrevolutionary America* (Durham: Duke University Press, 2010), chap. 1.

21. This explains Walker's rejection of repatriation plans proposed by the American Colonization Society. See Walker, *Appeal*, Article IV. For a forceful reading of the *Appeal* as a response to colonization plans, see David Kazanjian, *The Colonizing Trick: National Culture and Imperial Citizenship in Early America* (Minneapolis: University of Minnesota Press, 2003), chap. 2; Chris Apap, "'Let No Man of Us Budge One Step': David Walker and the Rhetoric of African American Emplacement," *Early American Literature* 46, no. 2 (2011): 319–50.

22. Sacvan Bercovitch, *The American Jeremiad* (Madison: University of Wisconsin Press, 1978); cf. David Howard-Pitney, *The Afro-American Jeremiad: Appeals for Justice in America* (Philadelphia: Temple University Press, 1990); Shulman, *American Prophecy*; Andrew R. Murphy, *Prodigal Nation: Moral Decline and Divine Punishment from New England to 9/11* (New York: Oxford University Press, 2009).

23. This democratic reading of the prophet echoes in different ways in Shulman, *American Prophecy*; Eddie Glaude, "On Prophecy and Critical Intelligence," *American Journal of Theology and Philosophy* 32, no. 2 (2011): 105–21.

24. Walker, *Appeal*, 5.

25. Jeremiah 5:21; cf. James Darsey, *The Prophetic Tradition and Radical Rhetoric in America* (New York: New York University Press, 1997), chap. 2.

26. Moses, *Golden Age of Black Nationalism*, 22.

27. For the full intellectual biography of the *Appeal* as well as the expansiveness of its circulation, see Hinks, *To Awaken My Afflicted Brethren*. For the legal implications of the *Appeal* on free speech, see Amy Reynolds, "The Impact of Walker's *Appeal* on Northern and Southern Conceptions of Free Speech in the Nineteenth Century," *Communication Law and Policy* 9, no. 1 (2004): 73–100.

28. Walker, *Appeal*, 4.

29. Walker's approach fits within the longer American pamphleteer tradition; see Bernard Bailyn, "The Transforming Radicalism of the American Revolution," in *Pamphlets of the American Revolution, 1750–1776*, ed. Bernard Bailyn and Jane Garrett (Cambridge, MA: Harvard University Press, 1965), 1; Richard Newman, Patrick Rael, and Philip Lapsansky, introduction to *Pamphlets of Protests: An Anthology of Early African-American Protest Literature, 1790–1860* (New York: Routledge, 2001), 1–32.

30. Walker, document 2, appendix, in *Appeal*, 88.

31. On the revival of rhetoric in democratic theory, see Bryan Garsten, "The Rhetoric Revival in Political Theory," *Annual Review of Political Science* 14 (2011): 159–80; cf. Garsten, *Saving Persuasion: A Defense of Rhetoric and Judgment* (Cambridge, MA: Harvard University Press, 2006); Danielle S. Allen, *Talking to Strangers: Anxieties of Citizenship since Brown v. Board of Education* (Chicago: University of Chicago Press, 2004).

32. Ronald Beiner, *Political Judgment* (Chicago: University of Chicago Press, 1983), 3.

33. Thomas Jefferson to David Harding, April 20, 1824, in *The Life and Selected Writings of Thomas Jefferson*, ed. Adrienne Koch and William Peden (New York: Modern Library, 2004), 651.

34. The works that underwrite this point include Thomas J. Davis, "Emancipation Rhetoric, Natural Rights, and Revolutionary New England: A Note on Four Black Petitions in Massachusetts, 1773–1777," *New England Quarterly* 62, no. 2 (1989): 248–63; Newman, Rael, and Lapsansky, introduction; Glen McClish, "William G. Allen's 'Orators and Oratory': Inventional Amalgamation, Pathos, and the Characterization of Violence in African-American Abolitionist Rhetoric," *Rhetoric Society Quarterly* 35, no. 1 (2005): 47–72; Jacqueline Bacon and Glen McClish, "Descendants of Africa, Sons of '76: Exploring Early African-American Rhetoric," *Rhetoric Society Quarterly* 36, no. 1 (2006): 1–29; Ivy Wilson, *Specters of Democracy: Blackness and the Aesthetics of Politics in the Antebellum U.S.* (New York: Oxford University Press, 2011), chap. 1.

35. Walker, *Appeal*, 18. The reader may be concerned with the gendered language at work in Walker's text. I will come back to this in the next chapter.

36. Ibid., 5.

37. Ibid., 13.

38. Walker, *Appeal*, 34–36; cf. Elizabeth McHenry, *Forgotten Readers: Recovering the Lost History of African American Literary Societies* (Durham: Duke University Press, 2002), chap. 1; Timothy Patrick McCarthy, "'To Plead Our Own Cause': Black Print Culture and the Origins of American Abolitionism," in *Prophets of Protest: Reconsidering the History of American Abolitionism*, ed. Timothy Patrick McCarthy and John Stauffer (New York: New Press, 2006), 136–37.

39. Walker, *Appeal*, 2.

40. *Boston Daily Evening Transcript*, September 28, 1830 (emphasis added); see also Walker, document 10, appendix, in *Appeal*, 109–10; cf. Hinks, *To Awaken My Afflicted Brethren*, chap. 5; cf. McHenry, *Forgotten Readers*, chap. 1. Nowhere are the textual effects of Walker's appeal more clearly laid out than in Marcy J. Dinius, *The Textual Effects of David Walker's Appeal: Print-Based Activism against Slavery, Racism, and Discrimination, 1829–1951* (Philadelphia: University of Pennsylvania Press, 2022).

41. Susan Zaeske, *Signatures of Citizenship: Petitioning, Antislavery and Women's Political Identity* (Chapel Hill: University of North Carolina Press, 2003), 3; cf. Edmund S. Morgan, *Inventing the People: The Rise of Popular Sovereignty in England and America* (New York: Norton, 1988), 223.

42. John Cowell, *Interpreter: Or Booke, Containing the Signification of Words* (London, 1637).

43. Nathan Bailey, *An Universal Etymological English Dictionary* (London, 1721).

44. Johnson, *Dictionary of the English Language*, 1:39.

45. Walker, *Appeal*, 2.

46. Samuel Cornish and John Brown Russwurm, "To Our Patrons," *Freedom's Journal*, March 16, 1827. Compare this to Cornish's claim as editor of *Rights of All*, the short-lived replacement for *Freedom's Journal*: "One general agent whose duty it shall be to continue travelling from one extremity of our country to the other, forming associations communicating with our people and the public generally, on all subjects of interest, collecting monies, and delivering stated lectures

on industry, frugality, enterprise &c., thereby [might link] together, by one solid claim, the whole free population, so as to make them think and feel and act, as one solid body, devoted to education and improvement." Cornish, *Rights of All*, September 18, 1829. For a more extended history of *Freedom's Journal*, see Jacqueline Bacon, *Freedom's Journal: The First African American Newspaper* (Lanham, MD: Lexington Press, 2007).

47. Kantrowitz, *More than Freedom*, 16. On virtual social identity, see Erving Goffman, *Stigma: Notes on the Management of Spoiled Identity* (1963; New York: Simon and Schuster, 2009), chaps. 1–2.

48. Walker, *Appeal*, 17 (emphasis added); cf. 30.

49. Bilder, "Origins of the Appeal," 942.

50. On the significance of black periodicals in circulating alternative narratives, see Todd Vogel, "The New Face of Black Labor," in *The Black Press: New Literary and Historical Essays*, ed. Todd Vogel (New Brunswick, NJ: Rutgers University Press, 2001), 37–54; Robert S. Levine, "Circulating the Nation: David Walker, the Missouri Compromise, and the Rise of the Black Press," in *The Black Press*, ed. Vogel, 17–36; Frankie Hutton, *The Early Black Press in America: 1827–1860* (Westport, CT: Greenwood Press, 1993), pt. 1; Bacon, *Freedom's Journal*.

51. Bilder, "Origins of the Appeal," 920–21. Cf. Bilder, *The Transatlantic Constitution: Colonial Legal Culture and the Empire* (Cambridge, MA: Harvard University Press, 2004), chaps. 2–4.

52. Moses Mather, "America's Appeal to the Impartial World" (1775), in *Political Sermons of the American Founding*, ed. Ellis Sandoz (Indianapolis: Liberty Fund, 1998), 1:441–92; James Forten, "Series of Letters by a Man of Color" (1813), in *Pamphlets of Protest*, ed. Newman, Rael, and Lapsansky, 66–74.

53. This description of the petitionary genre draws on Elizabeth R. Foster, "Petitions and the Petition of Right," *Journal of British Studies* 14, no. 1 (1974): 21–45; Morgan, *Inventing the People*, 223–30; Zaeske, *Signatures of Citizenship*, chap. 1. What is important to observe is that when read together, Foster, Morgan, and Zaeske can be seen as tracking the historical movement from the formal supplicatory quality of petitions in the sixteenth century to their informal subversive quality in the nineteenth century.

54. For an extended reflection on the "I-mode" and "we-mode" that underwrite social practices, see Raimo Tuomela, *The Philosophy of Social Practices: A Collective Acceptance View* (New York: Cambridge University Press, 2002).

55. Even in cases when we defy those expectations, we do so in light of norms that are largely shared. The notion of norms being shared is what makes expectations possible.

56. Nancy Fraser, *Justice Interruptus: Critical Reflections on the "Postsocialist Condition"* (New York: Routledge, 1997), 81; cf. Michael C. Dawson, *Black Visions: The Roots of Contemporary African-American Political Ideologies* (Chicago: University of Chicago Press, 2001), 23–35; Michael Warner, *Publics and Counterpublics* (New York: Zone Books, 2002), chap. 2.

57. Naturalization Act 1790, 1st Cong., sess. 2, chap. 1: 103; Militia Act 1792, 2nd Cong., sess. 1, chap. 33: 271. On this point, see Smith, *Civic Ideals*, chaps. 1 and 7; Kantrowitz, *More than Freedom*, 36.

58. Immanuel Kant, "What Is Enlightenment?" (1784), in *What Is Enlightenment? Eighteenth-Century Answers and Twentieth-Century Questions*, ed. James Schmidt (Berkeley: University of California Press, 1996), 58.

59. William Novak, "The Legal Transformation of Citizenship in Nineteenth-Century America," in *The Democratic Experiment: New Directions in American Political History*, ed. Meg Jacobs, William J. Novak, and Julian E. Zelizer (Princeton: Princeton University Press, 2003), 85–119; Kantrowitz, *More than Freedom*, 33–35.

60. I do not mean to suggest there were no attempts to settle the meaning of citizenship. David Ramsay, a prominent historian of the United States, used black folks as the defining marker of distinction between those who were citizens and those who were mere inhabitants. As he explained in 1789, "Any person living within a country or state, is an inhabitant of it, or resident in it. Negroes are inhabitants, but not citizens. Citizenship confers a right of voting at elections, and many other privileges not enjoyed by those who are no more than inhabitants. The precise difference may be thus stated: The citizen of a free state is so united to it as to possess an individual's proportion of the common sovereignty; but he who is no more than an inhabitant, or resident, has no farther connection with the state in which he resides, than such as gives him security for his person and property, agreeably to fixed laws, without any participation in its government." Ramsey, *A Dissertation on the Manners of Acquiring the Character and Privileges of a Citizen* (Charleston, SC, 1789), 3–4.

61. Walker, *Appeal*, 3 (emphasis added).

62. Letter to Editor, *The Liberator*, January 29, 1831.

63. V, "Walker's Appeal. No. 1," *The Liberator*, April 30, 1831.

64. Walker, *Appeal*, 64.

65. Although the point is clearly at work in Walker and Douglass, I am recasting Robert Brandom, *Reason in Philosophy* (Cambridge, MA: Harvard University Press, 2009), 3.

66. Johnson, *Dictionary of the English Language*, 1:39.

67. Morgan, *Inventing the People*, 223.

68. I should not be read as suggesting that this way of legitimizing power was a fact of social reality. It was not. Rather, I am noting a changed self-understanding internal to modernity that makes talk of popular assent and individual consent intelligible. This cultural shift is in line with what Jerome B. Schneewind describes as a shift from the "morality of obedience" to the "morality of self-governance"; see Schneewind, *The Invention of Autonomy: A History of Modern Moral Philosophy* (New York: Cambridge University Press, 1998), 4.

69. Schaar, *Legitimacy in the Modern State*, 25; Shulman, "Thinking Authority Democratically," 710.

70. Shulman, "Thinking Authority Democratically," 710.

71. Walker, *Appeal*, 5 (original emphasis).

72. Ibid., 2.

73. W.E.B. Du Bois, *The Souls of Black Folk* (1903; New York: Oxford University Press, 2007), 1.

74. Moses, *Golden Age of Black Nationalism*, 22 (emphasis added); cf. Moses, *Black Messiahs and Uncle Toms*, 41.

75. Reed, *Stirrings in the Jug*, 17–20. Obviously, Reed is not making a claim about black politics in the 1830s. In fact, he does not discern custodial-based black politics until the 1880s. I appropriate his term because of the alignment between its meaning and what Moses here suggests about Walker.

76. Reed, *Stirrings in the Jug*, 18–20; Gooding-Williams, *Shadow of Du Bois*, chaps. 4 and 6.

77. Coles, "To Make This Tradition Articulate," 51.

78. Walker, *Appeal*, 22.

79. Howard-Pitney, *Afro-American Jeremiad*, 3.

80. Jeremiah 1:10.

81. Walker, *Appeal*, 78–79.

82. Ibid., 78, 30–31.

83. Cf. Rufus Burrow Jr., *God and Human Responsibility: David Walker and Ethical Prophecy* (Macon, GA: Mercer University Press, 2003), 46–48.

84. Walker, *Appeal*, 13 note †; cf. King's much later but consistent formulation: "I have talked about the new age which is fastly coming into being. I have talked about the fact that God is working in history to bring about this new age. There is danger, therefore, that after hearing all of this you will go away with the impression that we can go home, sit down, and do nothing, waiting for the coming of the inevitable. You will somehow feel that this new age will roll in on the wheels of inevitability, so there is nothing to do but wait on it. If you get that impression you are the victims of an illusion wrapped in superficiality." King, "Facing the Challenge of a New Age" (1956), in *A Testament of Hope: The Essential Writings and Speeches of Martin Luther King, Jr.*, ed. James Melvin Washington (New York: HarperCollins, 1990), 141.

85. Walker, *Appeal*, 30.

86. Ibid.

87. Ibid., 5.

88. See Titus Livy, *The War with Hannibal*, in *The History of Rome from Its Foundation*, trans. Aubrey De Sélincourt, ed. Betty Radice (New York: Penguin Books, 1972), bk. 30. On Walker's specific reading habits, see Hinks, *To Awaken My Afflicted Brethren*, 180. In citing Livy here, I do not mean to suggest that Walker read the primary source, although there was an English version in existence: Livy, *The History of Rome*, trans. George Baker, 6 vols. (New York: Peter A. Mesier et al., 1823). It was common for pamphlets of this kind not to cite often; this was part of their sharply focused and academically pure quality. Nevertheless, throughout the *Appeal*, Walker often reveals that he is a careful student of classical and biblical history. As Hinks explains, "In terms of printed sources on which Walker relied, the *Appeal* shows that he used the studies of Josephus, Plutarch, Oliver Goldsmith on the Greeks, Jesse Toerry on the domestic slave trade, and Frederick Butler on America for a significant portion of his knowledge of history." Hinks, *To Awaken My Afflicted Brethren*, 180.

89. Walker, *Appeal*, 22.

90. The reference to Haiti is far more ambiguous. I surmise that Walker is referring to the internal conflict that ensued between two of Jean-Jacques Dessalines's former advisors in the wake of his assassination. If Walker is referring to this history, it is not clear what he intends to say. Does he mean to suggest that support for

Dessalines should have remained? Does he mean to say Dessalines's assassination was appropriate, given his autocratic style of governance but that unity should have resulted?

91. Walker, *Appeal*, 15.

92. Ibid., 9 (original emphasis).

93. John Stuart Mill, *On Liberty and Other Writings*, ed. Stefan Collini (1859; New York: Cambridge University Press, 1995), 66–67 (emphasis added).

94. W.E.B. Du Bois, *Darkwater: Voices from within the Veil* (1920; New York: Oxford University Press, 2014), 69.

Chapter 2. Living an Antislavery Life: Walker on the Demandingness of Freedom

1. David Walker, *Appeal to the Colored Citizens of the World*, ed. Peter P. Hinks (1829; University Park: Pennsylvania State University Press, 2000), 7, 64.

2. Ibid., 27. There is a partial affinity between the claims above and the argument advanced by Jeremy Waldron in his reading of John Locke. See Waldron, *God, Locke, and Equality: Christian Foundations in Locke's Political Thought* (New York: Cambridge University Press, 2002), chap. 3.

3. Walker, *Appeal*, 64.

4. Ibid., 5.

5. Stefan Wheelock rightly sees that "Walker endeavored to expose the perverse undertones of American republican freedom based on errant theology," but this account should not obscure the voluntarism of black agency that Walker intends to advance as a condition of performing one's freedom. See Wheelock, *Barbaric Culture and Black Critique: Black Antislavery Writers, Religion, and the Slaveholding Atlantic* (Charlottesville: University of Virginia Press, 2016), 101.

6. Walker, *Appeal*, 37 (original emphasis).

7. For a defense of this view of republicanism, see Philip Pettit, *Republicanism: A Theory of Freedom and Government* (New York: Oxford University Press, 1997); Pettit, *A Theory of Freedom: The Psychology and Politics of Agency* (New York: Oxford University Press, 2001); cf. Quentin Skinner, *Liberty before Liberalism* (New York: Cambridge University Press, 1998); Maurizio Viroli, *Republicanism* (New York: Hill and Wang, 2002). The argument here should not be seen as accepting the additional but controversial claim advanced by Pettit and Skinner (not Viroli) that this view of freedom is distinct from what one finds in liberalism or that this account of freedom exhausts what we might want to say about human agency. For the argument against drawing a distinction between republicanism and liberalism based on freedom, see Melvin L. Rogers, "Republican Confusion and Liberal Clarification," *Philosophy and Social Criticism* 34, no. 7 (2008): 799–824. For the argument that this view of freedom is incomplete, see Patchen Markell, "The Insufficiency of Non-Domination," *Political Theory* 36, no. 1 (2008): 9–36.

8. Danielle S. Allen, *Talking to Strangers: Anxieties of Citizenship since Brown v. Board of Education* (Chicago: University of Chicago Press, 2004), 5.

9. For a reading of the *Appeal* with which I am sympathetic and that presses the theme of existentialism in Walker's work, see Rufus Burrow Jr., *God and Human*

Responsibility: David Walker and Ethical Prophecy (Macon, GA: Mercer University Press, 2003), chap. 4.

10. Walker, *Appeal*, 64; cf. 7, 27.

11. Ibid., 65 (emphasis added).

12. Ibid., 12; cf. 21.

13. Ibid., 12.

14. Ibid.

15. David Brion Davis, *The Problem of Slavery in the Age of Emancipation* (New York: Alfred Knopf, 2014), 17; cf. Winthrop Jordan, *White over Black: American Attitudes toward the Negro, 1550–1812*, 2nd ed. (1968; Chapel Hill: University of North Carolina Press, 2012); George M. Frederickson, *The Black Image in the White Mind: The Debate on Afro-American Character and Destiny, 1817–1914* (Middletown, CT: Wesleyan University Press, 1968); Mia Bay, *The White Image in the Black Mind: African-American Ideas about White People, 1830–1925* (New York: Oxford University Press, 2000); Bruce Dain, *A Hideous Monster of the Mind: American Race Theory in the Early Republic* (Cambridge, MA: Harvard University Press, 2003); Wheelock, *Barbaric Culture*, chap. 3.

16. Hosea Easton, *A Treatise on the Intellectual Character, and Civil and Political Condition of the Colored People of the United States; and the Prejudice Exercised towards Them*, in *To Heal the Scourge of Prejudice: The Life and Writings of Hosea Easton*, ed. George R. Price and James Brewer Stewart (1837; Amherst: University of Massachusetts Press, 1999), 109.

17. Maria Stewart, "An Address Delivered at the African Masonic Hall" (1833), in *Maria W. Stewart, America's First Black Woman Political Writer: Essays and Speeches*, ed. Marilyn Richardson (Bloomington: Indiana University Press, 1987), 57 (emphasis added). A year earlier, she speaks of the souls of black men being constrained and as a result they "lose their ambition, and become worthless." Stewart, "Lecture Delivered at the Franklin Hall" (1832), in *Essays and Speeches*, 49.

18. Easton, *Treatise*, 104.

19. Frederick Douglass, *Narrative of the Life of Frederick Douglass, An American Slave* (1845), in *The Frederick Douglass Papers: Series Two, Autobiographical Writings*, ed. James Blassingame, John R. McKivigan, and Peter Hinks, vol. 1 (New Haven: Yale University Press, 1999), 49.

20. The uniqueness of modern chattel slavery is unlikely tied to debasement, as Walker suggests, but to the systematic confinement of debasement to a "race" of people. As David Brion Davis points out, many systems of slavery often involved the "bestializing aspects of dehumanization." When this was combined with racism, writes Davis, it "encouraged efforts at animalization in extreme and systematic forms" (*Problem of Slavery*, 13). Whatever we might think of the historical precision of Walker's point, his claim is ultimately about our self-description in light of slavery.

21. Walker, *Appeal*, 27.

22. Ibid., 21 (emphasis added).

23. Douglass, *Narrative*, 30.

24. Cf. Waldron, *God, Locke, and Equality*, 48.

25. Walker, *Appeal*, 18.

26. Ibid., 65.

27. Anna Julia Cooper, *A Voice from the South*, in *The Portable Anna Julia Cooper*, ed. Shirley Moody-Turner (1892; New York: Penguin Books, 2022), 158 (original emphasis).

28. William James, "Is Life Worth Living?" (1897), in *The Will to Believe and Other Essays in Popular Philosophy* (New York: Dover, 1956), 54 (original emphasis); cf. "The Will to Believe" (1896), in *Will to Believe*, 1–31.

29. I do not mean to suggest that the full expression of one's nature exclusively depends on an affirmation of it. For as we will see, Walker has something to say about conditions that must obtain—conditions that partly depend on white Americans. That our nature affords us a capacity to be free depends not only on us recognizing it but on the social world creating space in which that affordance can be realized. Compare Walker's thinking here to Stewart: "But 'I can't,' is a great barrier in the way. I hope it will soon be removed, and 'I will,' resume its place." Maria Stewart, "Religion and the Pure Principles of Morality, the Sure Foundation on Which We Must Build" (1831), in Richardson, *Essays and Speeches*, 35.

30. William Peden, introduction to Thomas Jefferson, *Notes on the State of Virginia*, ed. William Peden (Chapel Hill: University of North Carolina Press, 1955), xi. I will exclusively cite from the Library of America edition of Thomas Jefferson, *Notes on the State of Virginia* (1787), in *Jefferson: Writings*, ed. Merrill D. Peterson (New York: Library of America, 1984). For an extended reflection on the notes and its history, see Douglas L. Wilson, "Jefferson and the Republic of Letters," in *Jeffersonian Legacies*, ed. Peter Onuf (Charlottesville: University Press of Virginia, 1993), 50–76.

31. Jefferson, *Notes*, 264–71.

32. "It is not against experience to suppose, that different species of the same genus, or varieties of the same species, may possess different qualifications" (Jefferson, *Notes*, 270); cf. Walker, *Appeal*, 29. On the ambiguity of this moment in the *Notes*, see Dain, *Hideous Monster*, 30–36.

33. Cited in Walker, *Appeal*, 29 (emphasis provided by Walker); Jefferson, *Notes*, 270.

34. Walker, *Appeal*, 29.

35. Ibid., 30 (emphasis added).

36. Famously, Douglass does the same in his assessment of the humanity of African Americans, but now as a criticism of white Americans: "The manhood of the slave is conceded. It is admitted in the fact that Southern statute books are covered with enactments forbidding, under severe fines and penalties, the teaching of the slave to read or to write. When you can point to any such laws in reference to the beasts of the field, then I may consent to argue the manhood of the slave." Douglass, "What to the Slave Is the Fourth of July" (1852), in *The Frederick Douglass Papers: Series One, Speeches, Debates, and Interviews*, ed. John W. Blassingame, vol. 2 (New Haven: Yale University Press, 1982), 369–70.

37. Walker, *Appeal*, 7 (original emphasis).

38. John Locke, *Second Treatise*, ed. Ian Shapiro (1689; New Haven: Yale University Press, 2003), chap. 2, §6.

39. Henry Highland Garnet, "An Address to the Slaves of the United States" (1843), in *Black Nationalism in America*, ed. John Bracey, August Meier, and Elliott Rudwick (Indianapolis: Bobbs-Merrill, 1970), 71. For a full account of Garnet's speech, see

Eddie S. Glaude Jr., *Exodus!: Religion, Race, and Nation in Early Nineteenth-Century Black America* (Chicago: University of Chicago Press, 2000), chap. 8.

40. Cf. John McDowell, "Reason and Nature," in *Mind and World* (Cambridge, MA: Harvard University Press, 1996), 80, but especially 78–83; cf. McDowell, "Virtue and Reason," in *Mind, Value, and Reality* (Cambridge, MA: Harvard University Press, 1998), chap. 3; Sharon Krause, *Civil Passions: Moral Sentiment and Democratic Deliberation* (Princeton: Princeton University Press, 2008), 92–93.

41. Walker, *Appeal*, 13n.

42. Ibid., 23.

43. Ibid.

44. Charlton T. Lewis, *An Elementary Latin Dictionary* (New York: Harper and Brothers, 1890), 554.

45. Martin Jay, "Scopic Regimes of Modernity," in *Vision and Visuality*, ed. Hal Foster (New York: New Press, 1999), 3; Jonathan Crary, *Techniques of the Observer: On Vision and Modernity in the Nineteenth Century* (Cambridge, MA: MIT Press, 1992); Simon Gikandi, *Slavery and the Culture of Taste* (Princeton: Princeton University Press, 2011), 44. On the classical tradition specifically, see Quentin Skinner, *Reason and Rhetoric in the Philosophy of Hobbes* (New York: Cambridge University Press, 1996), chap. 5.

46. Sarah Mapps Douglass, "A Mother's Love," *Liberator*, July 28, 1832.

47. Lydia Maria Child, *An Appeal in Favor of That Class of Americans Called Africans* (1833; Amherst: University of Massachusetts Press, 1996), 11–12.

48. Cited in Radiclani Clytus, "'Keep It before the People': The Pictorialization of American Abolitionism," in *Early African American Print Culture*, ed. Lara Langer Cohen and Jordan Alexander Stein (Philadelphia: University of Pennsylvania Press, 2012), 294; Aston Gonzalez, *Visualizing Equality: African American Rights and Visual Culture in the Nineteenth Century* (Chapel Hill: University of North Carolina Press, 2020).

49. Easton, *Treatise*, 86.

50. Frederick Douglass, "Pictures and Progress" (1861), in *The Frederick Douglass Papers: Series One, Speeches, Debates, and Interviews*, ed. John W. Blassingame, vol. 3 (New Haven: Yale University Press, 1985), 456.

51. Karen Halttunen, "Humanitarianism and the Pornography of Pain in Anglo-American Culture," *American Historical Review* 100, no. 2 (1995): 307; cf. Elizabeth B. Clark, "'The Sacred Rights of the Weak': Pain, Sympathy, and the Culture of Individual Rights in Antebellum America," *Journal of American History* 82, no. 2 (1995): 463–93; Margaret Abruzzo, *Polemical Pain: Slavery, Cruelty, and the Rise of Humanitarianism* (Baltimore: Johns Hopkins University Press, 2011), chap. 4.

52. Glenn Hendler, *Structures of Feeling in Nineteenth-Century American Literature* (Chapel Hill: University of North Carolina Press, 2001), 2.

53. Theodore Dwight Weld to Angelina Grimke Weld, January 15, 1842, in *Letters of Theodore Dwight Weld and Angelina Grimke Weld and Sarah Grimke, 1822–1844*, ed. Gilbert H. Barnes and Dwight L. Duman (New York: Appleton-Century, 1934), 892.

54. Cited in Abruzzo, *Polemical Pain*, 129. For more on children's education in this regard, see pp. 129–31.

55. Walker, *Appeal*, 5 (emphasis added).

56. Ibid., 7.

57. Ibid., 24.

58. Adam Smith, *The Theory of Moral Sentiments* (1759; New York: Prometheus Books, 2000), 22.

59. Ibid., 4.

60. For the connection between the Scottish moral sense tradition and earlier American thinkers, which I will not rehearse, see Henry F. May, *The Enlightenment in America* (New York: Oxford University Press, 1976); Daniel Walker Howe, *Making the American Self: Jonathan Edwards to Abraham Lincoln* (New York: Oxford University Press, 2009).

61. David Hume, *A Treatise on Human Nature*, ed. L. A. Selby-Bigge and P. H. Nidditch, 2nd ed. (1740; New York: Oxford University Press, 1978), 414.

62. I borrow "shared physiology of feeling" from Nicole Eustace's analysis of eighteenth-century British American deployment of emotions. In her work, emotions are shared features of humanity that trouble distinctions between "feelings of the genteel and the selfish passions of the masses." Eustace, *Passion Is the Gale: Emotion, Power, and the Coming of the American Revolution* (Chapel Hill: University of North Carolina Press, 2008), 12, especially chaps. 8 and 9; cf. Andrew Burstein, *Sentimental Democracy: The Evolution of America's Romantic Self-Image* (New York: Hill and Wang, 1999).

63. Halttunen, "Humanitarianism," 318–22; cf. Clark, "'Sacred Rights'"; Clytus, "'Keep It before the People'"; Abruzzo, *Polemical Pain*.

64. Walker, *Appeal*, 24.

65. Theodore Dwight Weld, *American Slavery as It Is: Testimony of a Thousand Witnesses* (New York: American Anti-Slavery Society, 1839), 7 (emphasis added). Cf. "Husbands are torn from their wives, children from their parents, while the air is filled with the shrieks and lamentations of the bereaved." Child, *Appeal*, 12.

66. Mapps Douglass, "A Mother's Love."

67. David Hume, "Of the Standard of Taste," in *Essays: Moral, Political and Literary* (1760; Indianapolis: Liberty Fund Press, 1985), 234.

68. Krause, *Civil Passions*, 100–102.

69. Walker, *Appeal*, 25–26; "Affray and Murder," *Columbian Centinel*, September 9, 1829.

70. Walker, *Appeal*, 26 (original emphasis).

71. Cf. Barbara Herman, *Moral Literacy* (Cambridge, MA: Harvard University Press, 2007), 99.

72. Walker, *Appeal*, 27.

73. Ibid., 28.

74. Davis, *Problem of Slavery*, 42–43; cf. Daryl Michael Scott, *Contempt and Pity: Social Policy and the Image of the Damaged Black Psyche, 1880–1996* (Chapel Hill: University of North Carolina Press, 1997); Yuna Blajer de la Garza, "The Meek and the Mighty: Two Models of Oppression," *European Journal of Political Theory* 21, no. 3 (2022): 491–513.

75. Walker, *Appeal*, 14, 30, 35 ("sense"); 24, 28 ("common sense"); 32 ("sound sense"); 34 ("good sense").

76. Sophia Rosenfeld, *Common Sense: A Political History* (Cambridge, MA: Harvard University Press, 2011), chaps. 4–5; Daniel Coker, "A Dialogue between a Virginian and an African Minister" (1810), in *Pamphlets of Protest: An Anthology of Early African American Protest Literature, 1790–1860*, ed. Richard Newman, Patrick Rael, and Phillip Lapsansky (New York: Routledge, 2001), 54; Robert Purvis, "An Appeal of Forty Thousand Citizens, Threatened with Disfranchisement, to the People of Pennsylvania" (1837), in *Pamphlets of Protest*, ed. Newman, Rael, and Lapsansky, 136; William Whipper, "To the American People" (1837), in *Early Negro Writing: 1760–1837*, ed. Dorothy Porter (Baltimore: Black Classic Press, 1995), 205.

77. Rosenfeld, *Common Sense*, 73.

78. Walker, *Appeal*, 28. To clarify here, Walker slides from talking about black men referred to in the article to discussing the black woman and back again. But given that he moves seamlessly between the two, the argument being made seems to apply to both.

79. Stewart, "Address Delivered at the African Masonic Hall," 59. For a rich account of Stewart's thinking on this score, see Kristin Waters, *Maria W. Stewart and the Roots of Black Political Thought* (Jackson: University Press of Mississippi, 2022).

80. Stewart, "Lecture Delivered at the Franklin Hall," 46.

81. Cooper, *Voice*, 31 (original emphasis).

82. Still the reader may long for a more sustained discussion of this matter. After all, one might think, even if one grants that Walker has both men and women in mind, surely there are distinctive forms of domination with which women must contend. As Harriet Jacobs remarked, "Superadded to the burden common to all, [black women] have wrongs, and sufferings, and mortifications peculiarly their own." Jacobs, *Incidents in the Life of a Slave Girl—Written by Herself*, ed. Jean Fagan Yellin (1861; Cambridge, MA: Harvard University Press, 1987), 79. This is because, at least on one level, the reproductive capacities of women open them to another level of domination not shared by their male counterparts. I invite the reader to see my argument here as sufficiently agile to include this other level on which domination works. For richer engagements with this issue, see Stephanie Camp, *Closer to Freedom: Enslaved Women and Everyday Resistance in the Plantation South* (Chapel Hill: University of North Carolina Press, 2004); Deborah Gray White, *A'r'n't I a Woman: Female Slaves in the Plantation South* (New York: Norton, 1985); Shatema Threadcraft, *Intimate Justice: The Black Female Body and the Body Politic* (New York: Oxford University Press, 2016).

83. Walker, *Appeal*, 31.

84. Ibid.

85. Stewart, "Lecture Delivered at the Franklin Hall," 47.

86. Walker, *Appeal*, 31 (original emphasis).

87. Stewart, "Lecture Delivered at the Franklin Hall," 47.

88. Erica L. Ball, *To Live an Antislavery Life: Personal Politics and the Antebellum Black Middle Class* (Athens: University of Georgia Press, 2012), 30.

89. Walker, *Appeal*, 55.

90. Ball, *Antislavery Life*, 30.

91. Walker, *Appeal*, 31 (original emphasis).

92. Douglass, *Narrative*, 80.

93. Frederick Douglass, "An Address to the Colored People of the United States" (1848), in *Frederick Douglass: Selected Speeches and Writings*, ed. Eric Foner (Chicago: Lawrence Hill Books, 1999), 119; Douglass, *My Bondage and My Freedom* (1855; New York: Penguin, 2003), 140.

94. Douglass, *Narrative*, 80.

95. Walker, *Appeal*, 32.

96. Ibid.

97. There is an affinity between my claims here and Bernard Boxill's reading of Frederick Douglass, although integrity does not figure in his analysis. What Boxill discerns in Douglass is not unique to him but can be readily seen in Walker. See Boxill, "Fear and Shame as Forms of Moral Suasion in the Thought of Frederick Douglass," *Transactions of the Charles S. Peirce Society* 31, no. 4 (1995): 713–44.

98. Walker, *Appeal*, 25.

99. As Walker says in his reflections on a speech given by Elias B. Caldwell at the December 21, 1816, meeting of the American Colonization Society, "The real sense and meaning of the last part of Mr. Caldwell's speech is, get the free people of color away to Africa, from among the slaves, where they may at once be blessed and happy, and those who we hold in slavery, will be contented to rest in ignorance and wretchedness, to dig up gold and silver for us and our children." Later on Walker reiterates the point in his analysis of statements made by John Randolph, also made at the meeting. Randolph is clear in his speech that colonization of free blacks does not endanger the property of slaveholders. To this, Walker writes, "Here is a demonstrative proof, of a plan got up, by a gang of slave-holders to select the free people of color from among the slaves, that our more miserable brethren may be the better secured in ignorance and wretchedness, to work their farms and dig their mines, and thus go on enriching the Christians with their blood and groans" (*Appeal*, 54, 58). For the full speeches, see "The Meeting on the Colonization of Free Blacks," *National Intelligencer* (Washington, DC, December 24, 1816).

100. Walker, *Appeal*, 24.

101. Ibid., 41–42 (emphasis added).

102. Ibid., 79.

103. Danielle Allen provides the best reading of the Declaration that I am aware of: "The arc of the Declaration, then, is this: first the colonists declare themselves divorced from Britain; then, after confirming that divorce, they also declare that they are remarrying, now to one another." See Allen, *Our Declaration: A Reading of the Declaration of Independence in Defense of Equality* (New York: Norton, 2014), 95.

104. Walker, *Appeal*, 79 (emphasis added).

105. Ibid., 79n (emphasis added).

106. John Locke, *Some Thoughts Concerning Education*, ed. Ruth W. Grant and Nathan Tarcov (1693; Indianapolis: Hackett, 1996), 85, §115; Thomas Hobbes, *Leviathan*, ed. C. B. Macpherson (1651; New York: Penguin Classics, 1981), 188.

107. Amy Reynolds, "The Impact of Walker's *Appeal* on Northern and Southern Conceptions of Free Speech in the Nineteenth Century," *Communication Law and Policy* 9, no. 1 (2004): 73–100.

108. Jefferson, *Notes*, 264 (Query XIV) and 289 (Query XVIII). For an extended reflection on this theme, see Peter Onuf, "'To Declare Them a Free and Independent

People': Race, Slavery, and National Identity in Jefferson's Thought," *Journal of the Early Republic* 18, no. 1 (1998): 1–46.

109. V, "Walker's Appeal. No. 1," *The Liberator*, April 30, 1831.

110. Jack Turner, *Awakening to Race: Individualism and Social Consciousness in America* (Chicago: University of Chicago Press, 2012), 99.

111. Walker, *Appeal*, 23.

112. Ibid., 78.

113. Ibid., 78–79.

114. Michael Walzer, *Interpretation and Social Criticism* (Cambridge, MA: Harvard University Press, 1987), 39.

115. David Bromwich, *Moral Imagination* (Princeton: Princeton University Press, 2014), 17.

116. Ibid., 11.

117. Walker, *Appeal*, 5 (original emphasis).

Chapter 3. Being a Slave of the Community: Race, Domination, and Republicanism

1. For a discussion of republicanism and its reach in American political thought, see J.G.A. Pocock, *The Machiavellian Moment: Florentine Political Thought and the Atlantic Republican Tradition* (Princeton: Princeton University Press, 1975); M.N.S. Sellers, *American Republicanism: Roman Ideology in the United States Constitution* (New York: New York University Press, 1994). Contemporary affinities can be found in Michael J. Sandel, *Democracy's Discontent: America in Search of a Public Philosophy* (Cambridge, MA: Harvard University Press, 1996); Richard Dagger, *Civic Virtues: Rights, Citizenship, and Republican Liberalism* (New York: Oxford University Press, 1997); Maurizio Viroli, *Republicanism* (New York: Hill and Wang, 2002).

2. Quentin Skinner, "Machiavelli on the Maintenance of Liberty," *Politics* 18, no. 2 (1983): 3–15; Skinner, "The Idea of Negative Liberty," in *Philosophy of History: Essays on the Historiography of Philosophy*, ed. Richard Rorty, J. B. Schneewind, and Quentin Skinner (New York: Cambridge University Press, 1984), 193–221; Skinner, "The Republican Ideal of Political Liberty," in *Machiavelli and Republicanism*, ed. Gisela Bock, Quentin Skinner, and Maurizio Viroli (New York: Cambridge University Press, 1990), 239–309; Skinner, *Liberty before Liberalism* (New York: Cambridge University Press, 1998); Philip Pettit, *Republicanism: A Theory of Freedom and Government* (New York: Oxford University Press, 1997); Pettit, *On the People's Terms: A Republican Theory and Model of Democracy* (New York: Cambridge University Press, 2012); Pettit, *Just Freedom: A Moral Compass for a Complex World* (New York: Norton, 2014).

3. Chaim Wirszubski, *Libertas as a Political Ideal at Rome during the Late Republic and Early Principate* (New York: Cambridge University Press, 1968), 3.

4. For the rich diversity of the tradition of black American political thought, see Michael C. Dawson, *Black Visions: The Roots of Contemporary African-American Political Ideologies* (Chicago: University of Chicago Press, 2001). There are other texts that take up one or more of the traditions attended to by Dawson. A short selection includes Cornel West, *Prophesy Deliverance! An Afro-American Revolutionary*

Christianity (Philadelphia: Westminster Press, 1982); Cedric J. Robinson, *Black Marxism: The Making of the Black Radical Tradition* (London: Zed Press, 1983); Patricia Hill Collins, *Black Feminist Thought: Knowledge, Consciousness, and the Politics of Empowerment* (New York: Routledge, 1991); Eddie Glaude, *Exodus!: Religion, Race, and Nation in Early Nineteenth-Century Black America* (Chicago: University of Chicago Press, 2000).

5. My language of reconfiguration is taken from Michael Hanchard's important reflection on black political thought. As he puts it: "One of the challenges and contributions of black political thought is, to borrow from Toni Morrison in her discussion of African American literature, 'speaking things unspoken.' However, 'speaking things unspoken' also entails linking concepts and practices not normally associated with one another in order to see (*theorin*) differently." Hanchard, "Contours of Black Political Thought: An Introduction and Perspective," *Political Theory* 38, no. 4 (2010): 513; cf. Melvin L. Rogers and Jack Turner, "Political Theorizing in Black: An Introduction," in *African American Political Thought: A Collected History*, ed. Melvin L. Rogers and Jack Turner (Chicago: University of Chicago Press, 2021), 11–17.

6. Pettit, *Republicanism*, 50; cf. Pettit, *On the People's Terms*, chap. 1. For a powerful alternative way of understanding the relationship of republicanism to liberalism, see Andreas Kalyvas and Ira Katznelson, *Liberal Beginnings: Making a Republic for the Moderns* (New York: Cambridge University Press, 2008).

7. Skinner, *Liberty*, 96.

8. I extend appreciation to Davide Panagia for helping me understand this point. For a similar argument with which this account is sympathetic, see Barnor Hesse, "Escaping Liberty: Western Hegemony, Black Fugitivity," *Political Theory* 42, no. 3 (2014): 288–313; for one that focuses on labor rather than race, see Alex Gourevitch, *From Slavery to the Cooperative Commonwealth: Labor and Republican Liberty in the Nineteenth Century* (New York: Cambridge University Press, 2015).

9. My distinction here between "weak" and "strong" versions of racial solidarity is inspired by, although not consistent with, Tommie Shelby, *We Who Are Dark: The Philosophical Foundations of Black Solidarity* (Cambridge, MA: Harvard University Press, 2005), 27.

10. Frederick Douglass, "An Address to the Colored People of the United States" (1848), in *Frederick Douglass: Selected Speeches and Writings*, ed. Eric Foner (Chicago: Lawrence Hill Books, 1999), 119; cf. Douglass, *My Bondage and My Freedom* (1855; New York: Penguin, 2003), 140.

11. The most compelling rendering of this claim is found in Stephen Kantrowitz, *More than Freedom: Fighting for Black Citizenship in a White Republic, 1829–1889* (New York: Penguin, 2012). Although Neil Roberts would not follow Kantrowitz nor myself in tying the meaning of citizenship to affective states, he does rightly see that for black people under conditions of chattel slavery the meaning of freedom is not effectively realized through a legalistic framework. See Roberts, *Freedom as Marronage* (Chicago: University of Chicago Press, 2015), especially chap. 3.

12. Pettit, *On the People's Terms*, 5.

13. Derrick Darby gestures toward the need to think about the social basis of rights discourse in just this way: "The relevant social practices are not merely essential for the exercise or enjoyment of moral rights; they are essential for the very

existence or possession of moral rights." Darby, *Rights, Race, and Recognition* (New York: Cambridge University Press, 2009), 20. Recognizing the difficulty in ascertaining those social practices outside a formal juridical framework, he is left to fall back on the position "that affording a subject legal rights is a paradigm case of affording it institutional respect" (85). It may well seem trivially true that legal rights must be tied to institutional respect, but it is difficult to read Darby's text and not sense that he is after a form of social standing that exceeds the juridical framework and is bound up with the cultural logic of American life as such. Thus he writes, "But it does not follow from this that we must develop the idea of institutional respect using a legal model . . . we need not suppose that the only formal legal practices as opposed to more informal social practices can suffice" (85). I suggest that African Americans were after precisely this form of social standing, and it is for this reason that their appeals often assume the form that they did. We should therefore be careful not to slip, as Darby does, into relying primarily on the formal juridical framework. For several texts that do a better job of keeping informal social practices and interpersonal relationships in view and therefore understanding the ethical work required to affirm equality, see Christopher J. Lebron, *The Color of Our Shame: Race and Justice in Our Time* (New York: Oxford University Press, 2013); Axel Honneth, *Freedom's Right: The Social Foundations of Democratic Life* (New York: Columbia University Press, 2014); Sharon Krause, *Freedom beyond Sovereignty: Reconstructing Liberal Individualism* (Chicago: University of Chicago Press, 2015).

14. For a richer account of sentiment in the American context, see Karen Halttunen, "Humanitarianism and the Pornography of Pain in Anglo-American Culture," *American Historical Review* 100, no. 2 (1995): 307; Elizabeth B. Clark, " 'The Sacred Rights of the Weak': Pain, Sympathy, and the Culture of Individual Rights in Antebellum America," *Journal of American History* 82, no. 2 (1995): 463–93; Andrew Burstein, *Sentimental Democracy: The Evolution of America's Romantic Self-Image* (New York: Hill and Wang, 1999); Nicole Eustace, *Passion Is the Gale: Emotion, Power, and the Coming of the American Revolution* (Chapel Hill: University of North Carolina Press, 2008); Radiclani Clytus, " 'Keep It before the People': The Pictorialization of American Abolitionism," in *Early African American Print Culture*, ed. Lara Langer Cohen and Jordan Alexander Stein (Philadelphia: University of Pennsylvania Press, 2012), 290–317.

15. Eustace, *Passion*, 15.

16. Hosea Easton, *A Treatise on the Intellectual Character, and Civil and Political Condition of the Colored People of the United States; and the Prejudice Exercised towards Them*, in *To Heal the Scourge of Prejudice: The Life and Writings of Hosea Easton*, ed. George R. Price and James Brewer Stewart (1837; Amherst: University of Massachusetts Press, 1999), 90. Thinkers like Walker and Easton were not alone in believing this. Only several years earlier, undoubtedly influenced by Walker, the white abolitionist William Lloyd Garrison spoke of using his newspaper *The Liberator* to stimulate a "revolution in public sentiment." Garrison, "To the Public," *The Liberator*, January 1, 1831.

17. More details of Easton's upbringing and the discrimination he experienced are laid out in George R. Price and James Brewer Stewart, introduction to *Heal the Scourge of the Prejudice*, 1–47; cf. Bruce Dain, *A Hideous Monster of the Mind:*

American Race Theory in the Early Republic (Cambridge: MA: Harvard University Press, 2002), chap. 6.

18. Cicero, *On Duties*, ed. E. M. Atkins, trans. M. T. Griffin (New York: Cambridge University Press, 1991), 33. For a more careful analysis of this point that connects Aristotle and Cicero, see Iseult Honohan, *Civic Republicanism* (New York: Routledge, 2002), chap. 1.

19. John Adams to Mercy Otis Warren, April 16, 1776, in *The Founders' Constitution*, ed. Philip B. Kurland and Ralph Lerner, vol. 1, chap. 18, document 9, http://press -pubs.uchicago.edu/founders/documents/v1ch18s9.html.

20. In fairness to Madison, it is not that civic virtue goes out the window; rather, the strong faith that republicans placed in the virtue of humanity must be appropriately chastened. Madison thus argues that there is sufficient virtue present in humanity to sustain a self-governing society, but not so much virtue that we can do without the structure of constitutional government, whose mechanistic quality can function on its own. As Gordon Wood explains, the Constitution functioned to "cut through the structure of the states to the people themselves and yet was not dependent on the character of that people." Wood, *The Creation of the American Republic, 1776–1787* (1969; Chapel Hill: University of North Carolina Press, 1989), 497; Alexander Hamilton, James Madison, and John Jay, *The Federalist*, ed. J. R. Pole (1788; Indianapolis: Hackett Press, 2005), Federalist #51, #55.

21. Easton, *Treatise*, 90.

22. Ibid.

23. Ibid., 97–98.

24. Ibid., 117.

25. On the first point regarding Haiti, see the collection of essays found in Maurice Jackson and Jacqueline Bacon, eds., *Black Americans and the Haitian Revolution: Selected Essays and Historical Documents* (New York: Routledge, 2010); Brandon R. Byrd, *The Black Republic: African Americans and the Fate of Haiti* (Philadelphia: University of Pennsylvania Press, 2020). For more on these organizations, the reader might consult James Oliver Horton and Lois E. Horton, *In Hope of Liberty: Culture, Community, and Protest among Northern Free Blacks, 1700–1860* (New York: Oxford University Press, 1997), chap. 6; Todd Vogel, ed., *The Black Press: New Literary and Historical Essays* (New Brunswick, NJ: Rutgers University Press, 2001); Elizabeth McHenry, *Forgotten Readers: Recovering the Lost History of African American Literary Societies* (Durham: Duke University Press, 2002); Jacqueline Bacon, *Freedom's Journal: The First African American Newspaper* (Lanham, MD: Lexington Books, 2007); Erica L. Ball, *To Live an Antislavery Life: Personal Politics and the Antebellum Black Middle Class* (Athens: University of Georgia Press, 2012); Kantrowitz, *More than Freedom*.

26. Byrd, *The Black Republic*, 5.

27. This, of course, marks a departure from Shelby's use of the language of weak and strong. For him, "strong" racial solidarity affirms essentialism; Shelby, *We Who Are Dark*, 38–43. For my part, strong racial solidarity is less of a statement about some conception of blackness and more of a claim about the extent to which one's white counterparts are resistant to transformation.

28. Paul Taylor, *Race: A Philosophical Introduction* (Malden, MA: Polity Press, 2004), 15–16. See also West, *Prophesy Deliverance*, chap. 2.

29. Thomas Jefferson, *Notes on the State of Virginia* (1787), in *Jefferson: Writings*, ed. Merrill D. Peterson (New York: Library of America, 1984), 264–70.

30. Ibid., 270.

31. David Walker, *Appeal to the Colored Citizens of the World*, ed. Peter P. Hinks (1829; University Park: Pennsylvania State University Press, 2003), 32.

32. Maria Stewart, "Lecture Delivered at the Franklin Hall" (1832), in *Maria W. Stewart, America's First Black Woman Political Writer: Essays and Speeches*, ed Marilyn Richardson (Bloomington: Indiana University Press, 1987), 48.

33. Stewart, "An Address Delivered Before the African American Female Intelligence Society of America" (1832), 53. For several rich engagements with Stewart, see the classic text of Carla L. Peterson, *"Doers of the Word": African American Women Speakers and Writers in the North, 1830–1880* (New Brunswick, NJ: Rutgers University Press, 1995), chap. 3; Stefan M. Wheelock, *Barbaric Culture and Black Critique: Black Antislavery Writers, Religion, and the Slaveholding Atlantic* (Charlottesville: University of Virginia Press, 2016), chap. 4; Kristin Waters, *Maria W. Stewart and the Roots of Black Political Thought* (Jackson: University Press of Mississippi, 2022).

34. Glaude, *Exodus*, 54–55, 147–49.

35. *Minutes of the Fifth Annual Convention for the Improvement of the Free People of Color in the United States, 1835* (Philadelphia: William P. Gibbons, 1835), 14–15.

36. William Whipper, Alfred Niger, and Augustus Price, "To the American People," in *Minutes of the Fifth Annual Convention*, 26. Whipper continues this argument throughout the 1840s; see Whipper, "Opposition to Black Separatism: Three Letters by William Whipper," in *The Ideological Origins of Black Nationalism*, ed. Sterling Stuckey (Boston: Beacon Press, 1972), 252–60.

37. For an extended reflection on this, see Glaude, *Exodus*, 134–42; cf. Derrick R. Spires, *The Practice of Citizenship: Black Politics and Print Culture in the Early United States* (Philadelphia: University of Pennsylvania Press, 2019), chap. 3.

38. Peterson, *Doers of the Word*, 67.

39. Easton, *Treatise*, 91.

40. Quoted in Dorothy Sterling, *The Making of an Afro-American: Martin Robison Delany, 1812–1885: The Story of the Father of Black Nationalism* (New York: Doubleday, 1971), 130. For a richer narration of the medical school incident, see Nora N. Nercessian, *Against All Odds: The Legacy of Students of African Descent at Harvard Medical School before Affirmative Action, 1850–1968* (Hollis, NH: Harvard Medical School and Puritan Press, 2004), 7–23; Doris Y. Wilkinson, "The 1850s Harvard Medical Dispute and the Admission of African American Studies," *Harvard Library Bulletin* 3, no. 3 (1992): 13–27; Philip Cash, "Pride, Prejudice, and Politics," in *Blacks at Harvard: A Documentary History of African-American Experience at Harvard and Radcliffe*, ed. Werner Sollors, Caldwell Titcomb, and Thomas A. Underwood (New York: New York University Press, 1993), 22–31; Victor Ullman, *Martin Delany: The Beginnings of Black Nationalism* (Boston: Beacon Press, 1971), 122–35.

41. Quoted in Sterling, *Making of an Afro-American*, 132.

42. Quoted in ibid., 130.

43. Martin Robison Delany, *The Condition, Elevation, Emigration, and Destiny of the Colored People of the United States* (1852; New York: Arno Press, 1968).

44. The biographical content of this paragraph is largely drawn from Sterling, *The Making of an Afro-American*, chap. 4; Ullman, *Martin Delany*, 5–8.

45. It is important to note that Delany did not remain committed to this position. By the Civil War, Delany sees in the American polity the possibility for securing equal standing for blacks and even serves in the Union army. Of course, he returns to a modified version of this position after the collapse of Reconstruction. Notwithstanding, the concern here is not with the political philosophical development of Delany's thinking, and so I put this to the side.

46. Martin Delany to Frederick Douglass, July 14, 1848, in *Martin R. Delany: A Documentary Reader*, ed. Robert S. Levine (Chapel Hill: University of North Carolina Press, 2003), 109–16.

47. As early as 1797 this seemed clear. Absalom Jones, a prominent African American clergyman of Philadelphia and bishop of the newly formed African Methodist Episcopal Church, expressed objections to the Fugitive Slave Law in a petition he delivered to Congress on behalf of four fugitive slaves from North Carolina. "It was James Madison," writes Gary Nash, "who rose to assert that a petition from blacks 'had no claim on their attention' in Congress" (*Race and Revolution* [Lanham, MD: Rowman and Littlefield, 1990], 78). Madison framed the issue in a way that revealed the inescapable bind fugitive slaves were in: "If they are slaves," he said, "the Constitution gives them no hopes of being heard here." But if, however, "they are free by the laws of North Carolina, they ought to apply to those laws, and have their privilege established." Of course, given that they were fugitives, it followed that they could neither appeal to Congress nor appeal to North Carolina for a freedom they seemingly never had; see *Annals of Congress*, 4th Cong., 2nd sess., 2020, http://www.memory .loc.gov/cgi-bin/ampage?collId=llac&fileName=006/llac006.db&recNum=252.

48. Delany, *Condition*, 157.

49. Ibid., 158; cf. his earlier observation: "Moral theories have long been resorted to by us, as a means of effecting the redemption of our brethren in bonds, and the elevation of the free colored people in this country. Experience has taught us, that speculations are not enough; that the *practical* application of principles adduced, the thing carried out, is the only true and proper course to pursue" (41). Robert Gooding-Williams provides a careful account of how this worry sits at the heart of how Delany thinks about the principle of political inclusion. See Gooding-Williams, "Martin Delany's Two Principles, the Argument for Emigration, and Revolutionary Black Nationalism," in *African American Political Thought*, ed. Rogers and Turner, 77–94.

50. Cited in Kantrowitz, *More than Freedom*, 35.

51. Martin Delany to Frederick Douglass, July 10, 1852, in *Documentary Reader*, ed. Levine, 222. For more on Delany and Douglass's relationship, and Douglass's reception of *Uncle Tom's Cabin*, see Robert S. Levine, *Martin Delany, Frederick Douglass, and the Politics of Representative Identity* (Chapel Hill: University of North Carolina Press, 1997); Levine, "Uncle Tom's Cabin in Frederick Douglass' Paper: An Analysis of Reception," *American Literature* 64, no. 1 (1992): 71–93.

52. Levine, *Delany and Douglass*, 82. In this context, Levine also observes a more complicated relationship of Douglass to *Uncle Tom's Cabin* that seems less celebratory than Delany thinks.

53. Frederick Douglass, "What Are the Colored People Doing for Themselves?" *North Star*, July 14, 1848.

54. Frederick Douglass, "To Our Oppressed Countrymen," *North Star*, December 3, 1847.

55. Frances Ellen Watkins Harper, "The Colored Political in America" (1857), in *A Brighter Coming Day: A Frances Ellen Watkins Harper Reader*, ed. Frances Smith Foster (New York: Feminist Press, 1990), 99. For a very good text on Harper, see Utz McKnight, *Frances E. W. Harper: A Call to Conscience* (Indianapolis: Polity Press, 2020).

56. Frederick Douglass, "Is Civil Government Right?" (1851), in *The Essential Douglass: Selected Writings and Speeches*, ed. Nicholas Buccola (Indianapolis: Hackett Press, 2016), 46. Douglass retained this view well into the 1880s. As he explains in 1882, "I base my views of the propriety of this occasion not upon partisan, partial and temporary considerations, but upon the broad foundations of human nature itself. Man is neither wood nor stone. He is described by the great poet, as being looking before and after. He has a past, present and future. To eliminate either is a violation of his nature and an infringement upon his dignity. He is a progressive being, and memory, reason, and reflection are the resources of his improvement. With these perfections everything in the world, every great event has an alphabet, a picture, a voice to instruct." Douglass, "We Must Not Abandon the Observation of Decoration Day" (1882), in *The Frederick Douglass Papers: Series One, Speeches, Debates, and Interviews*, ed. John W. Blassingame and John R. McKivigan, vol. 5 (New Haven: Yale University Press, 1992), 45.

57. Frederick Douglass Papers, May 6, 1853, in *Documentary Reader*, ed. Levine, 237 (emphasis added); cf. Douglass, "Colonization" (1849), in *Frederick Douglass: Selected Speeches and Writings*, ed. Foner, 125–27.

58. Douglass was, of course, not beyond thinking that physical resistance and violence might be a possibility. See Douglass, "Is Civil Government Right?" 49.

59. Mary Ann Shadd, *A Plea for Emigration, or Notes of Canada West*, ed. Phanuel Antwi (1852; Peterborough: Broadview, 2016); James Theodore Holly, *A Vindication of the Capacity of the Negro Race for Self-Government, and Civilized Progress as Demonstrated by Historical Events of the Haytian Revolution* (New Haven, CT: William H. Stanley, 1857).

60. Shadd, *A Plea for Emigration*, 19.

61. Alexander Crummell, "Emigration, an Aid to the Civilization of Africa" (1863), in *Africa and America: Addresses and Discourses* (Springfield, MA: Willey & Co, 1891), 405–30; Crummell, "The Regeneration of Africa" (1865), in *Africa and America*, 431–66.

62. For Tocqueville's understanding of the social state, see Alexis de Tocqueville, *Democracy in America*, trans. George Lawrence, ed. J. P. Mayer (1835 and 1840; New York: Perennial Library, 1988), 356.

63. On Delany and Montesquieu, see Gooding-Williams, "Martin Delany's Two Principles, the Argument for Emigration, and Revolutionary Black Nationalism," 79–80. For a reception history of Tocqueville among the black public, see Alvin B. Tillery Jr., "Reading Tocqueville behind the Veil: African American Receptions of *Democracy in America*, 1835–1900," *American Political Thought: A Journal of Ideas, Institutions, and Culture* 7, no. 1 (2018): 1–25.

64. Delany, *Condition*, 39.

65. Ibid., 157 (original emphasis).

66. Frederick Douglass, "The Fugitive Slave Law" (1852), in *Frederick Douglass: Selected Speeches and Writings*, ed. Foner, 208–9.

67. Ibid., 209.

68. Delany, *Condition*, 49.

69. Ibid., 48–49. Although Delany uses the Constitution as a determination of political standing, he does argue that how we determine one's interest in the polity should, in some sense, be tied to contributions made. As he says, "hence an adopted citizen is required to reside a sufficient length of time, to form an attachment and establish some interest in the country of his adoption, before he can rightfully lay any claims to citizenship" (49–50). He then goes on to suggest that this is the great principle of "primitive right" and that upon this principle is founded "the rights of the colored man" (51). But this argument, located in chapter VII, "Claims of Colored Men as Citizens of the United States," is prefaced by his contention that one's natural or primitive right can be obstructed by unjust laws. Natural or primitive right seems to fall under the domain of moral law and not physical law.

70. Ibid., 156.

71. Tocqueville, *Democracy*, 356.

72. Martin Delany, "Political Destiny of the Colored Race on the American Continent" (1854), in *Documentary Reader*, ed. Levine, 248.

73. Ibid.

74. It is also true that Delany seems committed to underwriting his defense of solidarity with something stronger than this pragmatic argument. He does say that an "original" identity is the solid foundation upon which "the fabric of every substantial political structure in the world" rests and "which cannot exist without it; and so soon as a people or nation lose their original identity, just so soon must that nation or people become extinct" ("Political Destiny," 250). This is precisely what Tommie Shelby relies on to illuminate the essentialism in Delany's thinking. Shelby, *We Who Are Dark*, 38–52.

75. Delany, *Condition*, 160.

76. Cited in Francis A. Rollin, *Life and Public Services of Martin R. Delany* (Boston: Lee and Shepard, 1868), 76.

77. Pettit, *On the People's Terms*, 2.

78. Pettit, *Republicanism*, 52.

79. Cicero, *The Republic*, trans. Niall Rudd (New York: Oxford University Press, 1998), bk. 2, lines 43, 48–49; John Locke, *Two Treatises of Government*, ed. Ian Shapiro (1689; New Haven: Yale University Press, 2003), 107.

80. Pettit, *On the People's Terms*, 5; cf. chaps. 3–4.

81. The historian of republicanism will find this line very confusing: political slavery and chattel slavery were the same thing, at least for the Romans. Here, I only ask for patience. Whether it is in Aristotle or the American Founders, there is something like a political slave that loses a status previously enjoyed. This is to be distinguished from one that is fit for slavery or is a "natural" slave. In the American context, this latter description comes to be associated with chattel racial slavery. It may well be that during the Imperial Crisis, the thirteen colonies confused subjection and slavery.

After all, they were often criticized for having done so. But they thought of themselves as slaves all the same.

82. Mary Nyquist, *Arbitrary Rule: Slavery, Tyranny, and the Power of Life and Death* (Chicago: University of Chicago Press, 2013), 26; cf. David Brion Davis, *The Problem of Slavery in the Age of Emancipation* (New York: Knopf, 2014), 35–37.

83. Thomas Jefferson, "A Summary View of the Rights of British America," in *Jefferson: Writings*, ed. Peterson, 115.

84. Jefferson to John Randolph, August 25, 1775, in *Jefferson: Writings*, ed. Peterson, 749.

85. The reader may well be suspicious of this claim, especially given that I will say in chapter 4 that the American polity generally and Jefferson specifically relied on an aspirational view of the people—a people that may yet be—as the legitimating source of republicanism. I ask that the reader accept the claim above as the expression of one feature of an otherwise productive tension at the heart of the American polity—a way of thinking of the American people as realizing the rights of the past under properly administered constitutional conditions and a vision of the American people that exceeded its specific constitutional and ethical expression. Neorepublicanism, I am saying, relies on the first feature without attending to the second, and the workings of African American political thought (as we will see in chapter 4) holds both these themes in view, placing much of its emphasis on the power of the second half of this tension.

86. Cf. Pettit, *Republicanism*, 32–35.

87. Pettit does say that he takes "citizens in this discussion to comprise, not just citizens in the official sense, but all the more or less settled residents of a state who, being adult and able-minded, can play an informed role at any time in conceptualizing shared concerns and in shaping how the state acts in furthering those concerns" (*On the People's Terms*, 75). This move, of course, bypasses the historical problem with which African Americans were concerned—that is, how one achieves formal and informal standing in the eyes of one's fellows.

88. Douglass, "Address," 119. A little more than a year earlier in February 1847 during his time in England, Douglass made a similar point. See Douglass, "The Skin Aristocracy in America," in *The Frederick Douglass Papers: Series One, Speeches, Debates, and Interviews*, ed. John W. Blassingame, vol. 2 (New Haven: Yale University Press, 1982), 4.

89. Harper, "Colored Political," 99.

90. Walker, *Appeal*, 31 (emphasis added).

91. Dain, *Hideous Monster of the Mind*, 170.

92. Easton, *Treatise*, 105; cf. Delany, *Condition*, 154.

93. Racial stigmatization "entails doubting the person's worthiness and consigning him or her to a social netherworld. Indeed, although the language is somewhat hyperbolic, it means being skeptical about whether the person can be assumed to share a common humanity with the observer." Glenn Loury, *The Anatomy of Racial Inequality* (Cambridge, MA: Harvard University Press, 2003), 61; cf. R. A. Lenhardt, "Understanding the Mark: Race, Stigma, and Equality in Context," *New York University Law Review* 79, no. 3 (2004): 803–930; Lebron, *Color of Our Shame*, chap. 2.

94. Easton, *Treatise*, 108.

95. I am here appropriating the language of Clyde Taylor for other purposes. As he writes: "Black men are densely mythogenic, the object of layered fictions produced by others. Like other mythogenic people—Gypsies, Jews—the legend of the Black man outruns and awaits him through the course of his journey. 'What does it feel like to be a myth?' Du Bois might have written, instead of 'to be a problem?'" Taylor, "The Game," in *Black Male: Representations of Masculinity in Contemporary American Art*, ed. Thelma Golden (New York: Whitney Museum of American Art, 1994), 169.

96. Easton, *Treatise*, 103–4. In his book *The Color of Our Shame*, Christopher Lebron provides the closest contemporary analysis of this in which social devaluation at once recedes into the background of our institutions and evolves across time with institutional development. This ironically produces racial inequities in economic, education, and employment outputs as well as attention deficit in responding to these inequities. Lebron refers to this as *"the problem of social value—*the fact that blacks do not occupy an equal place in the scheme of normative attention and concern upon which our society depends in the first place to justify the distribution of benefits and burdens, as well as to identify those who are deserving or appropriate recipients" (*Color of Our Shame*, 46).

97. Charles Reason, "Introduction: The Colored People's 'Industrial College,'" in *Autographs for Freedom*, ed. Julia Griffiths (New York: Wanzer, Beardsley, and Co., 1854).

98. Frederick Douglass, "The Work of the Future" (1862), in *Frederick Douglass: Selected Speeches and Writings*, ed. Foner, 523.

99. Easton, *Treatise*, 103.

100. Ibid.

101. Ibid.

102. Ralph Ellison, "An Extravagance of Laughter" (1985), in *The Collected Essays of Ralph Ellison*, ed. John F. Callahan (New York: Modern Library, 2003), 644.

103. Easton, *Treatise*, 106 (original emphasis); cf. "Our children see this [commerce between master and slave], and learn to imitate it; for man is an imitative animal. This quality is the germ of all education in him. From his cradle to his grave he is learning to do what he sees others do. If a parent could find no motive either in his philanthropy or his self-love, for restraining the intemperance of passions toward his slave, it should always be a sufficient one that his child is present. But generally it is not sufficient. The parent storms, the child looks on, catches the lineaments of wrath, puts on the same airs in the circle of smaller slaves, gives loose to the worst of passions, and thus nursed, educated, and daily exercised in tyranny, cannot but be stamped by it with odious peculiarities." Jefferson, *Notes*, Query XVIII, 257. For more sustained reflections on the connection between white supremacy and children's books, see Donnarae MacCann, *White Supremacy in Children's Literature: Characterizations of African Americans, 1830–1900* (New York: Garland, 1998).

104. Ellison, "Extravagance of Laughter," 644.

105. Easton, *Treatise*, 105.

106. Speech by Theodore S. Wright, in *Black Abolitionist Papers*, ed. C. Peter Ripley, vol. 3 (1836; Chapel Hill: University of North Carolina Press, 1991), 184; Samuel Cornish, *Colored American*, June 9, 1838, in *Black Abolitionist Papers*, ed. Ripley, 3:265; Stephen A. Myers, *Northern Star and Freeman's Advocate*, March 3, 1842, in

Black Abolitionist Papers, ed. Ripley, 3:376; Charles B. Ray, R. Banks, P. McIntire, N. W. Jones, H. H. Garnet, T. Woodson, and S. H. Davis, "Report of the Committee upon the Press," in *Minutes of the National Convention of Colored Citizens* (New York: Piercy and Reed, 1843), 28; Frederick Douglass, *North Star*, July 7, 1848; James McCune Smith to Gerrit Smith, March 31, 1855, in *The Works of James McCune Smith*, ed. John Stauffer (New York: Oxford University Press, 2006), 317.

107. Easton, *Treatise*, 119.

108. See Benedict Anderson, *Imagined Communities: Reflections on the Origins and Spread of Nationalism*, rev. ed. (London: Verso, 2006); Richard Rorty, *Achieving Our Country: Leftist Thought in Twentieth-Century America* (Cambridge, MA: Harvard University Press, 1998), chaps. 3–4.

Part II. A Society That Never Was but May Yet Be

1. Iris Marion Young, *Justice and the Politics of Difference* (Princeton: Princeton University Press, 1990), 58–59.

2. Sophia Hatzisavvidou, *Appearances of Ethos in Political Thought: The Dimension of Practical Reason* (New York: Rowman and Littlefield, 2016), 4, 8; cf. Webb Keane, *Ethical Life: Its Natural and Social Histories* (Princeton: Princeton University Press, 2016). Rather than using "ethical life" or "ethos," Imani Perry deploys the term "culture" to capture the relationship between "physiological and sociocultural" in thinking about the emergence and persistence of racial disregard. Perry, *More Beautiful and More Terrible: The Embrace and Transcendence of Racial Inequality in the United States* (New York: New York University Press, 2011), 32–34.

3. Behind this is the deployment of Maeve Cooke's insight on what she calls "bad utopianism." "The focus is on the inability of the theory's emancipatory projections to connect with the particular constellations of reasons shaping the identities of its addressees: the theory stands accused of bad utopianism because it fails to offer reasons that its addressees can find affectively and intellectually compelling." Cooke, *Re-Presenting the Good Society* (Cambridge, MA: MIT Press, 2006), 162.

4. See generally ibid., chap. 7.

Chapter 4. The People's Two Bodies

1. Sheldon Wolin, "The People's Two Bodies," in *Fugitive Democracy and Other Essays*, ed. Nicholas Xenos (1981; Princeton: Princeton University Press, 2016); Edmund S. Morgan, *Inventing the People: The Rise of Popular Sovereignty in England and America* (New York: Norton, 1988); Bernard Yack, "The Myth of the Civic Nation," *Critical Review* 10, no. 2 (1996): 193–211; Rogers Smith, *Stories of Peoplehood* (New York: Cambridge University Press, 2003); Margaret Canovan, *The People* (Cambridge: Polity, 2005); Andreas Kalyvas, "Popular Sovereignty, Democracy, and the Constituent Power," *Constellations* 12, no. 2 (2005): 223–44; Sofia Nasstrom, "The Legitimacy of the People," *Political Theory* 35, no. 5 (2007): 624–58; Jason Frank, *Constituent Moments: Enacting the People in Postrevolutionary America* (Durham: Duke University Press, 2010); Paulina Ochoa Espejo, *The Time of Popular Sovereignty: Process and the Democratic State* (University Park: Pennsylvania State University Press, 2011);

Bonnie Honig, *Emergency Politics: Paradox, Law, Democracy* (Princeton: Princeton University Press, 2009); Kevin Olson, *Imagined Sovereignties: The Power of the People and Other Myths of the Modern Age* (New York: Cambridge University Press, 2016); Jonathan White and Lea Ypi, "The Politics of Peoplehood," *Political Theory* 45, no. 4 (2017): 439–65; Angélica Maria Bernal, *Beyond Origins: Rethinking Founding in a Time of Constitutional Democracy* (New York: Oxford University Press, 2017).

2. The exceptions to this argument include James Morone, *Democratic Wish: Popular Participation and the Limits of American Government*, rev. ed. (New Haven: Yale University Press, 1998); Danielle S. Allen, *Talking to Strangers: Anxieties of Citizenship since Brown v. Board of Education* (Chicago: University of Chicago Press, 2004); Frank, *Constituent Moments*.

3. Frank, *Constituent Moments*, 10.

4. Ibid., 3; Bernal, *Beyond Origins*, 163.

5. John Locke, *Second Treatise of Government* (1690), in *Two Treatises of Government and A Letter Concerning Toleration*, ed. Ian Shapiro (New Haven: Yale University Press, 2003), §§149, 155, 210, 221–22, 227–28, 230, 240; Thomas Paine, *The Rights of Man* (1792), in *Collected Writings*, ed. Eric Foner (New York: Library of America, 1995), pt. 2, 567. For the importance of trust to politics on which I rely, see John Dunn, "Trust and Political Agency," in *Interpreting Political Responsibility: Essays, 1981–1989* (Oxford: Blackwell, 1990), chap. 3.

6. See Benedict Anderson, *Imagined Communities: Reflections on the Origins and Spread of Nationalism*, rev. ed. (London: Verso, 2006); Richard Rorty, *Achieving Our Country: Leftist Thought in Twentieth-Century America* (Cambridge, MA: Harvard University Press, 1998), chaps. 3–4; Morone, *Democratic Wish*; cf. Christopher Looby, *Voicing America: Language, Literary Form, and the Origins of the United States* (Chicago: University of Chicago Press, 1996). To my mind, we get the best historical accounts of the idea of the community always in the making in explicit and implicit form in James Kloppenberg, *Toward Democracy: The Struggle for Self-Rule in European and American Thought* (New York: Oxford University Press, 2016); Manisha Sinha, *The Slave's Cause: A History of Abolition* (New Haven: Yale University Press, 2016).

7. Priscilla Wald, *Constituting Americans: Cultural Anxiety and Narrative Form* (Durham: Duke University Press, 1995), 2; Daniel Howe, *Making the American Self: Jonathan Edwards to Abraham Lincoln* (Cambridge, MA: Harvard University Press, 1997). Howe, in particular, charts a story in which self-transformation is supported by democratic institutions and cultures that are themselves susceptible to improvement.

8. Ralph Ellison, "The Little Man at Chehaw Station" (1978), in *The Collected Essays of Ralph Ellison*, ed. John F. Callahan (New York: Modern Library, 2003), 506.

9. Here I am following through on the insight of Cornel West. See West, "Pragmatism and the Tragic," in *Prophetic Thought in Postmodern Times* (Monroe, ME: Common Press, 1993), 32–33.

10. Frederick Douglass Papers, May 6, 1853, in *Martin R. Delany: A Documentary Reader*, ed. Robert S. Levine (Chapel Hill: University of North Carolina Press, 2003), 237; cf. Frederick Douglass, "Colonization" (1849), in *Frederick Douglass: Selected Speeches and Writings*, ed. Philip S. Foner (Chicago: Lawrence Hill Books, 1999), 125–27.

11. Thomas Jefferson to James Madison, September 6, 1789, in *The Writings of Thomas Jefferson* (hereafter *WTJ*), vol. 7, ed. Albert Ellery Bergh (Washington, DC: Thomas Jefferson Memorial Association, 1907), 454 (original emphasis); cf. Jefferson to John Wayles Eppes, June 24, 1813, in *WTJ*, 13:269–79; Jefferson to Governor William Plumer, July 21, 1816, in *WTJ*, 15:46–47; Jefferson to Thomas Earle, September 24, 1823, in *WTJ*, 15:470–71. All other citations to Jefferson's works will be from this collection unless otherwise noted.

12. Jefferson to Madison, September 6, 1789, in *WTJ*, 7:459.

13. Cf. David N. Mayer, *The Constitutional Thought of Thomas Jefferson* (Charlottesville: University of Virginia Press, 1995); Garrett Ward Sheldon, *The Political Philosophy of Thomas Jefferson* (Baltimore: Johns Hopkins University Press, 1993). For a thoughtful explication of Jefferson's own use of the language of generation, see Bernal, *Beyond Origins*, 175–89, especially 186–87.

14. Jefferson to Samuel Kercheval, July 12, 1816, in *WTJ*, 15:40–41; cf. Jefferson to John Adams, June 15, 1813, in *WTJ*, 13:252–56.

15. Judith Shklar, "Democracy and the Past: Jefferson and His Heirs," in *Redeeming American Political Thought*, ed. Stanley Hoffman and Dennis F. Thompson (Chicago: University of Chicago Press, 1998), 174. On the evolutionary character of Jefferson's thinking, see Ari Helo, *Thomas Jefferson's Ethics and the Politics of Human Progress: The Morality of a Slaveholder* (New York: Cambridge University Press, 2014), chaps. 1–2. On the idea that this was a general feature of the age, see Sophia Rosenfeld, *Democracy and Truth: A Short History* (Philadelphia: University of Pennsylvania Press, 2019), 26.

16. John Dewey, "Thomas Jefferson," in *The Essential Jefferson*, ed. John Dewey (1940; New York: Dover, 2008), 19; cf. Maurizio Valsania, *The Limits of Optimism: Thomas Jefferson's Dualistic Enlightenment* (Charlottesville: University of Virginia Press, 2011). We see a similar suggestion in Cornel West's identification of Jefferson, Emerson, and Dewey with the tradition of romanticism. See West, *The American Evasion of Philosophy: A Genealogy of Pragmatism* (Madison: University of Wisconsin Press, 1989), chap. 6.

17. Canovan, *People*, 29; cf. Nasstrom, "Legitimacy of the People," 624–58; Frank, *Constituent Moments*.

18. Frank, *Constituent Moments*, 8; cf. 18, 210.

19. Ibid., chap. 7.

20. Jefferson to John Randolph, August, 25, 1775, in *WTJ*, 4:28.

21. Hannah Arendt, "The Freedom to Be Free" (1966–67), *New England Review* 38, no. 2 (2017): 59; cf. Claude Lefort, *Democracy and Political Theory* (Minneapolis: University of Minnesota Press, 1988), 17.

22. See Kalyvas, "Popular Sovereignty," 223–44.

23. Sheldon Wolin, "Transgression, Equality, and Voice" (1996), in *Fugitive Democracy*, ed. Xenos, 54.

24. James Wilson, *Lectures on Law*, in *The Works of James Wilson*, vol. 1, ed. Robert Green McCloskey (1790–91; Cambridge, MA: Harvard University Press, 1967), 304. For a contrasting but earlier view, see Alexander Contee Hanson's remark that the notion of a sovereign people is "subversive of all government and law." Hanson (writing as *Aristides*) to the People, in *Representative Government and the Revolution: The*

Maryland Constitutional Crisis of 1787, ed. Melvin Yazawa (1787; Baltimore: Johns Hopkins University Press, 1975), 125.

25. Canovan, *People*, 123

26. In an earlier reading of the political philosophy of John Dewey, I argued for the importance of redemption to the polity and did so in order to guard against the compensatory idea. I am no longer confident, however, that this term "redemption" can be properly reconstructed given the history of racial disregard in the United States. On the defense of redemption, see Melvin Rogers, "The Fact of Sacrifice and Necessity of Faith: Dewey and the Ethics of Democracy," *Transactions of the Charles S. Peirce Society* 47, no. 3 (2011): 289–90.

27. Ralph Waldo Emerson, "Experience" (1844), in *Essays and Lectures* (New York: Library of America, 1983), 485.

28. Frederick Douglass, "The Dred Scott Decision" (1857), in *The Frederick Douglass Papers: Series One, Speeches, Debates, and Interviews*, ed. John W. Blassingame, vol. 3 (New Haven: Yale University Press, 1985), 172.

29. Walt Whitman, *Democratic Vistas: The Original Edition in Facsimile*, ed. Ed Folsom (1870–71; Iowa City: University of Iowa Press, 2010), 18.

30. W.E.B. Du Bois, *Darkwater: Voices from within the Veil* (1920; New York: Oxford University Press, 2007), 68.

31. Jefferson to Edward Carrington, January 16, 1787, in *Thomas Jefferson: Writings*, ed. Merrill D. Peterson (New York: Library of America, 1984), 880.

32. Jefferson to William Charles Jarvis, September 28, 1820, in *WTJ*, 15:278.

33. Samuel Johnson, *Dictionary: Selections from the 1755 Work That Defined the English Language*, ed. Jack Lynch (1755; New York: Levenger Press, 2003), 476. For Jefferson's recommendation of the *Dictionary* as an aid in fixing in us "the principles and practices of virtue," see Jefferson to Robert Skipwith, August 3, 1771, in *Writings*, ed. Peterson, 740–45.

34. Jefferson to Richard Price, February 1, 1785, in *Writings*, ed. Peterson, 798.

35. Jefferson to William Carmichael, 1786, in *WTJ*, 6:31. Three points should be noted here. First, this is not to deny Jefferson's belief in the importance of a natural aristocracy. He believes in the necessity of having "the real good and wise" at the helm; Jefferson to John Adams, October 28, 1813, in *Writings*, ed. Peterson, 1306. The disagreement between him and Adams, however, is about the precise relationship between the masses and the wise. On this point, Jefferson believes that one can appeal to the people's capacity for judgment, and he rejects the wholesale claim that one finds in Adams that the people are "addicted to Corruption and Venality." John Adams to Abigail Adams, July 3, 1776, in *Adams Family Correspondence*, vol. 2, ed. L. H. Butterfield (Cambridge, MA: Harvard University Press, 1963), 28. Second, I deliberately employ "may" to denote the uncertainty of appealing to the people's good sense. The capacity for good sense does not imply for Jefferson that the people will always employ it effectively. After all, Jefferson is clear that the citizenry is always in danger of having their capacities corrupted by their fellows or their institutions. This second point undercuts the long-standing attribution to Jefferson of blind optimism. For a longer critique of the attribution of optimism, see Valsania, *Limits of Optimism*. Third, precisely because the people's capacities can be corrupted, Jefferson—like others in the tradition of American and African American political thought—places

special emphasis on cultivating the moral and intellectual virtues of character. For a longer argument on the importance of character to Jefferson's thinking, see Jean Yarbrough, *American Virtues: Thomas Jefferson on the Character of a Free People* (Lawrence: University Press of Kansas, 1998).

36. Jefferson to Peter Carr, August 10, 1787, in *Writings*, ed. Peterson, 902. See more generally James Engell, *The Creative Imagination: Enlightenment to Romanticism* (Cambridge, MA: Harvard University Press, 1981), 155–57; cf. Daniel Wickberg, "What Is the History of Sensibilities? On Cultural Histories, Old and New," *American Historical Review* 112, no. 3 (2007): 666.

37. Whitman, *Democratic Vistas*, 9.

38. See generally Robert L. Tsai, *American's Forgotten Constitutions: Defiant Visions of Power and Community* (Cambridge, MA: Harvard University Press, 2014).

39. Espejo, *Time of Popular Sovereignty*, 176.

40. Nasstrom, "Legitimacy of the People," 645; cf. Bruce A. Ackerman, *We the People*, vol. 1, *Foundations* (Cambridge, MA: Harvard University Press, 1991); Ackerman, *We the People*, vol. 2, *Transformation* (Cambridge, MA: Harvard University Press, 1998); Ackerman, *We the People*, vol. 3, *The Civil Rights Revolution* (Cambridge, MA: Harvard University Press, 2014).

41. See Werner Sollors, *Beyond Ethnicity: Consent and Descent in American Culture* (New York: Oxford University Press, 1986), 6, 150–55; Tzvetan Todorov, *On Human Diversity: Nationalism, Racism, and Exoticism in French Thought*, trans. Catherine Porter (Cambridge, MA: Harvard University Press, 1993), 386. I am disaggregating race from the wider category of what Sollors calls ethnicity. See Sollors, *Beyond Ethnicity*, 36–39.

42. Reginald Horsman, *Race and Manifest Destiny: The Origins of American Racial Anglo-Saxonism* (Cambridge, MA: Harvard University Press, 1981), 15–22; Rogers M. Smith, *Civic Ideals: Conflicting Visions of Citizenship in U.S. History* (New Haven: Yale University Press, 1997), 72–77; Gregg D. Crane, *Race, Citizenship, and Law in American Literature* (New York: Cambridge University Press, 2002), 20–29.

43. Thomas Jefferson, "A Summary View of the Rights of British America" (1774), in *Writings*, ed. Peterson, 103–23; Jefferson, *Notes on Virginia* (1785), in *WTJ*, 14:179–208.

44. Todorov, *On Human Diversity*, 386.

45. Martin Robison Delany, *The Condition, Elevation, Emigration, and Destiny of the Colored People of the United States* (1852; New York: Arno Press, 1968), 154.

46. This paragraph relies on the analysis provided in Don E. Fehrenbacher, *The Dred Scott Case: Its Significance in American Law and Politics* (New York: Oxford University Press, 1978), chap. 14.

47. Dred Scott v. Sanford, 60 U.S. 393, [1857].

48. Jefferson, *Notes on Virginia*, in *WTJ*, 14:192.

49. Jefferson to David Harding, April 20, 1824, in *The Life and Selected Writings of Thomas Jefferson*, ed. Adrienne Koch and William Peden (New York: Modern Library, 2004), 651; cf. James L. Golden and Alan L. Golden, *Thomas Jefferson and the Rhetoric of Virtue* (Lanham, MD: Rowman and Littlefield, 2002).

50. Jefferson to Robert Skipwith, August 3, 1771, in *Writings*, ed. Peterson, 741.

51. See Allen, *Talking to Strangers*; Bryan Garsten, *Saving Persuasion: A Defense of Rhetoric and Judgment* (Cambridge, MA: Harvard University Press, 2006); Garsten, "The Rhetoric Revival in Political Theory," *Annual Review of Political Science* 14 (2011): 159–80.

52. "Letter from Dr. Delany," *The Liberator* 21, no. 4 (May 14, 1852; original emphasis). Garrison is one of the few excellent exceptions, as Delany makes clear in *Condition*. Referring to the cause of antislavery, he says, "Like Christianity, the principles are holy and of divine origin. And we believe, if wherever a man started right, with pure and holy motives, Mr. Garrison did; and that, had he the power of making the cause what it should be, it would all be right, and there never would have been any cause for the remarks we have made, though in kindness, and with the purest of motives" (29).

53. For Delany and Douglass's exchange on *Uncle Tom's Cabin*, see "Delany and Douglass on *Uncle Tom's Cabin*," in *Documentary Reader*, ed. Levine, 224–37.

54. Frederick Douglass Papers, May 6, 1853, in *Documentary Reader*, ed. Levine, 237; cf. Douglass, "Colonization," 125–27.

55. Patrick Shade, *Habits of Hope: A Pragmatic Theory* (Nashville: Vanderbilt University Press, 2001), 19; see also Adrienne M. Martin, *How We Hope: A Moral Psychology* (Princeton: Princeton University Press, 2014), chap. 1.

56. Delany, *Condition*, 157.

57. Ibid., 27, 29–30.

58. See generally Britt Rusert, *Fugitive Science: Empiricism and Freedom in Early African American Culture* (New York: New York University Press, 2017). On the complicated tradition of realism and empiricism in American and African American culture, see David E. Shi, *Facing Facts: Realism in American Thought and Culture, 1850–1920* (New York: Oxford University Press, 1995).

59. I have modified Terry Eagleton's formulation. See Eagleton, *Hope without Optimism* (Charlottesville: University of Virginia Press, 2015), chap. 2. A richer account of faith on which my reading partly relies can be found in Robert Merrihew Adams, *Finite and Infinite Goods: A Framework for Ethics* (New York: Oxford University Press, 1999), chap. 16; Ryan Preston-Roedder, "Faith in Humanity," *Philosophy and Phenomenological Research* 87, no. 3 (2013): 664–87; Preston-Roedder, "Three Varieties of Faith," *Philosophical Tropics* 46, no. 1 (2018): 173–99; Martin, *How We Hope*, chap. 4.

60. Delany, *Condition*, 11.

61. Ibid., 12.

62. Ibid., 8.

63. That the position of the pessimist often involves an ironic understanding of history is powerfully laid out in Joshua Foa Dienstag, *Pessimism: Philosophy, Ethic, Spirit* (Princeton: Princeton University Press, 2006).

64. Delany, *Condition*, 12 (emphasis added).

65. Martin Delany, "Political Destiny of the Colored Race on the American Continent" (1854), in *Documentary Reader*, ed. Levine, 246.

66. See Robert Gooding-Williams, "Martin Delany's Two Principles, the Argument for Emigration, and Revolutionary Black Nationalism," in *African American Political Thought: A Collected History*, ed. Melvin L. Rogers and Jack Turner (Chicago: University of Chicago Press, 2021), 77–94.

67. Frederick Douglass, "What to the Slave Is the Fourth of July" (1852), in *The Frederick Douglass Papers: Series One, Speeches, Debates, and Interviews*, ed. John W. Blassingame, vol. 2 (New Haven: Yale University Press, 1982), 360.

68. Ibid., 361.

69. Ibid., 363.

70. Ibid., 366; see Henry Wadsworth Longfellow, "A Psalm of Life" (1839), in *Henry Wadsworth Longfellow: Selected Poems*, ed. Lawrence Buell (New York: Penguin, 1988), 333–34.

71. Douglass, "Fourth of July," 368 (original emphasis).

72. Ibid., 368–69.

73. Frederick Douglass to William Lloyd Garrison, January 1, 1846, in *Frederick Douglass: Selected Speeches and Writings*, ed. Foner, 17 (emphasis added).

74. Douglass, "Fourth of July," 387.

75. Longfellow, "A Psalm of Life," 334.

76. Douglass, "Fourth of July," 368.

77. Frederick Douglass, "The Dred Scott Decision" (1857), in *Frederick Douglass Papers*, ed. Blassingame, 3:167. The religious character of Douglass's faith is carefully traced in David Blight, *Frederick Douglass: Prophet of Freedom* (New York: Simon & Schuster, 2018).

78. Frederick Douglass, "Is Civil Government Right?" (1851), in *The Essential Douglass: Selected Writings and Speeches*, ed. Nicholas Buccola (Indianapolis: Hackett Press, 2016), 46. For a careful reading of Douglass's account of human nature and the potential for its distortion, see Vincent W. Lloyd, *Black Natural Law* (New York: Oxford University Press, 2016), 12–16; Nicholas Buccola, "The Human Heart Is a Seat of Constant War: Frederick Douglass on Human Nature," in *A Political Companion to Frederick Douglass*, ed. Neil Roberts (Lexington: University of Kentucky Press, 2018), 252–82. In this sense, Douglass is essentially displaying what Preston-Roedder refers to as "faith in humanity." See Preston-Roedder, "Faith in Humanity."

79. Here, my view is heavily influenced by my reading of both Robert Gooding-Williams, *In the Shadow of Du Bois: Afro-Modern Political Thought in America* (Cambridge, MA: Harvard University Press, 2009), chap. 5 and Frank, *Constituent Moments*, chap. 7.

80. For this reading of Douglass's position, see Charles Mills, "Whose Fourth of July? Frederick Douglass and 'Original Intent,'" in *Frederick Douglass: A Critical Reader*, ed. Bill Lawson and Frank Kirkland (Malden, MA: Blackwell, 1999), 100–142; cf. David E. Schrader, "Natural Law in the Constitutional Thought of Frederick Douglass," in *Frederick Douglass: A Critical Reader*, ed. Lawson and Kirkland, 85–99.

81. Douglass, "Fourth of July," 368–69 (emphasis added). Douglass's view of the imperfections of the past that live in the present continues into the 1860s. In an address he delivers in Missouri in 1867, he tells his audience, "But wise and good as that instrument [referring to the Constitution] is; at this point and at many others, it is simply a human contrivance. It is the work of man and men struggling with many of the prejudices and infirmities common to man, and it is not strange that we should find in their constitution some evidences of their infirmity and prejudices." Douglass, "Sources of Danger to the Republic" (1867), in *The Frederick Douglass Papers: Series*

One, Speeches, Debates, and Interviews, ed. John Blassingame and John R. McKivigan, vol. 4 (New Haven: Yale University Press, 1991), 153.

82. Frederick Douglass, "A Nation in the Midst of a Nation" (1853), in *Frederick Douglass Papers*, ed. Blassingame, 2:424–25.

83. Frank Kirkland, "Enslavement, Moral Suasion, and the Struggles for Recognition: Frederick Douglass's Answer to the Question—What Is Enlightenment?" in *Frederick Douglass: A Critical Reader*, ed. Lawson and Kirkland, 244.

84. Douglass, "Fourth of July," 2:368.

85. What I am here referring to as "reinterprets the ethical content of liberty" finds a more general interpretative framework in Nick Bromell. He offers us a way of reading Douglass that squares the process of reimagining the ethical life of the community with Douglass's own foundationalism: "According to Douglass, it is endemic to democracy that although we must believe that democracy is sanctioned by immutable eternal principles (e.g., that 'all men are created equal'), as citizens we must also dare to act in ways that challenge or reject conventional, majoritarian understandings of those principles (e.g., by claiming, historical evidence to the contrary notwithstanding, that the word *men* in the Declaration of Independence includes black men as well as white men, women as well as men, homosexuals as well as heterosexuals, and so on)." Bromell, "'A Blending of Opposite Qualities': Frederick Douglass and the Demands of Democratic Citizenship," in *Political Companion to Douglass*, ed. Roberts, 421; cf. Bromell, *The Powers of Dignity: The Black Political Philosophy of Frederick Douglass* (Durham: Duke University Press, 2021), 119.

86. Frederick Douglass, "An Address to the Colored People of the United States" (1848), in *Frederick Douglass: Selected Speeches and Writings*, ed. Foner, 119; Douglass, *My Bondage and My Freedom* (1855; New York: Penguin, 2003), 140. This way of thinking about freedom as extending beyond the law is part of Douglass's post-Reconstruction outlook. See Douglass, "In Law Free; In Fact, a Slave" (1888), in *The Frederick Douglass Papers: Series One, Speeches, Debates, and Interviews*, ed. John Blassingame and John R. McKivigan, vol. 5 (New Haven: Yale University Press, 1992), 369.

87. Sharon Krause, "Frederick Douglass: Nonsovereign Freedom and the Plurality of Political Resistance," in *African American Political Thought*, ed. Rogers and Turner, 117.

88. It is worth noting my departure from Gooding-Williams's otherwise insightful reading of Douglass. He sees the narrative of decline as a substantive commitment that Douglass uses to berate those in the present "for not having kept faith with" the commitments as specified by the Founders (Gooding-Williams, *Shadow of Du Bois*, 195–94). But this account does not go far enough in capturing the "radical reconstruction" that Douglass offers and that Gooding-Williams takes himself to be explicating. The reason is that it misses, I suggest, the interior reworking of the idea of freedom. I therefore do not agree that "Douglass invokes the authority of the founding fathers to persuade his white contemporaries to make the common conscience of the founding fathers their own (to exchange their proslavery conscience for the founding fathers' conscience) and thereby to acquire a conscience whose demands accord with the principles and ideals they profess" (316n111). Douglass invokes the founding to create a shared rhetorical context, but he does so both to renarrate the principles of the past and to encourage his readers in the present to see themselves as now being

out of step with their treatment of black people. Here too, then, Douglass is not asking the present to live up to the "common conscience" as specified in its founding documents, since that conscience already contained the elements of its deformation. Bernard S. Boxill, "Fear and Shame as Forms of Moral Suasion in the Thought of Frederick Douglass," *Transactions of the Charles S. Peirce Society* 31, no. 4 (1995): 714. Rather, he is recharacterizing what that "common conscience" means and demands by both deploying the founding generation and supplanting it.

89. For classic interpretations of the Social Gospel as well as the crisis of faith during this period, see D. H. Meyer, "American Intellectuals and the Victorian Crisis of Faith," in *Victorian America*, ed. Daniel Walter Hose (Philadelphia: University of Pennsylvania Press, 1976), 59–77; James Turner, *Without God, Without Creed: The Origins of Unbelief in America* (Baltimore: Johns Hopkins University Press, 1983); T. J. Jackson Lears, *No Place of Grace: Antimodernism and the Transformation of American Culture, 1880–1920* (Chicago: University of Chicago Press, 1984); Donald K. Gorrell, *The Age of Social Responsibility: The Social Gospel in the Progressive Era, 1900–1920* (Macon, GA: Mercer University Press, 1988).

90. T. Thomas Fortune, *Black and White: Land, Labor, and Politics in the South* (1884; New York: Washington Square Press, 2007), 153.

91. Henry McNeal Turner, "The American Negro and His Father Land" (1895), in *Africa and the American Negro*, ed. J.W.E. Bowen (Atlanta: Gammon Theological Seminary, 1896), 195 (original emphasis). For a careful reading of Turner's pessimism, see Andrew E. Johnson, *No Future in This Country: The Prophetic Pessimism of Bishop Henry McNeal Turner* (Jackson: University Press of Mississippi, 2020).

92. John Dewey, "Philosophy and American National Life" (1904), in *John Dewey: The Middle Works, 1899–1924*, ed. Jo Ann Boydston, vol. 3 (Carbondale: Southern Illinois University Press, 2008), 75.

93. Although I do not take this up here, it is worth pointing out that this produced another distinct version of Social Gospel intervention that Gary Dorrien has brilliantly chronicled. See Dorrien, *The New Abolition: W.E.B. Du Bois and the Black Social Gospel* (New Haven: Yale University Press, 2015).

94. W.E.B. Du Bois, *The Souls of Black Folk* (1903; New York: Oxford University Press, 2007), 7.

95. On this point, I borrow from and modify Paul Taylor, "Pragmatism and Race," in *Pragmatism and the Problems of Race*, ed. Bill E. Lawson and Donald F. Koch (Bloomington: Indiana University Press, 2004); Eddie S. Glaude Jr., *In a Shade of Blue: Pragmatism and the Politics of Black America* (Chicago: University of Chicago Press, 2007).

96. Anna Julia Cooper, *A Voice from the South*, in *The Portable Anna Julia Cooper*, ed. Shirley Moody-Turner (1892; New York: Penguin Books, 2022), 5–6. Here I draw on Vivian M. May, *Anna Julia Cooper, Visionary Black Feminist: A Critical Introduction* (New York: Routledge, 2012), chap. 3.

97. Cooper, *Voice*, 157. For an extended reflection on Cooper with which I agree, see Carol Wayne White, *Black Lives and Sacred Humanity: Toward an African American Religious Naturalism* (New York: Fordham University Press, 2016), chap. 3, especially 64–66.

98. Cooper, *Voice*, 157 (original emphasis).

99. These two points help make sense of Cooper's contextualism. See Vivian M. May, "Thinking from the Margins, Acting at the Intersections: Anna Julia Cooper's *A Voice from the South*," *Hypatia* 19, no. 2 (2004): 74–91.

100. Cooper, *Voice*, 160. Williams James's reflections years later on the relationship between moral beliefs and faith often mirror the structure of Cooper's response to skepticism; see James, *The Will to Believe and Other Essays in Popular Philosophy* (1897; New York: Dover Press, 1956), especially 22–23. For a powerful reading of James's thinking with which I agree, see Eric MacGilvray, *Reconstructing Public Reason* (Cambridge, MA: Harvard University Press, 2004), chap. 2.

101. Adams, *Finite and Infinite Goods*, 386.

102. James, *Will to Believe*, 90; cf. 22–25; cf. John Dewey, *A Common Faith*, in *The Later Works: 1925–1953*, vol. 9, ed. Jo Ann Boydston (1932; Carbondale: Southern Illinois University Press, 1986), 16–17. For an interesting comparison of Cooper and James, see V. Denise James, "Reading Anna J. Cooper with William James: Black Feminist Visionary Pragmatism, Philosophy's Culture of Justification, and Belief," *The Pluralist* 8, no. 3 (2013): 32–45.

103. Dewey, *Common Faith*, 16 (emphasis added); cf. Cooper, *Voice*, 159–60.

104. Kalyvas, "Popular Sovereignty," 225.

105. Ibid., 227.

106. Ibid., 226. He says again, "Constituent politics might be seen as the explicit, lucid self-institution of society, whereby the citizens are jointly called to be the authors of their constitutional identity and to decide the central rules and higher procedures that will regulate their political and society life" (237).

107. Ibid., 227.

108. White and Ypi, "The Politics of Peoplehood," 447.

109. For this historical arc, see Ackerman's three-volume *We the People*.

110. A similar kind of problem besets Jack Balkin's reflections on political faith. I should say there is much in his account with which I agree. Similar to my argument, he emphasizes the future-oriented quality of legitimacy. He also sees an important role for storytelling and rhetoric in calling society to embrace new configurations of itself; Balkin, *Constitutional Redemption: Political Faith in an Unjust World* (Cambridge, MA: Harvard University Press, 2011), chap. 1. And as with my account, he sees faith as central to democratic development precisely because of the dependence on those over whom we have no control (chap. 3). But he seems to think about this exclusively through the prism of constitutionalism, which distorts the diverse range of political appeals that rely on constituent power and do so to reimagine who and what the polity takes itself to be. On the one hand, he means to identify what he calls constituent power with constitutional development, but on the other hand, he argues that the "ultimate goal of our constitutional order is to produce not merely democratic procedures but a *democratic culture*" (23 [original emphasis]). The invocation of democratic culture suggests that the commitment to the equal standing of persons must inform the web of beliefs that define the ethos of the community. This much he tells us: "Political egalitarianism must be nourished by cultural egalitarianism" (24). The problem with this account is that constitutional development cannot secure the kind of deep democratic culture he has in mind. For this reason, many of the thinkers discussed in this book direct their appeals to the people as such. In fairness, Balkin invokes faith in the

people, but the general tenor is to speak about political faith as faith in constitutional redemption. The problem, then, is that Balkin fails to disentangle faith in the people from faith in constitutional redemption. And in failing to do so, he narrows the expression of constituent power and excludes precisely those political actors that were interested in remaking the polity in precisely the way he means to defend.

111. Jürgen Habermas, "Constitutional Democracy: A Paradoxical Union of Contradictory Principles?" *Political Theory* 29, no. 6 (2001): 774.

112. Ibid.

113. Ibid.

114. Ibid., 775 (emphasis added).

115. My account has affinities with the one provided by Honig, although it moves in a different direction. See Honig, *Emergency Politics*, 29–35.

116. Admittedly, this claim stands in an uncomfortable relationship to the natural rights tradition to which someone like Walker or Douglass belonged. But this is only problematic if one removes the importance of *social practices* and the necessity of *action* in the logic of affirming rights. To be sure, for thinkers like Walker and Douglass, we have natural rights, but their mere existence does not entail their proper affirmation or execution. Regarding social practices, to have a right is to have a legitimate claim to enjoy goods of the community and to be taken by that community as a holder of a right. The first portion of this is about a social arrangement and the status human beings occupy that give them a legitimate claim to enjoy the goods of the community. The second portion of this claim, however, essentially says that the first is only as strong (practically) as those that affirm the status one believes they should enjoy. For Douglass, then, the appropriate social practices are necessary to affirming rights, and this is tied to the importance of action (by one's fellows) to having those rights expressively embodied. For a longer treatment that defends this way of understanding rights discourse, see Jeffrey Stout, *Democracy and Tradition* (Princeton: Princeton University Press, 2004), 204–9; Derrick Darby, *Rights, Race, and Recognition* (New York: Cambridge University Press, 2009), chap. 3.

117. In his "Popular Sovereignty as Procedures" (1988), an essay that also appeared as part of the appendix to his 1996 translated book *Between Facts and Norms*, Habermas appears to be sensitive to the position with which I am concerned; Habermas, "Popular Sovereignty as Procedures," in *Between Facts and Norms: Contributions to a Discourse Theory of Law and Democracy*, trans. William Rehg (Cambridge: Polity Press, 1996), 463–91. There he writes of the French and American Revolutions: "The revolutionary consciousness was expressed in the conviction that a new beginning could be made. This reflected a change in historical consciousness. Drawn together into a single process, world history became the abstract system of reference for a future-oriented action *considered capable of uncoupling the present from the past*. In the background lay the experience of a break with tradition: the threshold to dealing reflexively with cultural transmissions and social institutions was crossed" (467 [emphasis added]). Several pages later, he continues to explain the normative thrust of the revolution: "the revolutionary project overshoots the revolution itself: it eludes the revolution's own concepts. . . . It is only as a historical project that constitutional democracy points beyond its legal character to a normative meaning—a force at once explosive and formative" (471). But if there is a break with the past such that

its concepts do not overdetermine the present, it is not clear to me what Habermas means to say in the 2001 essay. He cannot retreat to the procedural rules of rights and the vision of recognition that inform that account, since it is precisely this description that is the problem. He must, instead, appeal to an account of the people that is itself discontinuous with the past, and never fully exhausted by the present in which contestation over the polity emerges. For it is here that we find the connection between the political and ethical standing of persons. At any rate, either he has changed his mind or his language betrays him. The first is a mistaken move for reasons I have already discussed, and the second is terribly unfortunate.

118. James Baldwin, "White Man's Guilt" (1965), in *Baldwin: Collected Essays*, ed. Toni Morrison (New York: Library of America, 1998), 722–23.

119. Frederick Douglass, "We Must Not Abandon the Observance of Decoration Day" (1882), in *Frederick Douglass Papers*, ed. Blassingame and McKivigan, 5:46; W.E.B. Du Bois, *The Souls of Black Folk* (1903; New York: Oxford University Press, 2007), 5.

120. Stokely Carmichael, "Berkeley Speech" (1966), in *Stokely Speaks: From Black Power to Pan-Africanism* (Chicago: Chicago Review Press, 2007), 55.

121. There is not much I can add to what has already been stated in the literature about the relationship between faith and courage. On this, the reader should see Paul Tillich, *Dynamics of Faith* (New York: Harper and Row, 1957), 16–22; Adams, *Finite and Infinite Goods*; Preston-Roedder, "Three Varieties of Faith"; Martin, *How We Hope*, chap. 4. It is nonetheless appropriate to say something about Tillich in this regard. Because his account of faith stands within a theological horizon, the certainty of faith is tied to the "experience of the holy" and is attended by doubt largely because we are finite creatures receiving the workings of faith; Tillich, *Dynamics of Faith*, 16. Doubt attends the faith-holder and courage becomes necessary, but the horizon in which these terms—doubt and courage—take hold is of a different kind than what I am suggesting in my reading of Douglass. Therefore, it is necessary to say that my description of faith, and the attendant features of doubt and courage, has the form akin to Tillich's account, even if it does not depend on the theological framework he describes. Hence Adrienne Martin explains: "there is such a thing as secular faith, an attitude that has the sustaining power and immunity to disappointment of religious faith" (*How We Hope*, 17). Faith thus functions as an orienting truth that stabilizes its holders and moves them through time, but it remains uncertain because its realization depends on those over whom one does not exercise final control, but on whom one must depend for affirmation. This allows us to say, now with Tillich and consistent with Douglass, "Whoever makes his nation his ultimate concern needs courage in order to maintain this concern" (*Dynamics of Faith*, 17).

122. Toni Morrison, "Moral Inhabitants" (1976), in *The Source of Self-Regard: Selected Essays, Speeches, and Meditations* (New York: Alfred Knopf, 2019), 47.

Chapter 5. Lynching and the Horrific: From Ida B. Wells to Billie Holiday

1. First published under the title "Bitter Fruit" in *New York Teacher* (January 1937); Peter Daniels, "'Strange Fruit': The Story of a Song," https://www.wsws.org/en/articles/2002/02/frut-f08.html. For a longer and helpful discussion of Meeropol,

see Nancy Kovaleff Baker, "Meeropol (a.k.a. Lewis Allen): Political Commentator and Social Conscience," *American Music* 20, no. 1 (2002): 25–79.

2. Billie Holiday, Frank Newton, and Café Society Band, *Strange Fruit*, Commodore Records, New York, 1939. For Holiday's 1959 performance, see https://www.youtube.com/watch?v=-DGY9HvChXk. The song's evolution is captured nicely in David Margolick, *Strange Fruit: The Biography of a Song* (New York: HarperCollins, 2001). I shall draw extensively from this work in the third section of the chapter, although for different ends. Holiday was not the first to sing the song, although it achieved its greatest popularity with her.

3. "bitter," *Oxford English Dictionary*, 2nd ed., 2012, http://www.oed.com.

4. See data source in Daniel T. Williams, "The Lynching Records at Tuskegee Institute," in *Eight Negro Bibliographies*, compiled by Daniel T. Williams (New York: Kraus-Reprint, 1969), 1–15. See also National Association for the Advancement of Colored People, *Thirty Years of Lynching in the United States, 1889-1918* (New York: National Association for the Advancement of Colored People, 1919); Fitzhugh W. Brundage, *Lynching in the New South: Georgia and Virginia, 1880–1930* (Urbana: University of Illinois Press, 1993); James H. Madison, *A Lynching in the Heartland: Race and Memory in America* (New York: Palgrave, 2001).

5. For powerful accounts that put on display the horror of lynching and vulnerability of black life in post-Reconstruction America, see Ida B. Wells, *Southern Horrors: Lynch Law in All Its Phases* (1892), in *The Light of Truth: Writings of an Anti-Lynching Crusader*, ed. Mia Bay (New York: Penguin Press, 2014), 57–82; Walter White, *Rope and Faggot: A Biography of Judge Lynch* (1929; New York: Knopf, 2001); W.E.B. Du Bois, *Black Reconstruction in America: An Essay toward a History of the Part which Black Folk Played in the Attempt to Reconstruct Democracy in America, 1860–1880* (1935; New York: Oxford University Press, 2007).

6. On the significance of fear and disgust to horror, see Noel Carroll, *The Philosophy of Horror or Paradoxes of the Heart* (New York: Routledge, 1990), 24–26.

7. Ida B. Wells, "Bishop Tanner's 'Ray of Light'" (1892), in *The Light of Truth*, ed. Bay, 53.

8. On the antilynching activism of Wells and the NAACP, see Ida B. Wells, *Crusade for Justice: The Autobiography of Ida B. Wells*, ed. Alfreda M. Duster (Chicago: University of Chicago Press, 1970); Paula J. Giddings, *Ida: A Sword among Lions* (New York: HarperCollins, 2008), especially chap. 8; Mia Bay, *To Tell the Truth Freely: The Life of Ida B. Wells* (New York: Hill and Wang, 2009); Robert Zangrando, *The NAACP Crusade against Lynching, 1909-1950* (Philadelphia: Temple University Press, 1980); Amy Helene Kirschke, *Art in Crisis: W.E.B. Du Bois and the Struggle for African American Identity and Memory* (Bloomington: Indiana University Press, 2007), chap. 3; Megan Ming Francis, *Civil Rights and the Making of the Modern American State* (New York: Cambridge University Press, 2014); Jenny Woodley, *Art for Equality: The NAACP's Cultural Campaign for Civil Rights* (Lexington: University Press of Kentucky, 2014).

9. Ida B. Wells, "The Requirements of Southern Journalism" (1893), in *The Light of Truth*, ed. Bay, 89. Although I put horror to a different use, my argument here has affinities with Alex Zamalin, *Struggle on Their Minds: The Political Thought of African American Resistance* (New York: Columbia University Press, 2017), 77–81.

10. Amy Louise Wood, *Lynching and Spectacle: Witnessing Racial Violence in America, 1890–1940* (Chapel Hill: University of North Carolina Press, 2009), 5; cf. Orlando Patterson, *Rituals of Blood: Consequences of Slavery in Two American Centuries* (Washington, DC: CIVITAS/Counterpoint, 1998), chap. 2; Shawn Michelle Smith, "The Evidence of Lynching Photographs," in *Lynching Photographs* (with Dora Apel) (Berkeley: University of California Press, 2007), 10–41; Dora Apel, "Lynching Photographs and the Politics of Public Shaming," in *Lynching Photographs* (with Shawn Michelle Smith), 42–78; Leigh Raiford, *Imprisoned in a Luminous Glare: Photography and the African American Freedom Struggle* (Chapel Hill: University of North Carolina Press, 2011)

11. On the status of race in Whitman, see Geoffrey Sill, "Whitman on 'The Black Question': A New Manuscript," *Walt Whitman Quarterly Review* 8, no. 2 (1990): 69–75; Martin Klammer, *Whitman, Slavery, and the Emergence of "Leaves of Grass"* (University Park: Pennsylvania State University Press, 1995); Ed Folsom, "Lucifer and Ethiopia: Whitman, Race, and Poetics before the Civil War and After," in *A Historical Guide to Walt Whitman*, ed. David S. Reynolds (New York: Oxford University Press, 2000), 45–95; Ed Folsom, "The Lost Black Presence in Whitman's Manuscripts," in *Whitman Noir: Black America and the Good Gray Poet*, ed. Ivy G. Wilson (Iowa City: University of Iowa Press, 2014), 3–31; George B. Hutchinson, "Race and the Family Romance: Whitman's Civil War," *Walt Whitman Quarterly Review* 20, no. 3 (2003): 134–50; Jack Turner, "Whitman's Undemocratic Vistas: Moral Anxiety, National Glory, White Supremacy," *American Political Science Review* (2022): 1–14 (online first), https://doi.org/10.1017/S0003055422000727.

12. The version of *Democratic Vistas* used here is Whitman's 1876 version. This is the second printing of his 1871 edition that contains Whitman's additions. See Walt Whitman, *Democratic Vistas*, ed. Ed Folsom (1876; Iowa City: University of Iowa Press, 2010). All other references to Whitman's writings will come from *Poetry and Prose*, ed. Justin Kaplan (New York: Library of America, 1996).

13. My account has the closest relationship to Nancy Rosenblum, "Strange Attractors: How Individualists Connect to Form Democratic Unity" (1990), in *A Political Companion to Walt Whitman*, ed. John E. Seery (Lexington: University Press of Kentucky, 2011), specifically at 55–57; cf. Jason Frank, *Constituent Moments: Enacting the People in Postrevolutionary America* (Durham: Duke University Press, 2010), chap. 6.

14. Cited in Margolick, *Strange Fruit*, 30.

15. Jefferson to Robert Skipwith, August 3, 1771, in *Thomas Jefferson: Writings*, ed. Merrill D. Peterson (New York: Library of America, 1984), 741.

16. See chapter 2.

17. Frederick Douglass, "Pictures and Progress" (1861), in *The Frederick Douglass Papers: Series One, Speeches, Debates, and Interviews*, ed. John W. Blassingame, vol. 3 (New Haven: Yale University Press, 1985), 456. There is some discrepancy about the dating of this speech, with Blassingame listing it as 1861 and others identifying it as being written between 1864 and 1865. For this latter view, see *Picturing Frederick Douglass: An Illustrated Biography of the Nineteenth Century's Most Photographed American*, ed. John Stauffer, Zoe Trodd, and Celeste-Marie Berner (New York: Norton, 2015), 161.

18. Ashton Gonzalez, *Visualizing Equality: African American Rights and Visual Culture in the Nineteenth Century* (Chapel Hill: University of North Carolina Press, 2020).

19. Whitman, *Democratic Vistas*, 59 (emphasis added).

20. Whitman, *Leaves of Grass*, in *Poetry and Prose*, 51.

21. Cf. Peter Coviello, "Intimate Nationality: Anonymity and Attachment in Whitman," *American Literature* 73, no. 1 (2001): 85–119; Nathanael O'Reilly, "Imagined America: Walt Whitman's Nationalism in the First Edition of Leaves of Grass," *Irish Journal of American Studies* 1 (2009): 1–9; Turner, "Whitman's Undemocratic Vistas."

22. Whitman, *Democratic Vistas*, 76.

23. Whitman, *Leaves of Grass*, in *Poetry and Prose*, 667; cf. Whitman, *Democratic Vistas*, 76.

24. John Dewey, *The Public and Its Problems*, ed. Melvin L. Rogers (1927; Athens, OH: Swallow Press, 2016), 204–5. For a richer account that aligns Whitman with Deweyan pragmatism, see Stephen John Mack, *The Pragmatic Whitman: Reimagining American Democracy* (Iowa City: University of Iowa Press, 2002).

25. Whitman, *Democratic Vistas*, 31. On the importance of Whitman to the Harlem Renaissance, see George B. Hutchinson, "Whitman and the Black Poet: Kelly Miller's Speech to the Walt Whitman Fellowships," *American Literature* (1989): 46–59; George B. Hutchinson, "The Whitman Legacy and the Harlem Renaissance," in *Walt Whitman: The Centennial Essays*, ed. Ed Folsom (Iowa City: University of Iowa Press, 1994), 201–16.

26. Hutchinson, "The Whitman Legacy and the Harlem Renaissance," 201–16.

27. Whitman, *Democratic Vistas*, 37.

28. William Stanley Braithwaite, ed., *Anthology of Magazine Verse for 1919 and Year Book of American Poetry* (Boston: Small, Maynard and Company, 1919), 297.

29. John Dewey, *Individualism: Old and New* (1930), in *John Dewey: The Later Works, 1925–1953*, vol. 5, ed. Jo Ann Boydston (Carbondale: Southern Illinois University Press, 1988), 76; cf. "For the mind, which alone builds the permanent edifice, haughtily builds it to itself. By it, with what follows it, are conveyed to mortal sense the culminations of the materialistic, the known, and a prophecy of the unknown." Whitman, *Democratic Vistas*, 49.

30. Whitman, *Democratic Vistas*, 42–43; cf. Whitman, *Leaves of Grass*, in *Prose and Poetry*, 475.

31. See Whitman, *Democratic Vistas*, 15, 18, 44, 50.

32. Ibid., 24.

33. George Kateb, *The Inner Ocean: Individualism and Democratic Culture* (Ithaca: Cornell University Press, 1992), 245.

34. Whitman, *Democratic Vistas*, 8–9.

35. Ibid., 36.

36. We should distinguish between this notion of aesthetics and its conventional notion as a study of the judgment of taste found in Immanuel Kant. See Robert Gooding-Williams, "Aesthetics and Receptivity: Kant, Nietzsche, Cavell, and Astaire," in *Look, A Negro!: Philosophical Essays on Race, Culture and Politics* (New York: Routledge, 2006), 43–67.

37. Thomas Carlyle, *Shooting Niagara: And After?* (London: Chapman and Hall, 1867).

38. Whitman, *Democratic Vistas*, 40; cf. Jeffrey Stout, *Democracy and Tradition* (Princeton: Princeton University Press, 2004), chap. 1.

39. Whitman, *Leaves of Grass*, in *Poetry and Prose*, 303.

40. Whitman, *Democratic Vistas*, 67. I focus on the capacity to listen, but on the theme of vision see Alan Trachtenberg, "Whitman's Visionary Politics," in *Walt Whitman of Mickle Street: A Centennial Collection*, ed. Geoffrey Sill (Knoxville: University of Tennessee Press, 1994), 94–108.

41. Whitman, *Democratic Vistas*, 56–57.

42. Ralph Waldo Emerson, "The Poet" (1844), in *Emerson: Essays and Lectures*, ed. Joel Porte (New York: Library of America, 1983), 458.

43. Douglass, "Lectures on Pictures" (1861), in *Picturing Frederick Douglass*, 132.

44. Whitman, *Democratic Vistas*, 67.

45. Ibid.

46. Whitman, *Leaves of Grass*, in *Poetry and Prose*, 28.

47. Ibid., 53. Of course, this is the theme that Alain Locke and Ralph Ellison in different ways exploit for inclusive ends.

48. Whitman, *Democratic Vistas*, 69.

49. Ida B. Wells, *Red Record: Tabulated Statistics and Alleged Causes of Lynchings in the United States, 1892-1893-1894* (1895), in *The Light of Truth*, ed. Bay, 228.

50. See Kirschke, *Art in Crisis*, chap. 3.

51. Trudier Harris, *Exorcising Blackness: Historical and Literary Lynching and Burning Rituals* (Bloomington: Indiana University Press, 1984); *Strange Fruit: Plays on Lynching by American Women*, ed. Kathy A. Perkins and Judith L. Stephens (Bloomington: Indiana University Press, 1998).

52. Whitman, *Democratic Vistas*, 70.

53. Ibid., 7–8 (emphasis added).

54. Ibid., 68. For a more sustained discussion of death in Whitman, see Jack Turner, "Whitman, Death, and Democracy," in *Political Companion to Whitman*, ed. Seery, 272–95.

55. On Wells's refusal of nostalgia, see Jill Locke, "Against Nostalgia: The Political Theory of Ida B. Wells," in *American Political Thought: An Alternative View*, ed. Jonathan Keller and Alex Zamalin (New York: Routledge, 2017).

56. For a discussion of empirical realism in Whitman, see David E. Shi, *Facing Facts: Realism in American Thought and Culture, 1850–1920* (New York: Oxford University Press, 1995), 29–33.

57. Cited in Shi, *Facing Facts*, 31.

58. Whitman, *Leaves of Grass*, in *Poetry and Prose*, 28.

59. Whitman, *Democratic Vistas*, 11.

60. Eddie Glaude, "The Magician's Serpent: Race and the Tragedy of American Democracy," *James Baldwin Review* 5, no. 1 (2019): 15. Jack Turner makes a stronger case that Whitman is not merely silent on this: "Thinking of the book's racial politics as one of absence misses half the picture. There is, in fact, a positive racial politics present in *Vistas*: a politics of American imperial developmentalism that travels west over the continental mainland and overseas into the Pacific. This American imperial developmentalism is whit in all but name" ("Whitman's Undemocratic Vistas," 5).

61. This very point led Langston Hughes to remark: "If, in his workaday editorials . . . Whitman sometimes contradicted his own highest ideals—just as Thomas Jefferson did by owning slaves yet writing about liberty—it is the best of him that we choose to keep and cherish, not his worst" (Hughes, "Like Whitman, Great Artists Are Not Always Good People," *Chicago Defender*, August 1, 1953, 11).

62. Whitman, *Democratic Vistas*, 36.

63. Wells, *Southern Horrors*, 58.

64. Cited in Francis, *Civil Rights*, 41.

65. W.E.B. Du Bois, *Dusk of Dawn: An Essay toward an Autobiography of a Race Concept* (1940; New York: Oxford University Press, 2007), 34.

66. There were conflicting reports on the size of the crowd, with the *Herald and Advertiser* estimating a crowd of five hundred while others suggesting two thousand. For more on the lynching of Sam Hose, see Edwin T. Arnold, *What Virtue There Is in Fire: Cultural Memory and the Lynching of Sam Hose* (Athens: University of Georgia Press, 2009); Donald G. Mathews, *At the Altar of Lynching: Burning Sam Hose in the American South* (New York: Cambridge University Press, 2017). For its effect on Du Bois, see David Levering Lewis, *W.E.B. Du Bois: Biography of a Race, 1868–1919* (New York: Henry Holt and Company, 1993), 226–29.

67. Du Bois, *Dusk of Dawn*, 34. Du Bois's retelling of this story is not consistent across his writings. There is some doubt that Hose's knuckles made it to Atlanta as quickly as Du Bois's account suggests. See Grace Elizabeth Hale, *Making Whiteness: The Culture of Segregation in the South, 1890–1940* (New York: Vintage Books, 1999), 214. In fact, Edwin Arnold notes in his research and interviews: "'Butcher shops all around Atlanta and Newnan display pig knuckles in their windows under a sign labeling them as the knuckles of Sam Hose'" (*What Virtue*, 172). Although the details of his retelling are inconsistent, what is consistent is the sense that Hose's lynching radically altered Du Bois's intellectual outlook and method of addressing racism.

68. C. Vann Woodward, *The Strange Career of Jim Crow* (1955; New York: Oxford University Press, 2002), 70.

69. Ibid., 69–74; Valerie Weaver, "The Failure of Civil Rights: 1875–1883 and Its Repercussions," *Journal of Negro History* 54, no. 4 (1969): 368–82; Richard Kluger, *Simple Justice: The History of Brown v. Board of Education and Black America's Struggle for Equality* (New York: Vintage, 1977), 51–69; Joel Williamson, *The Crucible of Race: Black-White Relations in the American South since Emancipation* (New York: Oxford University Press, 1984), 90–101; Michael Perman, *Struggle for Mastery: Disfranchisement in the South, 1888–1908* (Chapel Hill: University of North Carolina Press, 2001).

70. Here I think Rinaldo Walcott is right: "Yet the problem with utilizing a category such as 'extrajudicial' is that it assumes that Black life is recognizable as a life under and in the context of modernity and its orders of knowledge, juridical rules, and conditions that recognize some lives as a life." Walcott, *The Long Emancipation: Moving toward Black Freedom* (Durham: Duke University Press, 2021), 12.

71. Ida B. Wells, "Lynch Law," in *The Reason Why the Colored American Is Not in the World's Columbian Exposition*, ed. Robert W. Rydell (Urbana: University of Illinois Press, 1893/1999), 31; cf. Wells, *Red Record*, 255–68.

72. Wells, *Southern Horrors*, 77; Wells, *Lynch Law in Georgia* (1899), in *The Light of Truth*, 315.

73. Wells, "Lynch Law in America" (1900), in *The Light of Truth*, 394.

74. Wells, *Lynch Law in Georgia*, 315, but especially 322–25; Wells, "The Requirements of Southern Journalism," 89. For exceptional pieces on the importance of narrative form and truth-telling in Wells's thinking, see Jacqueline Goldsby, *A Spectacular Secret* (Chicago: University of Chicago Press, 2006), chap. 2; Lawrie Balfour, "Ida B. Wells and 'Color Line Justice': Rethinking Reparations in Feminist Terms," *Perspectives on Politics* 13, no. 3 (2015): 680–96; Naomi Murakawa, "Ida B. Wells on Racial Criminalization," in *African American Political Thought: A Collected History*, ed. Melvin L. Rogers and Jack Turner (Chicago: University of Chicago Press, 2021), 212–34.

75. Murakawa, "Ida B. Wells on Racial Criminalization," 214. As I shall do below, she borrowed the formulation from Khalil Muhammad, *The Condemnation of Blackness: Race, Crime, and the Making of Modern Urban America* (Cambridge, MA: Harvard University Press, 2010).

76. Wells, *Lynch Law in Georgia*, 315.

77. Cited in Wells, *Red Record*, 245; cf. Wells, *Lynch Law in Georgia*, 315.

78. Wells, *Southern Horrors*, 58, 70, 79; cf. Wells, *Red Record*, 221, 282, 285.

79. Wells, *Red Record*, 308. Compare this to the remark in the *London Inquirer* that Wells cites in *Crusade for Justice* referring to lynching: "These facts must be their own argument as the majority of our readers are anxious to know what those facts are" (190).

80. Cited in Shi, *Facing Facts*, 30

81. Wells, *Crusade for Justice*, 90.

82. Amelia Gere Mason, "Is Sentiment Declining," *Century* 61 (1901): 629. For an extended discussion of empiricism in the nineteenth and early twentieth centuries, see Shi, *Facing Facts*, chap. 4.

83. Tommy Curry, "The Fortune of Wells: Ida B. Wells-Barnett's Use of T. Thomas Fortune's Philosophy of Social Agitation as a Prolegomenon to Militant Civil Rights Activism," in *Transactions of the Charles S. Peirce Society* 48, no. 4 (2012): 456–82.

84. David T. Z. Mindich, *Just the Facts: How "Objectivity" Came to Define American Journalism* (New York: New York University Press, 1998), especially chap. 5.

85. Wood, *Lynching and Spectacle*, 75; cf. Smith, "Evidence of Lynching Photographs," 10–41; Mark Reinhardt, "Painful Photographs: From the Ethics of Spectatorship to Visual Politics," in *Ethics and Images of Pain*, ed. Asbjørn Grønstad and Henrik Gustafsson (New York: Routledge, 2012), 33–55; Goldsby, *A Spectacular Secret*, especially introduction, chap. 1.

86. Wells, "Lynch Law," in *The Reason Why*, 30. For an extended and useful reflection on Douglass and Wells's collaboration and friendship, see Bay, *To Tell the Truth*, 127–32.

87. Wells, *Red Record*, 228.

88. On epistemic inequality and injustice and the related debate, see Miranda Fricker, *Epistemic Injustice: Power and the Ethics of Knowing* (New York: Oxford University Press, 2010); Kristie Dotson, "A Cautionary Tale: On Limiting Epistemic Oppression," *Frontiers: A Journal of Women's Studies* 33, no. 1 (2012): 24–47; Jose Medina, *The Epistemology of Resistance: Gender and Racial Oppression* (New York: Oxford University Press, 2013).

89. Juliet Hooker, "Between Fact and Affect: Ida B. Wells and Harriet Jacobs on Black Loss" (unpublished manuscript). Importantly, by the time Wells was writing, journalism had developed an account of objectivity and impartiality that was taken to structure its self-understanding. This was part of the public understanding of journalism (Mindich, *Just the Facts*). Wells's reliance on journalism as a way to deal with lynching worked to trouble racial and gender discrimination, but it also permitted her to manage the affective and factual bases of her writing (see Hooker's essay once more).

90. Wells, "The Requirements of Southern Journalism," 89.

91. Cited in Bay, *To Tell the Truth*, 134.

92. Frederick Douglass, "Why Is the Negro Lynched?" (1894), in *Frederick Douglass: Selected Speeches and Writings*, ed. Philip Foner (Chicago: Lawrence Hill Books, 1999), 751, 752.

93. Mary Church Terrell, "Lynching from a Negro's Point of View," *North American Review* 178, no. 571 (1904): 858.

94. See Wells, *Southern Horrors*, 61, 70, 80; Ida B. Wells, "Lynch Law and the Color Line" (1893), in *The Light of Truth*, 119; Wells, *Red Record*, 240, 279.

95. See Wells, "Lynch Law," in *The Reason Why*; Wells, *Red Record*, 222, 223, 228, 249, 282, 283.

96. On dehumanization generally, see David Livingston Smith, *On Inhumanity: Dehumanization and How to Resist It* (New York: Oxford University Press, 2020), chap. 2, especially 19.

97. Muhammad, *Condemnation of Blackness*, 3.

98. White, *Rope and Faggot*, vii.

99. Wells, *Red Record*, 308.

100. Courtney R. Baker, *Humane Insight: Looking at Images of African American Suffering and Death* (Chicago: University of Illinois Press, 2015), 9.

101. Wells, *Red Record*, 309.

102. Ibid., 228.

103. Ibid., 239.

104. My way of laying things out may give the impression that the relationship between Wells and the NAACP was unproblematic. This is far from the truth. See Giddings, *Ida*, 491–501; Giddings, "Missing in Action: Ida B. Wells, the NAACP, and the Historical Record," *Meridians: Feminism, Race, Transnationalism* 1, no. 2 (2001): 1–17.

105. Francis, *Civil Rights*, 41; Zangrando, *NAACP Crusade*.

106. Woodley, *Art for Equality*.

107. Cited in Zangrando, *NAACP Crusade*, viii.

108. Wood, *Lynching and Spectacle*, 184; cf. Smith, "The Evidence of Lynching Photographs," 37–41; Apel, "Lynching Photographs," 42–78.

109. Cited in Wood, *Lynching and Spectacle*, 196.

110. It should be noted that the two men had already been savagely beaten and killed when they were subsequently staged for the lynching. See Madison, *Lynching in the Heartland*, 10–11.

111. See Reinhardt, "Painful Photographs," 33–55.

112. Margolick, *Strange Fruit*, 21.

113. Cited in ibid., 10.

114. Billie Holiday (with William Dufty), *Lady Sings the Blues* (New York: Penguin, 1956/1984), 84.

115. Cited in Margolick, *Strange Fruit*, 31.

116. Cited in ibid., 1.

117. Leon Forrest, "A Solo Long-Song for Lady Day," *Callaloo* 16, no. 2 (Spring 1993): 336; cf. to a similar invocation of "haunting" in Angela Davis, *Blues Legacies and Black Feminism: Gertrude "Ma" Rainey, Bessie Smith, and Billie Holiday* (New York: Vintage, 1998), 195; Farah Jasmine Griffin, *If You Can't Be Free, Be a Mystery: In Search of Billie Holiday* (New York: One World Book, 2001), 20.

118. Cited in Margolick, *Strange Fruit*, 30.

119. Ibid., 40.

120. See the performance at https://www.youtube.com/watch?v=-DGY9HvChXk.

121. Emily Lordi provides an insightful reading of Holiday's various performances. See Lordi, *Black Resonance: Iconic Women Singers and African American Literature* (New Brunswick, NJ: Rutgers University Press, 2013), 155–66.

122. Wilfred Mellers, "Round and About in Górecki's Symphony No. 3," *Tempo* 168, no. 3 (1989): 23.

123. Cited in Margolick, *Strange Fruit*, 30.

124. Cited in Lordi, *Black Resonance*, 139–40.

125. Ralph Ellison, *Going to the Territory* (1986), in *The Collected Essays of Ralph Ellison*, ed. John F. Callahan (New York: Modern Library, 2003), 761.

126. Whitman, *Leaves of Grass*, in *Poetry and Prose*, 11.

Chapter 6. Propaganda and Rhetoric: On W.E.B. Du Bois's "Criteria of Negro Art"

1. John O'Neil, "The Rhetoric of Deliberation: Some Problems in Kantian Theories of Deliberative Democracy," *Res Publica* 8, no. 3 (2002): 249–68; Danielle Allen, *Talking to Strangers: Anxieties of Citizenship since Brown v. Board of Education* (Chicago: University of Chicago Press, 2004); Bryan Garsten, *Saving Persuasion: A Defense of Rhetoric and Judgment* (Cambridge, MA: Harvard University Press, 2006); Bernard Yack, "Rhetoric and Public Reasoning: An Aristotelian Understanding of Political Deliberation," *Political Theory* 34, no. 4 (2006): 417–38.

2. Garsten, *Saving Persuasion*, 9.

3. W.E.B. Du Bois, *The Souls of Black Folk* (1903; New York: Oxford University Press, 2007), 1.

4. Arnold Rampersad, *The Art and Imagination of W.E.B. Du Bois* (New York: Schocken Books, 1976), 36.

5. W.E.B. Du Bois, *Dusk of Dawn: An Essay toward an Autobiography of a Race Concept* (1940; New York: Oxford University Press, 2007), 19–29; cf. Rampersad, *Art and Imagination*, 35–38. For an outline of some of Du Bois's course work, see Du Bois, *Against Racism: Unpublished Essays, Papers, Addresses, 1887–1961*, ed. Herbert Aptheker (Amherst: University of Massachusetts Press, 1985), 35–38.

6. Adams Sherman Hill, *The Principles of Rhetoric and Their Application* (New York: Harper and Brothers, 1878), iii; cf. to Hill's longer chapter titled "Persuasion," chap. 5.

7. Aristotle, *On Rhetoric: A Theory of Civic Discourse*, trans. George A. Kennedy, 2nd ed. (New York: Oxford University Press, 2007), 1.2, 1356a; Cicero, *On the Ideal Orator*, trans. James M. May and Jakob Wisse (New York: Oxford University Press, 2001), 2.35, 133. My understanding of Aristotle's and Cicero's rhetoric is owed to Eugene Garver, *Aristotle's Rhetoric: An Art of Character* (Chicago: University of Chicago Press, 1994); Garsten, *Saving Persuasion*, chaps. 4 and 5; Allen, *Talking to Strangers*, chap. 10; Wendy Olmsted, *Rhetoric: An Historical Introduction* (Malden, MA: Blackwell, 2006), chap. 1.

8. Rampersad, *Art and Imagination*, chap. 2. To my knowledge, Rampersad's text is the only one that explicitly takes up the importance of rhetoric to Du Bois.

9. The texts I have in mind include Manning Marable, *W.E.B. Du Bois: Black Radical Democrat* (Boston: Twayne, 1986); Shamoon Zamir, *Dark Voices: W.E.B. Du Bois and American Thought, 1888–1903* (Chicago: University of Chicago Press, 1995); Ross Posnock, *Color and Culture: Black Writers and the Making of the Modern Intellectual* (Cambridge, MA: Harvard University Press, 1996); Adolph L. Reed Jr., *W.E.B. Du Bois and American Political Thought: Fabianism and the Color Line* (New York: Oxford University Press, 1997); Eugene Victor Wolfenstein, *A Gift of the Spirit: Reading The Souls of Black Folk* (Ithaca: Cornell University Press, 2007); Robert Gooding-Williams, *In the Shadow of Du Bois: Afro-Modern Political Thought in America* (Cambridge, MA: Harvard University Press, 2009); Lawrie Balfour, *Democracy's Reconstruction: Thinking Politically with W.E.B. Du Bois* (New York: Oxford University Press, 2011).

10. Sheila Lloyd, "Du Bois and the Production of the Racial Picturesque," *Public Culture* 17, no. 2 (2005): 279.

11. W.E.B. Du Bois, "Criteria of Negro Art" (1926), in *Du Bois: Writings*, ed. Nathan Huggins (New York: Library of America, 1986), 1000.

12. Here I agree with Paul Taylor: "One of the keys to taking the history of philosophy seriously is the willingness to flirt with anachronism. We find contemporary language for views that earlier thinkers articulated in different ways, navigating all the while between the twin dangers of over-reading—assigning views that the thinker in question simply didn't, perhaps couldn't, hold—and insufficient generosity—assuming that the thinker in questions means whatever silly view the plain-language reading of his or her argument entails to us now." Taylor, *Black Is Beautiful: A Philosophy of Black Aesthetics* (Malden, MA: Blackwell, 2016), 93.

13. Although I extend my reflections on Du Bois's writings beyond the 1920s in this chapter and the next, I do so only to illuminate themes relevant to *Souls*. As such, I do not explore some of the primary concerns of two of his other significant works, *Black Reconstruction* (1935) and *Dusk of Dawn* (1940). This ultimately gives the impression that Du Bois's thinking remains relatively unchanged when, in fact, he comes to focus on the structural economic basis of racial oppression rather than its ethical-cultural logic that I emphasize here. I should explain, even if in this constrained context, why I have not treated those works with the care I accord "Criteria" and *Souls*.

Beginning in the late 1920s Du Bois's thinking undergoes a substantive development that makes the theoretical workings of political economy central to his analysis. Why then focus on the ethical life of the community and Du Bois's aesthetic and affective appeals? To answer this requires us to understand the relationship between *Souls* and his later works. It is not that Du Bois abandons his earlier thinking; after all, in

Souls, he argues that it is "work, culture, and liberty" that African Americans need (7). He often discusses (per the category of "work") the way racial animus and white supremacy structure economic relationships between blacks and whites and determine the status of black people within the economic framework of American life. In *Souls* and *Darkwater*, for example, he describes the economic habits of modern life which, when wedded to racial prejudice, affect black life in a distinct way. In the second of the two texts, Du Bois anchors his analysis of economic exploitation in an ethical discourse of culture and religion. In *Darkwater* the norms of white supremacy and racial disregard structure the relationship between the "darker peoples of the world" and white people. In this regard, Du Bois is sensitive to the socialist platform on display in the pages of *The Messenger*, edited by Chandler Owen and A. Philip Randolph; he also shows a concern with the logic of Western imperialism central to communists such as Cyril Briggs and Harry Haywood. *Darkwater* thus substantively expands the themes of race and capitalism only gestured to in *Souls*, but *Darkwater* serves to prepare the way for his work of the 1930s and 1940s.

Thus in *Black Reconstruction* and *Dusk of Dawn*, Du Bois centralizes political economy and in turn connects racial oppression and economic exploitation in ways that are descriptively acknowledged in his earlier works but not yet theoretically fleshed out. His slow embrace of and revision to Marxism help him understand how disposability and exploitation, although central to capitalism, are racialized and drive a wedge in American life that is both race- and class-based. What is significant to note about these later works is that Du Bois's slow philosophical development never abandons the ethical framework of his earlier works, even as it extends most explicitly to the workings of political economy. In all instances, Du Bois concerns himself with the kinds of habits that permit the disposability of black people, whether this happens via the lynching tree or the trade union. His turn to political economy is thus structured by the ethical, understood as a conceptual mode of analysis to examine the culture of American life and the standing of black people therein. He believes that the ethos of capitalism turns us into the wrong kinds of people and obstructs our ability to hear the cries of others. Some important works that move in this direction include: Andrew J. Douglas, *W.E.B. Du Bois and the Critique of the Competitive Society* (Athens: University of Georgia Press, 2019); Ella Myers, *The Gratification of Whiteness: W.E.B. Du Bois and the Enduring Rewards of Anti-Blackness* (New York: Oxford University Press, 2022). I thus focus on the initial ethical-cultural thread, believing that its substantive insights only amplify throughout his work.

14. William Stanley Braithwaite, "The Negro in American Literature" (1924), in *The William Stanley Braithwaite Reader* (Ann Arbor: University of Michigan Press, 1972), 68.

15. These next few sentences rely on Martha Jane Nadell's more careful treatment of the subject. See Nadell, *Enter the New Negroes: Images of Race in American Culture* (Cambridge, MA: Harvard University Press, 2004), chap. 1. See also Charles W. Chesnutt, "The Negro in Books" (1916), in *The New Negro: Readings on Race, Representation, and African American Culture, 1892–1938* (Princeton: Princeton University Press, 2007), 173–82 (hereafter *NN*).

16. Eric Sundquist, *To Wake the Nations: Race in the Making of American Literature* (Cambridge, MA: Harvard University Press, 1993), 336–38.

17. Regarding the relationship between culture, politics, and aesthetics, see George Hutchinson, *The Harlem Renaissance in Black and White* (Cambridge, MA: Harvard University Press, 1995); Nadell, *Enter the New Negroes*; Anne Elizabeth Carroll, *Word, Image, and the New Negro: Representation and Identity in the Harlem Renaissance* (Bloomington: Indiana University Press, 2005).

18. Alain Locke, "The New Negro," in *The New Negro: Voices of the Harlem Renaissance*, ed. Alain Locke (1925; New York: Simon and Schuster, 1992), 3; W.E.B. Du Bois, "The Social Origins of American Negro Art" (1925), in *Writings of W.E.B. Du Bois in Periodicals*, ed. Herbert Aptheker, vol. 2 (New York: Krause-Thomson, 1982), 269–71. See also Du Bois's earlier remark: "What is true of literature is true of art: here with a tenth of us colored, we see a colored face in an illustration, a painting or a bronze, on the stage or in a movie but rarely, and then usually in obvious caricature." Du Bois, "Review" of Mary White Ovington, *The Shadow*, in *Book Reviews by W.E.B. Du Bois*, ed. Herbert Aptheker (New York: KTO Press, 1977), 66.

19. Nadell, *Enter the New Negroes*, 25.

20. Walter Lippmann, *Public Opinion* (1922; New York: Free Press, 1965), 59. For my extended treatment of Lippmann, see Melvin Rogers, *The Undiscovered Dewey: Religion, Morality, and the Ethos of Democracy* (New York: Columbia University Press, 2009), 196–206.

21. Lippmann, *Public Opinion*, 63 (original emphasis).

22. Eric Walrond, "Art and Propaganda" (1921), in *NN*, 255; George S. Schuyler, "The Negro-Art Hokum" (1926), in *Voices from the Harlem Renaissance*, ed. Nathan Irvin Huggins (New York: Oxford University Press, 1995), 309–12; Langston Hughes, "The Negro Artist and the Racial Mountain" (1926), in *Voices from the Harlem Renaissance*, ed. Huggins, 305–9.

23. W.E.B. DuBois, "The Negro in Art: How Shall He Be Portrayed" (1926), in *NN*, 190–204, especially 192 (original emphasis).

24. For a sample of these kinds of readings, see David Levering Lewis, *W.E.B. Du Bois: The Fight for Equality and the American Century, 1919–1963* (New York: Henry Holt and Company, 2000), chap. 5, especially 174–82; Alessandra Lorini, "'The Spell of Africa Is upon Me': W.E.B. Du Bois's Notion of Art as Propaganda," in *Temples for Tomorrow: Looking Back at the Harlem Renaissance*, ed. Geneviève Fabre and Michel Feith (Bloomington: Indiana University Press, 2001), 159–76, at 160; Leonard Harris, "The Great Debate: W.E.B. Du Bois vs. Alain Locke on the Aesthetic," *Philosophia Africana* 7, no. 1 (2004): 15–39; Jeffrey W. Stewart, *The New Negro: The Life of Alain Locke* (New York: Oxford University Press, 2018), chap. 28.

25. Hughes, "The Negro Artist," 307.

26. Du Bois, "Criteria," 1000.

27. Ibid.

28. Lippmann, *Public Opinion*; Edward Louis Bernays, *Crystallizing Public Opinion* (New York: Boni and Liveright, 1923); Bernays, *Propaganda*, with introduction by Mark Crispin Miller (1928; New York: IG Publishing, 2005).

29. See Miller, introduction to *Propaganda*. The most recent reflection on this form of "support propaganda" can be found in Jason Stanley's wonderful work, *How Propaganda Works* (Princeton: Princeton University Press, 2015), 53, 110–13.

30. Du Bois, "Criteria," 1001.

31. W.E.B. Du Bois, "Negro Art" (1921), in *The Oxford W.E.B. Du Bois Reader*, ed. Eric J. Sundquist (New York: Oxford University Press, 1996), 310.

32. Du Bois's worry that the image of the criminal and prostitute will serve as a proxy for black life is one reason he comes to object so intensely to Claude McKay's *Home to Harlem*. As Du Bois says in his critical, and perhaps unfair, review, McKay catered to the "prurient demand on the part of white folk." For Du Bois, it was the protagonist Jake Brown, among others, whose freedom seemed wholly defined by self-indulgence. Although McKay sees this as an expression of the "real life" from which Du Bois is removed, for Du Bois this does not appear whole in its characterization of black people. See Du Bois, "Review" of Nella Larsen, *Quicksand*, Claude McKay, *Home to Harlem*, and Melville J. Herskovits, *The American Negro* (1928), in *Book Reviews*, 114. And for McKay's response: Claude McKay to W.E.B. Du Bois, June 18, 1928, in *The Correspondences of W.E.B. Du Bois: Selections, 1877–1934*, vol. 1, ed. Herbert Aptheker (Amherst: University of Massachusetts Press, 1973), 375. For an alternative reading that sees Du Bois's argument for propaganda as fueled by his aversion to emphasizing the complicated sexual desires of black people, see Stewart, *The New Negro: The Life of Alain Locke*, 528–29.

33. W.E.B. Du Bois, *Black Reconstruction in America: An Essay toward a History of the Part Which Black Folk Played in the Attempt to Reconstruct Democracy in America, 1860–1880* (1935; New York: Oxford University Press, 2007), 584–85.

34. Ibid., 585.

35. Harris, "The Great Debate," 16.

36. Taylor, *Black Is Beautiful*, 94.

37. Anna Julia Cooper, *A Voice from the South*, in *The Portable Anna Julia Cooper*, ed. Shirley Moody-Turner (1892; New York: Penguin Classics, 2022), 119.

38. Du Bois, *Souls*, 1.

39. Taylor, *Black Is Beautiful*, 95.

40. Although he offers a criticism of my reading of Du Bois, I think Robert Gooding-Williams and I are closer in our thinking about how goodness functions. See Gooding-Williams, "Beauty as Propaganda: On the Political Aesthetics of W.E.B. Du Bois," *Philosophical Topics* 49, no. 1 (2021): 13–34.

41. Du Bois, "Criteria," 1000.

42. In what I otherwise take to be an exemplary text, I think Taylor is too literal in his reading of inner compulsion. Inner compulsion, he writes, "is just the presumptive force assigned to the store of shared meanings and commitments that constitute a culture" (*Black Is Beautiful*, 96). This seems right, but it also strikes me as incomplete. It seems to ignore the creative impulse of the artist that wells up inside, shaping the aesthetic object that Du Bois means for us to note. John Coltrane's *A Love Supreme* is a musical journey whose elements musicians recognize, but it is one that Coltrane shapes for us in just the way he does in response to the world around him. Toni Morrison, for example, has a point of view that shapes *Beloved* into precisely the novel that it is so that we may come to see the power and danger of the past, even as the literary critic will likely recognize the tropes and elements central to the artistic practice in which Morrison participates. And Billie Holiday's styling of "Strange Fruit" discussed in the previous chapter channels the shared meanings by black people to lynching, but the mournful vision it projects exceeds the lyrics given the particular vocal arrangements she offers.

43. On the distinction between beauty and ugliness, see Gooding-Williams, "Beauty as Propaganda," 21–25.

44. Du Bois, "Criteria," 993; cf. Du Bois, *Souls*, 3; Du Bois, *Darkwater: Voices from within the Veil* (1920; New York: Oxford University Press, 2007), 15.

45. Hill, *Principles of Rhetoric*, 239.

46. See chapter 5.

47. Hill, *Principles of Rhetoric*, 167.

48. Du Bois, *Souls*, 1, 14.

49. It is worth noting that in the section of Hill's *Principles of Rhetoric* where he discusses narrative, he describes "movement" as involving "glimpses of a whole [story] from one point of view after another, or to bring part after part before the eye" (176). We might compare this to Cicero's more famous articulation of this in *On Invention* where he says we must speak "in language that does as much as possible to place the event in question before the eyes of our listeners." As Quentin Skinner rightly observes, the aim for classical rhetoricians was to transform "auditors into spectators." Cited in Skinner, *Reason and Rhetoric in the Philosophy of Hobbes* (New York: Cambridge University Press, 1996), 183.

50. Du Bois, "Criteria," 995.

51. Alain Locke, "The Negro Youth Speaks," in *The New Negro*, 50.

52. W.E.B. Du Bois, review of Alain Locke, *The New Negro*, in *Book Reviews*, 79.

53. Alain Locke, "The Message of the Negro Poets" (1927), in *The Works of Alain Locke*, ed. Charles Molesworth (New York: Oxford University Press, 2012), 69.

54. Alain Locke, "Art or Propaganda" (1928), in *The Critical Temper of Alain Locke: A Selection of His Essays on Art and Culture*, ed. Jeffrey C. Stewart (New York: Garland, 1983), 27.

55. In her dissertation, "The Art of Living: Recovering Alain Locke's Political Aesthetics," Michelle Rose carefully lays out the historical and philosophical context for understanding Locke's aversion to the utility of art. And she is keen to link his aversion to a worry over a kind of external imposition that leads to aesthetic partiality rather than expressive autonomy. My sense, as I argue here, is that this places Locke and Du Bois closer together given the latter's understanding of negative propaganda.

56. Locke, "The New Negro," 3–4.

57. Importantly, it is the New Negro that marks a departure: "The day of 'aunties,' 'uncles' and 'mammies' is equally gone. Uncle Tom and Sambo have passed on, and even the 'Colonel' and 'George' play barnstorm roles from which they escape with relief when the public spotlight is off. The popular melodrama has about played itself out, and it is time to scrap the fictions, garret the bogeys and settle down to a realistic facing of facts" (Locke, "The New Negro," 5).

58. Nancy Fraser, "Another Pragmatism: Alain Locke, Critical 'Race' Theory, and the Politics of Culture," in *The Critical Pragmatism of Alain Locke: A Reader on Value Theory, Aesthetics, Community, Culture, Race, and Education* (Lanham, MD: Rowman and Littlefield, 1999), 3–21; Henry Louis Gates Jr., "The Trope of the New Negro and the Reconstruction of the Image of the Black," *Representations* 24 (1988): 147.

59. For Locke's earlier reliance on Whitman, see Charles Molesworth, "Alain Locke and Walt Whitman: Manifesto and National Identity," in *The Critical Pragmatism of Alain Locke*, 175–89; George Hutchinson, "The Whitman Legacy and the

Harlem Renaissance," in *Walt Whitman: The Centennial Essays*, ed. Ed Folsom (Iowa City: University of Iowa Press, 1994), 202–7.

60. Walt Whitman, *Leaves of Grass* (1891–92), in *Whitman: Poetry and Prose*, ed. Justin Kaplin (New York: Library of America, 1996), 303.

61. Alain Locke, "The Ethics of Culture" (1925), in *Critical Temper*, 416. I am relying on the insight of George Hutchinson in his reflections on the aesthetics of John Dewey and Alain Locke in Hutchinson, *The Harlem Renaissance*, 48.

62. On this point, Locke is clear: "The especially cultural recognition they win should in turn provide the key to the revaluation of the Negro which must precede or accompany any further betterment of race relationships" ("The New Negro," 15). Cultural recognition, however, is independent of the self-worth achieved for oneself by virtue of one's art: "And so the social promise of our recent art is as great as the artistic. It has brought with it, first of all, that wholesome, welcome virtue of finding beauty in oneself" (Locke, "Negro Youth Speaks," 52).

63. Du Bois, "Criteria," 995.

64. Locke, "Art or Propaganda," 27.

65. George Hutchinson is thus correct when he says, "Locke's aestheticism carries a subtle social and political charge. . . . Aesthetic judgment becomes itself a form of social participation, essential to the building of community and the interactive orientation of diverse individuals and social groups to a common world" (*The Harlem Renaissance*, 49). I only wish he used this as the basis for drawing Du Bois and Locke together.

66. Du Bois, "Criteria," 993.

67. Du Bois, *Dusk of Dawn*, 2 (emphasis added). It is worth noting that when Du Bois places propaganda alongside the boycott and mob frenzy he is acknowledging, as did Locke, that "art cannot completely accomplish this [referring to political transformation]." Similar to Locke, Du Bois nonetheless believes "it can lead the way." Locke, "Art or Propaganda," 27.

68. Du Bois, "Criteria," 1001.

69. Ibid., 1002.

70. Ibid. It would take us too far afield to pursue the matter, but the form Du Bois's argument takes here represents Locke's later notion of the ethical wherein the "value reference is introverted or directed inwardly toward the self." Alain Locke, "Values and Imperatives," in *The Philosophy of Alain Locke: Harlem Renaissance and Beyond*, ed. Leonard Harris (Philadelphia: Temple University Press, 1989), 42.

71. W.E.B. Du Bois, "Review" (1920), in *Book Reviews*, 66.

72. Plato, *Gorgias*, trans. Donald J. Zeyl (Indianapolis: Hackett Publishing, 1987).

73. Peter Euben, "Reading Democracy: 'Socratic' Dialogues and the Political Education of Democratic Citizens," in *Demokratia: A Conversation on Democracies, Ancient and Modern*, ed. Josiah Ober and Charles Hedrick (Princeton: Princeton University Press, 1996), 337; cf. David Cohen, "The Politics of Deliberation: Oratory and Democracy in Classical Athens," in *A Companion to Rhetoric and Rhetorical Criticism*, ed. Walter Jost and Wendy Olmsted (Malden, MA: Blackwell, 2004), 22–37; Simone Chambers, "Rhetoric and the Public Sphere: Has Deliberative Democracy Abandoned Mass Democracy?" *Political Theory* 37, no. 3 (2009): 323–50.

74. There is a rich and long tradition that argues that to be free is to act according to one's authentic or true self. This tradition includes thinkers as diverse as John Stuart Mill, Karl Marx, and Alain Locke. Suffice it to say, acting against your true interest does not mean acting against your phenomenal, unreflective desires. This, of course, is partly how the manipulator works. Manipulators secure their own good by appealing to the phenomenal desires of the citizenry.

75. Garsten, *Saving Persuasion*, 7 and chap. 4; Allen, *Talking to Strangers*.

76. Hill, *Principles of Rhetoric*, 240.

77. As he says of the Freedmen's Bureau: "this Bureau set going a system of free labor, established a beginning of peasant proprietorship, secured the recognition of black freedmen before the *courts of law*, and founded the free common school in the South. On the other hand, it failed to begin the establishment of *good-will* between ex-masters and freedmen" (Du Bois, *Souls*, 18; emphasis added). In *Souls*, Du Bois attaches weight to both the law (see, for instance, his criticism of Booker T. Washington's willingness to abandon the franchise and civil equality in chapter 3, "Of Mr. Booker T. Washington and Others") and a deeper exchange and engagement among whites and blacks for improving the standing of each in the eyes of the other (see, for example, chapter 9, "Of the Sons of Master and Man," where he emphasizes the importance of social contact).

78. Cited in Lewis, *W.E.B. Du Bois*, 226. From William T. Ingersoll interview of W.E.B. Du Bois, June 1960, 146–47, http://credo.library.umass.edu/view/full/mums312-b237-i137.

79. Robert Stepto, *From behind the Veil: A Study of Afro-American Narrative*, 2nd ed. (1979; Urbana: University of Illinois Press, 1991), 53; cf. Wolfenstein, *Gift of the Spirit*, chap. 1.

80. W.E.B. Du Bois, "On *The Souls of Black Folk*" (1904), in *The Oxford W.E.B. Du Bois Reader*, ed. Eric J. Sundquist (New York: Oxford University Press, 1996), 305.

81. Du Bois, *Souls*, 1 (emphasis added).

82. Aristotle, *Rhetoric*, 1358b.

83. Tommie Shelby, *Dark Ghettos: Injustice, Dissent, and Reform* (Cambridge, MA: Harvard University Press, 2016), 97.

84. Du Bois, *Souls*, 3.

85. Gooding-Williams, *Shadow of Du Bois*, 3.

86. Du Bois, *Souls*, 23.

87. Ibid., 1. I do not mean to suggest that Du Bois was successful in consistently holding these two visions of politics together, but he did not unambiguously affirm rule as the model for understanding democracy. Admittedly, between *The Souls of Black Folk* and *Darkwater*, Du Bois slowly came to think about the foundations of leadership in wider—that is, popular—terms, amplifying and enriching his thinking from chapter 3. But the best way to think about this is in terms Francis Broderick articulated regarding Du Bois's developmental style: "Writing month after month on current events, he did not, of course, abruptly end one period of intellectual change and begin another. [Du Bois] might drop a hint, then wait twenty years before picking it up for future development" (Broderick, *W.E.B. Du Bois: Negro Leader in a Time of Crisis* [Palo Alto, CA: Stanford University Press, 1959], 123).

But even amid this development in Du Bois's thinking, the politics of rule achieved greater success with the Jamaican political activists and Black Nationalist Marcus

Garvey. Garvey's Universal Negro Improvement Association, with its mix of cultural nationalism, pessimism regarding transformation of the American polity, and vision of charismatic leadership, cast a long shadow over black politics in ways that have yet to be fully grasped. For two helpful pieces on the significance of Garvey, see Steven Hahn, *The Political Worlds of Slavery and Freedom* (Cambridge, MA: Harvard University Press, 2009), chap. 3; Michael Dawson, "Marcus Garvey: The Black Prince?" in *African American Political Thought: A Collected History*, ed. Melvin L. Rogers and Jack Turner (Chicago: University of Chicago Press, 2021), 260–89.

88. Robert Solomon, "The Politics of the Emotions," in *Bringing the Passions Back In: The Emotions in Political Philosophy*, ed. Rebecca Kingston and Leonard Ferry (Vancouver: University of British Columbia Press, 2008), 195, 198.

Chapter 7. Calling the People to a Higher Vision: *On* The Souls of Black Folk

1. Quoted in Gerald Horne, *Black and Red* (Albany: State University of New York Press, 1986), 345.

2. W.E.B. Du Bois, *The Souls of Black Folk* (1903; New York: Oxford University Press, 2007), 6.

3. Ibid., 74; compare this criticism to his reflections on abstract sociology in his 1905 essay, "Sociology Hesitant" (1905) *boundary 2* (2000): 37–44. For Du Bois's earlier division between research and normative advocacy work from which he departs by the time of *Souls*, see Du Bois, "The Study of the Negro Problems" (1898), in *Writings by W.E.B. Du Bois in Periodicals*, ed. Herbert Aptheker, vol. 1 (New York: Krause-Thomson, 1982), 40–52.

4. W.E.B. Du Bois, "The Souls of Black Folk" (1904), in *The Oxford W.E.B. Du Bois Reader*, ed. Eric J. Sundquist (New York: Oxford University Press, 1996), 34–35. On the revisions of the earlier essays and compositional coherence of *Souls*, see Robert Stepto, *From behind the Veil: A Study of Afro-American Narrative*, 2nd ed. (1979; Urbana: University of Illinois Press, 1991), chap. 3.

5. Du Bois, *Souls*, 1.

6. Sheila Lloyd, "Du Bois and the Production of the Racial Picturesque," *Public Culture* 17, no. 2 (2005): 278.

7. Frederick Douglass, "Pictures and Progress," in *The Frederick Douglass Papers: Series One, Speeches, Debates, and Interviews*, ed. John Blassingame, vol. 3 (New Haven: Yale University Press, 1985), 462.

8. Walt Whitman, *Democratic Vistas: The Original Edition in Facsimile*, ed. Ed Folsom (1870–71; Iowa City: University of Iowa Press, 2010), 76.

9. W.E.B. Du Bois, *Dusk of Dawn: An Essay toward an Autobiography of a Race Concept* (1940; New York: Oxford University Press, 2007), 14 (emphasis added). Importantly, *Dusk of Dawn* is the concluding text of the unintended trilogy that includes *The Souls of Black Folk* (1903) and *Darkwater* (1920); *Dusk of Dawn*, xxiii.

10. William H. Ferris, *The African Abroad*, vol. 1 (New Haven: Tuttle, Morehouse, and Taylor, 1913), 257.

11. Du Bois, *Souls*, 3.

12. Joseph Winters, *Hope Draped in Black: Race, Melancholy, and the Agony of Progress* (Durham: Duke University Press, 2016), 64.

13. For a good selection of texts that carefully explore Du Bois's gender politics, see Hazel Carby, *Race Men* (Cambridge, MA: Harvard University Press, 1998); Joy James, *Transcending the Talented Tenth* (New York: Routledge, 1997); Farah Jasmine Griffin, "Black Feminists and Du Bois: Respectability, Protection, and Beyond," *Annals of the American Academy of Political and Social Science* 568 (2000): 28–40; Susan Gillman and Alys Weinbaum, eds., *Next to the Color Line: Gender, Sexuality, and W.E.B. Du Bois* (Minneapolis: University of Minnesota Press, 2007); Lawrie Balfour, *Democracy's Reconstruction: Thinking Politically with W.E.B. Du Bois* (New York: Oxford University Press, 2011), 97–114; Shatema Threadcraft, *Intimate Justice: The Black Female Body and the Body Politic* (Oxford: Oxford University Press, 2016); Annie Menzel, "'Awful Gladness': The Dual Political Rhetorics of Du Bois's 'Of the Passing of the First-Born,'" *Political Theory* 47, no. 1 (2019): 32–56.

14. The exceptions to this include Edward Blum, *W.E.B. Du Bois: American Prophet* (Philadelphia: University of Pennsylvania Press, 2007), chap. 2; Jonathon S. Kahn, *Divine Discontent: The Religious Imagination of W.E.B. Du Bois* (New York: Oxford University Press, 2009), 64–70; Terrence L. Johnson, *Tragic Soul-Life: W.E.B. Du Bois and the Moral Crisis Facing American Democracy* (New York: Oxford University Press, 2012), chap. 2; Stephanie J. Shaw, *W.E.B. Du Bois and The Souls of Black Folk* (Chapel Hill: University of North Carolina Press, 2013), chap. 2; Anthony Appiah, *Lines of Descent: W.E.B. Du Bois and the Emergence of Identity* (Cambridge, MA: Harvard University Press, 2014), chap. 2.

15. For a rich account of these works with respect to Du Bois, see Blum, *American Prophet*, chap. 2.

16. Here I follow Ian Shapiro's analogy: "Think of the relations between foundational political commitment and the rest of our lives as roughly akin to the relations between the foundations of buildings and the structures and activities they support. One feature of foundational commitments brought out by this comparison is that although they are essential, by their nature they are incomplete and open-ended. Every house needs a foundation lest it fall over, yet a foundation is not to be confused with a house, much less with the lives of its inhabits." Shapiro, *Democratic Justice* (New Haven: Yale University Press, 1999), 22.

17. Du Bois, *Souls*, 103.

18. *Nation* 76, no. 1980 (June 11, 1903): 481–82.

19. John Spencer Bassett, "Two Negro Leaders," *South Atlantic Quarterly* 2 (1903): 267–72.

20. Ferris, *The African Abroad*, 273 (emphasis added). I do not mean to suggest that Ferris's estimation of Du Bois remained intact. For more on the complexity of Ferris's estimation of Du Bois, see Tommy Curry, "Author's Preface," and "Author's Introduction," in *The Philosophical Treatise of William H. Ferris: Selected Readings from the African Abroad, or, His Evolution in Western Civilization* (Lanham, MD: Rowman and Littlefield, 2016), 1–50.

21. William Braithwaite, "Some Contemporary Poets in the Negro Race" (1919), in *The William Stanley Braithwaite Reader* (Ann Arbor: University of Michigan Press, 1972), 53. Of course, so much of Du Bois's developed poetic sensibilities has been powerfully charted by Arnold Rampersad. See Rampersad, "W.E.B. Du Bois as a Man

of Literature," in *Critical Essays on W.E.B. Du Bois*, ed. William A. Andrews (Boston: Hall, 1985), 49–66; Rampersad, *The Art and Imagination of W.E.B. Du Bois* (New York: Schocken Books, 1976); Rampersad, "Slavery and the Literary Imagination: Du Bois's *The Souls of Black Folk*," in *Slavery and the Literary Imagination*, ed. Deborah E. McDowell and Arnold Rampersad (Baltimore, 1989), 104–24. See also Ross Posnock, *Color and Culture: Black Writers and the Making of the Modern Intellectual* (Cambridge, MA: Harvard University Press, 1996), chap. 4, on the insistence that aesthetics and politics are connected in Du Bois's thinking.

22. For a more extended account of this, see Charles Taylor, *Sources of the Self: The Making of the Modern Identity* (Cambridge, MA: Harvard University Press, 1989), chaps. 6–7. Also compare my discussion here with Kahn, *Divine Discontent*, 64–70; Johnson, *Tragic Soul-Life*, 46–48; Shaw, *W.E.B. Du Bois*, 24–25.

23. Kahn, *Divine Discontent*, 65.

24. William Wordsworth, *The Prelude* (1805), in *Wordsworth's Poetry and Prose*, ed. Nicholas Halmi (New York: W. W. Norton, 2014), 177–78; cf. James Engell, *The Creative Imagination: Enlightenment to Romanticism* (Cambridge, MA: Harvard University Press, 1981), 268–71.

25. Ralph Waldo Emerson, "The Poet" (1844), in *Emerson: Essays and Lectures*, ed. Joel Porte (New York: Library of America, 1983), 458.

26. Anna Julia Cooper, *A Voice from the South*, in *The Portable Anna Julia Cooper*, ed. Shirley Moody-Turner (1892; New York: Penguin Books, 2022), 150.

27. Cf. Paul Taylor, "What's the Use of Calling Du Bois a Pragmatist?" *Metaphilosophy* 35, no. 1/2 (2004): 103–4.

28. Frederick Douglass, *Narrative of the Life of Frederick Douglass, An American Slave* (1845), in *The Frederick Douglass Papers: Series Two, Autobiographical Writings*, ed. John W. Blassingame, John R. McKivigan, and Peter Hinks, vol. 1 (New Haven: Yale University Press, 1999), 20.

29. It is worth noting that this becomes central to his understanding of race in *Dusk of Dawn*: "But one thing is sure and that is the fact that since the fifteenth century these ancestors of mine and their other descendants have had a common history; have suffered a common disaster and have one long memory" (Du Bois, *Dusk of Dawn*, 59). On the connection between Douglass and Du Bois on the sorrow songs, see Winters, *Hope Draped in Black*, 43–45.

30. W.E.B. Du Bois, "The Souls of White Folk," *The Independent* 69 (1910): 339–42; Du Bois, "Of the Culture of White Folk," *Journal of Race Development* 7, no. 4 (1917): 434–47.

31. Cf. Ella Myers, *The Gratification of Whiteness: W.E.B. Du Bois and the Enduring Rewards of Anti-Blackness* (New York: Oxford University Press, 2022); Robert Gooding-Williams, "Beauty as Propaganda: On the Political Aesthetics of W.E.B. Du Bois," *Philosophical Topics* 49, no. 1 (2021): 14–21.

32. W.E.B. Du Bois, *Darkwater: Voices from within the Veil* (1920; New York: Oxford University Press, 2007), 18.

33. Ibid., 16, 22 (emphasis added).

34. This idea of the soul buckling under the weight of domination is informed by Lisa Tessman's argument of moral failure in *Moral Failure: On the Impossible Demands of Morality* (New York: Oxford University Press, 2015), chaps. 4 and 5.

35. Claudia Card, *The Unnatural Lottery: Character and Moral Luck* (Philadelphia: Temple University Press, 1996).

36. Du Bois, *Souls*, 2, 3.

37. I am here running together "prize" and "opportunity," the former of which denotes something deemed valuable that is given as a result of actions completed. It should be clear to the reader that opportunity (understood as chance) to secure what is valuable must exist.

38. Du Bois, *Souls*, 3 (emphasis added). Du Bois's sense of not being daunted repeats in *Darkwater*, 6.

39. Ibid., 33–34.

40. Ibid., 6.

41. Katie Stockdale, "Social and Political Dimensions of Hope," *Journal of Social Philosophy* 50, no. 1 (2019): 34. Although hope does not figure in her account, Lisa Tessman seems to be at work on a similar worry. See Tessman, *Moral Failure*, chaps. 4–5.

42. Du Bois, *Souls*, 100.

43. Ibid., 102.

44. To say that they should not have to bear this does not mean one can be totally saved from such thoughts and feelings. But we should never sit too comfortably with them. Tessman insists that there can be some failures in our lives, say, the inability of a parent to save a child from the racism over which they have no control, *"from which there can be no recovery,* not even the reassurance that one has learned a lesson for the future" (*Moral Failure*, 178). There is truth in this. Although Du Bois fails to discuss it in *Souls*, much later he would acknowledge that not only had he lost his son, but "in a sense my wife died too. Never after that was [Nina Du Bois] quite the same in her attitude toward life and the world" (cited in Lewis, *W.E.B. Du Bois: A Biography* [New York: Holt, 2009], 164).

45. Du Bois, *Souls*, 102 (emphasis added). Cornel West's now classic critique of Du Bois is his presumed failure to linger on the death of his son as well as Hose's death. See Cornel West and Henry Louis Gates Jr., *The Future of the Race* (New York: Vintage, 1997), 63–64.

46. Winters, *Hope Draped in Black*, 75.

47. Du Bois, *Souls*, 100.

48. Stepto, *Behind the Veil*, 53.

49. Shamoon Zamir, *Dark Voices: W.E.B. Du Bois and American Thought, 1888–1903* (Chicago: University of Chicago Press, 1995), 146.

50. Du Bois, *Souls*, 61.

51. Ibid., 7.

52. We should briefly take note of his sustained interest in this point. In his "Credo" in *Darkwater*, he writes: "I believe in Liberty for all men: the space to stretch their arms and their *souls*, the right to breathe and the right to vote, the freedom to choose their friends, enjoy the sunshine, and ride the railroads, uncursed by color; thinking, dreaming, working as they will in a kingdom of beauty and love" (1). That he distinguishes corporeal and spiritual activity is important. In his mind, it is very possible for African Americans to be free of external impediments and yet be constrained in the deepest recesses of themselves. Liberty is not merely about the

removal of external impediments (although important) but that more deadly form of white supremacy that tyrannizes over the soul and restricts thinking, dreaming, and what one works for.

53. Du Bois, *Souls*, 3 (emphasis added).

54. Du Bois pursues a parallel point in *Darkwater* but stops short of its political implications: "Of them I am singularly clairvoyant. I see in and through them. I view them from unusual points of vantage. Not as a foreigner do I come, for I am native, not foreign, bone of their thought and flesh of their language. Mine is not the knowledge of the traveler or the colonial composite of dear memories, words and wonder. Not yet is my knowledge that which servants have of masters, or mass of class, or capitalist of artisan. Rather I see these souls undressed and from the back and side. I see the workings of their entrails. I know their thoughts and they know that I know. This knowledge makes them now embarrassed, now furious!" (15). Here, black people have a kind of phenomenological knowledge born of social intimacy with white Americans that gives rise to an understanding of their needs and desires. This is largely because, on this version of the point, blackness is a production of white desires ("I am . . . bone of their thought and flesh of their language"). This point expands once more in *Dusk of Dawn* as this clairvoyance exposes both the conscious and subconscious character of racism and white supremacy (Du Bois, *Dusk of Dawn*, 2, 86–87). This is a point that becomes central to James Baldwin's much later thinking.

55. For a sustained reading of these and other aspects of this passage, see Paul Taylor, "W.E.B. Du Bois: Afro-modernism, Expressivism, and the Curse of Centrality," in *African American Political Thought: A Collected History*, ed. Melvin L. Rogers and Jack Turner (Chicago: University of Chicago Press, 2021), 235–59.

56. Charles Taylor, "The Politics of Recognition," in *Multiculturalism: Examining the Politics of Recognition*, ed. Amy Gutmann (Princeton: Princeton University Press, 1994), 26; cf. Sharon Krause, *Freedom beyond Sovereignty: Reconstructing Liberal Individualism* (Chicago: University of Chicago Press, 2015), chap. 2.

57. Tommie Shelby, *Dark Ghettos: Injustice, Dissent, and Reform* (Cambridge, MA: Harvard University Press, 2016), 35; cf. Krause, *Beyond Sovereignty*, 68–69. For a longer treatment of this as central to Du Bois's meaning of double-consciousness, see Dickson D. Bruce Jr., "W.E.B. Du Bois and the Idea of Double Consciousness," *American Literature: A Journal of Literary History, Critics, and Bibliography* 64, no. 2 (1992): 299–309. For my purposes, however, it is of little concern whether the idea of double-consciousness is owed to Hegel or William James. For three such competing accounts on Hegelian and Jamesian influences, respectively, see Zamir, *Dark Voices*, chap. 4; Shawn Michelle Smith, *Photography on the Color Line: W.E.B. Du Bois, Race, and Visual Culture* (Durham: Duke University Press, 2004), chap. 1; José Itzigsohn and Karida L. Brown, *The Sociology of W.E.B. Du Bois: Racialized Modernity and the Global Color Line* (New York: New York University Press, 2020), chap. 1.

58. Du Bois, *Souls*, 3; cf. William Wordsworth, "Ode [Intimations of Immortality]" (1807), in *Wordsworth's Poetry and Prose*, 432–39, especially at 436.

59. Ralf Haekel, *The Soul in British Romanticism: Negotiating Human Nature in Philosophy, Science and Poetry* (Trier: Wissenschaftlicher Verlag Trier, 2014), pt. 1; cf. Denise Gigante, *Life: Organic Form and Romanticism* (New Haven: Yale University Press, 2009), 29–30. For a more extended reflection on romanticism, see M. H. Abrams,

Natural Supernaturalism: Tradition and Revolution in Romantic Literature (New York: W. W. Norton, 1971).

60. Abrams, *Natural Supernaturalism*, 68.

61. Wordsworth, "Intimations Ode," 435–36.

62. Ralph Waldo Emerson, "The Transcendentalists" (1842), in *Essays and Lectures*, 193–209.

63. Robert Gooding-Williams, *In the Shadow of Du Bois: Afro-Modern Political Thought in America* (Cambridge, MA: Harvard University Press, 2009), 73; cf. this similar point although without reference to Wordsworth in Zamir, *Dark Voices*, 139–47.

64. Gooding-Williams, *Shadow of Du Bois*, 73.

65. Du Bois, *Souls*, 4.

66. David Levering Lewis also suggests this of Du Bois's analysis of life under conditions of slavery: "historians and sociologists assumed that 'every vestige of internal development disappeared, leaving the slaves not means of expression for their common life,' but Du Bois stopped short of making the southern plantation experience the equivalent of a lobotomy" (Lewis, *W.E.B. Du Bois: Biography of a Race, 1868–1919* [New York: Henry Holt and Company, 1993], 223).

67. James, *Transcending the Talented Tenth*, 35–36.

68. I shall always put "male" and "female" in scare quotes largely because they are meant to signal not merely someone that is legible to the viewer as "male" or "female" but someone whose legible identity and birth sex correspond ("cisgender," as we say today). This immediately brings into view the reproductive capacities of "males" and "females" but also obscures the space and lives of transgendered persons.

69. I am pulling from two different places in Carby's text. The first: "Gendered structures of thought and feeling permeate our lives and our intellectual work, including *The Souls of Black Folk* and other texts which have been regarded as *founding* texts written by the *founding fathers* of black American history and culture" (*Race Men*, 12–13). The second: "On the contrary, the metaphoric and symbolic characteristics of Josie and Atlanta determine that neither is a symbol of hope for the future of the African American folk, indeed neither have a viable political, social, and or intellectual future in Du Bois's text" (20).

70. Mary Church Terrell, "In Union There Is Strength," president's first address to the National Association of Colored Women, September 15, 1897, Mary Church Terrell Papers: Speeches and Writings, 1866–1953, Manuscript/Mixed Material, https://www.loc.gov/item/mss425490352/. For more on the National Association of Colored Women and the political thought that emerged from it, see Brittney C. Cooper, *Beyond Respectability: The Intellectual Thought of Race Women* (Urbana: University of Illinois Press, 2017), chap. 1.

71. Griffin, "Black Feminists and Du Bois," 28–40.

72. Threadcraft, *Intimate Justice*, 92.

73. Gail Bederman, *Manliness and Civilization: A Cultural History of Gender and Race in the United States, 1880–1917* (Chicago: University of Chicago Press, 1995), 21; cf. Martha S. Jones, *All Bound Up Together: The Woman Question in African American Public Culture, 1830–1900* (Chapel Hill: University of North Carolina Press, 2007).

74. Du Bois, *Souls*, 27; cf. 25.

75. Carby, *Race Men*, 39.

NOTES TO CHAPTER 7 [359]

77. Bederman, *Manliness and Civilization*, 27; cf. 18.

78. W.E.B. Du Bois, "The Overlook," *The Horizon*, December 1909. For an older but still useful survey of the perspective of black men in the nineteenth century on the inclusion of women, see Rosalyn Terborg-Penn, "Black Male Perspectives on the Nineteenth-Century Woman," in *The Afro-American Woman: Struggles and Images*, ed. Sharon Harley and Rosalyn Terborg-Penn (Baltimore: Black Classic Press, 1978), 28–42.

79. Du Bois, *Darkwater*, 78.

80. Du Bois, *Souls*, 33.

81. Ibid., 34.

82. Ibid., 35.

83. Winters, *Hope Draped in Black*, 61.

84. Du Bois, *Souls*, 34.

85. Ibid., 36.

86. For this critique, see Carby, *Race Men*, 17–20. See generally Winters's thoughtful pushback in *Hope Draped in Black*, 63–65.

87. Du Bois, *Souls*, 7.

88. Ibid., 103 (emphasis added).

89. Ibid., 108. The reader should note that none of Crummell's political philosophy comes through in this chapter. For a richer account of Crummell's life and philosophy the reader should consult Wilson Jeremiah Moses, *Alexander Crummell: A Study of Civilization and Discontent* (New York: Oxford University Press, 1989); Frank M. Kirkland, "Alexander Crummell's Three Visions of Black Nationalism," in *African American Political Thought*, ed. Rogers and Turner, 142–66.

90. Ronald Dworkin, *Justice for Hedgehogs* (Cambridge, MA: Harvard University Press, 2011), 197.

91. Du Bois, *Souls*, 108 (emphasis added).

92. Ibid., 109.

93. Ibid., 24.

94. Balfour, *Democracy's Reconstruction*, 73.

95. Shelby, *Dark Ghettos*, 97.

96. Du Bois, *Souls*, 104, 105, 106, 108.

97. I advanced a much earlier argument of this kind against the model of recognition proposed by Axel Honneth. See Rogers, "Rereading Honneth: Exodus Politics and the Paradox of Recognition," *European Journal of Political Theory* 8, no. 2 (2009): 183–206.

98. Du Bois, *Souls*, 7.

99. Ibid., 48–49.

100. Ibid., 80.

101. Ibid., 108.

102. Cf. Gooding-Williams, *Shadow of Du Bois*, 98–111.

103. Du Bois, *Souls*, 1.

104. Ibid., 66.

105. Ibid., 80.

106. Ibid., 104.

107. Ibid., 108.

108. Ibid., 89.

109. Ibid., 104.

110. For two critical views of shame, see Martha Nussbaum, *Hiding from Humanity: Disgust, Shame, and the Law* (Princeton: Princeton University Press, 2004); Jill Locke, *Democracy and the Death of Shame: Political Equality and Social Disturbance* (New York: Cambridge University Press, 2016).

111. Bernard Williams, *Shame and Necessity* (Berkeley: University California Press, 1994), 93; cf. Andrew Morrison, *The Culture of Shame* (New York: Ballantine Books, 1996); Christina Tarnopolsky, *Prudes, Perverts, and Tyrants: Plato's Gorgias and the Politics of Shame* (Princeton: Princeton University Press, 2010); Christopher J. Lebron, *The Color of Our Shame: Race and Justice in Our Time* (New York: Oxford University Press, 2014); Jennifer Jacquet, *Is Shame Necessary?: New Uses for an Old Tool* (New York: Pantheon, 2015).

112. Du Bois, *Souls*, 130.

113. See, for example, Williams, *Shame and Necessity*; Tarnopolsky, *Prudes, Perverts, and Tyrants*.

114. Williams, *Shame and Necessity*, 90; cf. Lebron, *Colour of Our Shame*, 21.

115. Williams, *Shame and Necessity*, 130.

116. Du Bois, *Souls*, 547 (original emphasis).

117. Plato, *Phaedrus*, 261b. Unsurprisingly and consistent with Du Bois's own view, Nathan Crick writes of *Phaedrus*: "In the *Phaedrus*, Socrates had proposed that the rhetorical art represents 'a way of directing the soul by means of speech,' meaning that rhetoric serves the end of virtue when it directs the soul toward the goal which dialectic has shown to be *good, beautiful, and true*." Crick, *Rhetoric and Power: The Drama of Classical Greece* (Columbia: University of South Carolina Press, 2014), 162 (emphasis added).

118. Cicero, *On the Ideal Orator*, trans. James M. May and Jakob Wisse (New York: Oxford University Press, 2001), 2.35, 133.

119. Gunnar Myrdal, *An American Dilemma: The Negro Problem and Modern Democracy*, vol. 1 (1944; New Brunswick, NJ: Transaction, 1996), 214, lxxix.

Conclusion: James Baldwin's Gift

1. Pew Research Center, "Race in America 2019," https://www.pewresearch.org/social-trends/2019/04/09/race-in-america-2019/; Pew Research Center, "Deep Divisions in Americans' Views of the Nation's Racial History—and How to Address It," 2021, https://www.pewresearch.org/politics/2021/08/12/deep-divisions-in-americans-views-of-nations-racial-history-and-how-to-address-it/; Pew Research Center, "Most Americans Say There Is Too Much Economic Inequality in the U.S., but Fewer than Half Call It a Top Priority," 2020, https://www.pewresearch.org/social-trends/2020/01/09/most-americans-say-there-is-too-much-economic-inequality-in-the-u-s-but-fewer-than-half-call-it-a-top-priority/; World Meteorological Organization, *State of the Global Climate* (Geneva: World Meteorological Organization, 2021).

2. Gunnar Myrdal, *An American Dilemma: The Negro Problem and Modern Democracy*, with an introduction by Sissela Bok, 2 vols. (1944; New Brunswick, NJ:

Transaction, 2009). For three significant histories of Myrdal's project, see David Southern, *Gunnar Myrdal and Black-White Relations: The Use and Abuse of An American Dilemma, 1944–1969* (Baton Rouge: Louisiana State University Press, 1987); Walter Jackson, *Gunnar Myrdal and America's Conscience* (Chapel Hill: University of North Carolina Press, 1990); Maribel Morey, *White Philanthropy: Carnegie Corporation's An American Dilemma and the Making of a White World Order* (Chapel Hill: University of North Carolina Press, 2021).

3. I do not mean this in the sense that Charles Mills has in mind when he invokes the term "racial liberalism." For his account, see Mills, "Racial Liberalism," *PMLA* 123, no. 4 (2008): 1380–97.

4. Here I liberally appropriate the language of "once-born" from William James. See James, *The Varieties of Religious Experience: A Study of Human Nature* (1902; New York: Modern Library 1999), lectures IV and V.

5. "Dixie's Hesitation Waltz: You Lead, We Might Follow," *Variety*, May 29, 1963, 3.

6. A great deal has been written on Baldwin, and as of late. For those with whom I share the most and have learned the most from in thinking about Baldwin, see Lawrie Balfour, *The Evidence of Things Not Said: James Baldwin and the Promise of American Democracy* (Ithaca: Cornell University Press, 2000); George Shulman, *American Prophecy: Race and Redemption in American Political Culture* (Minneapolis: University of Minnesota Press, 2008), chap. 4; Jack Turner, *Awakening to Race: Individualism and Social Consciousness in America* (Chicago: University of Chicago Press, 2012), chap. 5; Nick Bromell, *The Time Is Always Now: Black Thought and the Transformation of US Democracy* (New York: Oxford University Press, 2013), chap. 3; Nicholas Buccola, *The Fire Is upon Us: James Baldwin, William F. Buckley Jr., and the Debate over Race in American* (Princeton: Princeton University Press, 2019); Eddie S. Glaude Jr., *Begin Again: James Baldwin's America and Its Urgent Lessons for Our Own* (New York: Crown Press, 2020); John E. Drabinski, "James Baldwin: Democracy between Nihilism and Hope," in *African American Political Thought: A Collected History*, ed. Melvin L. Rogers and Jack Turner (Chicago: University of Chicago Press, 2021), 481–96.

7. My idea of "critical responsiveness" moves in a different direction than William Connolly's more famous iteration of the term, although I don't think my use of it is incompatible with his. See Connolly, *The Ethos of Pluralization* (Minneapolis: University of Minnesota Press, 1995).

8. Saidiya V. Hartman, "The Time of Slavery," *South Atlantic Quarterly* 101, no. 4 (2002): 759.

9. James Baldwin, *The Fire Next Time* (1963), in *Baldwin: Collected Essays*, ed. Toni Morrison (New York: Library of America, 1998), 292. All references to Baldwin's works will be from this collection (*CE*) unless otherwise noted.

10. Myrdal, *American Dilemma*, vol. 1, lxxxiii, lxxxv, 307.

11. See Southern, *Gunnar Myrdal and Black-White Relations*, especially chaps. 5 and 7; Jackson, *Gunnar Myrdal and American's Conscience*, 210–11; Gary Gerstle, "The Protean Character of American Liberalism," *American Historical Review* 99, no. 4 (1994): 1043–73; Leah N. Gordon, *From Power to Prejudice: The Rise of Racial Individualism in Midcentury America* (Chicago: University of Chicago Press, 2016), chap. 1; Morey, *White Philanthropy*, chap. 10; Daniel Geary, *Beyond Civil Rights:*

The Moynihan Report and Its Legacy (Cambridge, MA: Harvard University Press, 2017). For another important angle on the growing conservative bent of analysis on race and the use of Myrdal in this regard, see Penny M. Von Eschen, *Race against Empire: Black Americans and Anticolonialism, 1937-1957* (Ithaca: Cornell University Press, 1997).

12. On the distinction between "beginning" and "origin," see Edward Said, *Beginnings: Intention and Method* (1975; New York: Columbia University Press, 1985), xii–xiii; cf. 372–73. On beginning as a structural theme in Baldwin, see Glaude, *Begin Again*.

13. Myrdal, *American Dilemma*, lxxxviii (emphasis added).

14. Here I borrow this term from Eddie S. Glaude Jr., *In a Shade of Blue: Pragmatism and the Politics of Black America* (Chicago: University of Chicago Press, 2007), 51–55.

15. James, *Varieties*, 101.

16. Ibid., 531; cf. "but provisionally and as a mere matter of program and method, since the evil facts are as genuine parts of nature as the good ones, the philosophic presumption should be that they have some rational significance, and that systematic healthy-mindedness, failing as it does to accord to sorrow, pain, and death any positive and active attention whatever, is formally less complete than systems that try at least to include these elements in their scope" (ibid., 185).

17. Ibid., 185.

18. Myrdal, *American Dilemma*, lxxix.

19. Ibid., lxxx.

20. Ibid., lxxxiii.

21. See chapters 2, 5, and 7 of this book.

22. Sacvan Bercovitch, *The Rites of Assent* (New York: Routledge, 1993), 29.

23. On what is now called the "contingent symbiosis" thesis, see Rogers Smith, "The 'Liberal Tradition' and American Racism," in *The Oxford Handbook of Racial and Ethnic Politics in the United States*, ed. David L. Leal, Taeku Lee, and Mark Sawyer (New York: Oxford University Press, 2018); cf. Smith, "Understanding the Symbiosis of American Rights and American Racism," in *The American Liberal Tradition Reconsidered: The Contested Legacy of Louis Hartz* (Lawrence: University Press of Kansas, 2010), 55–89. For a similar idea, see Charles W. Mills, *Black Rights/White Wrongs: The Critique of Racial Liberalism* (New York: Oxford University Press, 2017).

24. Myrdal, *American Dilemma*, 24. In the same context, he refers to the "century-long lag of public morals," by which he means that the practical norms underwriting institutions and actions were out of step with the higher values of the American Creed.

25. For a more sustained discussion of this crisis, see Mark Greif, *The Age of the Crisis of Man: Thought and Fiction in America, 1933-1973* (Princeton: Princeton University Press, 2015); Christopher Lasch, *The True and Only Heaven: Progress and Its Critics* (New York: Norton, 1991).

26. Reinhold Niebuhr, *The Nature and Destiny of Man: A Christian Interpretation*, 2 vols. (1939; Louisville, KY: Westminster John Knox Press, 1996), 23; cf. *The Children of Light and the Children of Darkness* (1944; Chicago: University of Chicago Press, 2011), chap. 1. On the divide between Niebuhr's orientation and Myrdal's, see David L. Chappell, "Niebuhrisms and Myrdaleries: The Intellectual Roots of the Civil

Rights Movement Reconsidered," in *The Role of Ideas in the Civil Rights South*, ed. Ted Ownby (Jackson: University Press of Mississippi, 2002), 3–18.

27. W.E.B. Du Bois, *Dusk of Dawn: An Essay toward an Autobiography of a Race Concept* (1940; New York: Oxford University Press, 2007), 66.

28. Karl Mannheim, *Man and Society in an Age of Reconstruction: Studies in Modern Social Structure* (New York: Harcourt, Brace, and World, 1940), 39.

29. Morey, *White Philanthropy*, 200.

30. Cited in ibid., 201.

31. Myrdal, *American Dilemma*, 2:997–98; cf. 1024. This is a piece of his idea of "cumulative causation" in which positive transformation on one or more factors relating to racial inequality stimulates an upward trajectory (ibid., 1:75–78; cf. ibid., vol. 2, appendix 3, 1065–72). How to secure the positive transformation in the first place involves acting on a "rank order of discrimination"—that is, an order in which you begin with the form of discrimination to which white Americans are least attached to, thus preparing the way to challenge those forms of discrimination on which they seemingly depend. Ibid., 1:60–67.

32. Jackson, *Gunnar Myrdal*, 187.

33. In her insightful but brief review Margaret Jarman Hagood captures the point very nicely: "After more than a thousand pages of critical appraisal of our culture and behavior . . . [Myrdal] 'makes up' by expressing great confidence in America's future role as the most powerful *white nation and in the inherent goodness of American people.*" *Land Policy Review*, 7, no. 3 (1944): 31. Relatedly, Jeanne Morefield explores how this is not merely a feature of domestic liberalism but also part of its imperial logic. See Morefield, *Empires without Imperialism: Anglo-American Decline and the Politics of Deflection* (New York: Oxford University Press, 2014), introduction.

34. See generally Myrdal, *American Dilemma*, vol. 2, appendix 2, 1035–64.

35. James Baldwin, "The White Problem" (1964), in *The Cross of Redemption: Uncollected Writings*, ed. Randall Kenan (New York: Vintage Books, 2010), 95.

36. Balfour, *Evidence of Things Not Said*, 27–29; cf. Shulman, *American Prophecy*, 143–50.

37. Baldwin, "The White Problem," *CE*, 91.

38. James Baldwin, *Notes of a Native Son* (1955), *CE*, 32.

39. Baldwin, *The Fire Next Time*, 294.

40. Baldwin did not think black people were immune to the force of the origin story, but given the distribution of power he was less concerned about this. See James Baldwin and Margaret Mead, *A Rap on Race* (New York: Dell Publishing, 1971), 34–35.

41. James Baldwin, "The White Man's Guilt" (1965), *CE*, 723.

42. James Baldwin, *Nobody Knows My Name* (1961), *CE*, 135. To this we should add the striking passage from *The Fire Next Time* where we now see that to be divested of a crutch is to court death: "Perhaps the whole root of our trouble, the human trouble, is that we will sacrifice all the beauty of our lives, will imprison ourselves in totems, taboos, crosses, blood sacrifices, steeples, mosques, races, armies, flags, nations, in order to deny the fact of death, which is the only fact we have" (339). Baldwin's preoccupation with identity is twofold. I have discussed the first as it relates to an American identity, but something, even in passing, must be said about the second. The United States' evasion of freedom is a species of a primordial problem for

Baldwin. This issue relates to his philosophical anthropology. In *Notes of a Native Son*, he puts the matter this way: "But our humanity is our burden, our life; we need not battle for it; we need only to do what is infinitely more difficult—that is, accept it" (18). Contained in our humanity are forces of good and evil, and the problem of American identity is a manifestation of this fact.

43. Avery Gordon, *Ghostly Matters: Haunting and the Sociological Imagination* (Minneapolis: University of Minnesota Press, 2008), xvi.

44. "A Conversation with James Baldwin" (1963), interviewed by Kenneth B. Clark, in *Conversations with James Baldwin*, ed. Fred L. Standley and Louis H. Pratt (Jackson: University Press of Mississippi, 1989), 41. For helpful discussions of that meeting, see David Leeming, *James Baldwin: A Biography* (New York: Arcade Publishing, 1994), 222–26; Peniel E. Joseph, *The Sword and the Shield: The Revolutionary Lives of Malcolm X and Martin Luther King Jr.* (New York: Basic Books, 2020), 142–46.

45. Baldwin, "A Conversation with James Baldwin," 41.

46. Baldwin, *Notes of a Native Son, CE*, 20.

47. "Liberalism and the Negro: A Roundtable Discussion," *Commentary* 37, no. 3 (March 1964): 25–42.

48. On the Baldwin-Glazer disagreement, see Turner, *Awakening to Race*, 93–95; Louis Menand, *The Free World: Art and Thought in the Cold War* (New York: Farrar, Straus and Giroux, 2021), 629–31.

49. "Liberalism and the Negro," 34.

50. Sidney Hook, "Report on the International Day against Dictatorship and War," *Partisan Review* 16, no. 7 (1949). Baldwin was also critical of Wright but from a very different angle. By the 1960s, he came to see something of the truth in Wright's criticisms of the United States. On this point, see Baldwin, *Notes of a Native Son, CE*, 11–18; Baldwin, *Nobody Knows My Name, CE*, 247–68.

51. "Liberalism and the Negro," 38.

52. The character of my critique is owed to Tommie Shelby's idea of the medical model ameliorating social problems. See Shelby, *Dark Ghettos: Injustice, Dissent, and Reform* (Cambridge, MA: Harvard University Press, 2016), 2–4.

53. Iris Marion Young, *Responsibility for Justice* (New York: Oxford University Press, 2011), 97–104.

54. Baldwin, *Fire Next Time*, 292.

55. Baldwin, *Notes of a Native Son, CE*, 22.

56. Baldwin and Mead, *Rap on Race*, 166.

57. Baldwin, *Notes of a Native Son, CE*, 23.

58. *Washington Post*, June 18, 2019, https://www.washingtonpost.com/politics/mcconnell-says-hes-against-reparations-for-slavery-it-would-be-pretty-hard-to-figure-out-who-to-compensate/2019/06/18/9602330c-9205-11e9-b58a-a6a9afaa0e3e_story.html.

59. Baldwin and Mead, *Rap on Race*, 166.

60. James Baldwin, "Words of a Native Son" (1964), *CE*, 713.

61. Baldwin, *Rap on Race*, 166.

62. Baldwin, "Words of a Native Son," *CE*, 713; cf. "Race, Hate, Sex, and Colour: A Conversation with James Baldwin and Colin MacInnes" (1965), in *Conversations with James Baldwin*, 52–53; Baldwin and Mead, *Rap on Race*, 56.

63. Young, *Responsibility for Justice*, 110. In connecting Baldwin and Young as I do I am under no illusions that this will settle matters. Students of policy will likely raise many complicated and empirical questions. The point here is to get us to see that whether we can suggest that there is something like historical racial injustices will depend on the point of view we assume when thinking about responsibility.

64. Saddling Hook with the total weight of this view of the American Creed minimizes his complexity. His early 1947 *Commentary* essay "Intelligence and the Evil in Human History" and his 1960 American Philosophical Association address, "Pragmatism and the Tragic Sense of Life," suggest a different mode of engagement than was on display in 1964. Still, this is not the argumentative path he takes when engaging Baldwin. See Sidney Hook, *Pragmatism and the Tragic Sense of Life* (New York: Basic Books, 1974); cf. Hook, *Political Power and Personal Freedom: Critical Studies in Democracy, Communism and Civil Rights* (1959; New York: Collier Books, 1962), especially chaps. 6–8. For helpful even if conflicting interpretations of Hook, see Cornel West, *The American Evasion of Philosophy: A Genealogy of Pragmatism* (Madison: University of Wisconsin Press, 1989), 114–24; Neil Jumonville, *Critical Crossings: The New York Intellectuals in Postwar America* (Berkeley: University of California Press, 1991), 17–28.

65. Daniel Moynihan, *The Moynihan Report: The Negro Family: The Case for National Action*, Office of Policy Planning and Research of the U.S. Department of Labor (1965; New York: CosimReports, 2018), 47. For a very helpful annotated version and important reflection on the report, see Daniel Geary, "The Moynihan Report: An Annotated Edition," *The Atlantic*, September 15, 2015, https://www.theatlantic.com/politics/archive/2015/09/the-moynihan-report-an-annotated-edition/404632/; Geary, *Beyond Civil Rights*.

66. Moynihan, *Moynihan Report*, preface.

67. Daryl Michael Scott, *Contempt and Pity: Social Policy and the Image of the Damaged Black Psyche, 1880–1996* (Chapel Hill: University of North Carolina Press, 1997), 137–59; cf. Lawrence D. Bobo, "Somewhere between Jim Crow and Post-Racialism: Reflections on the Racial Divide in America Today," *Daedalus* 140 (2011): 11–36.

68. We must proceed with care here. The point is not that society via the state has no role in helping African Americans. On the contrary, one of the results of racial liberalism from Myrdal to Moynihan was the need for government intervention to secure the conditions of equal access and treatment to better integrate black Americans into the existing norms of society. This marked an enormous improvement when compared to the nineteenth-century struggles for racial equality and proper regard. As Edwin C. Berry of the Chicago Urban League put the matter in support of Moynihan's thinking, the state must be "affirmatively color-conscious" if a color-blind society founded on equality is to be realized. "Transcript of the American Academy Conference on the Negro American" [1965], *Daedalus* 95, no. 1 (1966): 351. But government intervention was thought necessary to create a healthy context of choice, and whether black people would rightly make use of that context depended on them and their cultural tendencies. The necessity of state intervention retained the logic of pathology, but it did so in the following way. Will African Americans be able to make use of a context of choice, given their existing cultural tendencies?

69. For a recent text that does a much better job than I can do on these contemporary matters, see Shelby, *Dark Ghettos*.

70. Baldwin, "The White Man's Guilt," 723.

71. Ibid.

72. James Baldwin, "What Price Freedom?" (1964), in *The Cross of Redemption*, 95; Baldwin, "The White Man's Guilt," *CE*, 722.

73. Ralph Ellison, *Shadow and Act* (1964), in *The Collected Essays of Ralph Ellison*, ed. John F. Callahan (New York: Modern Library, 2003), 280.

74. "Liberalism and the Negro," 27.

75. Josiah Royce, *The Problem of Christianity* (1913; Washington, DC: Catholic University of America Press, 2001), 161.

76. Baldwin, *Fire Next Time*, 294.

77. Ibid., 346–47 (emphasis added).

78. Ibid., 294.

79. Baldwin and Mead, *Rap on Race*, 163.

80. Ibid., 164.

81. Ibid.

82. Royce, *Problem of Christianity*, 175.

83. Jesse McCarthy, *Who Will Pay Reparations on My Soul? Essays* (New York: W. W. Norton, 2021), 234.

84. James Baldwin, "The Artist's Struggle for Integrity" (1962), in *The Cross of Redemption*, 50.

appeals, 26, 37; affect and, 91–97; cultivating perceptual capacities and, 74–90,
266; generic conventions of, 47–53;
judgment and, 39–44, 48–55; national
character and, 91–99; prophecy and,
55–61; standing and, 44–47, 50–55.
See also specific appeals
"Appeal to Christian Women of the South"
(Grimke), 47
"Appeal to Forty Thousand Citizens,
Threatened with Disfranchisement, to
the People of Pennsylvania" (Purvis), 47
*Appeal to the Colored Citizens of the World,
But in Particular, and Very Expressly,
to Those of the United States of America*
(Walker), 24, 37, 39–44, 48–53, 55–61,
63–97, 104–5, 130, 147, 302n4
"An Appeal to the People on the Causes
and Consequences of a War with Great
Britain" (Lowell), 47
"An Appeal to the Public for Religious
Liberty" (Backus), 47
"An Appeal to the World or a Vindication
of the Town of Boston" (Adams), 47
arbitrary power, 7–8, 35, 100, 103–4, 122,
277–78. *See also* domination; freedom
Arendt, Hannah, 146
Aristotle, 54, 98, 106, 123–24, 207, 224,
302n8
Arnold, Edwin, 342n67
Arnold, Matthew, 174
art, 183–88, 197–200. *See also* "Criteria
of Negro Art" (Du Bois); Harlem
Renaissance; horror; judgment;
rhetoric
"Art and Propaganda" (Walrond), 211
"Art or Propaganda" (Locke), 220–21
aspiration, 7, 14, 25, 28–29, 131, 140–55, 167,
189, 226–34, 242–46, 264–65, 287–90,
324n85. *See also* democracy; future-
not-yet; people, the; perfectionism;
transformation; United States
atonement, 288–90
awakening, 41–44, 61–62, 66–74, 263

Backus, Isaac, 47
Bailey, Nathan, 48
Baker, Courtney, 196
Baldwin, James: African American
theoretical tradition and, 5, 93, 149;

character and, 20; critical responsive-
ness and, 268, 279–86; faith and, 269,
287; history and, 14, 172, 187–88, 265,
268, 275–76, 278–90, 363n40; Hook
and, 279–80; reconstitution and, 149;
rhetoric of, 16, 278–79
Balfour, Lawrie, 254, 275
Balkin, Jack, 335n110
Baraka, Amiri, 222
Bassett, John Spencer, 234
Bederman, Gail, 249
Beiner, Ronald, 45, 55
Beitler, Lawrence, 176
beliefs, 166–68. *See also* faith
Bercovitch, Sacvan, 272
Bernal, Angelica, 140
Bernays, Edward, 213–14
Berry, Edwin C., 365n68
betrayal, 83–85, 279
Bilder, Mary, 41, 49
Birmingham riot, 275
Biscoe, Hamp, 197
"Bitter Fruit" (Meeropol), 176, 201
Black and White (Fortune), 164
black internationalism, 10, 42, 293n27
black nationalism, 42, 55, 113, 303n16.
See also Delany, Martin Robison
Black Power movement, 256, 278, 285
Black Reconstruction (Du Bois), 215–16,
236–37, 346n13
Blake, William, 245
bootblack. *See* enslaved free man
Boston Daily Evening Transcript, 47, 52
Braithwaite, William Stanley, 182, 209–12,
234–35
Briggs, Cyril, 346n13
Broderick, Francis, 352n87
Bromell, Nick, 333n85
Bromwich, David, 95
Brooklyn Edge, 188
Brown, James, 201
Brown, Vincent, 34
Burke, Kenneth, 143

Café Society, 16, 201–3
Caldwell, Elias B., 315n99
Canovan, Margaret, 146–48
Carby, Hazel, 247, 249, 252, 358n69
carceral state, 3
Card, Claudia, 238

cultural imperialism, 134–35
culture, 23–24, 135–37. *See also* character;
    freedom; funded experience; slavery;
    white supremacy

Darby, Derrick, 317n13
Dark Princess (Du Bois), 216
Darkwater (Du Bois), 1, 211, 218, 236–37,
    346n13, 352n87, 356n52, 357n54
Davis, David Brion, 68, 310n20
Dawson, Michael, 8
debt peonage, 3, 243
deceit, 81–90
Declaration of Independence, 41, 50, 57,
    90–97, 120–24, 134–35, 147, 160–63,
    271, 280
Delany, Martin Robison, 37; African
    American theoretical tradition and, 5;
    black separatism of, 91, 96, 107, 111–14,
    119–20, 134–35; civic virtue and, 102;
    Douglass and, 26–27, 114–16, 118, 130,
    141–42, 144, 153, 155–63, 167–69, 173–75,
    285; Du Bois and, 230–31; faith and,
    21–22, 126, 134, 323n74, 331n52;
    Jefferson and, 151–52; law and, 117–18;
    the people and, 131, 135–36, 323n69;
    pessimism of, 26, 37–38, 155–65, 174,
    193, 228–29, 234, 321n45; Walker and,
    120, 158–59
Delany, Patti, 112–14
democracy: aesthetics of, 180–88, 209–23;
    African American thought traditions
    and, 2–14, 234–35; agency in, 10, 208,
    262–63; aspiration and, 14–15, 266;
    constitutionalism and, 24–25, 141–42,
    146, 149–50, 155, 168–73, 335n110;
    definition of, 9; ethical vision of, 7, 10,
    27–28, 31–38, 140–42, 154–55, 184–85;
    faith and, 1, 7–9, 26–29, 54–55, 133–37,
    142–55, 170–72, 266; historical vision
    and, 13–14, 172, 187–88, 265, 268,
    275–90, 363n40; judgment and, 15,
    24–25, 32–33, 37, 39–44, 48–53, 133–37;
    legitimacy of, 14–15, 26, 144, 149–51,
    155, 162–63, 272, 289; the people and,
    5–7, 55–61, 131, 139–54; perfectionism
    and, 11–24, 26, 31–38, 131, 133–37, 141–54,
    163, 171–72, 182–83, 187–88, 192–93,
    223–29, 232–46, 256–66, 272, 276,
    279–90; propaganda and, 223–29;

rationality in, 42–47, 54–55; rhetoric
    and, 15, 37, 43–44, 160–63, 180–88,
    206–8, 224–25, 266, 296n40; sov-
    ereignty's relation to, 15, 18, 21, 145,
    169–70; vulnerability and, 21–22, 278.
    See also critical responsiveness; equal-
    ity; freedom; habits; reconstitution
    (of American democracy); sensibilities;
    standing; transformation; voting;
    white supremacy
Democracy in America (Tocqueville),
    292n19
Democratic Vistas (Whitman), 27, 149–50,
    179–88, 191, 211
demotic rationality, 42–47, 54–55, 130
despair, 256
Dessalines, Jean-Jacques, 308n90
development (human), 66–74
Dewey, John, 19, 29, 32–33, 99, 146, 165,
    167–68, 182–83, 211, 329n26
Dictionary of the English Language
    (Johnson), 40, 149
disavowal, 13–14, 285
discrimination (racial), 17
Dixon, Thomas, 209
domination: appeals to counter, 42–43,
    74–90; arbitrary power and, 7–8, 35;
    aspiration and, 25; character discourse
    and, 18–19, 104–12; chattel slavery
    as special case of, 60–61; equality as
    operating against, 39–44; freedom
    and, 25, 63–66, 102–12, 133–37, 260,
    272, 277–78, 292n18; horrors of, 66–67;
    human nature and, 66–90; racial dis-
    regard and, 43–44, 101, 133–37; racial
    solidarity in the face of, 25, 37, 60–65,
    86–90, 99–115, 121–31, 236, 317n8,
    319n27; republicanism and, 99–112, 130;
    white supremacy and, 25–26, 28–29.
    See also freedom; habits; sovereignty;
    white supremacy
Douglass, Frederick, 5, 37; aesthetics and,
    76–77, 95, 180–81, 194–95, 231, 236;
    civic virtue and, 102–4, 333n88; Covey
    and, 69–70; Crummell and, 13; Delany
    and, 26–27, 114–16, 118, 130, 141–42, 144,
    153, 155–63, 167–69, 173–75, 285; faith
    and, 141, 148, 159–63, 217, 236, 322n56,
    332n81, 336n116, 337n121; fear and, 92;
    feelings of freedom and, 89, 126; the

A NOTE ON THE TYPE

THIS BOOK has been composed in Miller, a Scotch Roman typeface designed by Matthew Carter and first released by Font Bureau in 1997. It resembles Monticello, the typeface developed for The Papers of Thomas Jefferson in the 1940s by C. H. Griffith and P. J. Conkwright and reinterpreted in digital form by Carter in 2003.

Pleasant Jefferson ("P. J.") Conkwright (1905–1986) was Typographer at Princeton University Press from 1939 to 1970. He was an acclaimed book designer and AIGA Medalist.

The ornament used throughout this book was designed by Pierre Simon Fournier (1712–1768) and was a favorite of Conkwright's, used in his design of the *Princeton University Library Chronicle*.